The Individual Investor's Guide to No-Load Mutual Funds
Seventh Edition

The Individual Investor's Guide to No-Load Mutual Funds

Seventh Edition

American Association of Individual Investors

International Publishing Corporation
Chicago

The American Association of Individual Investors is an independent, non-profit corporation formed for the purpose of assisting individuals in becoming effective managers of their own assets through programs of education, information and research.

American Association of Individual Investors
625 North Michigan Avenue, Department NLG
Chicago, IL 60611
(312) 280-0170

ISBN 0-942 641-05-1
Library of Congress Catalog Card Number: 87-80864

Published by: International Publishing Corporation

Data in this guide were gathered from company releases. Factual material is not guaranteed but has been obtained from sources believed to be reliable.

Preface

Abrupt moves in the common stock and bond markets, along with an increasing supply of specialized and general purpose mutual funds, have made investment selection and portfolio planning more complex. Without a well-formulated and appropriate long-term investment plan, sharp market volatility may cause investors to make short-term decisions that prove to be less than optimal. Whenever the market spikes—up or down—some mutual funds and fund categories will perform substantially better or worse than others. As always, but perhaps highlighted by recent market behavior, getting mutual fund information to evaluate and compare performance and to effectively establish or modify investment plans is crucial.

Our continuing goal for the Guide is to present comprehensive, accurate, and useful information on no-load mutual funds. To that end, we have developed a format and a data analysis framework that is efficient in making fund comparisons. Individual investors using this Guide can spend more time evaluating funds, making portfolio decisions, and structuring long-term investment plans, rather than devoting substantial time and effort to simply gathering data.

As always, we have refrained from making any value judgments on the funds we report: Included in our lists are both exceptional performers as well as the mediocre and the outright terrible. Judgments are not made as to whether performance qualifies a fund for inclusion in the Guide, but we do have other criteria that must be met. If a fund has a load—front-end or back-end—it is excluded from the Guide no matter what the load percentage is. Funds that have fees that are significant and continual as well as funds that have redemption fees that do not eventually disappear are considered to be effectively loaded and are excluded from the Guide. In a special section, we continue to report on the performance of funds closed to new investors that would otherwise meet the criteria for inclusion in the Guide.

One particular problem that the October market upheaval caused was in our method for reinvesting capital gains and interest and dividend distributions. Our policy is to reinvest all distributions made during the month at the end of the month. Normally, the difference in annual returns between reinvesting on the actual distribution date rather than the end of the month is small. However, because funds liquidated some holdings during the last quarter of 1987 and realized in some cases significant gains, large distributions to shareholders were made in November and December. Funds that made exceptionally large distributions at the beginning of the month, particularly in December, would show different total returns if reinvested when distributed rather than at the end of the month. Where we felt that the difference was substantial and might affect investor decisions, we recalculated the return to reflect reinvestment on the distribution date.

Another change prompted by the stock market's performance in late 1987 was our bear market designation for calculating down market performance. Previously, we have used July 1981 through July 1982—now a distant period. To include newer funds in the down market calculation and to acknowledge the market collapse in 1987, we have changed our bear market period to the September 1987 through December 1987 period. Again, to include more funds and to examine a more recent bull market period, August 1984 through August 1987 now represents our up market period.

Because of the relatively low return for most funds in 1987, five-year total return figures will decline, in some cases dramatically. For example, the five-year total return on the Standard & Poor's index of 500 stocks was 146.1% through yearend 1986, but through yearend 1987 the five-year return dropped to 113.2%. Picking up 1987 with a 5.2% return and dropping 1982 with a 21.4% return accounted for the five-year total return decline.

There are 42 more funds in this edition, for a total of 358 no-load funds with comprehensive share data for six years, total returns, risk measures, up and down market performance, investment objectives, portfolio composition, shareholder services, telephone numbers and addresses. Funds that were new in 1987 but did not have a full year of operations are included in a separate section with a brief description. These 31 funds that made the NASD mutual fund listing sometime in 1987 plus the 358 funds that were listed and had full-year data comprise the 389 funds covered by our Guide.

We gather the mutual fund data for the Guide from each fund's prospectus and from direct communication with the fund. All the statistics we report are calculated by us and we make every effort to verify our figures. Our standard continues to be full and accurate disclosure. We believe that this Guide provides a sound and informed basis for your investment decisions.

All the data collection activities and the risk and return calculations were the responsibility of William H. Anderson Jr., financial analyst for AAII. Marie Anderson, research assistant, contacted funds and collected data. Maria Crawford Scott, editor of the AAII Journal, and her staff provided editorial guidance and support.

Chicago
June 1988

John Markese, Ph.D.
Vice President
Director of Research

Table of Contents

Introduction

A mutual fund is an open-ended investment company that pools investors' money to invest in securities. It is open-ended because it continuously issues new shares when investors want to invest in the fund, and it redeems shares when investors want to sell. A mutual fund trades directly with its shareholders, and the share price of the fund represents the market value of the securities that the fund holds.

There are several advantages that mutual funds offer individual investors. They provide:

- Professional investment management at a very low cost,
- A diversified group of securities that only a large portfolio can provide,
- Information through prospectuses and annual reports that facilitates comparisons among funds,
- Special services such as checkwriting, dividend reinvestment plans, telephone switching, periodic withdrawal and investment plans, etc.,
- Recordkeeping statements that make it easy to track the value of one's own holdings and that ease the paperwork at tax time.

Many individuals feel that they can achieve better results by investing their money directly in stocks rather than in mutual funds. Whether this is true for you is a question only you can answer. Many individual investors find it difficult to measure their own performance accurately and to make a valid comparison of their results versus a mutual fund. Mutual fund performance figures, in contrast, are easily available from sources such as this guide.

If you can do better than the average mutual fund over a relatively long time period, then individual stock selection makes financial sense. The next question is, can you do it as efficiently? Successful investing takes time and effort. Investors must spend a considerable amount of energy searching for opportunities and monitoring each investment.

Professional investment management comes relatively cheaply with mutual funds. The typical advisor charges about 0.5% annually for managing a fund's assets. For an individual making a $10,000 investment, that comes to only $50 a year. If you value your time, you can see that your money might be well spent by paying someone else to do the work.

Of course, mutual fund investing does not preclude investing in securities on your own. One useful strategy would be to invest in mutual funds and individual securities. The mutual funds would insure your participation in overall market moves and lend diversification to your portfolio while the individual securities would provide you with the opportunity to beat the market.

Diversification

If there is one ingredient to successful investing that is universally agreed upon, it is the benefit of diversification. The concept is so commonsensical that it is a piece of folk wisdom: "Don't put all your eggs in one basket." It is also a concept that is backed up by a great deal of research and market experience.

The benefit that diversification provides is risk reduction. Risk to investors is frequently defined as volatility of return—in other words, by how much each year an investment's returns might vary. Investors prefer returns that are relatively predictable, and thus less volatile. On the other hand, they want returns that are high. Diversification eliminates some of the risk, without reducing potential returns.

Mutual funds, because of their size, provide investors with a significant amount of diversification that might be difficult for an individual to duplicate. This is true not only for common stock funds, but also for bond funds, municipal bond funds, gold funds, international funds—in fact, for almost all mutual funds. Even the sector funds offer diversification within an industry. The degree of diversification will vary among funds, but most will provide investors with some amount of diversification.

Why No-Loads?

This book is dedicated to no-load mutual funds. Investors have learned that:

- A load is a sales commission that goes to whoever sells fund shares to an investor;

- A load does not go to anyone responsible for managing the fund's assets, and does not serve as an incentive for the fund manager to perform better;
- Funds with loads, on average, consistently underperform no-load funds when the load is taken into consideration in performance calculations;
- For every high-performing load fund, there exists a similar no-load fund that can be purchased instead;
- Loads understate the real commission charged because they reduce the total amount being invested: $10,000 invested in an 8.5% front-end load fund results in an $850 sales charge and only a $9,150 investment in the fund. The load actually represents 9.3% of the net funds invested;
- If a load fund is held over a long time period, the effect of the load is not diminished as quickly as many people believe because the load is paid up front; if that money had been working for you, as in a no-load fund, it would have been compounding over the whole time period.

The bottom line in any investment is how it performs for you, the investor. There may be some load funds that will do better even factoring in the load, but you have no way of finding that fund in advance. The only guide you have is historical performance, which is not necessarily an indication of future performance. With a load fund, you are starting your investment with a loss—the load. Start even. Stick with no-loads.

Sorting Out Charges

Although it is best to stick with no-load funds, they are becoming more difficult to distinguish from load funds. On the one hand, full front-end load funds have declined in popularity, and some are now turning to other kinds of charges. Some mutual funds sold by brokerage firms, for example, have lowered their loads to 4%, and others have introduced back-end loads—sales commissions paid when exiting the fund. In both instances, the load is often accompanied by 12b-1 plan charges.

On the other hand, some no-load funds have found that to compete, they must market themselves much more aggressively. To do so, they have introduced charges of their own.

The result has been the introduction of low loads, redemption fees and 12b-1 plans. Low loads are simply up-front sales charges that are lower than the traditional 8.5% rate, which used to be the standard. Some low loads are as little as 1%.

Redemption fees work just like back-end loads: You pay when you get out. Some funds have sliding scale redemption fees, so that the longer you remain invested, the lower the charge when you leave. Some funds use redemption fees to discourage short-term trading, a policy that is designed to protect longer-term investors. These funds, by and large, have redemption fees that disappear after six months.

The most confusing charge involves the 12b-1 plan. The adoption of a 12b-1 plan by a fund permits the advisor to use fund assets to pay for distribution costs, including advertising, distribution of fund literature such as prospectuses and annual reports, and sales commissions paid to brokers. Some funds use 12b-1 plans as masked load charges: They levy very high rates on the fund, and use the money to pay brokers to sell the fund. Since the charge is annual and based on the value of the investment, this can result in a total cost to a long-term investor that exceeds the old 8.5% up-front sales load, yet it allows the fund to be classified as a no-load. Other funds use money from 12b-1 plans to pay only distribution costs, and still others have 12b-1 plans but don't use them to levy charges against fund assets. In some instances, the fund advisor may use the 12b-1 plan to pay distribution expenses from his own pocket. The new fee table now required in all prospectuses should clarify the impact of a 12b-1 plan.

In this guide, we include mutual funds that have 12b-1 plans if there is no front-end or back-end load or any redemption fee that continues beyond six months. For some of these funds, however, the 12b-1 plan may result in charges equivalent to substantial loads. How can you analyze this?

One solution is to convert the annual percentage 12b-1 charge into an approximately equivalent front-end load. Figure 1 allows you to do that. For instance, a 0.25% annual 12b-1 charge is equivalent to a 1% front-end load, if you remain invested in the fund for four years; a 1.25% annual 12b-1 charge is equivalent to an astronomical 12.50% front-end load if you remain invested in the fund for 10 years. The comparison depends upon an assumed investment time horizon and investment growth rate, since 12b-1 charges are levied

Figure 1
Front-End Equivalent of 12b-1 Charges

Holding Period (Years)	If the annual 12b-1 charge is:					
	0.10%	0.25%	0.50%	0.75%	1.00%	1.25%
	The front-end load equivalent would be:					
1	0.10%	0.25%	0.50%	0.75%	1.00%	1.25%
2	0.20	0.50	1.00	1.50	2.00	2.50
3	0.30	0.75	1.50	2.25	3.00	3.75
4	0.40	1.00	2.00	3.00	4.00	5.00
5	0.50	1.25	2.50	3.75	5.00	6.25
10	1.00	2.50	5.00	7.50	10.00	12.50
20	2.00	5.00	10.00	15.00	20.00	25.00
30	3.00	7.50	15.00	22.50	30.00	37.50

annually on the total value of the mutual fund. We have included a variety of time horizons in the table, and investors must make their own assumptions here.

Remember, too, that the bottom line in analyzing charges is total expenses. The 12b-1 charge is included in the "ratio of expenses to net assets" figure; a fund with a 12b-1 charge may have a lower expense ratio than a fund without a 12b-1 charge. The introduction of fee tables, required by the SEC in all prospectuses after May 1, should make the comparison of total expenses among funds easier. Chapter 2 describes this table in more detail.

The decision as to what constitutes a load is difficult, but we took a very hard-line approach in this guide:

- All funds with front-end or back-end loads were excluded, regardless of the size of the load;
- Funds that had redemption fees were excluded if they extended beyond six months, since that cuts into investor flexibility;
- Funds with 12b-1 plans were not excluded from the guide; we note, however, if the fund has a 12b-1 plan and what the maximum annual charge is. Investors should assess these plans individually.

Investing in No-Load Funds

Selecting a mutual fund, while less time-consuming than investing in individual securities, does require some homework. No individual should put money into an investment that he does not understand. This does not require a detailed investigation of the fund's investments, but it does require some understanding of the possible risks involved along with the possible returns.

This guide is designed to provide you with that understanding. We have kept the chapters brief and to the point, so that individuals new to mutual fund investing will not be overwhelmed with unnecessary details. Those who are familiar with mutual funds may want to skip directly to Chapters 4 and 5, which describe how to use this guide most effectively.

In **Chapter 1,** we provide you with an overview of the kinds of mutual funds that are available. We have divided them into categories based on shared characteristics, primarily investment objective. The category will provide a generalized guide to the kinds of investments the fund will make, and the riskiness of the fund.

In **Chapter 2,** we have described the information that is provided by the mutual fund. Much of this information is 'must reading' for the mutual fund investor, and you need to have an idea of what to look for, where to look for it and what it means.

Chapter 3 gives recordkeeping hints, as well as some things to keep in mind regarding the tax treatment of mutual funds.

Chapter 4 provides a systematic approach to selecting a mutual fund. It is really the heart of this book, and describes an approach that will allow you to pick an individual mutual fund or a group of funds that will fit your investment needs. It is an approach that takes into consideration your risk tolerance, and it is what we have structured the statistical section around.

Finally, **Chapter 5** presents an explanation of the performance data and the information on the individual fund data pages. It also provides a key to the statistical section on the data pages, including a guide to the abbreviations used.

Once you are familiar with mutual funds and the systematic approach to analyzing and forming a mutual fund portfolio that we have suggested, you will want to take a look at the summaries of historical performance in **Chapter 6.** While past performance is no indication of the future, it may indicate quality and consistency of fund management. From this section, you should pick out several mutual funds that meet your investment objectives and risk tolerance. These funds can be examined more closely in the full-page fund data pages in **Chapter 7.** Call or write the funds to get a copy of the prospectus and annual report, and make sure you read the prospectus carefully before investing in any mutual fund. Information on tax-exempt bond funds can be found in the half-page data pages in **Chapter 8.**

No-load mutual funds that started in 1987 are listed in the New Funds section at the back of this guide. Also at the back is a list of funds that are reported as 'no-loads' by the financial press but that did not meet our criteria and are thus not included in this book. And, we have provided a list at the back of the guide of no-load fund families that have two or more funds. We have listed all of the funds in a family in this section, including load funds.

1

Mutual Fund Categories

Mutual funds come in all shapes and sizes; there are close to 400 funds covered in this book alone, each with its own characteristics. Many mutual funds have similar investment objectives, however. These shared investment objectives generally lead to other characteristics that are similar, particularly as measured by long-term returns and risk in terms of volatility of return.

These shared characteristics allow us to divide mutual funds into several broad categories. This chapter defines the mutual fund categories we used for this book. Figure 1-1 indicates the financial characteristics of the different fund categories. In this book, the individual fund data pages appear alphabetically; however, the fund's category is indicated beneath the fund's name.

Aggressive Growth Funds

The investment objective of aggressive growth funds is maximum capital gains. They invest aggressively in common stocks and tend

Figure 1-1
Characteristics of Mutual Funds by Investment Objective*

Fund Objective	1987 Return (%)	5-Year Return (%)	Bear Market Return† (%)	Bull Market Return‡ (%)	Risk (Beta)
Aggressive Growth	(2.3)	47.1	(26.0)	56.7	1.11
Growth	1.0	67.6	(22.1)	64.5	0.93
Growth & Income	(0.4)	80.2	(20.1)	60.5	0.80
Balanced	(0.3)	98.7	(14.7)	54.9	0.61
Bond	1.1	68.5	1.9	26.7	0.08
Tax-Exempt Bond	(0.9)	63.4	0.2	20.0	0.13
International	10.8	167.8	(15.3)	125.7	0.67
Precious Metals	28.5	28.9	(25.2)	171.9	0.48
S&P 500	5.2	113.2	(24.3)	144.7	1.00

*For all funds covered in this guide for time period ending December 31, 1987. Returns include reinvestment of distributions.
†September 1, 1987 through December 31, 1987.
‡August 1, 1984 through August 31, 1987.

to stay fully invested over the market cycle. Sometimes, these funds will use leverage (borrowed funds), and some may engage in trading listed stock options or take positions in stock index futures.

Aggressive growth funds typically provide low income distributions. This is because they tend to be fully invested in common stocks and do not earn a significant amount of interest income. In addition, the common stocks they invest in are generally growth-oriented stocks that do not pay significant cash dividends.

Many aggressive growth funds concentrate their assets in particular industries or segments of the market, and their degree of diversification may not be as great as other types of funds. These investment strategies result in increased risk. Thus, they tend to perform better than the overall market during bull markets, but fare worse during bear markets.

In general, long-term investors who need not be concerned with monthly or yearly variation in investment return will find investment in this class of funds the most rewarding. Because of the extreme volatility of return, however, risk-averse investors with a short-term investment horizon may find that these funds lie well outside their comfort zones. The riskiness of these funds can be offset by a greater allocation of an investor's total assets to a relatively risk-free investment, such as a money market fund (this portfolio strategy is further described in Chapter 4 in the section on risk.) During prolonged market declines, aggressive growth funds can sustain severe declines in net asset value.

Market timing is not a strategy we recommend, particularly over the short term. Although the transaction costs of switching in and out of no-load mutual funds are near zero, it can create significant tax liabilities. In addition, the ability to consistently time the market correctly in the short term, after adjusting for risk, costs and taxes, has not been demonstrated. However, aggressive growth funds, with their high volatility and fully invested position, do make ideal vehicles for those who believe they possess the insight to guess the next market move. The investment strategy would be to invest in aggressive growth funds during up markets, and to switch to money market funds during down markets.

Growth Funds

The investment objective of growth funds is to obtain long-term growth of invested capital. They generally do not engage in speculative tactics such as using financial leverage or short selling. On occasion, these funds will use stock or index options to reduce risk by hedging their portfolio positions.

Growth funds typically are more stable than aggressive growth funds. Generally, they invest in growth-oriented firms that are older, larger, and pay larger cash dividends. You are likely to find companies such as IBM, Pepsico and McDonald's in the portfolios of growth funds. The degree of concentration of assets is not as severe as with aggressive growth funds. Additionally, these funds tend to move from fully invested to partially invested positions over the market cycle. They build up cash positions during uncertain market environments.

In general, growth fund performance tends to mirror the market during bull and bear markets. Some growth funds have been able to perform relatively well during recent bear markets because their managers were able to change portfolio composition by a much greater degree or to maintain much higher cash positions than aggressive growth fund managers. However, higher cash positions can also cause the funds to underperform aggressive growth funds during bull markets.

Aggressive investors should consider holding both growth fund shares and aggressive growth fund shares in their overall portfolios. This is an especially appealing strategy for investors who hold aggressive growth mutual funds that invest in small stock growth firms. The portfolios of these funds complement the portfolios of growth funds, leading to greater overall diversification. The combination produces overall returns that will tend to be less volatile than an investment in only aggressive growth funds.

As with the aggressive growth funds, these funds can sustain severe declines in net asset value during prolonged bear markets. Since some portfolio managers of growth funds attempt to time the market over the longer market cycle, using these funds for market timing may be counterproductive.

Growth & Income Funds

Growth and income funds generally invest in the common stocks and convertible securities of seasoned, well-established, cash-dividend-paying companies. The funds attempt to provide shareholders with significant income along with long-term growth. They generally attempt to avoid excessive fluctuations in net asset value. One tends to find a high concentration of public utility common stocks and corporate convertible bonds in the portfolios of growth and income funds. The funds also provide higher income distributions, less variability in return, and greater diversification than growth and aggressive growth funds.

Because of the high current income offered by these kinds of funds, potential investors should keep the tax consequences in mind. Remember that, although capital gains are now taxed at the same rate as income, an effective tax strategy is to defer paying taxes whenever possible. The distributions from these funds are frequent and are fully taxable in the year paid. High tax bracket individuals should consider investing in these kinds of funds by using IRAs, Keoghs and 401(k)s.

Balanced Funds

The balanced fund category has become less distinct in recent years, and a significant overlap in fund objectives exists between growth and income funds and balanced funds. In general, the portfolios of balanced funds consist of investments in common stocks and substantial investments in bonds and convertible bonds. The proportion of stocks and bonds that will be held is usually stated in the investment objective, but it may be variable. Various names, such as equity-income, income, and total return, have been attached to funds that have all the characteristics of traditional balanced funds.

Balanced funds are generally less volatile than aggressive growth, growth, and growth and income funds.

As with growth and income funds, balanced funds provide a high dividend yield. Similarly, high tax bracket investors that want to invest in these funds should consider using tax-sheltered money.

Bond Funds and Tax-Exempt Bond Funds

Bond mutual funds, not surprisingly, invest in bonds. They are attractive to bond investors because they provide diversification and liquidity that is not as readily available in direct bond investments.

Bond funds hold various kinds of fixed-income securities in their portfolios. Some specialize in municipal bond issues; others invest in only U.S. government bonds or agency issues, such as Ginnie Maes. Still others invest in corporate bonds. 'High yield' bond funds invest in lower-rated corporate and municipal bonds with a higher default risk; these bonds must offer higher yields to compensate for the greater risk. These bond funds are commonly referred to as 'junk' bond funds.

Bond funds have portfolios with a wide range of average maturities. Many funds use their names to characterize their maturity structure. Generally, short term means that the portfolio has a weighted average maturity of less than three years. Intermediate implies an average maturity of three to 10 years, and long term is over 10 years. The longer the maturity, the greater the change in fund value when interest rates change. Longer-term bond funds are riskier than shorter-term funds, and they tend to offer higher yields.

Since bond funds can (and do) provide investors with diversification, investors should invest in funds that are large. Large bond funds hold many more bond issues than do smaller funds, and as a result of sliding scale management fees, they tend to charge a lower percentage fee.

Bond funds that hold principally corporate or U.S. government debt obligations appear among the regular fund data listings in this book. Tax-exempt bond funds, which invest in municipal bonds, follow the regular fund listings in a separate section. Tax-exempt bond funds are similar in structure to other bond funds, but are sometimes very specialized tax shelter vehicles—state-specific tax-exempt funds are an example.

Precious Metals Funds

Precious metals mutual funds specialize in investments in both foreign and domestic companies that mine gold and other precious metals. Some funds also hold gold directly through investments in gold coins or bullion. Gold options are another method used to invest in the industry. Mutual fund investments in precious metals range from the conservative to the highly speculative.

Gold and precious metals mutual funds offer advantages similar to bond funds: They allow investors interested in this area to invest in a more liquid and diversified vehicle than would be available through a direct purchase.

The appeal of gold and precious metals is that they have performed well during extreme inflationary periods. Over the short term, the price of gold moves in response to a variety of political, economic and psychological forces. As world tension and anxiety rise, so does the price of gold. In periods of peace and stability, the price of gold declines. Because gold tends to perform in an inverse relationship to stocks, bonds, and cash, it can be used as a stabilizing component in one's portfolio. Silver and platinum react in a fashion similar to gold. Precious metals funds, like the metal itself, are very volatile, often shooting from the bottom to the top and back to the bottom in fund rankings over the years. Investors should understand, however, that because most gold funds invest in the stock of gold mining companies, they are still subject to some stock market risk.

International Funds

International funds invest in securities of firms located in different countries. Some funds specialize in regions, such as the Pacific or Europe, and others invest worldwide. In addition, some funds—usually termed 'global funds'—invest in both foreign and U.S. stocks.

International funds provide investors with added diversification. The most important factor when diversifying a portfolio is selecting assets that do not behave similarly to each other under similar economic scenarios. Within the U.S., investors can diversify by selecting securities of firms in different industries. In the international realm, investors must take the diversification process one step further by holding securities of firms in different countries. The more independently these foreign markets move in relation to the U.S. market, the greater will be the diversification potential for the U.S. investor, and ultimately, the lower his risk.

In addition, international funds overcome some of the difficulties investors would face in making foreign investments directly. For instance, individuals would have to thoroughly understand the foreign brokerage process, be familiar with the various foreign marketplaces and their economies, be aware of currency fluctuation trends, and have access to reliable financial information. Obviously this can be a monumental task for the individual investor.

There are some risks to investing internationally. In addition to the risk inherent in investing in any security, there is an additional exchange rate risk. The return to a U.S. investor from a foreign security depends on both the security's return in its own currency plus the rate at which that currency can be exchanged for U.S. dollars. Another uncertainty is political risk, which includes government restriction, taxation, or even total prohibition of the exchange of one currency into another. Of course, the more the mutual fund is diversified among various countries, the less the risk involved.

Other Funds

There are many specialized mutual funds that do not have their own categories. Instead, they will be found in one of the various categories mentioned above. These funds are classified by their investment objectives rather than by their investment strategies. For instance, several funds specialize in specific industries, but one industry-specific fund does not necessarily appear in the same category as another industry-specific fund. Other specialized funds that may appear in various categories include the option-income funds, the 'socially conscious' funds, funds designed solely for tax-sheltered plans, and geographically specific funds.

One other fund category deserves a special mention—the index fund. An example of an index fund is Vanguard's Index Trust, categorized as a growth and income fund. This fund was designed to match the Standard & Poor's 500 stock index, and does so by investing in all 500 stocks in the S&P 500; the amounts invested in each stock are proportional to the firm's market value representation in the S&P 500. Statistics on this fund are quite useful for comparison with other funds, since it is a representation of the market.

2

Understanding
Mutual Fund Statements

One of the advantages of mutual fund investing is the wealth of information that must be provided to fund investors and prospective investors. Taken together, the various reports provide investors with vital information concerning financial matters and how the fund is managed, both key elements in the selection process. In fact, mutual fund statements, along with performance statistics, are the only other sources of information most investors will need in the selection process.

To new mutual fund investors, the information may seem overwhelming. However, regulations covering the industry have standardized the reports: Once you know where to look for information, the location will hold true for almost all funds.

There are basically five types of statements produced by the mutual fund: the prospectus; the Statement of Additional Information; annual, semiannual and quarterly reports; marketing brochures; and account statements. Actually, the second report—the Statement of Additional Information—is part of the prospectus. However, the Securities and Exchange Commission has allowed mutual funds to simplify and streamline the prospectus by dividing it into two parts: Part A, which all prospective investors must receive, and Part B—the Statement of Additional Information—which the fund must send investors if they specifically request it. In practice, when most people (including the funds) refer to the prospectus, they are referring to Part A. For simplicity, that is what we will do here, as well.

The Prospectus

The prospectus is the single most important document produced by the mutual fund, and it is must reading for investors before investing. By law, prospective investors must receive a prospectus before the fund can accept initial share purchases. In addition, current shareholders must receive new prospectuses when they are updated, at least once a year.

The prospectus is generally organized into sections, and although it must cover specific topics, the overall structure may differ somewhat among funds. The cover usually gives a quick synopsis of the fund: investment objective, sales or redemption charges, minimum investment, retirement plans available, address, and telephone number. More detailed descriptions are in the body of the prospectus.

Fee Table: Under a recent Securities and Exchange Commission ruling, all mutual fund prospectuses must include a table near the front that delineates all fees and charges to the investor. The table contains three sections: The first section lists all transaction charges to the investor, including all front-end and back-end loads and redemption fees; the second section lists all annual fund operating expenses as a percentage of net assets; and the third section is an illustration of the total cost of these fees and charges to an investor over time. The illustration assumes an initial investment of $1,000 and a 5% growth rate for the fund, and states the total dollar cost to an investor if he were to redeem his shares at the end of one year, three years, five years and 10 years.

Condensed Financial Information: One of the most important sections of the prospectus contains the condensed financial information, which provides statistics on income and capital changes per share of the fund (an example is shown in Figure 2-1). The per-share figures are given for the life of the fund or 10 years, whichever is less. Also included are important statistical summaries of investment activities throughout each period. Occasionally these financial statements are only referred to in the prospectus and are actually contained in the annual report, which in this instance would accompany the prospectus.

The per-share section summarizes the financial activity over the year to arrive at the end-of-year net asset value for the fund. The financial activity summarized includes increases in net asset value due to dividend and interest payments received and capital gains from investment activity. Decreases in net asset value are due to capital losses from investment activity, investment expenses and payouts to fund shareholders in the form of distributions.

Figure 2-1
The Condensed Financial Information Statement: An Example

	1977	1978	1979	1980	1981	1982	1983	1984	1985	1986	Six Months Ended June 30, 1987*
Net Asset Value, Beginning of Period	$14.73	$13.01	$13.11	$14.64	$17.84	$15.52	$17.56	$19.70	$19.52	$22.99	$24.27
Investment Activities											
Income	.64	.69	.79	.89	.90	.89*	.93	.93	.97	.96	.47
Expenses	(.07)	(.04)	(.04)	(.06)	(.07)	(.06)	(.06)	(.05)	(.06)	(.07)	(.04)
Net Investment Income	.57	.65	.75	.83	.83	.83	.87	.88	.91	.89	.43
Net Realized and Unrealized Gain (Loss) on Investments	(1.72)	.10	1.59	3.73	(1.76)	2.29	2.85	.30	5.08	3.30	6.18
Total from Investment Activities	(1.15)	.75	2.34	4.56	(.93)	3.12	3.72	1.18	5.99	4.19	6.61
Distributions											
Net Investment Income	(.57)	(.65)	(.75)	(.83)	(.83)	(.83)	(.87)	(.88)	(.91)	(.89)	(.36)
Realized Net Gain	—	—	(.06)	(.53)	(.56)	(.25)	(.71)	(.48)	(1.61)	(2.02)	—
Total Distributions	(.57)	(.65)	(.81)	(1.36)	(1.39)	(1.08)	(1.58)	(1.36)	(2.52)	(2.91)	(.36)
Net Asset Value, End of Period	$13.01	$13.11	$14.64	$17.84	$15.52	$17.56	$19.70	$19.52	$22.99	$24.27	$30.52
Ratio of Expenses to Average Net Assets	.46%[1]	.36%[1]	.30%[1]	.35%	.42%	.39%	.28%	.27%	.28%	.28%	.27%**
Ratio of Net Investment Income to Average Net Assets	4.50%	5.43%	5.28%	5.06%	4.91%	5.38%	4.22%	4.53%	4.09%	3.40%	3.06%**
Portfolio Turnover Rate	6%	8%	29%	18%	12%	11%	35%	14%	36%	29%	4%**
Shares Outstanding, End of Period (thousands)	1,617	5,046	5,395	5,535	5,879	6,266	11,861	14,841	17,148	19,984	29,692

[1] Includes .10%, .06% and .04% representing amortization of deferred organization and offering expenses for the years ended December 31, 1977, 1978 and 1979, respectively.
*Unaudited
**Annualized

Source: Vanguard Index Trust

Potential investors may want to note the line items in this section. *Investment income* represents the dividends and interest earned by the fund during its fiscal year. *Expenses* reflect such fund costs as the management fee, legal fees, transfer agent fees and the like. These expenses are given in detail in the statement of operations section of the annual report. *Net investment income* is investment income less expenses. This line is important for investors to note because it reflects the level and stability of net income over the time period. A high net investment income would most likely be for funds that have income rather than growth as their investment objective. Since net investment income must be distributed to shareholders to maintain the conduit status of the fund and avoid taxation of the fund, a high net investment income has the potential of translating into a high tax liability for the investor.

Net realized and unrealized gain (loss) on investments is the change in the value of investments that have been sold or that continue to be held by the fund.

Distributions to fund shareholders are also detailed. These distributions will include dividends from net investment income from the current and sometimes previous fiscal periods. The new tax law requires that all income earned must be distributed in the calendar year earned. Also included in distributions will be any realized net capital gains.

The last line in the per-share section will be the *net asset value* at the end of the year, which reflects the value of one share of the fund. It is calculated by determining the total assets of the fund and dividing by the number of mutual fund shares outstanding. The figure will change for a variety of reasons, including changes in investment income, expenses, gains, losses and distributions. Depending upon the source of change, a decline in net asset value may or may not be due to poor performance. For instance, a decline in net asset value may be due to a significant distribution of realized gains on securities.

The selected financial ratios at the bottom of the per-share financial data are important indicators of fund performance and strategy. The *expense ratio* relates expenses incurred by the fund to average net assets. These expenses include the investment advisory fee, legal and accounting fees, and 12b-1 charges to the fund; they do not include brokerage fees. A high expense ratio detracts from your investment return. In general, common stock funds have higher expense ratios than bond funds, and smaller funds have higher expense ratios than larger funds. The average for all funds is about 1.25%. Funds with expense ratios above 1.5% are high, and those above 2.0% should be carefully scrutinized.

The *ratio of net investment income to average net assets* is very similar to a dividend yield. This, too, should reflect the investment objective of the fund. Common stock funds with income as part of their investment objective would be expected to have a ratio of about 3% under current market conditions, and aggressive growth funds would have a ratio closer to 0%.

The *portfolio turnover rate* is the lower of purchases or sales divided by average net assets. It reflects how frequently securities are bought and sold by the fund. For purposes of determining the turnover for common stock funds, fixed-income securities with a maturity of less than a year are excluded, as are all government securities, short- and long-term. For bond funds, however, long-term U.S. government bonds are included.

Investors should take note of the portfolio turnover rate, because the higher the turnover, the greater the brokerage costs incurred by the fund. Brokerage costs are not reflected in the expense ratio but instead are directly reflected in a decrease in net asset value. In addition, funds with high turnover rates generally have higher capital gains distributions, which are taxed in the year of distribution. Aggressive growth mutual funds are most likely to have high turnover rates. Some bond funds also have very high portfolio turnover rates. A 100% portfolio turnover rate indicates that securities in the portfolio have been on average held for one year; a 200% portfolio turnover indicates that securities on average have been traded every six months. The portfolio turnover rate for the average mutual fund falls between 80% and 100%.

Investment Objective/Policy: The investment objective section of the prospectus elaborates on the brief sentence or two on the cover. In this section, the fund describes the types of investments it will make—whether it is bonds, stocks, convertible securities, options, etc.—along with some general guidelines as to the proportions these securities will represent in the fund's portfolio. In common stock funds, a statement usually indicates whether it will be oriented toward capital gains or income. In this section, the management will also briefly discuss approaches to market timing, risk assumption, and the anticipated level of portfolio turnover. Some prospectuses may indicate any investment restrictions they have placed on the fund, such as purchasing securities on margin, short sales, industry or firm concentration, foreign securities, lending of securities, and allowable proportions in certain investment categories. This investment restrictions section is usually given in more detail in the Statement of Additional Information.

Fund Management: The fund management section names the investment advisor and gives the advisory fee schedule. Most advisors charge a management fee on a sliding scale that decreases as assets under management increase. Occasionally, some portion of the fund advisors' fees are subject to their performance relative to the market.

Some prospectuses will describe the fund's officers and directors, with a short biography of affiliations and relevant experience. For most funds, however, this information is provided in more detail in the Statement of Additional Information. The board of directors is elected by fund shareholders; the fund advisor is selected by the board of directors. The advisor is usually a firm operated by or affiliated with officers of the fund. Information on fund officers and directors is not critical to fund selection. Rarely mentioned in either the prospectus or the Statement of Additional Information, however, is the portfolio manager for the fund. The portfolio manager is responsible for the day-to-day purchases of the fund, and is employed by the fund advisor.

Other Important Sections: There are several other sections in a mutual fund prospectus that investors should be aware of. They will appear under various headings, depending upon the prospectus, but they are not difficult to find.

Mutual funds that have 12b-1 plans must have a description of them in the prospectus. Under new SEC rules, a description of these plans—also known as distribution plans—must be prominently and clearly placed in the prospectus. The distribution plan details the marketing aspects of the fund and how it relates to fund expenses. For instance, advertising, distribution of fund literature, and any arrangements with brokers would be included in the marketing plan; the 12b-1 plan pays for these distribution expenses. Sometimes, these plans do not charge the fund for the expenses but rather allow the advisor to pay for them. The actual cost to the fund of a 12b-1 plan will also be listed at the front of the prospectus in the fee table.

The capital stock, or fund share characteristics section, provides shareholders with a summary of their voting rights, participation in dividends and distributions, and the number of authorized and issued shares of the fund. Often, a separate section will discuss the tax treatment that will apply to fund distributions, which may include dividends, interest and capital gains.

The how-to-buy-shares section gives the minimum initial investment and any subsequent minimums; it will also list load charges or fees. In addition, information on mail, wire, and telephone purchases is provided, along with dividend and/or capital gains distribution reinvestment options, and any automatic withdrawal or retirement options.

The how-to-redeem-shares section discusses telephone, written, and wire redemption options, with a special section on signature guarantees and other documents that may be needed. Also detailed are any fees for reinvestment or redemption. Shareholder services are usually outlined here, with emphasis on switching among funds in a family of funds. This will include any fees for switching, and any limits on the number of switches allowed.

Statement of Additional Information

This document elaborates on the prospectus. The investment objectives section is more in-depth, with a list and description of investment restrictions. The management section gives brief biographies of directors and officers, and provides the number of fund shares owned beneficially by the officers and directors named. The investment advisor section, while reiterating the major points made in the prospectus, gives all the expense items and contract provisions of the agreement between the advisor and the fund. If the fund has a 12b-1 plan, further details will likely be in the Statement of Additional Information.

Many times, the Statement of Additional Information will include much more information on the tax consequences of mutual fund distributions and investment. Conditions under which withholding for federal income tax will take place are also provided. The fund's financial statements are incorporated by reference to the annual report to shareholders, and generally do not appear in the Statement of Additional Information. Finally, the independent auditors give their opinion on the representativeness of the fund's financial statements.

Annual, Semiannual and Quarterly Reports

All funds must send their shareholders audited annual and semiannual reports. Mutual funds are allowed to combine their prospectus and annual report; some do this, but most do not.

The annual report describes the fund activities over the past year, and provides a listing of all investments of the fund at market value as of the end of the fiscal year. Usually, the cost basis of the investment is also given for each. Looking in-depth at individual securities held by the fund is probably a waste of time. However, it is helpful to be aware of the overall investment categories. For instance, investors should look at the percentage invested in common stocks, bonds, convertible bonds, and any other holdings. In addition, a look at the types of common stocks held gives the investor some indication of how the portfolio will fare in various market environments.

The annual report will also have a balance sheet, which lists all assets and liabilities of the fund by general category. This holds little interest for investors.

The statement of operations, similar to an income statement, is of interest only in that the fund expenses are broken down. For most funds, the management fee is by far the largest expense; the expense ratio in the prospectus conveys much more useful information. The statement of changes in net assets is very close to the financial information provided in the prospectus, but the information is not on a per-share basis. Per-share information will, however, frequently be detailed in the annual report in a separate section. Footnotes to the financial statements elaborate on the entries, but other than any pending litigation against the fund, they are most often routine.

The quarterly or semiannual reports are current accounts of the investment portfolio, and provide more timely views of the fund's investments than does the annual report.

Marketing Brochures and Advertisements

These will generally provide a brief description of the fund. However, the most important bit of information will be the number to call to receive the fund prospectus and annual report, if you have not received them already.

A new SEC ruling has tightened and standardized the rules regarding mutual fund advertising. All mutual funds that use performance figures in their ads must now include one-, three-, five- and ten-year total return figures. Bond funds that quote yields must use a standardized method for computing yield, and they must include total return figures, as well. Finally, any applicable sales commissions must be mentioned in the advertisement.

Account Statements

Mutual funds send out periodic account statements detailing reinvestment of dividend and capital gains distributions, new purchases or redemptions, and any other account activity such as service fees. The statement provides a running account balance by date with share accumulations, account value to date and a total of distributions made to date. These statements are invaluable for tax purposes and should be saved. The fund will also send out, in January, a Form 1099-Div for any distributions made the previous year, and a Form 1099-B if any mutual fund shares were sold.

Mutual Fund Recordkeeping
and Taxes

Mutual funds can be advantageous in that they minimize some of the more mundane details involved in investing. Of course, these details are not eliminated entirely, and they primarily relate to recordkeeping and taxes.

Recordkeeping

Mutual fund investing, as with any other investment, demands some amount of recordkeeping. This is made easier by the statements sent out by the individual funds.

Purchases and redemptions are acknowledged by mutual funds through a confirmation statement sent to the investor. These statements should be retained both for tax purposes, and in case any dispute with the fund arises. Most mutual funds send shareholders periodic statements of their account activity, including any investments and distributions received over a certain time period. At yearend, the fund will send a summary of the yearly account activity. In addition, the fund will send separate forms (1099-Div and 1099-B) noting all the activity in the shareholder's account that will be reported to the IRS for tax purposes. These statements should be saved, both for your own information and as backup documentation that may be necessary for income tax filings.

Investors should also make it a habit to save the latest prospectus issued by the fund, so that future purchases, exchanges, and/or redemptions can be made in accordance with the fund's latest business procedures.

Taxes

It is the unfortunate fate of investors that, eventually, they all must face IRS regulations. Mutual fund investors are no different, but mutual funds do have certain tax consequences that are not readily apparent to those unfamiliar with the area.

Investors incur two distinct types of tax liabilities from mutual funds. The first results from distributions a shareholder receives from the mutual fund, and the second results from the sale of mutual fund shares. The tax implications are quite different, and are discussed below.

Distributions From Mutual Funds: The IRS treats mutual funds as conduits between their shareholders and the corporations whose securities the fund holds. This means that the mutual fund itself is not taxed. In addition, the mutual fund itself does not pay dividends; it merely passes on income from dividends, interest and capital gains to shareholders.

Mutual funds earn income over the tax year from cash dividends and interest received from the fund's investments. The fund earns capital gains resulting from price changes of the securities it holds. Capital gains and losses can be realized through the sale of the securities during the tax year, or unrealized if the securities continue to be held by the fund at the end of the tax year. All income earned by the fund, and any capital gains and losses (realized or unrealized), cause the value of the fund's assets to increase or decrease. This is reflected in the fund's per-share net asset value.

In order to receive conduit status from the IRS, mutual funds must distribute 98% of all net investment income and net realized capital gains received during the calendar year. They do so in the form of distributions to shareholders. Under the new tax laws, mutual funds are required to make these distributions by the end of the calendar year, regardless of when the fund's fiscal year ends. The result is that many funds must make distributions late in the year to assure that they have distributed all income and gains through yearend.

Mutual funds are allowed to net out any investment expenses before distributions, and are not required to make a distribution if investment expenses are greater than net investment income. However, starting in 1988, investors may be taxed on most of those investment expenses. This result of the new tax laws was to have started in 1987, but was postponed one year after intense lobbying by the mutual fund industry. The lobbying continues. If these expenses are taxed, however, they may be included with all other investment expenses incurred by a taxpayer, and any amount above 2% of adjusted gross income is deductible if you itemize.

Fund distributions are simply a transferal of assets from the fund to the shareholder. This means that when a distribution is made, the net total assets of the fund drop, and so, too, does the per-share net asset value. In fact, it drops by exactly the amount of the distribution.

Once the distribution is paid to the shareholder it is taxable, regardless of whether or not the shareholder reinvests the distribution. The tax depends on the source of the income to the fund. The kinds of distributions that a mutual fund shareholder may receive include ordinary dividends, capital gains, exempt-interest dividends and return of capital (non-taxable) distributions. Mutual funds notify shareholders of the underlying sources of the distribution when it is made.

In addition, mutual funds are required to send their shareholders at the end of each year a form for tax purposes, known as Form 1099-DIV (Statement for Recipients of Dividends and Distributions). This form indicates what a shareholder must report or take into consideration on his federal income tax return concerning all fund distributions for the taxable year; an example of the 1987 version is presented in Figure 3-1. This form contains the following information:

Figure 3-1
Form 1099-DIV

Type or print PAYER'S Federal identifying number, name, address, and ZIP code below.	This is important tax information and is being furnished to the Internal Revenue Service. If you are required to file a return, a negligence penalty will be imposed on you if this dividend income is taxable and the IRS determines that it has not been reported.	Statements for Recipients of Dividends and Distributions Copy B For Recipient	**1987**
Recipient's identifying number	1 Gross dividends and other distributions on stock	2 Investment expenses included in Box 1	3 Captial gain distributions	4 Federal income tax withheld
Type or print RECIPIENT'S name, address, and ZIP code below.	5 Nontaxable distributions (if determinable)		6 Foreign tax paid
	Liquidation Distributions		
	8 Cash		9 Non-cash (show fair market value)
	7 Foreign Country or U.S. Possession		

Form 1099-DIV   Department of the Treasury-Internal Revenue Service

- The amount that you must report as ordinary dividends,
- The capital gains distributions that you must report,
- The non-taxable distributions (return of capital) that usually will reduce your stock basis,
- The foreign tax paid that you may claim as a deduction or credit,
- Any federal income tax withheld, such as the 20% tax on reportable payments under backup withholding.

Capital losses realized by the fund are not passed on to shareholders, but are used by the fund to offset capital gains. The fund is allowed to carry the loss forward to net against future gains for up to eight years.

There is one important tax implication of mutual fund distributions that prospective investors should consider. Since mutual fund cash distributions result in an immediate decline in per-share net asset value equal to the per-share distribution, individuals who purchase mutual fund shares before the ex-distribution date effectively have a portion of their investment capital returned to them upon distribution. Since the distribution is taxable unless the fund is held in a tax-sheltered account (IRA, Keogh, etc.), the investor is left worse off by the amount of the tax he must pay on the distribution. Therefore, under normal circumstances, taxpaying investors should wait and make significant fund purchases after the ex-distribution date. The income and capital gains distribution months are given when available in the one-page fund summaries in this guide.

Mutual Fund Sales: The other type of tax liability mutual fund investors are likely to incur are gains and losses that result from the purchase and subsequent sale, exchange or redemption of mutual fund shares themselves. The amount of the gain or loss is the difference between the adjusted basis in the shares and the amount realized from the sale, exchange or redemption.

Mutual fund investors should keep detailed records of prior purchases in order to determine and substantiate the magnitude of gain or loss once the shares are sold.

It is equally important for investors to understand the various identification methods for determining which shares were sold if the entire holdings are not liquidated.

For income tax purposes, the cost, or basis, of mutual fund shares that have subsequently been sold can be determined by the 'first in, first out' (FIFO) method, by the identifiable cost method, or by an averaging method.

The FIFO method assumes that the shares sold were the first ones acquired. Using the FIFO method when shares have appreciated over time may result in a substantial capital gain and tax due. The most productive strategy would be to sell those shares with the highest cost and thereby minimize the tax liability or generate a loss that can be used to offset other gains. The identifiable cost method is useful for that purpose.

The identifiable cost method requires that the shares sold be specifically identified as the ones acquired on a specific date at a specific acquisition cost. The IRS states: "If you can definitely identify within the fund the shares of stock you sold, the basis is the cost or other basis of those shares of stock. However, when a number of shares are acquired and sold at various times in different quantities and the shares you sell cannot be identified with certainty, the basis of the shares you sell is the basis of the securities acquired first." When using the identifiable cost method of accounting for share costs, the IRS places the burden of proof on the taxpayer. That is, the taxpayer must be able to trace a sale to a specific block of shares. One method for doing this is to periodically request that the fund send stock certificates that represent the investor's holdings. When a sale is made, the investor should record the certificate number(s) and the date of acquisition, along with the original cost and proceeds received. This method, however, is time-consuming and cumbersome, and requires safeguarding of the certificates.

If the shares are left on deposit with the fund, as most fund investors do, shareholders should keep detailed records of each purchase. When a sale is desired, the shareholder should write to the fund (or telephone and follow up with a letter) and instruct the fund to sell a specific block of shares acquired on a specific date; these shares identified for sale would have the highest cost basis in order to minimize any tax liability. He should also request that the fund confirm the sale in writing. A copy of the original letter and the confirmation letter should both be saved.

Other methods allowed by the tax code provide investors with averaging techniques to compute the basis of shares sold, as long as certain requirements are met. These approaches are somewhat complex and are explained in IRS Publication 564.

Taxpayers who are determining their basis for tax purposes should remember that, when liquidating holdings, some of the shares may have been acquired through automatic reinvestment of distributions. Thus, the cost basis for these shares is the per-share net asset value at the time of reinvestment. The taxpayer will have already partially satisfied the income tax liability on these shares, since taxes were paid on the distribution. Ignoring the cost of shares acquired this way could result in an overpayment of income taxes. For example, suppose an individual invested $2,000 in a mutual fund two years ago. Since the per-share net asset value at that time was $10, he acquired 200 shares. Recently, he liquidated his holdings in this fund and received $3,000. It might appear in this instance that he must pay taxes on $1,000 of long-term capital gains. However, suppose that the fund made two distributions during this period totaling $600, and suppose that those distributions were reinvested. Income tax on the distribution was paid; in essence, the taxpayer used the distribution to purchase new shares totaling $600. The shareholder's basis in the fund is really $2,600, and the investment gain subject to taxation at the time of liquidation is only $400 ($3,000 − $2,600). This illustrates the need to maintain good mutual fund account records.

Taxpayers should be aware that brokers, including mutual funds, underwriters of the fund or agents of the fund, are required to report to the IRS the proceeds from sales, exchanges or redemptions. They will send shareholders a written statement, Form 1099-B, detailing the transactions by January 31 of the year following the calendar year in which the transaction occurred. This is not required, though, for transactions in money market mutual funds.

Since the tax aspects of investing and mutual fund trading are among the greatest causes of investor confusion, it is a good idea for all potential mutual fund investors to familiarize themselves with federal tax reporting requirements before they invest. The fund prospectus gives some information on the taxation of distributions and the reporting of account activity. An excellent source of information is prepared by the IRS itself, Publication 564. In addition to listing the tax rules, the booklet gives numerous examples to illustrate how the rules apply in different situations.

4

A Systematic Approach to Fund Selection

Financial data and summaries of mutual fund services are presented in Chapters 7 and 8 for nearly 400 no-load mutual funds. Without an efficient approach and a firm idea of your financial goals and needs, searching through these funds for appropriate investments may consume a substantial amount of your time and energy. This chapter provides a guide for establishing a systematic approach, and the information we supply in the data pages will enable you to implement that approach.

Important Considerations

Mutual fund investments should reflect a number of variables that are defined by the individual investor. These are:

- Risk tolerance,
- Anticipated holding period,
- Liquidity needs,
- Income requirements, and
- Tax exposure.

Risk tolerance refers to the potential volatility of an investment—fluctuations in return—that an investor finds acceptable. For well-diversified portfolios, a relative measure of volatility is 'beta,' a concept that we will discuss shortly.

The anticipated holding period is important for the investor to define, because it helps determine the investor's risk tolerance. Time is a form of diversification; longer holding periods provide greater diversification across different market environments. Thus, investors who anticipate longer holding periods can take on more risk.

The liquidity needs of an investor help define the types of funds investors should consider. Liquidity implies preservation of capital, so that withdrawals from a mutual fund can be made at any time with a reasonable certainty that the per-share value will not have dropped sharply. Highly volatile aggressive growth funds are the least liquid, and short-term fixed-income funds are the most liquid.

Income requirements are a concern if the mutual fund investment must generate some consistent level of income for the investor on a periodic basis. Bond funds produce much more reliable income flows than common stock mutual funds. However, no matter what the investment objective of a fund, there are usually periodic withdrawal programs available if certain income flows are required.

Tax exposure presents an important decision point for investors. High tax bracket investors should seek mutual funds that are unlikely to make large distributions. The tax initiative ideally should be up to the investor, who can make the decision by timing the sale of mutual fund shares. Conversely, high tax-bracket investors can advantageously relegate high distribution funds to their tax-sheltered accounts such as IRAs or Keoghs.

Life Cycles

These investment parameters can be viewed as a function of the point in your life cycle. Table 4-1 below gives some generalized investment circumstances.

Many individuals, of course, do not fit neatly into life cycle categories, but they may still have similar circumstances. For instance, individuals in their early career phase may be intermediate-term, medium-risk investors, rather than long-term, high-risk investors. The important considerations are the investment circumstances themselves, because they will affect the kinds of funds chosen. Polar examples of mutual fund choices that reflect the different sets of

Figure 4-1
The Life Cycle: Risk Tolerance, Holding Period and Tax Exposure

	Early Career	Mid Career	Late Career	Retirement
Risk Tolerance	High	High	Medium	Low
Holding Period	Long	Long	Intermediate	Intermediate
Tax Exposure	Low	High	High	Low

circumstances are:

- The high-risk, long-term, high-tax-exposure individual, who would tend to hold aggressive growth and growth common stock mutual funds that have growth potential but low dividend yields, and who would tend to use shorter-term municipal bond funds to meet liquidity needs; versus
- The low-risk, shorter-term, low-tax-exposure individual, who would tend to hold growth and income and balanced common stock mutual funds that have some growth potential but that also pay a significant dividend, and who would tend to use shorter-term, high-yield bond or money market funds to meet liquidity needs.

Of course, these circumstances continually change, sometimes dramatically; the mutual fund portfolio must be viewed dynamically.

Beta: A Closer Look at Risk

Of the circumstances we discussed above, risk is the most difficult concept for many investors to define, and yet much of the selection question depends on this definition. For instance, the amount of money invested in money market or bond funds is a function of your anticipated liquidity needs, and your tax bracket dictates whether mutual fund investments should generate high or low levels of income. Which funds to choose, then, and how much to invest in each, becomes a function primarily of your risk tolerance.

The measure for risk that we use in this guide is beta. It is an important concept to understand, because beta can be used as a measure of risk for a single fund and for your entire portfolio. Thus if you define your risk in terms of beta, you can select funds with betas that, taken in combination, reflect your own risk tolerance.

Beta is a measure of the relative volatility inherent in a mutual fund investment. This volatility is measured relative to the market, which is usually defined as the Standard & Poor's Index of 500 common stocks. The market's beta is always 1.0, and a money market fund's beta is always 0. If you hold a mutual fund with a beta of 1.0, it will move on average in tandem with the market: If the market is up 10%, the fund will be up on average 10%, and if the market drops 10%, the fund will drop on average 10%. A mutual fund with a beta of 1.5 is 50% more volatile: If the market is up 10%, the fund will be up on average 50% more or 15%, and conversely, if the market is down 10%, the fund on average will be down 15%. A negative beta implies that the mutual fund moves inversely in some magnitude to the market. A few of the bond funds have negative betas that are near zero.

The higher the fund's beta, the greater the volatility of the investment in the fund and the less appropriate the fund would be for shorter holding periods. It should be remembered that beta is a relative measure: A low beta only implies that the fund's movement is not volatile relative to the market. Its return, however may be quite variable. For instance, industry-specific sector fund moves may not be related to market volatility, but changes in the industry may cause their returns to fluctuate widely. For a well-diversified stock fund, beta is a very useful measure of risk, but for concentrated funds, beta only captures a portion of the variability that the fund may experience. Beta is also less useful for measuring the risk inherent in bond funds or mutual funds with large bond holdings, since these funds may move relatively independent of the stock market. Betas for precious metals funds can be even more misleading. Precious metals funds often have relatively low betas, but these funds are extremely volatile. Their volatility stems from factors that do not affect the common stock market as much. In addition, the betas of precious metals funds sometimes change significantly from year to year.

Although betas can be misleading risk measures for some mutual funds, they can be helpful in determining the market risk of an investor's overall portfolio.

The beta of a mutual fund portfolio is the weighted sum of the betas of the individual mutual fund investments, based on their percentage representation (at market value) in the portfolio. For example, if a portfolio is divided among three mutual funds, with equal investments (based on the current market value of the funds) in each, the portfolio beta would be:

$(0.33 \times \text{beta Fund A}) + (0.33 \times \text{beta Fund B}) + (0.33 \times \text{beta Fund C})$

The examples below illustrate the approach. However, they only represent four of the infinite combinations of mutual funds and proportions invested in each. The betas used in the examples are averages for the class of mutual fund suggested (See Figure 1-1 in

Chapter 1); if you were determining your own portfolio's beta, you would use individual mutual fund betas.

The higher-risk, longer-term holding period, higher-tax-exposure individual with minimum liquidity needs: One portfolio combination might be 90% in aggressive common stock mutual funds (high capital gains potential, low dividend yield; average beta of 1.11), and 10% in tax-exempt money market funds (beta of 0). The portfolio beta is:

$$(0.90 \times 1.11) + (0.10 \times 0) = 1.00$$

The lower-risk, shorter-term holding period, lower-tax-exposure individual with higher liquidity needs: One portfolio might have 40% in growth common stock mutual funds (average beta of 0.93), 40% in growth and income common stock mutual funds (with an average beta of 0.80), and 20% in taxable money market funds (beta of 0). The portfolio beta is:

$$(0.40 \times 0.93) + (0.40 \times 0.80) + (0.20 \times 0) = 0.69$$

Alternatively, this same risk level can be achieved with a different mix: 84% in growth and income common stock mutual funds, and 16% in a bond fund (average beta of 0.08). The portfolio beta remains the same:

$$(0.84 \times 0.80) + (0.16 \times 0.08) = 0.69$$

The lower-risk, higher-tax-exposure individual: One possible portfolio would use the same funds as the first example, but would increase the investment in money market funds so that the risk is the same as the second example. Under this scenario, 62% is in aggressive growth common stocks, and 38% is in tax-exempt money market funds. The portfolio beta is:

$$(0.62 \times 1.11) + (0.38 \times 0) = 0.69$$

Defining your risk tolerance level is a crucial step in the fund selection process. Even if you do not go through the calculations described above, you should have some idea of how the riskiness of the fund you choose will affect your overall portfolio. The individual fund beta figures, provided in the data section, will help you do this. Once you have determined your own risk tolerance, you will have a better idea of which category to choose from in selecting a mutual fund. After defining your investment parameters (taxes, liquidity, holding period, income, risk) you are ready to look at the individual mutual funds themselves.

5

An Explanation of the Mutual Fund Statistics

When choosing among mutual funds, most investors start with performance statistics: How well have the various mutual funds performed in the past? If past performance could only perfectly predict future performance, the selection would be easy. But, of course, it can't.

What past performance can tell you is how well the fund's management has handled different market environments, how consistent the fund has been, and how well the fund has done relative to its risk level, relative to other similar funds and relative to the market. We present performance statistics in Chapter 6 in several different forms. First, we provide an overall picture, with the average performance of each mutual fund category for the last five years, along with stock market, bond market and Treasury bill benchmarks. The top 20 and bottom 20 no-load mutual fund performers for 1987 are given for a recent reference. The list changes each year and reflects the cyclical nature of financial markets and the changing success of individual mutual fund managers. A list of the top 50 mutual funds ranked by five-year total return is given for a long-term perspective on investment performance.

Since the performance of a fund must be judged relative to similar funds, we have also grouped the funds by category and ranked the funds according to their total return performance for 1987; funds that are closed but would otherwise meet criteria for inclusion in the guide have their performance reported in a separate category. To make the comparison easier, we have also provided other data in this chapter. The fund's five-year total return figure gives a longer-term perspective on the performance of the fund; the letter (superscript) indicates the fund's performance relative to all other funds that have five years of data—an 'A' indicates the fund was in the top 20% in terms of performance, and an 'E' indicates the fund was in the bottom 20%. Consistency of performance is indicated by the actual returns during bull and bear markets, and the accompanying letter designates the relative bull and bear market performance ranking for the period compared to all other funds. We also included the fund's beta as a measure of risk. Betas were not determined for tax-exempt funds.

Individual Funds

After reviewing the performance rankings, you can find more in-depth information on the individual funds in the one-page financial summaries for each no-load fund in Chapter 7 and in the half-page summaries for tax-exempt funds in Chapter 8. The funds here are presented alphabetically, not by category. Their categories, however, are indicated at the top of the page, under the fund's name. These pages provide six years of per-share data, performance and risk statistics, a summary of investment objectives, portfolio composition, services, and the telephone number and address of the fund.

Some of this information is taken directly from mutual fund reports (the prospectus, annual and quarterly reports), while other statistics, such as fund performance and risk, were calculated by us.

The following provides definitions and explanations of the terms we have used in the summaries of the individual funds. The explanations are listed in the order in which the data appear on the fund summary pages.

Years Ending: This indicates over what time period the per-share data applies, and varies with the fiscal year of the fund. Funds with fiscal years ending in June, in particular, have year-old data. Most funds have more recent data, since the fiscal year ends near or at the end of the calendar year. The fiscal yearend is when the fund's per-share data is made available to the shareholders. The performance statistics are always calculated on a calendar-year basis no matter what fiscal year the fund uses.

Net Investment Income: Dividend and interest income earned by the fund, stated in per-share amounts.

Dividends from Net Investment Income: Per-share income distributions reported in the fiscal year.

Net Gains (Losses) on Investments: Per-share realized and unrealized capital gains. The difference between beginning value or cost incurred during the year and current market or realized value.

Distributions from Net Realized Capital Gains: Per-share distributions from realized capital gains after netting out realized losses. These distributions vary each year with both the investment success of the fund and the amount of securities sold.

Net Asset Value End of Year: Net asset value is the sum of all securities held, based on their market value, divided by the number of mutual fund shares outstanding at the end of the fiscal year.

Ratio of Expenses to Net Assets: The sum of administrative fees plus advisor management fees and 12b-1 fees divided by the average net asset value of the fund, stated as a percentage. Brokerage costs incurred by the fund are not included in the expense ratio but are instead reflected directly in net asset value.

Portfolio Turnover Rate: A measure of the trading activity of the fund, which is computed by dividing the lesser of purchases or sales for the fiscal year by the monthly average value of the securities owned by the fund during the year. Securities with maturities of less than one year are excluded from the calculation. The result is expressed as a percentage, with 100% implying a complete portfolio turnover within one year.

Total Assets: Aggregate year-end fund value in millions of dollars.

Annual Rate of Return: This is a total return figure, expressed as a percentage increase (decrease), and was computed using monthly net asset values per share and shareholder distributions during the year. Distributions were assumed to be reinvested at the end of the month in which they were paid. Return on investment is calculated on the basis of the calendar year, regardless of the fund's fiscal year.

Five-Year Total Return: Assuming investment on January 1, 1983, the total percentage increase (decrease) in investment value if held through December 31, 1987. All distributions are assumed to have been reinvested at the end of the month in which they were paid. The letter superscript indicates the fund's five-year ranking among all funds: An 'A' indicates the fund was among the top 20%, an 'E' indicates the fund was among the bottom 20%, with 'B', 'C' and 'D' falling in between.

An Explanation of the Mutual Fund Statistics **31**

Degree of Diversification: Diversification is a relative concept. We have measured fund diversification relative to the S&P 500, under the assumption that the market represents a well-diversified portfolio. The diversification rankings were assigned after statistically determining how closely the returns of the fund matched the overall market during the three-year period starting January 1, 1985, and ending December 31, 1987. The more closely the returns matched the market during that period, the higher the diversification ranking. Common stock funds that did not track the market well, and therefore had lower diversification rankings, many times had industry or special concentrations, such as sector, gold, and international funds. Some funds, however, had lower diversification rankings due to high cash positions, even though they were not sector or specialty funds. Diversification should be thought of as market-tracking ability rather than number or type of investments. We ranked all of the funds based on market-tracking ability and divided them into five groups. An 'A' represents the group that most closely tracked the market; 'E' represents the group that tracked the market the least. The others fall into the remaining groups. The lower the degree of diversification ranking, the greater the chance that the fund's return will not follow the market. This figure was not calculated for balanced, bond and tax-exempt bond funds, due to their investments in fixed-income securities.

Beta: A risk measure that relates the volatility in returns of the fund to the market. The higher the beta of a fund, the higher the risk of the fund. The figure is based on monthly returns for the 36 months from the beginning of 1985 through the end of 1987. A beta of 1.0 indicates that the fund's returns will on average be as volatile as the market and move in the same direction; a beta higher than 1.0 indicates that if the market rises or falls, the fund will rise or fall respectively but to a greater degree; a beta of less than 1.0 indicates that if the market rises or falls, the fund will rise or fall to a lesser degree. The S&P 500 index always has a beta of 1.0; money market funds will always have a beta of 0. Occasionally, a fund will have a negative beta. This means that on average the fund's return moves inversely to the market. Negative beta funds usually have beta values near 0 and are concentrated in the precious metals and bond fund categories.

Bull: The rating reflects the fund's performance in the most recent bull (up) market, starting August 1, 1984, and continuing through August 31, 1987. The funds were ranked relative to all other funds according to their total return for the period. They were then divided into five groups. Group A reflects the top 20%, Group B the next 20%, and Group E reflects the bottom 20%. Funds ranked A and B performed better than average during the bull market, funds ranked C performed average, and funds ranked D and E performed worse than average during the bull market.

Bear: The rating reflects the fund's performance in the most recent bear (down) market, from September 1, 1987, through December 31, 1987. The funds were ranked relative to all other funds according to their total return for the period. They were then divided into five groups. Group A reflects the top 20%, Group B the next 20%, and Group E reflects the bottom 20%. Funds ranked A and B performed better than average during the bear market, funds ranked C performed average, and funds ranked D and E performed worse than average during the bear market.

NA: Indicates that the statistic was not available. For the five-year total return figure, the statistic would not be available for funds that have been operating for less than five years. For the beta and degree of diversification figures, funds operating for less than 36 months would not have the statistics available. Balanced funds, bond funds and tax-exempt bond funds do not have diversification statistics. For the bull and bear ratings, funds not operating during the entire bull or bear market period would not have these statistics available.

Information on portfolio composition was obtained directly from the fund's annual and quarterly reports, and we have indicated the date on which the information is based. Please note that some funds employ leverage, borrowing to buy securities, and this may result in the portfolio composition exceeding 100%.

The months in which income and capital gains distributions to shareholders are made is indicated when available. If a fund has a 12b-1 plan, the maximum amount that can be charged is given; remember, though, that while no fund can be charged more than the maximum, some funds are charged less than the maximum, and some are not charged at all. If the fund's advisor pays the charge, it is so noted. The minimum initial and subsequent investments in the fund are also detailed. Often, funds will have lower minimums for IRAs; this is also indicated.

Investor services provided by the fund are detailed. These include the availability for IRA, Keogh, corporate pension and profit-sharing plans, simplified employee pension plans and non-profit group retirement plans (indicated by **IRA, Keogh, Corp, SEP,** and **403(b)**, respectively); whether the fund allows the automatic and systematic withdrawal of monies from the fund (indicated by **Withdraw**); and if the fund allows for automatic investments through an investor's checking account **(Deduct)**. Since all funds have automatic reinvestment of distribution options, this service was not specifically noted.

Telephone exchanges with other funds in the family are also listed. If exchange privileges are allowed, we have indicated whether the family includes a money market fund.

Finally, we list the states in which the fund is registered. If the fund is not registered in the state in which you reside, you will not be able to open an account in the fund.

Other Lists

We have also included a list of new funds at the end of the mutual fund summaries. These funds appear in NASD newspaper listings but were less than one year old as of December 31, 1987, and therefore financial data or analysis was either not useful or not possible.

Mutual funds that are shown to be no-load in the financial press but that do not appear in this book are listed after the new fund section. Examples would be funds closed to new investors, funds for institutional or corporate customers only, funds limited to employees or members of a particular organization, and 'no-load' funds with redemption fees that continue after six months.

Our last list is of fund families that contain primarily no-load funds. All of the funds within a family, including load funds, are listed.

6

Mutual Fund Performance Rankings

On the following pages, we have ranked all of the no-load mutual funds listed in this guide by their investment performance. The funds were ranked according to several different criteria. These are:

The performance statistics also include information on bull and bear market performance, and risk as measured by beta. **Chapter 5 presents a detailed explanation of the performance statistics; a summary is presented on the following page.**

A summary of total return performance is presented below, along with stock, bond, and money market indexes for comparison.

Mutual Fund Categories and Total Return Performance Summary

Category	Total Return (%)						
	1982	1983	1984	1985	1986	1987	5-Year
Aggressive Growth	22.7	19.0	(11.5)	26.9	10.7	(2.3)	47.1
Growth	21.6	19.7	(2.3)	25.9	11.7	1.0	67.6
Growth & Income	20.6	21.1	4.1	25.8	13.9	(0.4)	80.2
Balanced	24.6	20.9	9.1	25.3	17.5	(0.3)	98.7
Bond	27.8	9.6	11.5	20.5	14.4	1.1	68.5
Tax-Exempt	33.5	9.5	8.5	17.5	16.6	(0.9)	63.4
International	0.1	30.4	(5.0)	33.4	51.1	10.8	167.8
Precious Metals	39.0	(1.5)	(26.2)	(7.3)	39.3	28.5	28.9
S&P 500	21.4	22.4	6.1	31.6	18.6	5.2	113.2
Salomon Bond Index	42.5	6.3	16.9	30.1	19.9	2.6	98.9
T-Bills	10.5	8.8	9.9	7.7	6.2	5.9	44.8

Key to Performance Rankings

Annual & Five-Year Total Return: Includes the change in net asset value and all distributions, and assumes reinvestment of distributions at the end of each month. Five-year total returns are ranked (A through E). The letter 'A' indicates the fund was in the top performance group and the letter 'E' indicates the fund was in the bottom group. The letters 'B,' 'C' and 'D' indicate the fund was in the 2nd, 3rd or 4th performance group.

Bull: Fund performance and ranking (A through E) over the most recent bull market, from August 1984 through August 1987. For the rankings, 'A' indicates the fund was in the top group and 'E' indicates the fund was in the bottom group; funds ranked 'B,' 'C' and 'D' fell in between.

Bear: Fund performance and ranking (A through E) over the most recent bear market, from September 1987 through December 1987. For the rankings, 'A' indicates the fund was in the top group and 'E' indicates the fund was in the bottom group; funds ranked 'B,' 'C' and 'D' fell in between.

Beta: A measure of risk relative to the market. The market's beta is always 1.0; a beta higher than 1.0 indicates fund returns were more volatile than the market and a beta lower than 1.0 indicates fund returns were less volatile than the market.

For more complete descriptions, see Chapter 5.

Key to Fund Types

A	— Aggressive Growth	**GI**	— Growth & Income
Bal	— Balanced	**Intl**	— International
Bd	— Bond	**M**	— Precious Metals
G	— Growth	**TE**	— Tax-Exempt

The Top 20 Performers: 1987

Type	Fund	Return (%)
M	Lexington Goldfund	46.3
Intl	Nomura Pacific Basin Fund	33.8
M	US Gold Shares	31.6
M	US New Prospector	31.1
M	Bull & Bear Gold Investors Ltd.	30.3
Intl	T. Rowe Price International Bond	28.1
G	Mathers	26.2
Intl	Vanguard/Trustees' Commingled—Int'l.	23.4
Intl	Ivy International	19.6
G	Rightime	19.5
G	T. Rowe Price New Era	17.5
M	Financial Strategic Portfolio—Gold	16.0
M	USAA Gold	15.8
A	100 Fund	15.7
G	IAI Stock	15.4
G	Columbia Growth	14.7
G	IAI Apollo	13.9
Bal	Loomis-Sayles Mutual	13.6
G	Permanent Portfolio	13.1
A	20th Century Growth	13.0

The Bottom 20 Performers: 1987

Type	Fund	Return (%)
A	44 Wall Street	(34.6)
GI	Steadman Associated	(23.9)
G	Bowser Growth	(19.3)
A	Bruce	(18.0)
G	Steadman Investment	(17.5)
Bd	Benham Target Maturities Trust Series 2010	(15.2)
G	Cumberland Growth	(15.0)
A	US LoCap	(13.2)
G	Janus Value	(11.7)
G	Unified Growth	(11.6)
Bal	Unified Income	(11.6)
Bal	Stratton Monthly Dividend Shares	(11.3)
A	US Growth	(11.2)
A	Financial Strategic Portfolio—Financial Services	(11.0)
G	Afuture	(11.0)
A	Neuwirth	(10.7)
GI	Vanguard Convertible Securities	(10.7)
A	Legg Mason Special Investment Trust	(10.6)
Bd	Benham Target Maturities Trust Series 2005	(10.4)
G	T. Rowe Price New America Growth	(9.9)

Top 50 Funds: Five-Year Total Return
(1983 through 1987)

Type	Fund	Return (%)
Intl	T. Rowe Price International	204.9
Intl	Transatlantic Fund	190.6
Intl	Scudder International	190.3
Bal	Mutual Shares	146.3
GI	Dodge & Cox Stock	145.0
Bal	Mutual Qualified Income	144.1
A	Lehman Opportunity	128.0
Bal	Lindner Dividend	123.7
Bal	Loomis-Sayles Mutual	123.2
G	Boston Co. Capital Appreciation	120.2
G	T. Rowe Price New Era	119.6
G	Manhattan	118.7
GI	Selected American Shares	118.0
Bal	Evergreen Total Return	114.6
Bal	Vanguard/Wellington	114.1
G	Legg Mason Value Trust	113.8
Bal	Financial Industrial Income	113.0
Bal	Safeco Income	110.6
A	Fairmont	109.6
GI	Vanguard Index Trust	109.2
G	Acorn	109.1
Bal	Dodge & Cox Balanced	108.2
GI	Ivy Growth	108.2
G	Mathers	107.9
A	Quest for Value	106.5
A	New Beginning Growth	106.0
A	Twentieth Century Select	105.1
Bal	Vanguard/Wellesley	104.5
GI	Partners	104.4
A	SteinRoe Special	104.2
A	20th Century Growth	101.9
G	Century Shares Trust	100.9
GI	Founders Blue Chip	99.4
G	IAI Stock	98.8
G	IAI Regional	97.5
Bd	Fidelity High Income	96.4
GI	Gintel ERISA	95.1
GI	Penn Square Mutual	95.0
G	101 Fund	95.0
G	Nicholas	94.7
G	Scudder Capital Growth	93.1
Bal	Dreyfus Convertible Securities	93.0
Bd	Northeast Investors Trust	91.7
GI	UMB Stock	90.3
A	Evergreen	90.3
G	T. Rowe Price Growth Stock	89.2
GI	Fidelity Fund	89.1
GI	Unified Mutual Shares	88.3
Bal	Stratton Monthly Dividend Shares	87.3
G	Lexington Research	86.9

Aggressive Growth Funds
Ranked By 1987 Total Return

Fund	Total Return (%) 1987	Total Return (%) 5-Year	Market Cycle Performance (%) Bear	Market Cycle Performance (%) Bull	Beta
100 Fund	15.7	63.1[D]	(10.7)[C]	88.1[C]	0.89
20th Century Growth	13.0	101.9[A]	(26.8)[E]	168.3[A]	1.27
Fidelity Freedom	8.9	NA	(25.5)[E]	143.9[A]	1.12
SteinRoe Cap. Opp.	8.7	47.2[E]	(27.0)[E]	119.7[B]	1.21
FSP—Health Sciences	7.1	NA	(24.9)[E]	166.4[A]	1.26
T. Rowe Price Cap. App.	5.9	NA	(10.8)[C]	NA	NA
20th Century Select	5.7	105.1[A]	(23.9)[D]	147.3[A]	1.10
New Beginning Growth	5.5	106.0[A]	(24.6)[D]	132.9[A]	1.13
Founders Special	5.3	56.3[D]	(24.2)[D]	102.4[B]	1.09
Janus Venture	5.1	NA	(17.3)[C]	NA	NA
Reich & Tang Equity	5.1	NA	(19.6)[D]	NA	NA
SteinRoe Stock	5.1	60.5[D]	(26.1)[E]	127.3[A]	1.12
FSP—Energy	4.9	NA	(28.2)[E]	102.5[B]	0.88
Lehman Opportunity	4.5	128.0[A]	(20.0)[D]	114.2[B]	0.80
Financial Dynamics	3.7	39.0[E]	(30.3)[E]	116.5[B]	1.32
SteinRoe Special	3.5	104.2[A]	(21.6)[D]	122.8[B]	1.00
Columbia Special	3.0	NA	(30.0)[E]	NA	NA
Tudor	1.1	77.5[B]	(27.7)[E]	126.8[A]	1.24
FSP—Leisure	0.7	NA	(25.0)[E]	127.7[A]	1.11
Sherman, Dean	0.2	(29.2)[E]	(37.9)[E]	47.3[E]	0.58
Lexington Growth	0.0	47.7[E]	(25.9)[E]	135.1[A]	0.99
USAA Sunbelt Era	(0.8)	30.6[E]	(26.1)[E]	85.4[C]	1.16
GIT Equity Special Growth	(1.4)	NA	(20.0)[D]	119.6[B]	0.98
Fund Trust Agg. Growth	(1.4)	NA	(22.1)[D]	NA	0.79
Scudder Development	(1.6)	34.5[E]	(26.5)[E]	80.1[C]	1.18
Medical Technology	(1.9)	36.7[E]	(25.2)[E]	126.1[A]	1.19
Quest for Value	(2.1)	106.5[A]	(21.1)[D]	95.6[C]	0.78
American Investors	(2.2)	(9.8)[E]	(28.3)[E]	62.9[D]	1.26
SteinRoe Discovery	(3.2)	NA	(28.1)[E]	100.9[C]	1.36
Evergreen	(3.5)	90.3[B]	(24.7)[D]	116.7[B]	0.91
Leverage Fund of Boston	(4.0)	27.0[E]	(34.9)[E]	126.8[A]	1.38
Bull & Bear Capital Growth	(4.3)	39.8[E]	(28.4)[E]	93.7[C]	1.12
Vanguard Explorer II	(4.5)	NA	(27.5)[E]	NA	NA
FSP—Utilities	(4.9)	NA	(11.0)[C]	NA	NA
Dreyfus New Leader	(5.3)	NA	(28.5)[E]	NA	NA
FSP—Technology	(5.3)	NA	(30.4)[E]	114.9[B]	1.34
Gradison Opp. Growth	(5.4)	NA	(22.0)[D]	93.4[C]	0.89
Axe-Houghton Stock	(6.2)	42.7[E]	(35.8)[E]	141.6[A]	1.34
Gintel Capital Apprec.	(7.1)	NA	(21.4)[D]	NA	NA
Naess & Thomas Special	(7.2)	(0.2)[E]	(31.6)[E]	60.5[D]	1.23
Fairmont	(7.6)	109.6[A]	(26.2)[E]	117.4[B]	1.08
T. Rowe Price New Horizons	(7.6)	20.8[E]	(28.4)[E]	65.5[D]	1.20
Steadman Oceanographic	(8.5)	(31.6)[E]	(37.5)[E]	15.1[E]	1.46
Fiduciary Capital Growth	(9.0)	45.4[E]	(27.0)[E]	70.4[D]	1.02
Babson Enterprise	(9.5)	NA	(28.0)[E]	110.5[B]	1.05

Continued on next page

Aggressive Growth Funds
Ranked By 1987 Total Return

Fund	Total Return (%)		Market Cycle Performance (%)		Beta
	1987	5-Year	Bear	Bull	
Continued from previous page					
Value Line Special Sit.	(9.8)	2.1ᴱ	(29.1)ᴱ	65.3ᴰ	1.29
Legg Mason Special	(10.6)	NA	(29.8)ᴱ	NA	NA
Neuwirth	(10.7)	42.8ᴱ	(29.4)ᴱ	110.8ᴮ	1.14
FSP—Financial Services	(11.0)	NA	(18.4)ᶜ	NA	NA
US Growth	(11.2)	NA	(27.2)ᴱ	57.6ᴰ	1.05
US LoCap	(13.2)	NA	(33.6)ᴱ	NA	NA
Bruce	(18.0)	NA	(17.6)ᶜ	108.1ᴮ	0.72
44 Wall Street	(34.6)	(80.1)ᴱ	(42.1)ᴱ	(37.1)ᴱ	1.66
Average	**(2.3)**	**47.1**	**(26.0)**	**102.2**	**1.11**

Growth Funds
Ranked By 1987 Total Return

Fund	Total Return (%) 1987	5-Year	Market Cycle Performance (%) Bear	Bull	Beta
Mathers	26.2	107.9[A]	(3.7)[C]	117.3[B]	0.73
Rightime	19.5	NA	2.5[A]	NA	NA
T. Rowe Price New Era	17.5	119.6[A]	(19.1)[C]	131.3[A]	0.95
IAI Stock	15.4	98.8[A]	(18.3)[C]	121.0[B]	0.87
Columbia Growth	14.7	86.4[B]	(17.0)[C]	121.0[B]	0.96
IAI Apollo	13.9	NA	(20.3)[D]	NA	0.95
Permanent Portfolio	13.1	32.5[E]	(3.5)[B]	48.1[E]	0.24
Gradison Established Growth	12.4	NA	(13.1)[C]	134.9[A]	0.84
Founders Growth	10.2	79.2[B]	(21.4)[D]	131.7[A]	1.01
Flex—Retirement Growth	10.1	62.2[D]	(14.0)[C]	59.3[D]	0.67
Wayne Hummer Growth	9.3	NA	(19.4)[D]	114.2[B]	0.97
Flex Growth	7.6	NA	(13.4)[C]	NA	NA
Nicholas II	7.2	NA	(19.1)[C]	124.2[A]	0.81
Safeco Growth	7.0	59.7[D]	(19.8)[D]	80.4[C]	0.95
WPG	6.8	80.7[B]	(22.9)[D]	123.8[B]	1.07
Growth Industry Shares	6.6	56.3[D]	(18.5)[C]	85.4[C]	0.94
Dreyfus Growth Opportunity	6.4	84.6[B]	(22.0)[D]	108.2[B]	0.87
USAA Growth	5.5	49.3[D]	(21.9)[D]	97.2[C]	1.01
Beacon Hill Mutual	5.4	80.5[B]	(21.8)[D]	114.0[B]	0.94
IAI Regional	5.0	97.5[A]	(18.1)[C]	139.2[A]	0.89
Vanguard/W.L. Morgan Gr.	4.7	77.7[B]	(25.2)[E]	117.0[B]	1.05
Value Line Fund	4.7	38.3[E]	(20.2)[D]	126.7[A]	1.10
Acorn	4.3	109.1[A]	(20.6)[D]	129.4[A]	0.86
T. Rowe Price Growth	3.3	89.2[B]	(22.1)[D]	142.5[A]	0.94
Babson Growth	3.1	84.8[B]	(24.9)[E]	138.2[A]	1.01
Value Line Leveraged	3.0	59.0[D]	(23.4)[D]	136.2[A]	1.13
Harbor Growth	2.9	NA	(25.2)[E]	NA	NA
National Industries	2.6	35.4[E]	(22.0)[D]	70.9[C]	0.92
Brandywine Fund	2.6	NA	(29.9)[E]	NA	NA
Vanguard Star	1.6	NA	(13.4)[C]	NA	NA
Salem Growth	1.6	NA	(21.6)[D]	NA	NA
Steadman American Industry	0.9	(28.5)[E]	(28.0)[E]	14.4[E]	0.98
Gateway Growth Plus	0.7	NA	(22.8)[D]	NA	NA
US Good and Bad Times	0.6	58.2[D]	(23.6)[D]	100.3[C]	0.95
Selected Special Shares	0.6	63.3[C]	(26.7)[E]	102.4[B]	1.02
Boston Co. Capital Apprec.	0.4	120.2[A]	(20.1)[D]	136.6[A]	0.90
Manhattan	0.4	118.7[A]	(27.5)[E]	153.8[A]	1.11
AARP Capital Growth	0.1	NA	(24.7)[D]	NA	NA
Armstrong Associates	0.1	32.3[E]	(23.9)[D]	84.4[C]	0.90
Financial Industrial	0.0	58.2[D]	(25.9)[E]	112.3[B]	1.06
Lexington Research	0.0	86.9[B]	(22.9)[D]	120.7[B]	0.90
Scudder Capital Growth	(0.8)	93.1[B]	(25.4)[E]	133.0[A]	1.09
Fund Trust Growth	(1.1)	NA	(19.4)[D]	NA	0.73
Nicholas	(1.3)	94.7[B]	(19.1)[C]	101.5[B]	0.68
SteinRoe Universe	(1.6)	39.9[E]	(26.7)[E]	100.3[C]	1.11

Continued on next page

Growth Funds
Ranked By 1987 Total Return

Fund	Total Return (%) 1987	5-Year	Market Cycle Performance (%) Bear	Bull	Beta
Continued from previous page					
AMA Growth	(1.8)	52.6[D]	(24.8)[D]	100.8[C]	1.02
Fidelity Contrafund	(2.1)	58.5[D]	(30.3)[E]	132.8[A]	1.09
Vanguard Primecap	(2.3)	NA	(24.3)[D]	NA	1.06
101 Fund	(2.6)	95.0[B]	(19.2)[D]	84.8[C]	0.80
SBSF Fund	(3.1)	NA	(20.6)[D]	92.0[C]	0.70
Newton Growth	(3.6)	53.3[D]	(31.2)[E]	105.7[B]	1.07
Sound Shore	(3.7)	NA	(21.6)[D]	NA	NA
Rainbow	(4.0)	55.9[D]	(24.7)[D]	88.4[C]	0.90
Fidelity Trend	(4.2)	70.7[C]	(28.4)[E]	119.4[B]	1.16
Stratton Growth	(4.3)	62.4[D]	(22.7)[D]	89.9[C]	0.95
Northeast Investors Growth	(4.3)	85.2[B]	(27.2)[E]	149.7[A]	0.99
Boston Co. Special Growth	(4.4)	71.0[C]	(25.4)[E]	96.8[C]	1.06
Vanguard World—U.S. Gr.	(6.1)	NA	(23.9)[D]	NA	NA
Legg Mason Value Trust	(7.2)	113.8[A]	(26.4)[E]	116.2[B]	0.95
Century Shares Trust	(8.0)	100.9[A]	(20.2)[D]	127.6[A]	0.80
Calvert—Equity Portfolio	(8.2)	29.4[E]	(28.9)[E]	92.3[C]	1.01
Copley Tax-Managed	(8.3)	86.2[B]	(13.2)[C]	86.7[C]	0.49
Fidelity Value	(8.6)	54.7[D]	(26.2)[E]	95.4[C]	0.92
T. Rowe Price New America	(9.9)	NA	(26.4)[E]	NA	NA
Afuture	(11.0)	(7.6)[E]	(24.1)[D]	39.0[E]	0.94
Unified Growth	(11.6)	51.2[D]	(26.7)[E]	99.1[C]	1.01
Janus Value	(11.7)	NA	(26.1)[E]	NA	NA
Cumberland Growth	(15.0)	26.2[E]	(25.9)[E]	67.8[D]	0.84
Steadman Investment	(17.5)	(7.8)[E]	(30.9)[E]	50.7[D]	0.92
Bowser Growth	(19.3)	NA	(40.2)[E]	NA	1.03
Average	**1.0**	**67.6**	**(22.1)**	**105.7**	**0.93**

Growth & Income Funds
Ranked By 1987 Total Return

Fund	Total Return (%) 1987	Total Return (%) 5-Year	Market Cycle Performance (%) Bear	Market Cycle Performance (%) Bull	Beta
Dodge & Cox Stock	12.5	145.0[A]	(20.2)[D]	165.1[A]	0.94
Rushmore Index Plus	8.9	NA	(21.5)[D]	NA	NA
UMB Stock	5.1	90.3[B]	(19.4)[D]	102.8[B]	0.87
Penn Square Mutual	4.9	95.0[B]	(21.3)[D]	112.2[B]	0.85
Vanguard Index Trust	4.7	109.2[A]	(24.5)[D]	143.5[A]	1.00
Valley Forge	4.6	53.3[D]	(3.6)[C]	31.9[E]	0.15
Analytic Optioned Equity	4.2	70.5[C]	(11.6)[C]	67.7[D]	0.54
Partners	4.2	104.4[A]	(19.5)[D]	122.3[B]	0.79
Janus	3.9	81.3[B]	(17.1)[C]	85.1[C]	0.68
Primary Trend Fund	3.7	NA	(13.2)[C]	NA	NA
T. Rowe Price Equity Inc.	3.5	NA	(15.8)[C]	NA	NA
Scudder Growth & Income	3.4	78.8[B]	(18.0)[C]	128.6[A]	0.86
Vanguard Quantitative	3.3	NA	(24.4)[D]	NA	NA
Viking Equity Index	3.3	NA	(24.6)[D]	NA	NA
Babson Value	3.3	NA	(25.4)[E]	NA	1.00
Fidelity Fund	3.1	89.1[B]	(23.2)[D]	124.5[A]	0.99
Dreyfus Third Century	2.5	69.4[C]	(20.1)[D]	95.8[C]	0.80
Founders Blue Chip	2.4	99.4[A]	(23.1)[D]	128.5[A]	0.96
Istel (Lepercq)	2.3	47.5[E]	(17.1)[C]	74.9[C]	0.71
General Securities	2.0	66.4[C]	(9.0)[C]	87.9[C]	0.56
Vanguard/Trustees'—U.S.	1.6	77.3[B]	(27.3)[E]	122.3[B]	1.03
AARP Growth & Income	0.7	NA	(19.2)[C]	NA	NA
Energy	0.6	73.9[C]	(23.8)[D]	97.2[C]	0.84
Selected American Shares	0.2	118.0[A]	(21.4)[D]	126.3[A]	0.78
Dividend/Growth—Dividend	(0.2)	58.9[D]	(22.0)[D]	85.0[C]	0.90
Guardian Mutual	(1.0)	86.9[B]	(26.2)[E]	121.0[B]	0.92
Gintel ERISA	(1.1)	95.1[B]	(18.4)[C]	97.7[C]	0.78
Ivy Growth	(1.8)	108.2[A]	(21.7)[D]	117.4[B]	0.74
Vanguard Windsor II	(2.1)	NA	(23.4)[D]	NA	NA
Unified Mutual Shares	(2.3)	88.3[B]	(19.3)[D]	106.9[B]	0.78
Noddings Convertible	(2.9)	NA	(9.4)[C]	NA	NA
Bartlett Basic Value	(3.8)	NA	(20.9)[D]	NA	0.62
T. Rowe Price Growth & Inc.	(4.3)	67.1[C]	(23.2)[D]	86.3[C]	0.88
Fund Trust Growth & Inc.	(4.5)	NA	(18.6)[C]	NA	0.66
Calamos Convertible	(4.5)	NA	(16.9)[C]	NA	NA
Safeco Equity	(4.8)	77.1[B]	(29.2)[E]	130.2[A]	1.04
Gateway Option Income	(5.7)	47.1[E]	(16.5)[C]	61.1[D]	0.53
Pine Street	(5.8)	76.2[C]	(24.8)[E]	112.5[B]	0.94
LMH	(6.4)	NA	(14.5)[C]	71.2[C]	0.50
Reserve Equity Contrarian	(6.8)	NA	(30.6)[E]	140.2[A]	0.97
Legg Mason Total Return	(7.5)	NA	(24.6)[D]	NA	NA
Flex—Income and Growth	(7.6)	NA	(10.6)[C]	NA	NA
Vanguard Convertible	(10.7)	NA	(19.2)[D]	NA	NA
Steadman Associated	(23.9)	(8.0)[E]	(31.0)[E]	38.9[E]	1.04
Average	(0.4)	80.2	(20.1)	102.9	0.80

Balanced Funds
Ranked By 1987 Total Return

Fund	Total Return (%)		Market Cycle Performance (%)		Beta
	1987	5-Year	Bear	Bull	
Loomis-Sayles Mutual	13.6	123.2[A]	(12.9)[C]	154.3[A]	0.92
USAA Cornerstone	9.0	NA	(18.5)[C]	NA	0.61
BB&K Diversa Fund	8.2	NA	(8.4)[C]	NA	NA
Dodge & Cox Balanced	7.7	108.2[A]	(13.4)[C]	121.2[B]	0.63
Mutual Qualified Income	7.6	144.1[A]	(15.6)[C]	105.6[B]	0.61
Mutual Shares	6.2	146.3[A]	(15.7)[C]	104.7[B]	0.60
Financial Industrial Income	4.8	113.0[A]	(17.9)[C]	120.8[B]	0.80
Strong Income	4.3	NA	(1.6)[B]	NA	NA
Vanguard/Wellington	2.3	114.1[A]	(15.2)[C]	112.7[B]	0.65
Founders Equity Income	1.9	69.1[C]	(13.9)[C]	69.3[D]	0.53
SteinRoe Total Return	0.4	76.1[C]	(13.2)[C]	89.3[C]	0.60
Vanguard/Wellesley	(1.9)	104.5[A]	(4.0)[C]	78.5[C]	0.29
Value Line Income	(2.4)	54.1[D]	(17.5)[C]	94.4[C]	0.68
Dreyfus Convertible	(3.0)	93.0[B]	(19.3)[D]	103.8[B]	0.57
Axe-Houghton Fund B	(4.0)	85.5[B]	(19.6)[D]	120.5[B]	0.76
Lindner Dividend	(4.1)	123.7[A]	(9.2)[C]	65.8[D]	0.30
US Income	(4.3)	NA	(8.4)[C]	36.3[E]	0.39
Bull & Bear Equity-Income	(4.7)	71.4[C]	(18.6)[C]	95.5[C]	0.69
Adtek	(4.9)	NA	(26.0)[E]	NA	0.83
Safeco Income	(5.9)	110.6[A]	(21.6)[D]	118.9[B]	0.77
Value Line Convertible	(6.1)	NA	(17.1)[C]	NA	NA
Evergreen Total Return	(8.9)	114.6[A]	(16.3)[C]	100.2[C]	0.56
Stratton Monthly Dividend	(11.3)	87.3[B]	(11.3)[C]	92.4[C]	0.46
Unified Income	(11.6)	37.4[E]	(18.2)[C]	56.6[D]	0.55
Average	**(0.3)**	**98.7**	**(14.7)**	**96.9**	**0.61**

Bond Funds
Ranked By 1987 Total Return

Fund	Total Return (%) 1987	5-Year	Market Cycle Performance (%) Bear	Bull	Beta
Treasury First Fund	8.9	NA	5.0ᴬ	NA	NA
IAI Reserve	5.9	NA	2.1ᴬ	NA	NA
American Investors Income	5.8	61.4ᴰ	(4.5)ᶜ	56.8ᴰ	0.29
Boston Co. Managed Income	5.7	NA	1.8ᴬ	NA	0.09
Neuberger Money Market Plus	5.5	NA	2.2ᴬ	NA	NA
Bull & Bear U.S. Gov't.	5.4	NA	2.1ᴬ	NA	NA
Delaware Treasury Reserves	5.3	NA	2.2ᴬ	NA	NA
T. Rowe Price Short-Term	5.2	NA	3.3ᴬ	NA	0.01
Rodney Square Benchmark	4.7	NA	6.5ᴬ	NA	NA
Baker—U.S. Government	4.5	NA	3.5ᴬ	NA	NA
Vanguard Short-Term Bond	4.4	66.5ᶜ	2.8ᴬ	42.9ᴱ	0.03
SteinRoe High-Yield Bonds	4.0	NA	3.0ᴬ	NA	NA
Fidelity Short-Term Bond	3.9	NA	2.3ᴬ	NA	NA
20th Century U.S. Gov't.	3.8	54.8ᴰ	3.2ᴬ	35.4ᴱ	0.00
Financial Bond—High Yield	3.6	NA	(2.3)ᴮ	NA	0.19
USAA Income	3.5	75.0ᶜ	2.9ᴬ	50.1ᴰ	0.06
Strong Gov't. Securities	3.4	NA	9.4ᴬ	NA	NA
Value Line U.S. Gov't.	3.4	67.2ᶜ	3.1ᴬ	52.5ᴰ	0.01
UMB Bond	2.9	59.8ᴰ	3.3ᴬ	43.5ᴱ	0.02
T. Rowe Price High Yield	2.9	NA	(4.0)ᶜ	NA	0.21
Scudder Target Gen'l. 1990	2.9	53.3ᴰ	2.2ᴬ	48.8ᴰ	0.03
Merit U.S. Government	2.9	NA	4.4ᴬ	NA	NA
Benham GNMA Income	2.8	NA	3.7ᴬ	NA	NA
Bartlett Fixed Income	2.8	NA	1.0ᴮ	NA	NA
Vanguard High Yield	2.7	82.0ᴮ	(2.1)ᴮ	64.1ᴰ	0.19
Fidelity Mortgage	2.6	NA	2.6ᴬ	NA	0.01
Nicholas Income	2.6	75.3ᶜ	0.2ᴮ	53.7ᴰ	0.11
Dreyfus GNMA	2.5	NA	2.1ᴬ	NA	NA
Newton Income	2.5	58.0ᴰ	2.1ᴬ	31.4ᴱ	0.02
WPG Gov't. Securities	2.5	NA	3.5ᴬ	NA	NA
Benham Target—1990	2.4	NA	3.1ᴬ	NA	NA
Vanguard GNMA	2.3	72.1ᶜ	3.3ᴬ	50.3ᴰ	(0.01)
Fidelity Intermediate	2.1	73.4ᶜ	2.7ᴬ	51.4ᴰ	0.06
T. Rowe Price New Income	2.1	68.0ᶜ	4.3ᴬ	40.6ᴱ	(0.05)
IAI Bond	2.1	71.4ᶜ	3.0ᴬ	52.3ᴰ	0.03
AARP GNMA & U.S. Treas.	2.0	NA	2.3ᴬ	NA	NA
Babson Bond Trust	1.9	73.4ᶜ	3.1ᴬ	50.3ᴰ	0.04
Axe-Houghton Income	1.8	85.3ᴮ	1.4ᴬ	70.0ᴰ	0.16
Scudder Gov't. Mortgage	1.5	NA	2.2ᴬ	NA	NA
Columbia Fixed Income	1.4	NA	3.1ᴬ	46.1ᴱ	0.01
California U.S. Gov't.	1.2	NA	2.5ᴬ	NA	NA
Fidelity High Income	1.2	96.4ᴬ	(4.0)ᶜ	72.8ᶜ	0.21
AARP General Bond	1.2	NA	3.1ᴬ	NA	NA
Vanguard Bond Market	1.2	NA	3.1ᴬ	NA	NA
Fidelity Ginnie Mae	1.2	NA	2.5ᴬ	NA	NA

Continued on next page

Bond Funds
Ranked By 1987 Total Return

Fund	Total Return (%) 1987	Total Return (%) 5-Year	Market Cycle Performance (%) Bear	Market Cycle Performance (%) Bull	Beta
Continued from previous page					
SteinRoe Managed Bonds	1.1	72.6ᶜ	3.3ᴬ	51.6ᴰ	0.06
Fidelity Gov't. Securities	1.0	60.9ᴰ	2.6ᴬ	45.5ᴱ	0.05
Safeco U.S. Gov't.	0.9	NA	1.2ᴬ	NA	NA
Scudder Income	0.8	74.9ᶜ	2.7ᴬ	53.8ᴰ	0.08
Lexington GNMA	0.8	60.4ᴰ	1.7ᴬ	45.6ᴱ	(0.02)
T. Rowe Price GNMA	0.8	NA	1.5ᴬ	NA	NA
Boston Company GNMA	0.7	NA	1.9ᴬ	NA	NA
Mutual of Omaha America	0.7	55.7ᴰ	3.6ᴬ	37.4ᴱ	0.02
Fund Trust Income	0.4	NA	(2.0)ᴮ	NA	0.15
Vanguard Investment Grade	0.3	70.3ᶜ	3.8ᴬ	51.9ᴰ	0.05
Northeast Investors Trust	0.1	91.7ᴮ	(5.1)ᶜ	80.7ᶜ	0.16
Fidelity Flexible Bond	0.1	63.9ᶜ	2.6ᴬ	48.8ᴰ	0.05
Dreyfus A Bond Plus	(0.4)	68.9ᶜ	2.4ᴬ	52.8ᴰ	0.08
AMA Income	(0.6)	56.9ᴰ	0.9ᴮ	42.1ᴱ	0.09
Flex Bond	(0.7)	NA	(0.3)ᴮ	NA	NA
Git Income—A-Rated	(1.1)	NA	2.7ᴬ	55.9ᴰ	0.06
Cap. Preservation T-Note	(1.3)	57.9ᴰ	3.4ᴬ	39.8ᴱ	0.04
US GNMA	(1.3)	NA	3.3ᴬ	NA	NA
Financial Bond—Select	(1.5)	58.9ᴰ	0.5ᴮ	57.0ᴰ	0.15
Value Line Aggressive Inc.	(2.0)	NA	(8.0)ᶜ	NA	NA
GIT Income—Maximum	(2.8)	NA	(5.9)ᶜ	52.9ᴰ	0.19
Vanguard U.S. Treasury Bond .	(2.9)	NA	4.0ᴬ	NA	NA
Rightime Gov't. Securities	(3.1)	NA	2.6ᴬ	NA	NA
Benham Target—1995	(3.9)	NA	4.2ᴬ	NA	NA
Liberty	(4.6)	68.8ᶜ	(8.0)ᶜ	60.7ᴰ	0.26
Financial Bond—U.S. Gov't.	(5.1)	NA	(0.3)ᴮ	NA	NA
Benham Target—2000	(6.0)	NA	7.9ᴬ	NA	NA
Bull & Bear High Yield	(6.4)	NA	(9.2)ᶜ	42.8ᴱ	0.21
Benham Target—2005	(10.4)	NA	9.8ᴬ	NA	NA
Benham Target—2010	(15.2)	NA	9.3ᴬ	NA	NA
Average	**1.1**	**68.5**	**1.9**	**50.9**	**0.08**

Tax-Exempt Bond Funds
Ranked By 1987 Total Return

	Total Return (%)		Market Cycle Performance (%)		
Fund	1987	5-Year	Bear	Bull	Beta
U.S.T. Int. Tax-Exempt	4.5	NA	3.3[A]	NA	NA
Vanguard Short Term Muni	4.1	34.2[E]	1.2[A]	22.0[E]	0.03
Calvert Tax-Free Ltd. Term	3.5	39.1[E]	0.9[B]	25.2[E]	0.05
AARP Tax Free Short Term	3.3	NA	1.2[A]	NA	NA
Scudder Tax-Free Target 1990 ...	3.2	NA	0.6[B]	31.1[E]	0.06
USAA Tax Exempt Short	2.8	39.9[E]	2.4[A]	24.0[E]	0.04
Scudder Tax-Free Target 1993 ...	2.6	NA	0.4[B]	38.9[E]	0.08
Benham Nat'l. Tax-Free Int.	2.2	NA	0.4[B]	25.2[E]	0.09
T. Rowe Price TF Short-Int.	2.2	NA	1.1[B]	25.4[E]	0.05
Vanguard Intermediate Munis ...	1.7	61.7[D]	1.2[A]	44.0[E]	0.11
SteinRoe Intermediate Munis	1.7	NA	0.4[B]	NA	NA
Scudder Tax-Free Target 1996 ...	1.5	NA	1.3[A]	NA	NA
Fidelity Aggressive Tax-Free	1.4	NA	(1.2)[B]	NA	NA
California Muni Fund	1.4	NA	0.7[B]	NA	0.09
Park Ave. N.Y. Tax Exempt	1.4	NA	0.5[B]	NA	0.12
Fidelity Limited Term Munis ..	1.1	65.0[C]	0.3[B]	43.2[E]	0.11
Dreyfus Inter. Tax Exempt	1.1	NA	(0.2)[B]	NA	0.12
USAA Tax Exempt Inter..........	1.0	58.5[D]	1.8[A]	38.4[E]	0.10
Benham Calif. Intermediate	0.8	NA	0.4[B]	32.6[E]	0.07
Value Line TE High Yield	0.5	NA	(0.6)[B]	NA	0.15
T. Rowe Price TF High Yield .	0.3	NA	(0.6)[B]	NA	NA
Fidelity Short-Term Tax-Free ..	0.2	NA	0.1[B]	NA	NA
Unified Municipal—Indiana	0.2	NA	0.5[B]	NA	NA
Safeco Municipal	0.2	77.1[B]	0.4[B]	54.3[D]	0.15
SteinRoe Managed Munis	0.1	84.4[B]	2.3[A]	53.2[D]	0.16
Vanguard Muni. Insured Long	0.1	NA	0.6[B]	NA	0.12
Lexington Tax Exempt Bond ...	0.0	NA	0.4[B]	NA	NA
US Tax Free	(0.2)	NA	1.1[A]	NA	0.07
Scudder Managed Municipals ..	(0.3)	64.7[C]	(0.3)[B]	47.1[E]	0.15
SteinRoe High-Yield Munis	(0.3)	NA	(1.0)[B]	NA	0.16
GIT Tax-Free High Yield	(0.6)	NA	(0.1)[B]	49.9[D]	0.16
Scudder New York Tax-Free ...	(0.7)	NA	0.1[B]	NA	0.15
Fidelity Texas Tax-Free	(0.7)	NA	(0.7)[B]	NA	NA
Bull & Bear Tax-Free Income ..	(0.9)	NA	0.1[B]	52.2[D]	0.16
Kentucky Tax-Free Income	(1.0)	62.7[D]	1.4[A]	39.8[E]	0.11
Unified Municipal—General	(1.0)	NA	0.2[B]	NA	NA
Vanguard Long-Term Munis ...	(1.1)	69.6[C]	0.9[B]	49.3[D]	0.14
Calif. Tax Free Income	(1.2)	NA	(0.4)[B]	NA	NA
Fidelity Massfree	(1.3)	NA	(0.9)[B]	NA	0.15
Vanguard Pennsylvania Ins.	(1.3)	NA	0.9[B]	NA	NA
AARP Tax Free Bond	(1.4)	NA	0.4[B]	NA	NA
Strong Tax-Free Income	(1.4)	NA	2.9[A]	NA	NA
Fidelity Municipal	(1.5)	68.4[C]	(0.2)[B]	50.1[D]	0.13
Vanguard High-Yield Munis	(1.6)	73.6[C]	0.4[B]	50.5[D]	0.16

Continued on next page

Tax-Exempt Bond Funds
Ranked By 1987 Total Return

	Total Return (%)		Market Cycle Performance (%)		
Fund	1987	5-Year	Bear	Bull	Beta
Continued from previous page					
Dreyfus California Tax Ex.	(1.7)	NA	(0.8)ᴮ	NA	0.15
Scudder California Tax Free	(1.7)	NA	0.2ᴮ	NA	0.19
Dreyfus Tax Exempt	(1.7)	67.0ᶜ	(0.4)ᴮ	45.9ᴱ	0.13
Babson Tax-Free Income	(1.9)	65.9ᶜ	0.2ᴮ	48.0ᴱ	0.13
USAA Tax Exempt High-Yd. ..	(1.9)	68.8ᶜ	1.5ᴬ	41.9ᴱ	0.13
Dreyfus Insured Tax Exempt ...	(1.9)	NA	(0.1)ᴮ	NA	NA
Safeco California Tax-Free	(2.1)	NA	0.5ᴮ	50.6ᴰ	0.16
Fidelity Insured Tax-Free	(2.2)	NA	0.6ᴮ	NA	NA
Fidelity Ohio Tax-Free	(2.4)	NA	(0.7)ᴮ	NA	NA
Fidelity N.Y. TF High Yield ...	(2.4)	NA	(0.4)ᴮ	NA	0.14
T. Rowe Price New York TF ...	(2.5)	NA	0.9ᴮ	NA	NA
Merit Pennsylvania Tax-Free ...	(2.5)	NA	0.2ᴮ	NA	NA
Dreyfus New York Tax Ex.	(2.7)	NA	(1.5)ᴮ	NA	0.16
Fidelity High-Yield Munis	(2.9)	78.6ᴮ	(1.4)ᴮ	50.6ᴰ	0.15
Fidelity N.Y. Tax-Free Ins.	(3.2)	NA	0.5ᴮ	NA	NA
Fidelity Michigan Tax-Free	(3.2)	NA	(0.6)ᴮ	NA	NA
Dreyfus Mass. Tax-Ex.	(3.4)	NA	(1.4)ᴮ	NA	NA
Vanguard N.Y. Insured TF	(3.5)	NA	0.6ᴮ	NA	NA
Fidelity Calif. TF High Yield ...	(3.6)	NA	(0.3)ᴮ	39.1ᴱ	0.13
Vanguard Calif. TF Insured	(3.9)	NA	0.6ᴮ	NA	NA
Financial Tax-Free Income	(4.0)	69.8ᶜ	(0.1)ᴮ	52.2ᴰ	0.18
Fidelity Minnesota Tax-Free	(4.1)	NA	(0.9)ᴮ	NA	NA
T. Rowe Price Tax-Free Inc.	(4.2)	55.0ᴰ	(0.9)ᴮ	41.3ᴱ	0.16
Benham Calif. Tax-Free Long ..	(4.6)	NA	(0.7)ᴮ	41.8ᴱ	0.20
Fidelity Penn. TF High Yield ..	(5.8)	NA	(2.0)ᴮ	NA	NA
Benham Nat'l. Tax-Free Long .	(6.7)	NA	(2.5)ᴮ	NA	0.17
T. Rowe Price Calif. Tax-Free ...	(6.8)	NA	0.0ᴮ	NA	NA
New York Muni	(7.3)	NA	(2.0)ᴮ	39.8ᴱ	0.21
Average	**(0.9)**	**63.4**	**0.2**	**41.0**	**0.13**

International Funds
Ranked By 1987 Total Return

Fund	Total Return (%) 1987	5-Year	Market Cycle Performance (%) Bear	Bull	Beta
Nomura Pacific Basin	33.8	NA	(9.6)ᶜ	NA	NA
T. Rowe Price Int'l. Bond	28.1	NA	18.6ᴬ	NA	NA
Vanguard/Trustees'—Int'l.	23.4	NA	(12.8)ᶜ	216.4ᴬ	0.53
Ivy International	19.6	NA	(21.6)ᴰ	NA	NA
Vanguard World—Int'l.	12.4	NA	(11.0)ᶜ	NA	NA
FSP—Pacific Basin	9.8	NA	(27.9)ᴱ	252.3ᴬ	0.68
Transatlantic Fund	9.2	190.6ᴬ	(16.9)ᶜ	223.6ᴬ	0.60
T. Rowe Price International	8.0	204.9ᴬ	(17.5)ᶜ	233.1ᴬ	0.62
International Equity Trust	3.3	NA	(18.1)ᶜ	NA	NA
Scudder Global	2.9	NA	(22.9)ᴰ	NA	NA
World of Technology	2.4	NA	(18.2)ᶜ	79.1ᶜ	0.92
Pax World	2.2	85.5ᴮ	(14.9)ᶜ	86.9ᶜ	0.62
Scudder International	1.0	190.3ᴬ	(21.8)ᴰ	212.3ᴬ	0.70
FSP—European	(4.6)	NA	(20.3)ᴰ	NA	NA
Average	**10.8**	**167.8**	**(15.3)**	**186.2**	**0.67**

Precious Metal Funds
Ranked By 1987 Total Return

Fund	Total Return (%) 1987	5-Year	Market Cycle Performance (%) Bear	Bull	Beta
Lexington Goldfund	46.3	56.5ᴰ	(15.5)ᶜ	133.6ᴬ	0.38
US Gold Shares	31.6	(5.8)ᴱ	(18.3)ᶜ	45.7ᴱ	0.32
US New Prospector	31.1	NA	(28.2)ᴱ	NA	NA
Bull & Bear Gold	30.3	35.9ᴱ	(23.3)ᴰ	125.3ᴬ	0.46
FSP—Gold	16.0	NA	(31.3)ᴱ	95.2ᶜ	0.65
USAA Gold	15.8	NA	(34.7)ᴱ	NA	0.62
Average	**28.5**	**28.9**	**(25.2)**	**99.9**	**0.48**

Statistics for Closed Funds

Type	Fund	Total Return (%) 1987	5-Year	Market Cycle Performance (%) Bear	Bull	Beta
G	Lindner	8.8	107.7ᴬ	(15.0)ᶜ	74.0ᶜ	0.55
A	Loomis-Sayles Cap. Dev. .	15.9	131.1ᴬ	(18.8)ᶜ	128.4ᴬ	1.37
G	Sequoia	7.2	132.4ᴬ	(11.7)ᶜ	65.6ᴰ	0.53
A	Vanguard Explorer	(7.0)	0.8ᴱ	(25.4)ᴱ	5.4ᴱ	0.93
Bal	Vanguard High-Yd. Stock .	(4.7)	151.3ᴬ	(18.7)ᶜ	70.3ᴰ	0.54
GI	Vanguard Windsor	1.4	142.6ᴬ	(22.3)ᴰ	93.0ᶜ	0.78

7

Mutual Fund Data Summaries

On the following pages, we present in-depth information on 286 no-load mutual funds. The funds are listed alphabetically; their category is indicated at the top of the page under the fund's name. Below are brief definitions and explanations of some of the terms used on the data pages.

For more complete descriptions, see **Chapter 5.**

Years Ending: The fiscal year-end for the per-share data information, which varies among funds. All performance information, however, is calculated on a calendar-year basis.

Annual & Five-Year Total Return: Includes the change in net asset value and all distributions, and assumes reinvestment of distributions at the end of each month. Five-year total returns are also ranked: An 'A' indicates the fund was in the top performing group and an 'E' indicates the fund was in the lowest group.

Degree of Diversification: Measured relative to the S&P 500. Funds were ranked according to how closely their returns tracked the S&P 500. An 'A' indicates the fund was in the group that most closely tracked the market; an 'E' indicates the fund was in the group that tracked the market the least.

Beta: A measure of risk relative to the market. The market's beta is always 1.0; a beta higher than 1.0 indicates fund returns are more volatile than the market and a beta lower than 1.0 indicates fund returns are less volatile than the market.

Bull: Fund performance and ranking (A through E) over the most recent bull market, from August 1984 through August 1987.

Bear: Fund performance and ranking (A through E) over the most recent bear market, from September 1987 through December 1987.

Distributions: Months in which distributions are paid were provided when available.

12b-1: Indicates whether the fund has a 12b-1 plan. If the fund has a 12b-1 plan, either the maximum charge is indicated or it is stated that the advisor pays any distribution charges.

Investor Services: IRA, Keogh, Corp, 403(b) and **SEP** indicate the availability of IRA, Keogh, corporate pension and profit-sharing plans, non-profit group retirement plans, and simplified employee pension plans. **Withdraw** indicates if the fund allows for the automatic and systematic withdrawal of monies, and **Deduct** indicates if the fund allows for automatic investments through an investor's checking account. All funds offer automatic reinvestment of distributions.

AARP CAPITAL GROWTH

Growth

Scudder Fund Distributors
175 Federal Street
Boston, MA 02110-2267
(800) 253-2277

| | Years Ending 9/30 | | | | | |
	1982	1983	1984	1985 (10 mos.)	1986	1987
Net Investment Income ($)	—	—	—	.12	.18	.11
Dividends from Net Investment Income ($)	—	—	—	—	.09	.19
Net Gains (Losses) on Investments ($)	—	—	—	1.83	4.28	7.40
Distributions from Net Realized Capital Gains ($)	—	—	—	—	.19	.90
Net Asset Value End of Year ($)	—	—	—	16.95	21.13	27.55
Ratio of Expenses to Net Assets (%)	—	—	—	1.50	1.44	1.24
Portfolio Turnover Rate (%)	—	—	—	42	46	54
Total Assets: End of Year (Millions $)	—	—	—	20.6	55.7	115.9
Annual Rate of Return (%) Years Ending 12/31	—	—	—	—	15.9	0.1

Five-Year Total Return(%)	NA	Degree of Diversification	NA	Beta	NA	Bull (%)	NA	Bear (%)	(24.7)ᴰ

Objective: Seeks long-term capital appreciation through investment in common stocks and convertible securities. Looks for undervalued stocks with above average long-term earnings growth potential. Can invest in debt securities and put and call options.

Portfolio: (9/30/87) Common stocks 92%, short-term securities 7%, preferred stocks 1%. Largest stock holdings: media and service 25%, technology 15%.

Distributions: **Income:** Annually   **Capital Gains:** Annually

12b-1: No

Minimum: **Initial:** $250   **Subsequent:** None

Min IRA: **Initial:** $250   **Subsequent:** None

Services: IRA, Keogh, Withdraw, Deduct

Tel Exchange: Yes   **With MMF:** Yes

Registered: All states

AARP GENERAL BOND

Bond

Scudder Fund Distributors
175 Federal Street
Boston, MA 02110-2267
(800) 253-2277

	Years Ending 9/30					
	1982	1983	1984	1985 (10 mos.)	1986	1987
Net Investment Income ($)	—	—	—	1.06	1.41	1.22
Dividends from Net Investment Income ($)	—	—	—	1.06	1.41	1.22
Net Gains (Losses) on Investments ($)	—	—	—	.31	.61	(1.19)
Distributions from Net Realized Capital Gains ($)	—	—	—	—	.05	.23
Net Asset Value End of Year ($)	—	—	—	15.31	15.87	14.45
Ratio of Expenses to Net Assets (%)	—	—	—	1.50	1.30	1.18
Portfolio Turnover Rate (%)	—	—	—	54	63	193
Total Assets: End of Year (Millions $)	—	—	—	45.3	88.4	108.0
Annual Rate of Return (%) Years Ending 12/31	—	—	—	—	10.7	1.2

Five-Year Total Return(%)	NA	Degree of Diversification	NA	Beta	NA	Bull (%)	NA	Bear (%)	3.1[A]

Objective: Seeks high level of current income consistent with preservation of capital. Invests in short-, intermediate- and long-term government securities and in high quality corporate bonds. Normally has 65% of assets invested in government and corporate bonds.

Portfolio: (9/30/87) Long-term bonds 66%, intermediate-term bonds 32%, other assets 3%. Largest holdings: U.S. Treasury & agency 25%, utilities 16%.

Distributions: **Income:** Monthly   **Capital Gains:** Annually

12b-1: No

Minimum: **Initial:** $250   **Subsequent:** None

Min IRA: **Initial:** $250   **Subsequent:** None

Services: IRA, Keogh, Withdraw, Deduct

Tel Exchange: Yes   **With MMF:** Yes

Registered: All states

AARP GNMA & U.S. TREASURY
Bond

Scudder Fund Distributors
175 Federal Street
Boston, MA 02110-2267
(800) 253-2277

			Years Ending 9/30			
	1982	1983	1984	1985 (10 mos.)	1986	1987
Net Investment Income ($)	—	—	—	1.17	1.54	1.35
Dividends from Net Investment Income ($)	—	—	—	1.17	1.54	1.35
Net Gains (Losses) on Investments ($)	—	—	—	.52	.50	(1.09)
Distributions from Net Realized Capital Gains ($)	—	—	—	—	.03	.01
Net Asset Value End of Year ($)	—	—	—	15.52	15.99	14.89
Ratio of Expenses to Net Assets (%)	—	—	—	1.03	.90	.88
Portfolio Turnover Rate (%)	—	—	—	67	62	51
Total Assets: End of Year (Millions $)	—	—	—	322.1	1,963	2,827.6

Annual Rate of Return (%) Years Ending 12/31	—	—	—	—	11.4	2.0

Five-Year Total Return(%)	NA	Degree of Diversification	NA	Beta	NA	Bull (%)	NA	Bear (%)	2.3ᴬ

Objective: Seeks high level of current income consistent with preservation of capital. Invests primarily in GNMA securities and other debt instruments backed by the U.S. Government.

Portfolio: (9/30/87) GNMAs 50%, U.S. Treasury obligations 48%, repurchase agreements 2%.

Distributions: **Income:** Monthly   **Capital Gains:** Annually

12b-1: No

Minimum: **Initial:** $250   **Subsequent:** None

Min IRA: **Initial:** $250   **Subsequent:** None

Services: IRA, Keogh, Withdraw, Deduct

Tel Exchange: Yes   **With MMF:** Yes

Registered: All states

AARP GROWTH & INCOME

Growth & Income

Scudder Fund Distributors
175 Federal Street
Boston, MA 02110-2267
(800) 253-2277

	1982	1983	1984	1985 (10 mos.)	1986	1987
Net Investment Income ($)	–	–	–	.39	.73	.52
Dividends from Net Investment Income ($)	–	–	–	.19	.70	.49
Net Gains (Losses) on Investments ($)	–	–	–	1.64	4.10	5.51
Distributions from Net Realized Capital Gains ($)	–	–	–	–	.09	.88
Net Asset Value End of Year ($)	–	–	–	16.84	20.88	25.54
Ratio of Expenses to Net Assets (%)	–	–	–	1.50	1.21	1.08
Portfolio Turnover Rate (%)	–	–	–	13	37	43
Total Assets: End of Year (Millions $)	–	–	–	26.7	99.3	357.6

Years Ending 9/30

Annual Rate of Return (%) Years Ending 12/31	–	–	–	–	19.2	0.7

Five-Year Total Return(%)	NA	Degree of Diversification	NA	Beta	NA	Bull (%)	NA	Bear (%)	(19.2)c

Objective: Seeks long-term growth of capital, current income and growth of income. Invests primarily in common stocks and convertible securities. Looks for companies with good earnings growth potential that pay dividends.

Portfolio: (9/30/87) Common stocks 73%, convertible securities 21%, short-term securities 5%, preferred stocks 2%. Largest stock holdings: producer durables 12%, utilities 10%.

Distributions: Income: Feb, May, Aug, Nov   **Capital Gains:** Annually

12b-1: No

Minimum: Initial: $250   Subsequent: None

Min IRA: Initial: $250   Subsequent: None

Services: IRA, Keogh, Withdraw, Deduct

Tel Exchange: Yes   **With MMF:** Yes

Registered: All states

ACORN
Growth

Harris Associates, L.P.
Two N. LaSalle St.
Chicago, IL 60602-3790
(312) 621-0630

	Years Ending 12/31					
	1982	1983	1984	1985	1986	1987
Net Investment Income ($)	1.14	.60	.67	.58	.67	.73
Dividends from Net Investment Income ($)	1.03	1.04	.55	.51	.50	.77
Net Gains (Losses) on Investments ($)	2.87	5.95	.58	8.72	5.35	.61
Distributions from Net Realized Capital Gains ($)	.04	1.04	1.63	1.86	6.07	5.42
Net Asset Value End of Year ($)	27.35	31.82	30.89	37.82	37.27	32.42
Ratio of Expenses to Net Assets (%)	.92	.85	.85	.78	.79	.82
Portfolio Turnover Rate (%)	32	22	33	32	34	52
Total Assets: End of Year (Millions $)	132.4	173.8	210.2	317.5	414.6	417.8

Annual Rate of Return (%) Years Ending 12/31	17.5	25.1	4.5	31.4	16.7	4.3

Five-Year Total Return(%)	109.1^	Degree of Diversification	D	Beta	.86	Bull (%)	129.4^	Bear (%)	(20.6)^D

Objective: Seeks capital growth through investment in common stocks and convertibles of smaller companies that are not yet widely recognized as growth companies. May invest in foreign securities.

Portfolio: (12/31/87) Common stocks 87%, money markets 9%, fixed income 4%. Largest stock holdings: information group 28%, foreign securities 17%.

Distributions: Income: July, Dec   **Capital Gains:** Dec

12b-1: No

Minimum: Initial: $4,000   Subsequent: $1,000

Min IRA: Initial: $200   Subsequent: $200

Services: IRA, Keogh, SEP, Withdraw, Deduct

Tel Exchange: Yes   **With MMF:** Yes

Registered: All states except AL, AR, MS, ND, NH, NM, UT, VT

ADTEK
Balanced

Heath, Schneider, Mueller & Toll
4920 W. Vliet St.
Milwaukee, WI 53208
(414) 257-1842

	Years Ending 5/31					
	1982	1983	1984	1985	1986	1987
Net Investment Income ($)	–	–	–	.30	.37	.22
Dividends from Net Investment Income ($)	–	–	–	–	.29	.41
Net Gains (Losses) on Investments ($)	–	–	–	.80	1.70	1.66
Distributions from Net Realized Capital Gains ($)	–	–	–	–	.18	.72
Net Asset Value End of Year ($)	–	–	–	11.10	12.70	13.45
Ratio of Expenses to Net Assets (%)	–	–	–	1.95	1.87	1.73
Portfolio Turnover Rate (%)	–	–	–	179	232	107
Total Assets: End of Year (Millions $)	–	–	–	23.9	29.6	39.9

| Annual Rate of Return (%) Years Ending 12/31 | – | – | – | 13.5 | 16.0 | (4.9) |

| Five-Year Total Return(%) | NA | Degree of Diversification | NA | Beta | .83 | Bull (%) | NA | Bear (%) | (26.0)ᴱ |

Objective: Seeks long-term capital appreciation and protection of capital through a balance of common stocks of established companies, corporate bonds and money market instruments. The particular balance is determined by economic and market conditions indicated by various technical and fundamental analysis techniques. May enter into repos.

Portfolio: (11/30/87) Cash equivalents 70%, common stocks 30%. Largest stock holdings: consumer non-durables 11%, capital goods 6%.

Distributions: Income: Annually   **Capital Gains:** Annually

12b-1: No

Minimum: Initial: $250   Subsequent: $50

Min IRA: Initial: $250   Subsequent: $50

Services: IRA, Keogh, Corp, 403(b), Withdraw, Deduct

Tel Exchange: No

Registered: FL, IL, WI

AFUTURE

Growth

Carlisle-Asher Management Co.
Legal Arts Building
Front & Lemon Sts.
Media, PA 19063
(800) 523-7594/(215) 565-3131

	Years Ending 12/31					
	1982	1983	1984	1985	1986	1987
Net Investment Income ($)	.86	.09	.07	.10	(.02)	.09
Dividends from Net Investment Income ($)	.50	.82	.09	.08	.11	.12
Net Gains (Losses) on Investments ($)	2.58	1.77	(2.78)	2.28	(.76)	(1.05)
Distributions from Net Realized Capital Gains ($)	1.23	.96	2.01	—	—	2.14
Net Asset Value End of Year ($)	15.81	15.89	11.08	13.38	12.49	9.27
Ratio of Expenses to Net Assets (%)	1.60	1.60	1.60	1.60	1.40	1.60
Portfolio Turnover Rate (%)	160	152	121	193	200	355
Total Assets: End of Year (Millions $)	33.1	34.6	24.9	24.6	16.2	9.9
Annual Rate of Return (%) Years Ending 12/31	27.7	12.2	(19.2)	21.5	(5.9)	(11.0)

Five-Year Total Return(%)	(7.6)[E]	Degree of Diversification	C	Beta	.94	Bull (%)	39.0[E]	Bear (%)	(24.1)[D]

Objective: Capital appreciation through long-term holdings in common stock of large, well-established companies. Current dividend income is not a substantial factor in selecting investments. May take defensive posture in debt securities.

Portfolio: (12/31/87) Common stocks 54%, other assets 36%, short-term notes 10%. Largest stock holdings: consumer/miscellaneous products & services 17%, technology 16%.

Distributions: Income: Jan   **Capital Gains:** Jan

12b-1: No

Minimum: Initial: $500   Subsequent: $30

Min IRA: Initial: $500   Subsequent: $30

Services: IRA, Keogh, Withdraw, Deduct

Tel Exchange: No

Registered: All states except AK, AR, CT, ID, KS, KY, LA, ME, MS, ND, NH, NM, NV, SC, SD, UT, VA, VT, WY

AMA CLASSIC GROWTH FUND
(formerly AMA GROWTH)
Growth

AMA Advisers, Inc.
5 Sentry Pkwy. W., Suite 120
P.O. Box 1111
Blue Bell, PA 19422
(800) 262-3863/(215) 825-0400

| | Years Ending 9/30 | | | | | 12/31 | |
	1982	1983	1984	1985	1986	1986* (3 mos.)	1987
Net Investment Income ($)	.27	.22	.33	.32	.14	.03	.15
Dividends from Net Investment Income ($)	.23	.26	.26	.38	.16	.05	.16
Net Gains (Losses) on Investments ($)	.28	2.45	(.62)	.73	2.12	.44	(.17)
Distributions from Net Realized Capital Gains ($)	—	—	—	—	.41	1.79	2.16
Net Asset Value End of Year ($)	7.70	10.11	9.56	10.23	11.92	10.56	8.22
Ratio of Expenses to Net Assets (%)	1.26	1.26	1.30	1.32	1.34	1.73	1.65
Portfolio Turnover Rate (%)	77	114	129	158	127	146	148
Total Assets: End of Year (Millions $)	35.6	35.1	29.6	26.9	26.8	37.6	36.3

Annual Rate of Return (%) Years Ending 12/31	21.2	7.5	5.4	23.5	11.0	*	(1.8)

Five-Year Total Return(%)	52.6ᴰ	Degree of Diversification	A	Beta 1.02	Bull (%)	100.8ᶜ	Bear (%)	(24.8)ᴰ

Fiscal year changed from 9/30 to 12/31. All annual return figures are for full years ending 12/31.

Objective: Seeks capital appreciation. Fund favors equity investments in companies that have potential for above-average, long-term growth in sales and earnings on a sustained and predictable basis.

Portfolio: (9/30/87) Common stocks 81%, commercial paper 20%, other assets 1%. Largest stock holdings: technology 16%, basic materials 14%.

Distributions: Income: Jan, April, July, Oct   **Capital Gains:** Annually

12b-1: Yes   **Amount:** 0.50%

Minimum: Initial: $1,000   **Subsequent:** None

Min IRA: Initial: $500   **Subsequent:** $50

Services: IRA, Keogh, SEP, Corp, 403(b), Withdraw, Deduct

Tel Exchange: Yes   **With MMF:** Yes

Registered: All states

AMA CLASSIC INCOME
(formerly AMA INCOME)
Bond

AMA Advisers
5 Sentry Pkwy. W.
Suite 120, P.O. Box 1111
Blue Bell, PA 19422
(800) 262-3863/(215) 825-0400

	Years Ending 3/31					
	1982	1983	1984	1985	1986	1987
Net Investment Income ($)	.97	.85	.81	.86	.77	.60
Dividends from Net Investment Income ($)	.97	.89	.79	.87	.80	.63
Net Gains (Losses) on Investments ($)	(.49)	1.64	(.60)	.02	1.13	.05
Distributions from Net Realized Capital Gains ($)	–	–	–	–	–	–
Net Asset Value End of Year ($)	7.31	8.91	8.33	8.34	9.44	9.46
Ratio of Expenses to Net Assets (%)	1.16	1.16	1.25	1.50	1.39	1.65
Portfolio Turnover Rate (%)	122	256	105	62	147	67
Total Assets: End of Year (Millions $)	20.1	23.7	21.2	19.7	19.2	39.4

Annual Rate of Return (%) Years Ending 12/31		31.7	9.1	8.4	18.3	12.7	(.6)
Five-Year Total Return(%) 56.9ᴰ	Degree of Diversification NA	Beta .09	Bull (%) 42.1ᴱ	Bear (%) .9ᴮ			

Objective: Seeks the highest investment income available consistent with preservation of capital. At least 80% of assets are in short-term money market instruments or marketable debt securities of only the three highest investment ratings. May enter into repurchase agreements comprising no more than 10% of fund's assets.

Portfolio: (9/30/87) Non-convertible bonds 60%, U.S. Treasury securities 23%, temporary investments 10%, convertible bonds 7%.

Distributions: Income: Jan, Apr, July, Oct   **Capital Gains:** Apr

12b-1: Yes   **Amount:** 0.50%

Minimum: Initial: $1,000   **Subsequent:** None

Min IRA: Initial: $500   **Subsequent:** $50

Services: IRA, Keogh, Corp, 403(b), SEP, Withdraw, Deduct

Tel Exchange: Yes   **With MMF:** Yes

Registered: All states

AMERICAN INVESTORS GROWTH

Aggressive Growth

D.H. Blair Advisors, Inc.
777 W. Putnam Ave.
P.O. Box 2500
Greenwich, CT 06836
(800) 243-5353/(203) 531-5000

	Years Ending 12/31					
	1982	1983	1984	1985	1986	1987
Net Investment Income ($)	.22	.08	.12	.17	.02	.03
Dividends from Net Investment Income ($)	–	.23	.14	.19	–	.05
Net Gains (Losses) on Investments ($)	(2.30)	.26	(1.95)	.80	(.14)	(.17)
Distributions from Net Realized Capital Gains ($)	–	.76	–	.44	.60	.75
Net Asset Value End of Year ($)	9.45	8.80	6.83	7.17	6.45	5.51
Ratio of Expenses to Net Assets (%)	1.20	1.14	1.41	1.33	1.40	1.66
Portfolio Turnover Rate (%)	53	59	127	204	161	158
Total Assets: End of Year (Millions $)	138.1	116.7	85.0	80.1	64.2	53.1

Annual Rate of Return (%) Years Ending 12/31	(18.0)	3.6	(20.8)	14.3	(1.7)	(2.2)

Five-Year Total Return(%)	(9.8)ᴱ	Degree of Diversification	B	Beta 1.26	Bull (%) 62.9ᴰ	Bear (%) (28.3)ᴱ

Objective: Growth of investment capital through investment in common stocks. Securities are almost exclusively chosen on the basis of market action determined through statistics and charts of industry, company and market. Uses technical analysis of banking and money. May take defensive posture in debt investments.

Portfolio: (12/31/87) Common stocks 96%, convertible bonds 3%, notes 1%. Largest stock holdings: machinery 22%, oil 11%.

Distributions: Income: Dec   **Capital Gains:** Dec

12b-1: Yes   Amount: 0.50%

Minimum: Initial: $1,000   Subsequent: $100

Min IRA: Initial: $400   Subsequent: $100

Services: IRA, Keogh, SEP, Withdraw, Deduct

Tel Exchange: Yes   With MMF: Yes

Registered: All states

AMERICAN INVESTORS INCOME

Bond

D.H. Blair Advisors, Inc.
777 W. Putnam Ave.
P.O. Box 2500
Greenwich, CT 06836
(800) 243-5353/(203) 531-5000

	Years Ending 6/30					
	1982	1983	1984	1985	1986	1987
Net Investment Income ($)	1.27	1.21	1.26	1.12	1.12	1.13
Dividends from Net Investment Income ($)	1.27	1.21	1.25	1.12	1.12	1.14
Net Gains (Losses) on Investments ($)	(2.78)	3.01	(2.46)	.27	.16	(.44)
Distributions from Net Realized Capital Gains ($)	—	—	—	—	—	—
Net Asset Value End of Year ($)	8.25	11.26	8.81	9.08	9.24	8.79
Ratio of Expenses to Net Assets (%)	1.47	1.56	1.55	1.51	1.41	1.54
Portfolio Turnover Rate (%)	71	132	77	117	97	72
Total Assets: End of Year (Millions $)	12.7	18.2	16.4	20.2	23.4	23.1
Annual Rate of Return (%) Years Ending 12/31	12.6	26.9	(8.5)	22.7	7.0	5.8

Five-Year Total Return(%)	61.4D	Degree of Diversification	NA	Beta	.29	Bull (%)	56.8D	Bear (%)	(4.5)C

Objective: High current income. Invests in high yielding, lower-rated bonds and preferred stocks, most of which will reflect speculative characteristics being of medium or lower grade (Ba or BB or lower). May buy convertible fixed-income and convertible preferred stocks.

Portfolio: (6/30/87) Bonds 87%, preferred stocks 7%, commercial paper 5%, common stocks 1%. Largest holdings: savings & loan 14%, steel 12%.

Distributions: Income: Jan, April, July, Oct   **Capital Gains:** Jan

12b-1: Yes   **Amount:** 0.50%

Minimum: Initial: $1,000   **Subsequent:** $100

Min IRA: Initial: $400   **Subsequent:** $100

Services: IRA, Keogh, Corp, SEP, Withdraw, Deduct

Tel Exchange: Yes   **With MMF:** Yes

Registered: All states

ANALYTIC OPTIONED EQUITY

Growth & Income

Analytic Investment Mgmt., Inc.
2222 Martin St., #230
Irvine, CA 92715-1454
(714) 833-0294

	Years Ending 12/31					
	1982* (6 mos.)	1983	1984	1985	1986	1987
Net Investment Income ($)	.25	.46	.47	.56	.45	.38
Dividends from Net Investment Income ($)	.12	.60	.44	.48	.45	.46
Net Gains (Losses) on Investments ($)	1.55	1.86	.44	1.65	1.06	.24
Distributions from Net Realized Capital Gains ($)	—	.24	.02	1.20	2.20	2.48
Net Asset Value End of Year ($)	12.38	13.86	14.31	14.84	13.70	11.38
Ratio of Expenses to Net Assets (%)	1.48	1.23	1.30	1.23	1.18	1.17
Portfolio Turnover Rate (%)	28	49	45	54	64	84
Total Assets: End of Year (Millions $)	29.0	54.2	76.7	85.5	76.4	74.8
Annual Rate of Return (%) Years Ending 12/31	10.3	19.3	6.7	16.5	10.2	4.2

Five-Year Total Return(%)	70.5[c]	Degree of Diversification	A	Beta	.54	Bull (%)	67.7[D]	Bear (%)	(11.6)[c]

Year-end changed from 6/30 to 12/31.
All per share data is adjusted for a 10 for 1 stock split on 6/30/86.

Objective: Obtain a greater long-term total return and smaller fluctuations in quarterly total return from a diversified, optioned common stock portfolio than would be realized from the same portfolio unoptioned.

Portfolio: (12/31/87) Common stocks 81%, other assets 19%, put and call options 1%, short-term securities 1%. Largest stock holdings: telephone utilities 8%, computer equipment 8%.

Distributions: Income: Quarterly   **Capital Gains:** Annually
12b-1: No
Minimum: Initial: $5,000   Subsequent: $500
Min IRA: Initial: None   Subsequent: None
Services: IRA, Keogh, Corp, 403(b), SEP, Withdraw
Tel Exchange: No
Registered: All states except AR, MT, ND, NH, NM, OK, RI, SC, VT

ARMSTRONG ASSOCIATES
Growth

Armstrong Associates, Inc.
1445 Roff Ave.
Lock Box 212, Suite 1490
Dallas, TX 75202
(214) 720-9101

	Years Ending 6/30					
	1982	1983	1984	1985	1986	1987
Net Investment Income ($)	.41	.21	.16	.24	.14	.10
Dividends from Net Investment Income ($)	.19	.43	.20	.14	.24	.16
Net Gains (Losses) on Investments ($)	(1.28)	3.72	(2.51)	1.02	1.17	1.51
Distributions from Net Realized Capital Gains ($)	1.21	.38	.38	.76	—	.51
Net Asset Value End of Year ($)	7.10	10.22	7.29	7.65	8.72	9.66
Ratio of Expenses to Net Assets (%)	1.70	1.60	1.60	1.70	1.6	1.70
Portfolio Turnover Rate (%)	34	59	96	53	54	51
Total Assets: End of Year (Millions $)	7.7	12.9	9.8	11.0	11.7	12.3

Annual Rate of Return (%) Years Ending 12/31	15.5	11.0	(11.5)	21.0	11.3	.1

Five-Year Total Return(%)	32.3ᴱ	Degree of Diversification	B	Beta	.90	Bull (%)	84.4ᶜ	Bear (%)	(23.9)ᴰ

Objective: Seeks growth of capital through investment in common stock of large, established companies expected to have growth in earnings over a one- to three-year period. May invest in short-term debt securities as a defensive measure.

Portfolio: (9/30/87) Common stocks 84%, short-term debt and cash 16%. Largest stock holdings: electronics & electrical equipment 15%, retail & related 12%.

Distributions: Income: Oct   **Capital Gains:** Oct

12b-1: No

Minimum: Initial: $250   Subsequent: None

Min IRA: Initial: $250   Subsequent: None

Services: IRA, Keogh, Withdraw, Deduct

Tel Exchange: No

Registered: AR, LA, NM, TX

AXE-HOUGHTON FUND B
Balanced

Axe-Houghton Management, Inc.
400 Benedict Avenue
Tarrytown, NY 10591
(800) 431-1030/(914) 631-8131

	Years Ending 10/31					
	1982	1983	1984	1985	1986	1987
Net Investment Income ($)	.59	.68	.62	.71	.72	.44
Dividends from Net Investment Income ($)	.51	.59	.59	.66	.66	.58
Net Gains (Losses) on Investments ($)	1.24	.73	(.09)	1.23	2.90	(.48)
Distributions from Net Realized Capital Gains ($)	.13	.13	.13	—	.70	2.86
Net Asset Value End of Year ($)	8.99	9.68	9.49	10.77	13.03	9.55
Ratio of Expenses to Net Assets (%)	.76	.73	.76	.74	.98	1.18
Portfolio Turnover Rate (%)	19	64	88	97	239	324
Total Assets: End of Year (Millions $)	147.5	147.7	141.2	152.6	190.0	172.7

Annual Rate of Return (%) Years Ending 12/31	26.1	11.1	6.3	32.9	23.1	(4.0)

Five-Year Total Return(%)	85.5[B]	Degree of Diversification	NA	Beta	.76	Bull (%)	120.5[B]	Bear (%)	(19.6)[D]

Objective: Seeks conservation of capital, reasonable income, and long-term capital growth. May not invest more than 75% of its assets in common stocks at one time. Also invests in bonds and preferred stocks.

Portfolio: (10/31/87) Common stocks 54%, bonds and other notes 41%, short-term notes 6%, convertible preferred stocks 1%. Largest stock holdings: consumer staples 23%, health 9%.

Distributions: Income: Jan, April, July, Oct   **Capital Gains:** Jan

12b-1: Yes   Amount: 0.45%

Minimum: Initial: $1,000   Subsequent: None

Min IRA: Initial: $25   Subsequent: $25

Services: IRA, Keogh, Corp, 403(b), Withdraw, Deduct

Tel Exchange: Yes   **With MMF:** Yes

Registered: All states

AXE-HOUGHTON INCOME

Bond

Axe-Houghton Management, Inc.
400 Benedict Avenue
Tarrytown, NY 10591
(800) 431-1030/(914) 631-8131

	Years Ending 11/30					
	1982	1983	1984	1985	1986	1987
Net Investment Income ($)	.52	.47	.49	.51	.50	.53
Dividends from Net Investment Income ($)	.50	.50	.50	.50	.50	.50
Net Gains (Losses) on Investments ($)	.47	(.10)	.08	.45	.51	(.47)
Distributions from Net Realized Capital Gains ($)	–	–	–	–	–	–
Net Asset Value End of Year ($)	4.65	4.52	4.59	5.05	5.56	5.12
Ratio of Expenses to Net Assets (%)	1.02	1.01	1.09	1.04	1.37	1.42
Portfolio Turnover Rate (%)	55	30	13	90	90	269
Total Assets: End of Year (Millions $)	35.2	33.9	35.3	40.2	48.5	51.9

Annual Rate of Return (%) Years Ending 12/31	31.0	7.5	15.5	26.6	15.8	1.8

Five-Year Total Return(%)	85.3[B]	Degree of Diversification	NA	Beta	.16	Bull (%)	70.0[D]	Bear (%)	1.4[A]

Objective: Seeks high current income consistent with prudent investment risk. Invests in bonds and debentures, dividend-paying common stocks, convertible preferred stocks and bonds, government notes and short-term money market instruments.

Portfolio: (11/30/87) Bonds and other notes 96%, short-term notes 2%, other assets 2%. Largest holdings: bank and finance 23%, mortgage-backed 20%.

Distributions: Income: Jan, April, July, Oct   **Capital Gains:** Jan

12b-1: Yes   **Amount:** 0.45%

Minimum: Initial: $1,000   **Subsequent:** None

Min IRA: Initial: $25   **Subsequent:** $25

Services: IRA, Keogh, Corp, 403(b), Withdraw, Deduct

Tel Exchange: Yes   **With MMF:** Yes

Registered: All states

AXE-HOUGHTON STOCK

Aggressive Growth

Axe-Houghton Management, Inc.
400 Benedict Avenue
Tarrytown, NY 10591
(800) 431-1030/(914) 631-8131

	Years Ending 12/31					
	1982	1983	1984	1985	1986	1987
Net Investment Income ($)	.05	.07	.05	.06	.01	—
Dividends from Net Investment Income ($)	.05	.02	.05	—	.04	.04
Net Gains (Losses) on Investments ($)	2.33	2.66	(2.16)	2.07	.96	(.28)
Distributions from Net Realized Capital Gains ($)	—	.20	5.01	—	1.80	2.26
Net Asset Value End of Year ($)	11.51	14.02	6.85	8.98	8.11	5.53
Ratio of Expenses to Net Assets (%)	.88	.84	.95	.95	1.28	1.41
Portfolio Turnover Rate (%)	89	119	134	191	218	306
Total Assets: End of Year (Millions $)	160.5	150.8	87	107.3	96.2	65.6

Annual Rate of Return (%) Years Ending 12/31	26.1	23.7	(15.5)	31.1	10.9	(6.2)

Five-Year Total Return(%)	42.7ᴱ	Degree of Diversification	B	Beta	1.34	Bull (%) 141.6ᴬ	Bear (%) (35.8)ᴱ

Objective: Primary objective is long-term capital growth. Looks to invest in companies with above-average growth prospects. Also invests in convertible preferred and foreign stocks. For defensive purposes the fund can invest in bonds.

Portfolio: (12/31/87) Common stocks 96%, short-term notes 7%, convertible preferred stocks 1%. Largest stock holdings: technology 29%, consumer staples 26%.

Distributions: Income: Annually   **Capital Gains:** Annually
12b-1: Yes   **Amount:** 0.45%
Minimum: Initial: $1,000   **Subsequent:** None
Min IRA: Initial: $25   **Subsequent:** $25
Services: IRA, Keogh, Corp, 403(b), Withdraw, Deduct
Tel Exchange: Yes   **With MMF:** Yes
Registered: All states

BABSON BOND TRUST
Bond

Jones and Babson, Inc.
3 Crown Center
2440 Pershing Rd.
Kansas City, MO 64108
(800) 821-5591/(816) 471-5200

	Years Ending 11/30					
	1982	1983	1984	1985	1986	1987
Net Investment Income ($)	.17	.17	.17	.16	.16	.15
Dividends from Net Investment Income ($)	.17	.17	.12	.21	.16	.11
Net Gains (Losses) on Investments ($)	.10	Nil	(.01)	.11	.10	(.14)
Distributions from Net Realized Capital Gains ($)	—	—	—	—	—	—
Net Asset Value End of Year ($)	1.48	1.48	1.52	1.58	1.68	1.58
Ratio of Expenses to Net Assets (%)	.75	.75	.92	.98	.97	.97
Portfolio Turnover Rate (%)	91	49	42	39	41	72
Total Assets: End of Year (Millions $)	32.8	37.1	42.1	54.7	69.7	65.0

Annual Rate of Return (%) Years Ending 12/31	28.1	9.6	12.9	20.7	13.9	1.9

Five-Year Total Return(%)	73.4ᶜ	Degree of Diversification	NA	Beta	.04	Bull (%)	50.3ᴅ	Bear (%)	3.1ᴬ

Objective:	Seeks current regular income and stability of principal. Long-term capital growth is a secondary aim. Maturity structure is conservative, with all issues rated A or higher. Most agency securities are mortgages.
Portfolio:	(11/30/87) Corporate bonds 85%, U.S. government bonds 11%, other assets 3%, repos 2%. Largest bond holdings: banks and finance 25%, transportation 21%.
Distributions:	Income: Feb, May, Aug, Nov **Capital Gains:** Nov
12b-1:	No
Minimum:	Initial: $500 Subsequent: $50
Min IRA:	Initial: $250 Subsequent: $25
Services:	IRA, Keogh, SEP, Withdraw
Tel Exchange:	Yes **With MMF:** Yes
Registered:	All states

BABSON
ENTERPRISE
Aggressive Growth

Jones & Babson, Inc.
3 Crown Center
2440 Pershing Rd.
Kansas City, MO 64108
(800) 821-5591/(816) 471-5200

			Years Ending 11/30			
	1982	1983	1984 (11 mos.)	1985	1986	1987
Net Investment Income ($)	–	–	.07	.07	.04	.03
Dividends from Net Investment Income ($)	–	–	–	.07	.05	.05
Net Gains (Losses) on Investments ($)	–	–	(.77)	3.35	1.51	(2.15)
Distributions from Net Realized Capital Gains ($)	–	–	–	.13	.47	1.28
Net Asset Value End of Year ($)	–	–	9.30	12.52	13.56	10.12
Ratio of Expenses to Net Assets (%)	–	–	1.67	1.58	1.37	1.35
Portfolio Turnover Rate (%)	–	–	14	38	32	104
Total Assets: End of Year (Millions $)	–	–	7.3	34.5	47.9	35.6
Annual Rate of Return (%) Years Ending 12/31	–	–	(5.0)	38.6	9.0	(9.5)

Five-Year Total Return(%)	NA	Degree of Diversification	D	Beta	1.05	Bull (%)	110.5B	Bear (%)	(28.0)E

Objective: Seeks long-term capital growth through investment in smaller, faster-growing companies whose capitalization is between $15 million and $300 million.

Portfolio: (11/30/87) Common stocks 96%, repos 5%. Largest stock holdings: building and construction 13%, consumer products 12%.

Distributions: Income: Nov   **Capital Gains:** Nov
12b-1: No
Minimum: Initial: $1,000   Subsequent: $100
Min IRA: Initial: $250   Subsequent: $25
Services: IRA, Keogh, SEP, Withdraw
Tel Exchange: Yes   **With MMF:** Yes
Registered: All states

BABSON GROWTH
Growth

Jones & Babson, Inc.
3 Crown Center
2440 Pershing Rd.
Kansas City, MO 64108
(800) 821-5591/(816) 471-5200

	Years Ending 6/30					
	1982	1983	1984	1985	1986	1987
Net Investment Income ($)	.45	.38	.35	.39	.34	.30
Dividends from Net Investment Income ($)	.44	.38	.38	.21	.55	.15
Net Gains (Losses) on Investments ($)	(2.29)	4.96	(1.90)	2.38	3.64	3.08
Distributions from Net Realized Capital Gains ($)	.79	.23	1.62	.01	3.21	.60
Net Asset Value End of Year ($)	9.67	14.40	10.85	13.40	13.62	16.25
Ratio of Expenses to Net Assets (%)	.60	.61	.76	.76	.75	.74
Portfolio Turnover Rate (%)	22	26	52	35	20	14
Total Assets: End of Year (Millions $)	205.8	249.2	208.2	215.4	253.8	288.8
Annual Rate of Return (%) Years Ending 12/31	14.5	15.9	0.2	29.7	19.0	3.1

Five-Year Total Return(%)	84.8[B]	Degree of Diversification	A	Beta	1.01	Bull (%)	138.2[A]	Bear (%)	(24.9)[E]

Objective: Invests in common stocks that are selected for their long-term possibilities of both capital and income growth. Invests in common stocks of established, well-managed companies in growing industries deemed to have potential for maintaining earnings and dividend growth.

Portfolio: (9/30/87) Common stocks 95%, short-term corporate notes 3%, repos 1%. Largest stock holdings: consumer cyclicals 19%, consumer staples 15%.

Distributions: Income: Jan, July   **Capital Gains:** July

12b-1: No

Minimum: Initial: $500   Subsequent: $50

Min IRA: Initial: $250   Subsequent: $25

Services: IRA, Keogh, SEP, Withdraw

Tel Exchange: Yes   **With MMF:** Yes

Registered: All states

BABSON VALUE
Growth & Income

Jones & Babson, Inc.
3 Crown Center
2440 Pershing Rd.
Kansas City, MO 64108
(800) 821-5591/(816) 471-5200

	Years Ending 11/30					
	1982	1983	1984	1985	1986	1987
Net Investment Income ($)	–	–	–	.56	.49	.55
Dividends from Net Investment Income ($)	–	–	–	.09	.87	.63
Net Gains (Losses) on Investments ($)	–	–	–	1.90	3.01	(1.33)
Distributions from Net Realized Capital Gains ($)	–	–	–	–	.18	.04
Net Asset Value End of Year ($)	–	–	–	12.59	15.04	13.59
Ratio of Expenses to Net Assets (%)	–	–	–	.93	1.20	1.08
Portfolio Turnover Rate (%)	–	–	–	13	28	52
Total Assets: End of Year (Millions $)	–	–	–	2.8	6.9	13.5
Annual Rate of Return (%) Years Ending 12/31	–	–	–	26.5	20.7	3.3

Five-Year Total Return(%)	NA	Degree of Diversification	NA	Beta	NA	Bull (%)	NA	Bear (%)	(25.4)ᴇ

Objective: Seeks long-term growth of capital and income through investment in common stocks of companies rated B– or better (by Standard & Poor's or Value Line) in terms of growth and stability of earnings and dividends. Holds contrarian attitude seeking undervalued stocks.

Portfolio: (11/30/87) Common stocks 92%, repos 4%, convertible bonds 3%. Largest stock holdings: financial services 14%, utilities 10%.

Distributions: Income: Nov   **Capital Gains:** Nov

12b-1: No

Minimum: Initial: $1,000   Subsequent: $100

Min IRA: Initial: $250   Subsequent: $25

Services: IRA, Keogh, SEP, Withdraw

Tel Exchange: Yes   **With MMF:** Yes

Registered: All states

BAKER—
U.S. GOVERNMENT SERIES
Bond

James Baker & Company
1601 Northwest Expressway
20th Floor
Oklahoma City, OK 73118
(405) 842-1400

	Years Ending 12/31					
	1982	1983	1984	1985	1986 (3 mos.)	1987
Net Investment Income ($)	–	–	–	–	.28	1.06
Dividends from Net Investment Income ($)	–	–	–	–	–	.87
Net Gains (Losses) on Investments ($)	–	–	–	–	.37	(.63)
Distributions from Net Realized Capital Gains ($)	–	–	–	–	–	.01
Net Asset Value End of Year ($)	–	–	–	–	15.65	15.20
Ratio of Expenses to Net Assets (%)	–	–	–	–	.98	1.00
Portfolio Turnover Rate (%)	–	–	–	–	98	740
Total Assets: End of Year (Millions $)	–	–	–	–	3.5	19.1
Annual Rate of Return (%) Years Ending 12/31	–	–	–	–	–	4.5

Five-Year Total Return(%)	NA	Degree of Diversification	NA	Beta	NA	Bull (%)	NA	Bear (%)	3.5^

Objective: Seeks both current income and capital appreciation through investment in debt obligations of the U.S. government and its agencies, including Treasury bills, notes and bonds. May emphasize capital appreciation or current income depending on the level of interest rates. May also use put and call options.

Portfolio: (12/31/87) U.S. Treasury bonds 78%, U.S. Treasury bills 22%.

Distributions: Income: Monthly   **Capital Gains:** Annually

12b-1: Yes   **Amount:** 0.50%

Minimum: Initial: $1,000   Subsequent: $100

Min IRA: Initial: $1,000   Subsequent: $100

Services: IRA, Keogh, Withdraw, 403(b), Corp

Tel Exchange: Yes   **With MMF:** No

Registered: Call for availability

BARTLETT BASIC VALUE
Growth & Income

Bartlett & Company
36 E. Fourth St.
Cincinnati, OH 45202
(800) 543-0863/(513) 621-0066

	Years Ending 3/31					
	1982	1983	1984 (11 mos.)	1985	1986	1987
Net Investment Income ($)	–	–	.58	.63	.48	.46
Dividends from Net Investment Income ($)	–	–	.46	.57	.49	.45
Net Gains (Losses) on Investments ($)	–	–	.08	.80	3.28	1.07
Distributions from Net Realized Capital Gains ($)	–	–	–	.18	1.02	1.25
Net Asset Value End of Year ($)	–	–	10.20	10.88	13.13	12.96
Ratio of Expenses to Net Assets (%)	–	–	1.99	1.78	1.56	1.28
Portfolio Turnover Rate (%)	–	–	8	36	82	58
Total Assets: End of Year (Millions $)	–	–	12.4	22.8	52.7	91.1

Annual Rate of Return (%) Years Ending 12/31	–	–	–	25.6	13.7	(3.8)

Five-Year Total Return(%)	NA	Degree of Diversification	D	Beta	.62	Bull (%)	NA	Bear (%)	(20.9)D

Objective: Seeks capital appreciation and secondarily current income through investment in common stocks and convertible securities considered to be undervalued and having at least three years' history. May temporarily invest in investment grade debt securities and cash as defensive move. May enter into repos, invest in foreign securities, lend its securities, and hedge its portfolio with options, futures contracts and options on futures contracts.

Portfolio: (9/30/87) Common stocks 78%, commercial paper 15%, corporate bonds 3%, collateralized mortgage obligations 2%, repos 2%. Largest stock holdings: banking 10%, natural gas distribution 9%.

Distributions: Income: Mar, June, Sep, Dec   **Capital Gains:** Mar
12b-1: Yes   **Amount:** Pd. by Advisor
Minimum: Initial: $5,000   Subsequent: $100
Min IRA: Initial: $250   Subsequent: $50
Services: IRA, Keogh, Corp, 403(b)
Tel Exchange: Yes   **With MMF:** Yes
Registered: AZ, CA, CO, DC, FL, IL, IN, HI, KY, MA, MI, MN, MO, NY, OH, PA, TX, WV

BARTLETT FIXED INCOME

Bond

Bartlett & Company
36 East Fourth Street
Cincinnati, OH 45202
(800) 543-0863/(513) 621-0066

	Years Ending 3/31					
	1982	1983	1984	1985	1986	1987 (11 mos.)
Net Investment Income ($)	–	–	–	–	–	.87
Dividends from Net Investment Income ($)	–	–	–	–	–	.87
Net Gains (Losses) on Investments ($)	–	–	–	–	–	.18
Distributions from Net Realized Capital Gains ($)	–	–	–	–	–	–
Net Asset Value End of Year ($)	–	–	–	–	–	10.18
Ratio of Expenses to Net Assets (%)	–	–	–	–	–	.93
Portfolio Turnover Rate (%)	–	–	–	–	–	192
Total Assets: End of Year (Millions $)	–	–	–	–	–	145.2

Annual Rate of Return (%) Years Ending 12/31	–	–	–	–	–	2.8

Five-Year Total Return(%)	NA	Degree of Diversification	NA	Beta	NA	Bull (%)	NA	Bear (%)	1.0B

Objective: Seeks high level of current income. Capital appreciation is of secondary importance. Invests in a broad range of fixed-income securities including U.S. government, corporate and mortgage-backed bonds. May also invest in high-yielding equity securities.

Portfolio: (9/30/87) U.S. government obligations 53%, corporate obligations 32%, temporary cash investments 11%, other assets 4%. Largest bond holdings: industrial 80%, utilities 13%.

Distributions: Income: Monthly   **Capital Gains:** Annually
12b-1: Yes   **Amount:** Pd. by Advisor
Minimum: Initial: $5,000   Subsequent: $100
Min IRA: Initial: $250   Subsequent: $50
Services: IRA, Keogh, Corp, 403(b)
Tel Exchange: Yes   **With MMF:** Yes
Registered: AZ, CA, CO, DC, FL, IL, IN, HI, KY, MA, MI, MN, MO, NY, OH, PA, TX, WV

BB&K DIVERSA
Balanced

Bailard, Biehl & Kaiser, Inc.
951 Mariner's Island Boulevard
Suite 700
San Mateo, CA 94404
(415) 571-6002

	Years Ending 9/30					
	1982	**1983**	**1984**	**1985**	**1986**	**1987** (10 mos.)
Net Investment Income ($)	–	–	–	–	–	.21
Dividends from Net Investment Income ($)	–	–	–	–	–	–
Net Gains (Losses) on Investments ($)	–	–	–	–	–	1.49
Distributions from Net Realized Capital Gains ($)	–	–	–	–	–	–
Net Asset Value End of Year ($)	–	–	–	–	–	11.70
Ratio of Expenses to Net Assets (%)	–	–	–	–	–	1.02
Portfolio Turnover Rate (%)	–	–	–	–	–	66
Total Assets: End of Year (Millions $)	–	–	–	–	–	91.7

Annual Rate of Return (%) Years Ending 12/31	–	–	–	–	–	8.2

Five-Year Total Return(%)	NA	Degree of Diversification	NA	Beta	NA	Bull (%)	NA	Bear (%)	(8.4)^c

Objective: Seeks above average total return with below average risk through multiple asset allocation. Invests in five classes of securities: stocks, bonds, foreign securities, real estate and cash. Will hold at least 5% of each category but no more than 50% of any one.

Portfolio: (9/30/87) International securities 32%, domestic common stocks 22%, government bonds 13%, corporate bonds 10%, short-term notes 9%, real estate portfolio 5%, other assets 9%.

Distributions: Income: Annually   **Capital Gains:** Annually

12b-1: No

Minimum: Initial: $25,000   Subsequent: $2,000

Min IRA: Initial: $10,000   Subsequent: $2,000

Services: IRA, Keogh, Corp, SEP, 403(b), Withdraw

Tel Exchange: No

Registered: CA, CO, GA, HI, NY, UT, WI

BEACON HILL MUTUAL
Growth

Beacon Hill Management, Inc.
75 Federal St.
Boston, MA 02110
(617) 482-0795

	Years Ending 6/30					
	1982	**1983**	**1984**	**1985**	**1986**	**1987**
Net Investment Income ($)	.05	.03	(.02)	(.03)	(.22)	(.43)
Dividends from Net Investment Income ($)	.05	.03	—	—	—	—
Net Gains (Losses) on Investments ($)	(.67)	4.69	(1.00)	4.60	7.35	3.80
Distributions from Net Realized Capital Gains ($)	—	—	—	—	—	.99
Net Asset Value End of Year ($)	12.07	16.76	15.74	20.31	27.44	29.82
Ratio of Expenses to Net Assets (%)	4.00	3.70	3.40	3.30	3.50	3.70
Portfolio Turnover Rate (%)	1	20	0	2	8	0
Total Assets: End of Year (Millions $)	2.0	2.6	2.3	2.9	3.9	3.8
Annual Rate of Return (%) Years Ending 12/31	12.7	16.6	3.8	33.5	6.0	5.4

Five-Year Total Return(%)	80.5[B]	Degree of Diversification	B	Beta	.94	Bull (%)	114.0[B]	Bear (%)	(21.8)[D]

Objective:	Seeks long-term capital growth through investment in common stocks of well-established companies. As defensive measure, may hold debt securities.
Portfolio:	(6/30/87) Common stocks 96%, other assets 4%. Largest stock holdings: drugs & cosmetics 22%, food products 14%.

Distributions: Income: July   **Capital Gains:** July
12b-1: No
Minimum: Initial: None   Subsequent: None
Min IRA: Initial: None   Subsequent: None
Services: IRA, Keogh, Corp, Withdraw
Tel Exchange: No
Registered: Call for information—many pending

BENHAM
GNMA INCOME
Bond

Benham Management Corp.
755 Page Mill Road
Palo Alto, CA 94304-1018
(800) 227-8380/(415) 858-3600

	Years Ending 3/31					
	1982	1983	1984	1985	1986 (6 mos.)	1987
Net Investment Income ($)	–	–	–	–	.56	.92
Dividends from Net Investment Income ($)	–	–	–	–	.58	.93
Net Gains (Losses) on Investments ($)	–	–	–	–	.45	.02
Distributions from Net Realized Capital Gains ($)	–	–	–	–	–	–
Net Asset Value End of Year ($)	–	–	–	–	10.42	10.42
Ratio of Expenses to Net Assets (%)	–	–	–	–	.29	.74
Portfolio Turnover Rate (%)	–	–	–	–	264	566
Total Assets: End of Year (Millions $)	–	–	–	–	169.7	393.2
Annual Rate of Return (%) Years Ending 12/31	–	–	–	–	11.3	2.8

Five-Year Total Return(%)	NA	Degree of Diversification	NA	Beta	NA	Bull (%)	NA	Bear (%)	3.7A

Objective:	Seeks high level of current income through investment in GNMAs and other U.S. government-backed debt securities. At least 65% of the portfolio must be invested in GNMAs.
Portfolio:	(9/30/87) GNMAs 88%, repos 12%.
Distributions:	**Income:** Monthly **Capital Gains:** Annually
12b-1:	No
Minimum:	**Initial:** $1,000 **Subsequent:** $100
Min IRA:	**Initial:** $100 **Subsequent:** None
Services:	IRA, Keogh
Tel Exchange:	Yes **With MMF:** Yes
Registered:	All states

BENHAM TARGET MATURITIES TRUST SERIES 1990
Bond

Benham Management Corp.
755 Page Mill Road
Palo Alto, CA 94304-1018
(800) 227-8380/(415) 858-2400

	Years Ending 12/31					
	1982	1983	1984	1985	1986	1987
Net Investment Income ($)	–	–	–	4.00	5.39	5.58
Dividends from Net Investment Income ($)	–	–	–	–	–	–
Net Gains (Losses) on Investments ($)	–	–	–	7.41	5.57	(3.68)
Distributions from Net Realized Capital Gains ($)	–	–	–	–	–	–
Net Asset Value End of Year ($)	–	–	–	68.16	79.12	81.02
Ratio of Expenses to Net Assets (%)	–	–	–	.53	.70	.70
Portfolio Turnover Rate (%)	–	–	–	46	113	88
Total Assets: End of Year (Millions $)	–	–	–	4.1	5.9	9.6

Annual Rate of Return (%) Years Ending 12/31	–	–	–	–	16.1	2.4

Five-Year Total Return(%)	NA	Degree of Diversification	NA	Beta	NA	Bull (%)	NA	Bear (%)	3.1^

Objective: Seeks highest attainable return through investment in zero coupon U.S. Treasury securities and other full coupon Treasury securities. The trust will terminate on December 31 of its target maturity year of 1990 and will be liquidated during the January following the termination.

Portfolio: (12/31/87) Zero coupon bonds due in 1990, 100%. Largest bond holdings: separate trading of interest and principal of securities (STRIPS) 51%, Treasury receipts (TR) 34%.

Distributions: Income: Annually   **Capital Gains:** Annually

12b-1: No

Minimum: Initial: $1,000   Subsequent: $100

Min IRA: Initial: $100   Subsequent: None

Services: IRA, Keogh

Tel Exchange: Yes   **With MMF:** Yes

Registered: All states

BENHAM TARGET MATURITIES TRUST SERIES 1995

Bond

Benham Management Corp.
755 Page Mill Road
Palo Alto, CA 94304-1018
(800) 227-8380/(415) 858-2400

	Years Ending 12/31					
	1982	1983	1984	1985	1986	1987
Net Investment Income ($)	–	–	–	2.51	3.69	3.99
Dividends from Net Investment Income ($)	–	–	–	–	–	–
Net Gains (Losses) on Investments ($)	–	–	–	7.37	7.65	(6.10)
Distributions from Net Realized Capital Gains ($)	–	–	–	–	–	–
Net Asset Value End of Year ($)	–	–	–	42.99	54.33	52.22
Ratio of Expenses to Net Assets (%)	–	–	–	.53	.70	.70
Portfolio Turnover Rate (%)	–	–	–	–	89	86
Total Assets: End of Year (Millions $)	–	–	–	2.2	5.1	7.0
Annual Rate of Return (%) Years Ending 12/31	–	–	–	–	26.4	(3.9)

Five-Year Total Return(%)	NA	Degree of Diversification	NA	Beta	NA	Bull (%)	NA	Bear (%)	4.2^

Objective: Seeks highest attainable return through investment in zero coupon U.S. Treasury securities and other full coupon Treasury securities. The trust will terminate on December 31 of its target maturity year of 1995 and will be liquidated the following January.

Portfolio: (12/31/87) Zero coupon bonds due in 1995, 100%. Largest bond holdings: Separate trading of interest and principal of securities (STRIPS) 53%, Treasury receipts (TR) 26%.

Distributions: Income: Annually   **Capital Gains:** Annually
12b-1: No
Minimum: Initial: $1,000   Subsequent: $100
Min IRA: Initial: $100   Subsequent: None
Services: IRA, Keogh
Tel Exchange: Yes   **With MMF:** Yes
Registered: All states

BENHAM TARGET MATURITIES TRUST SERIES 2000
Bond

Benham Management Corp.
755 Page Mill Road
Palo Alto, CA 94304-1018
(800) 227-8380/(415) 858-2400

	Years Ending 12/31					
	1982	1983	1984	1985	1986	1987
Net Investment Income ($)	–	–	–	1.53	2.40	2.68
Dividends from Net Investment Income ($)	–	–	–	–	–	–
Net Gains (Losses) on Investments ($)	–	–	–	5.73	6.27	(4.79)
Distributions from Net Realized Capital Gains ($)	–	–	–	–	–	–
Net Asset Value End of Year ($)	–	–	–	26.77	35.44	33.33
Ratio of Expenses to Net Assets (%)	–	–	–	.52	.70	.70
Portfolio Turnover Rate (%)	–	–	–	34	39	73
Total Assets: End of Year (Millions $)	–	–	–	2.2	5.1	6.3
Annual Rate of Return (%) Years Ending 12/31	–	–	–	–	32.4	(6.0)

Five-Year Total Return(%)	NA	Degree of Diversification	NA	Beta	NA	Bull (%)	NA	Bear (%)	7.9ᴬ

Objective: Seeks highest attainable return through investment in zero coupon U.S. Treasury securities and other full coupon Treasury securities. The trust will terminate on December 31, 2000, and will be liquidated the following January.

Portfolio: (12/31/87) Zero coupon bonds due in 2000, 100%. Largest bond holdings: separate trading of interest and principal of securities (STRIPS) 49%, Treasury receipts (TR) 19%.

Distributions: Income: Annually   **Capital Gains:** Annually

12b-1: No

Minimum: Initial: $1,000   **Subsequent:** $100

Min IRA: Initial: $100   **Subsequent:** None

Services: IRA, Keogh

Tel Exchange: Yes   **With MMF:** Yes

Registered: All states

BENHAM TARGET MATURITIES TRUST SERIES 2005
Bond

Benham Management Corp.
755 Page Mill Road
Palo Alto, CA 94304
(800) 227-8380/(415) 858-2400

	Years Ending 12/31					
	1982	1983	1984	1985 (9 mos.)	1986	1987
Net Investment Income ($)	–	–	–	1.14	1.59	1.77
Dividends from Net Investment Income ($)	–	–	–	–	–	–
Net Gains (Losses) on Investments ($)	–	–	–	3.67	5.46	(4.23)
Distributions from Net Realized Capital Gains ($)	–	–	–	–	–	–
Net Asset Value End of Year ($)	–	–	–	16.69	23.74	21.28
Ratio of Expenses to Net Assets (%)	–	–	–	.47	.70	.70
Portfolio Turnover Rate (%)	–	–	–	37	50	68
Total Assets: End of Year (Millions $)	–	–	–	.8	2.9	3.7

Annual Rate of Return (%) Years Ending 12/31	–	–	–	–	42.2	(10.4)

Five-Year Total Return(%)	NA	Degree of Diversification	NA	Beta	NA	Bull (%)	NA	Bear (%)	9.8ᴬ

Objective: Seeks highest attainable return through investment in zero coupon U.S. Treasury securities and other full coupon Treasury securities. The trust will terminate on December 31, 2005, and will be liquidated the following January.

Portfolio: (12/31/87) Zero coupon bonds due in 2005, 100%. Largest bond holdings: separate trading of registered interest and principal of securities (STRIPS) 54%, Treasury receipts (TR) 15%.

Distributions: Income: Annually   **Capital Gains:** Annually

12b-1: No

Minimum: Initial: $1,000   Subsequent: $100

Min IRA: Initial: $100   Subsequent: None

Services: IRA, Keogh

Tel Exchange: Yes   **With MMF:** Yes

Registered: All states

BENHAM TARGET MATURITIES TRUST SERIES 2010
Bond

Benham Management Corp.
755 Page Mill Road
Palo Alto, CA 94304-1018
(800) 227-8380/(415) 858-2400

	Years Ending 12/31					
	1982	1983	1984	1985	1986	1987
Net Investment Income ($)	—	—	—	.76	1.09	1.23
Dividends from Net Investment Income ($)	—	—	—	—	—	—
Net Gains (Losses) on Investments ($)	—	—	—	2.83	5.13	(3.92)
Distributions from Net Realized Capital Gains ($)	—	—	—	—	—	—
Net Asset Value End of Year ($)	—	—	—	11.43	17.65	14.96
Ratio of Expenses to Net Assets (%)	—	—	—	.49	.70	.70
Portfolio Turnover Rate (%)	—	—	—	18	91	84
Total Assets: End of Year (Millions $)	—	—	—	1.2	4.9	9.3

Annual Rate of Return (%) Years Ending 12/31	—	—	—	—	54.4	(15.2)

Five-Year Total Return(%)	NA	Degree of Diversification	NA	Beta	NA	Bull (%)	NA	Bear (%)	9.3[A]

Objective: Seeks highest attainable return through investment in zero coupon U.S. Treasury securities and other full coupon Treasury securities. The trust will terminate on December 31, 2010, and will be liquidated the following January.

Portfolio: (12/31/87) Zero coupon bonds due in 2010, 100%. Largest bond holdings: Separate trading of interest and principal of securities (STRIPS) 100%.

Distributions: Income: Annually   **Capital Gains:** Annually

12b-1: No

Minimum: Initial: $1,000   Subsequent: $100

Min IRA: Initial: $100   Subsequent: None

Services: IRA, Keogh

Tel Exchange: Yes   **With MMF:** Yes

Registered: All states

BOSTON CO.
CAPITAL
APPRECIATION
Growth

The Boston Company Advisors
One Boston Place
Boston, MA 02108
(800) 225-5267/(800) 343-6324

	Years Ending 12/31					
	1982	1983	1984	1985	1986	1987
Net Investment Income ($)	.73	.71	.86	1.00	.90	.76
Dividends from Net Investment Income ($)	.81	.64	.69	.74	.50	1.32
Net Gains (Losses) on Investments ($)	1.95	4.80	.73	7.50	5.69	(.41)
Distributions from Net Realized Capital Gains ($)	3.37	.82	2.91	1.56	5.80	5.36
Net Asset Value End of Year ($)	23.87	27.92	25.91	32.11	32.40	26.07
Ratio of Expenses to Net Assets (%)	1.07	.98	1.00	.96	.95	.95
Portfolio Turnover Rate (%)	86	47	26	59	37	46
Total Assets: End of Year (Millions $)	212.9	238.1	259.7	369.7	452.9	431.6

Annual Rate of Return (%) Years Ending 12/31	13.6	24.0	6.9	35.0	22.5	0.4

Five-Year Total Return(%)	120.2^A	Degree of Diversification	A	Beta	.90	Bull (%)	136.6^A	Bear (%)	(20.1)^D

Objective: Seeks long-term growth of capital through investment in companies with strong growth features and that meet other investment criteria based on studies of trends in industries and companies. May engage in repos, invest in foreign securities and employ leverage.

Portfolio: (12/31/87) Common stocks 96%, municipal bonds 1%, U.S. Treasury obligations 1%, other assets 1%. Largest stock holdings: financial services 20%, basic industries 13%.

Distributions: Income: Jan, April, July, Oct   **Capital Gains:** Jan
12b-1: Yes   **Amount:** 0.45%
Minimum: Initial: $1,000   **Subsequent:** None
Min IRA: Initial: $500   **Subsequent:** None
Services: IRA, Keogh, Corp, Withdraw
Tel Exchange: Yes   **With MMF:** Yes
Registered: All states

BOSTON CO.
GNMA
Bond

The Boston Company Advisors
One Boston Place
Boston, MA 02108
(800) 225-5267/(800) 343-6324

	Years Ending 12/31					
	1982	1983	1984	1985	1986 (10 mos.)	1987
Net Investment Income ($)	–	–	–	–	.88	.99
Dividends from Net Investment Income ($)	–	–	–	–	.88	.99
Net Gains (Losses) on Investments ($)	–	–	–	–	.13	(.88)
Distributions from Net Realized Capital Gains ($)	–	–	–	–	–	–
Net Asset Value End of Year ($)	–	–	–	–	12.63	11.75
Ratio of Expenses to Net Assets (%)	–	–	–	–	.65	1.04
Portfolio Turnover Rate (%)	–	–	–	–	85	122
Total Assets: End of Year (Millions $)	–	–	–	–	15.4	13.6

Annual Rate of Return (%) Years Ending 12/31	–	–	–	–	–	0.7

Five-Year Total Return(%)	NA	Degree of Diversification	NA	Beta	NA	Bull (%)	NA	Bear (%)	1.9ᴬ

Objective:	Seeks high current income consistent with preservation of capital. Invests in U.S. government-backed debt obligations—principally GNMA mortgage-backed securities.
Portfolio:	(12/31/87) Mortgage-backed securities 58%, U.S. government obligations 37%, repos 12%.
Distributions:	**Income:** Monthly **Capital Gains:** Annually
12b-1:	Yes **Amount:** 0.45%
Minimum:	**Initial:** $1,000 **Subsequent:** None
Min IRA:	**Initial:** $500 **Subsequent:** None
Services:	IRA, Keogh, Corp, Withdraw
Tel Exchange:	Yes **With MMF:** Yes
Registered:	All states

BOSTON CO.
MANAGED INCOME
Bond

The Boston Company Advisors
One Boston Place
Boston, MA 02108
(800) 225-5267/(800) 343-6324

	Years Ending 12/31					
	1982	1983	1984	1985*	1986	1987
Net Investment Income ($)	–	–	–	1.20	.86	1.20
Dividends from Net Investment Income ($)	–	–	–	.99	.96	1.20
Net Gains (Losses) on Investments ($)	–	–	–	.99	.28	(.52)
Distributions from Net Realized Capital Gains ($)	–	–	–	–	.07	.10
Net Asset Value End of Year ($)	–	–	–	11.80	11.91	11.29
Ratio of Expenses to Net Assets (%)	–	–	–	1.48	.88	.94
Portfolio Turnover Rate (%)	–	–	–	173	71	306
Total Assets: End of Year (Millions $)	–	–	–	16.7	49.3	51.8
Annual Rate of Return (%) Years Ending 12/31	–	–	–	21.8	14.9	5.7

Five-Year Total Return(%)	NA	Degree of Diversification	NA	Beta	.09	Bull (%)	NA	Bear (%)	1.8ᴬ

Objectives changed Nov. 1984; prior history not meaningful.

Objective: Seeks high current income through investment in debt securities such as corporate bonds, debentures, convertibles, preferred stocks, U.S. government obligations and money market instruments. May engage in repos and in foreign securities.

Portfolio: (12/31/87) Corporate bonds 71%, U.S. government and agency obligations 22%, repos 3%, preferred stocks 2%, other assets 2%. Largest bond holdings: banking and finance 26%, industrial 12%.

Distributions: Income: Monthly   **Capital Gains:** Jan
12b-1: Yes   **Amount:** 0.45%
Minimum: Initial: $1,000   **Subsequent:** None
Min IRA: Initial: $500   **Subsequent:** None
Services: IRA, Keogh, Corp, Withdraw
Tel Exchange: Yes   **With MMF:** Yes
Registered: All states

BOSTON CO.
SPECIAL GROWTH
Growth

The Boston Company Advisors
One Boston Place
Boston, MA 02108
(800) 225-5267/(800) 343-6324

	Years Ending 12/31					
	1982 (8 mos.)	1983	1984	1985	1986	1987
Net Investment Income ($)	.22	.50	.38	.36	.13	.63
Dividends from Net Investment Income ($)	—	—	.09	.35	.31	.81
Net Gains (Losses) on Investments ($)	3.27	4.67	(2.36)	5.07	1.40	(.91)
Distributions from Net Realized Capital Gains ($)	—	.61	.11	—	4.96	4.10
Net Asset Value End of Year ($)	13.49	18.05	15.87	20.95	17.21	12.02
Ratio of Expenses to Net Assets (%)	1.43	1.49	1.50	1.35	1.32	1.49
Portfolio Turnover Rate (%)	102	247	261	258	192	322
Total Assets: End of Year (Millions $)	1.4	25.5	27.6	53.6	35.9	30.7
Annual Rate of Return (%) Years Ending 12/31	—	38.3	(10.9)	34.7	7.7	(4.4)

Five-Year Total Return(%) 71.0ᶜ	Degree of Diversification C	Beta 1.06	Bull (%) 96.8ᶜ	Bear (%) (25.4)ᴱ

Objective: Seeks above-average growth of capital through investment in securities thought to have significant growth potential—primarily common stocks and convertible securities of smaller companies, and larger, more established companies with above-average growth potential. May engage in repos, invest in foreign securities, and employ leverage.

Portfolio: (12/31/87) Common stocks 84%, repos 12%, convertible bonds 3%, other assets 1%. Largest stock holdings: financial services 19%, basic industries 12%.

Distributions: Income: Jan   **Capital Gains:** Jan
12b-1: Yes   **Amount:** 0.45%
Minimum: Initial: $1,000   **Subsequent:** None
Min IRA: Initial: $500   **Subsequent:** None
Services: IRA, Keogh, Corp, Withdraw
Tel Exchange: Yes   **With MMF:** Yes
Registered: All states

BOWSER GROWTH
Growth

Commonwealth Capital Mgmt.
1500 Forest Ave., Suite 223
Richmond, VA 23229
(800) 527-9500/(804) 285-8211

	Years Ending 12/31					
	1982	1983	1984 (10 mos.)	1985	1986	1987
Net Investment Income ($)	–	–	.02	–	(.06)	(.08)
Dividends from Net Investment Income ($)	–	–	–	.03	.01	–
Net Gains (Losses) on Investments ($)	–	–	(.49)	(.13)	(.49)	(.28)
Distributions from Net Realized Capital Gains ($)	–	–	–	–	–	–
Net Asset Value End of Year ($)	–	–	2.53	2.37	1.81	1.45
Ratio of Expenses to Net Assets (%)	–	–	4.94	3.93	4.77	4.93
Portfolio Turnover Rate (%)	–	–	–	9	47	59
Total Assets: End of Year (Millions $)	–	–	3.1	3.8	2.5	1.9

Annual Rate of Return (%) Years Ending 12/31	–	–	–	(5.7)	(23.7)	(19.3)

Five-Year Total Return(%)	NA	Degree of Diversification	D	Beta 1.03	Bull (%)	NA	Bear (%)	(40.2)E

Objective: Seeks capital appreciation through investment in common stocks that are undervalued, based on the underlying financial strength of the company and its future prospects. May take defensive posture in debt securities. May invest in repos and lend its portfolio securities.

Portfolio: (12/31/87) Common stocks 93%, bonds 3%, repos 3%, other assets 2%. Largest stock holdings: health care & toiletries 22%, diversified 15%.

Distributions: Income: Annually   **Capital Gains:** Annually

12b-1: Yes   **Amount:** 0.50%

Minimum: Initial: $1,000   Subsequent: $100

Min IRA: Initial: $1,000   Subsequent: $100

Services: IRA, Deduct

Tel Exchange: Yes   **With MMF:** No

Registered: AK, CA, CO, DC, DE, FL, GA, HI, ID, IL, IN, KS, KY, MA, MD, MN, MO, MS, ND, NE, NV, NY, OR, TN, TX, UT, VA, WA, WI, WV, WY

BRANDYWINE FUND
Growth

Friess Associates, Inc.
Suite C-205, Greenville Center
Greenville, DE 19807
(302) 656-6200

		Years Ending 9/30				
	1982	1983	1984	1985	1986 (10 mos.)	1987
Net Investment Income ($)	–	–	–	–	.03	(.02)
Dividends from Net Investment Income ($)	–	–	–	–	–	.03
Net Gains (Losses) on Investments ($)	–	–	–	–	.98	6.04
Distributions from Net Realized Capital Gains ($)	–	–	–	–	–	–
Net Asset Value End of Year ($)	–	–	–	–	11.01	17.00
Ratio of Expenses to Net Assets (%)	–	–	–	–	1.3	1.2
Portfolio Turnover Rate (%)	–	–	–	–	58	147
Total Assets: End of Year (Millions $)	–	–	–	–	58.0	127.8
Annual Rate of Return (%) Years Ending 12/31	–	–	–	–	16.4	2.6

Five-Year Total Return(%)	NA	Degree of Diversification	NA	Beta	NA	Bull (%)	NA	Bear (%)	(29.9)E

Objective: Primary objective is to produce long-term capital appreciation through investment in common stocks of lesser known companies moving from a lower to a higher market share position within their industry groups. Not more than 5% of the fund's assets may be invested in companies having an operating history of less than three years.

Portfolio: (12/31/87) Common stocks 93%, short-term securities 10%. Largest stock holdings: computer systems 21%, health & medical products 14%.

Distributions: Income: Annually   **Capital Gains:** Annually

12b-1: No

Minimum: Initial: $25,000   Subsequent: $1,000

Min IRA: Initial: NA   Subsequent: NA

Services: NA

Tel Exchange: No

Registered: AR, AZ, CA, CO, CT, DC, DE, FL, HI, MA, MD, ME, MI, MO, NC, NJ, NV, NY, OH, PA, SC, TN, TX, UT, VA, WA, WI

BRUCE FUND
Aggressive Growth

Bruce and Co.
20 North Wacker Dr.
Suite 1425
Chicago, IL 60606
(312) 236-9160

	Years Ending 6/30					
	1982	1983	1984	1985	1986	1987
Net Investment Income ($)	–	–	7.17	5.63	2.21	2.77
Dividends from Net Investment Income ($)	–	–	3.74	8.25	10.20	1.29
Net Gains (Losses) on Investments ($)	–	–	(36.82)	36.65	42.16	(6.55)
Distributions from Net Realized Capital Gains ($)	–	–	29.56	99.23	36.94	–
Net Asset Value End of Year ($)	–	–	185.44	120.24	117.47	112.40
Ratio of Expenses to Net Assets (%)	–	–	2.92	4.89	2.68	1.64
Portfolio Turnover Rate (%)	–	–	99	85	0	11
Total Assets: End of Year (Millions $)	–	–	1.1	1.0	2.9	7.0

Annual Rate of Return (%) Years Ending 12/31	–	–	6.2	37.0	29.6	(18.0)

Five-Year Total Return(%)	NA	Degree of Diversification	E	Beta	.72	Bull (%)	108.1[B]	Bear (%)	(17.6)[C]

Objective:	Seeks long-term capital appreciation; dividend income is a secondary consideration. Can invest in stocks, bonds and convertible securities. May also invest in unseasoned companies where the risks are greater than for established companies.
Portfolio:	(6/30/87) Common stocks 51%, U.S. government bonds 44%, municipal bonds 6%. Largest stock holdings: data processing services 26%, energy services 19%.
Distributions:	**Income:** Annually **Capital Gains:** Annually
12b-1:	No
Minimum:	**Initial:** $1,000 **Subsequent:** $500
Min IRA:	**Initial:** $1,000 **Subsequent:** $500
Services:	IRA
Tel Exchange:	No
Registered:	CA, CO, CT, FL, GA, IL, IN, KY, LA, MA, MD, MI, MN, MO, MS, NJ, NV, NY, OH, OK, OR, PA, SC, TN, TX, VA, WA, WI

BULL & BEAR
CAPITAL GROWTH
Aggressive Growth

Bull & Bear Advisers
11 Hanover Sq.
New York, NY 10005
(800) 847-4200/(212) 363-1100

	Years Ending 12/31					
	1982	1983	1984	1985	1986	1987
Net Investment Income ($)	.26	.33	.09	.14	(.02)	(.03)
Dividends from Net Investment Income ($)	.27	.23	.30	.13	.20	—
Net Gains (Losses) on Investments ($)	1.24	1.80	(.89)	3.34	.69	(.42)
Distributions from Net Realized Capital Gains ($)	—	—	1.96	.35	5.91	1.57
Net Asset Value End of Year ($)	13.97	15.87	12.81	15.81	10.37	8.35
Ratio of Expenses to Net Assets (%)	1.42	1.23	1.33	1.41	2.25	2.20
Portfolio Turnover Rate (%)	34	67	94	78	78	112
Total Assets: End of Year (Millions $)	72.7	76.1	63.6	91.8	61.7	64.6

Annual Rate of Return (%) Years Ending 12/31	12.6	15.5	(4.3)	27.8	3.6	(4.3)

Five-Year Total Return(%)	39.8ᴱ	Degree of Diversification	A	Beta 1.12	Bull (%) 93.7ᶜ	Bear (%) (28.4)ᴱ

Objective: Seeks long-term capital appreciation through a diversified portfolio consisting primarily of common stocks of emerging growth companies and in special situations. May invest in foreign securities, may employ leverage and may engage in repos.

Portfolio: (12/31/87) Common stocks 99%, convertible securities 1%. Largest stock holdings: multi-line companies 15%, financial services 13%.

Distributions: Income: Annually   **Capital Gains:** Annually

12b-1: Yes   **Amount:** 1.00%

Minimum: Initial: $1,000   **Subsequent:** $100

Min IRA: Initial: $100   **Subsequent:** $100

Services: IRA, Keogh, 403(b), SEP, Withdraw, Deduct

Tel Exchange: Yes   **With MMF:** Yes

Registered: All states

BULL & BEAR
EQUITY-INCOME
Balanced

Bull & Bear Advisers
11 Hanover Sq.
New York, NY 10005
(800) 847-4200/(212) 363-1100

	Years Ending 12/31					
	1982	1983	1984	1985	1986	1987
Net Investment Income ($)	.75	.65	.71	.67	.38	.44
Dividends from Net Investment Income ($)	.75	.65	.70	.70	.38	.44
Net Gains (Losses) on Investments ($)	.88	.64	.04	1.82	1.63	(.92)
Distributions from Net Realized Capital Gains ($)	.65	–	.25	1.31	2.01	.21
Net Asset Value End of Year ($)	10.49	11.13	10.93	11.41	11.03	9.90
Ratio of Expenses to Net Assets (%)	2.02	2.03	1.98	2.14	3.00	2.57
Portfolio Turnover Rate (%)	21	36	155	103	93	91
Total Assets: End of Year (Millions $)	4.4	5.3	4.5	6.3	11.3	13.3
Annual Rate of Return (%) Years Ending 12/31	18.3	12.4	7.2	25.8	18.7	(4.7)

Five-Year Total Return(%)	71.4[c]	Degree of Diversification	NA	Beta	.69	Bull (%)	95.5[c]	Bear (%)	(18.6)[c]

Objective: Intends to provide current income and long-term growth through investment in large, major corporations' common stock and senior convertibles. May also invest in corporate bonds and money market instruments.

Portfolio: (12/31/87) Convertible bonds 49%, common stocks 26%, U.S. government obligations 15%, convertible preferred stocks 9%. Largest stock holdings: consumer products 8%, miscellaneous 3%.

Distributions: Income: Mar, June, Sept, Dec   **Capital Gains:** Dec
12b-1: Yes   **Amount:** 1.00%
Minimum: Initial: $1,000   **Subsequent:** $100
Min IRA: Initial: $100   **Subsequent:** $100
Services: IRA, Keogh, 403(b), SEP, Withdraw, Deduct
Tel Exchange: Yes   **With MMF:** Yes
Registered: All states

BULL & BEAR GOLD INVESTORS LTD.
(formerly GOLCONDA INVESTORS LTD.)

Precious Metals

Bull & Bear International
Advisers, Inc.
11 Hanover Square
New York, NY 10005
(800) 847-4200/(212) 363-1100

	Years Ending 6/30					
	1982	1983	1984	1985	1986	1987
Net Investment Income ($)	.68	.40	.16	.11	.02	(.02)
Dividends from Net Investment Income ($)	.75	.50	.20	.12	.04	.03
Net Gains (Losses) on Investments ($)	(4.46)	4.72	(2.03)	(1.82)	(.21)	8.83
Distributions from Net Realized Capital Gains ($)	—	—	—	—	—	—
Net Asset Value End of Year ($)	9.49	14.11	12.04	10.21	9.98	18.76
Ratio of Expenses to Net Assets (%)	2.02	1.71	1.71	1.74	2.39	2.46
Portfolio Turnover Rate (%)	107	12	31	30	32	66
Total Assets: End of Year (Millions $)	6.2	23.4	23.0	21.6	20.6	62.2
Annual Rate of Return (%) Years Ending 12/31	6.4	0.6	(25.2)	2.6	35.0	30.3

Five-Year Total Return(%)	35.9ᴱ	Degree of Diversification	E	Beta	.46	Bull (%)	125.3ᴬ	Bear (%)	(23.3)ᴰ

Objective: Seeks capital appreciation by concentrating its investments in gold bullion, stocks of companies mining, processing or dealing in gold and other foreign securities. May hold any or all of its cash in foreign currencies including gold coins.

Portfolio: (6/30/87) Common stocks 71%, gold bullion 18%, silver bullion 4%, platinum bullion 3%, convertible bonds 2%, convertible preferred stocks 1%. Largest stock holdings: North American mining companies 32%, Pacific Rim mining companies 22%.

Distributions: Income: Jan   **Capital Gains:** Jan

12b-1: Yes   **Amount:** 1.00%

Minimum: Initial: $1,000   **Subsequent:** $100

Min IRA: Initial: $100   **Subsequent:** $100

Services: IRA, Keogh, SEP, 403(b), Withdraw, Deduct

Tel Exchange: Yes   **With MMF:** Yes

Registered: All states except WI

BULL & BEAR
HIGH YIELD
Bond

Bull & Bear Management Corp.
11 Hanover Square
New York, NY 10005
(800) 847-4200/(212) 363-1100

			Years Ending 6/30			
	1982	1983	1984 (10 mos.)	1985	1986	1987
Net Investment Income ($)	—	—	1.62	1.94	1.89	1.76
Dividends from Net Investment Income ($)	—	—	1.62	1.94	1.89	1.74
Net Gains (Losses) on Investments ($)	—	—	(1.75)	1.17	.54	(1.92)
Distributions from Net Realized Capital Gains ($)	—	—	—	—	—	.02
Net Asset Value End of Year ($)	—	—	13.25	14.42	14.96	13.04
Ratio of Expenses to Net Assets (%)	—	—	.99	1.16	1.37	1.50
Portfolio Turnover Rate (%)	—	—	95	127	77	85
Total Assets: End of Year (Millions $)	—	—	8.7	33.5	113.1	206.2
Annual Rate of Return (%) Years Ending 12/31	—	—	7.8	20.9	6.0	(6.4)

Five-Year Total Return(%)	NA	Degree of Diversification	NA	Beta	.21	Bull (%)	42.8ᴱ	Bear (%)	(9.2)ᶜ

Objective: Seeks the highest income over the long term through investment in high-yield fixed-income debt securities of short-, intermediate-, or long-term maturities graded in the lower categories. Value of shares subject to influence by changes in interest rates. May invest up to 15% of assets in foreign securities and may enter into repos.

Portfolio: (6/30/87) Corporate bonds 97%, cash and other assets 3%. Largest holdings: real estate & home building 13%, communications & media 11%.

Distributions:	**Income:** Monthly		**Capital Gains:** Annually
12b-1:	Yes	**Amount:** 0.50%	
Minimum:	**Initial:** $1,000	**Subsequent:** $100	
Min IRA:	**Initial:** $100	**Subsequent:** $100	
Services:	IRA, Keogh, SEP, 403(b), Withdraw, Deduct		
Tel Exchange:	Yes	**With MMF:** Yes	
Registered:	All states		

BULL & BEAR
U.S. GOVERNMENT
GUARANTEED
SECURITIES
Bond

Bull & Bear Management Corp.
11 Hanover Square
New York, NY 10005
(800) 847-4200/(212) 363-1100

	Years Ending 6/30					
	1982	1983	1984	1985	1986 (4 mos.)	1987
Net Investment Income ($)	–	–	–	–	.58	1.47
Dividends from Net Investment Income ($)	–	–	–	–	.47	1.42
Net Gains (Losses) on Investments ($)	–	–	–	–	(.27)	(.21)
Distributions from Net Realized Capital Gains ($)	–	–	–	–	–	–
Net Asset Value End of Year ($)	–	–	–	–	14.84	14.68
Ratio of Expenses to Net Assets (%)	–	–	–	–	1.21	2.06
Portfolio Turnover Rate (%)	–	–	–	–	31	185
Total Assets: End of Year (Millions $)	–	–	–	–	8.8	46.8

Annual Rate of Return (%) Years Ending 12/31	–	–	–	–	–	5.4

Five-Year Total Return(%)	NA	Degree of Diversification	NA	Beta	NA	Bull (%)	NA	Bear (%)	2.1^

Objective: Seeks high level of current income, liquidity, and safety of principal. Invests in U.S. Treasury and government agency securities including bills, notes, bonds, GNMAs, and Federal Housing Administration bonds. Can also write covered call options on securities it owns.

Portfolio: (6/30/87) GNMAs 108%.

Distributions: Income: Monthly   **Capital Gains:** Annually

12b-1: Yes   **Amount:** 1.00%

Minimum: Initial: $1,000   **Subsequent:** $100

Min IRA: Initial: $100   **Subsequent:** $100

Services: IRA, Keogh, SEP, 403(b), Withdraw, Deduct

Tel Exchange: Yes   **With MMF:** Yes

Registered: All states

CALAMOS CONVERTIBLE INCOME
(formerly NODDINGS-CALAMOS CONVERTIBLE INCOME)

Growth & Income

Calamos Asset Management, Inc.
2001 Spring Road, #750
Oak Brook, IL 60521
(800) 323-9943/(312) 571-7115

	Years Ending 4/30					
	1982	1983	1984	1985	1986 (10 mos.)	1987
Net Investment Income ($)	–	–	–	–	.32	.52
Dividends from Net Investment Income ($)	–	–	–	–	.25	.54
Net Gains (Losses) on Investments ($)	–	–	–	–	1.92	.50
Distributions from Net Realized Capital Gains ($)	–	–	–	–	–	.53
Net Asset Value End of Year ($)	–	–	–	–	11.99	11.94
Ratio of Expenses to Net Assets (%)	–	–	–	–	2.00	1.30
Portfolio Turnover Rate (%)	–	–	–	–	26	45
Total Assets: End of Year (Millions $)	–	–	–	–	10.2	23.6

Annual Rate of Return (%) Years Ending 12/31	–	–	–	–	16.1	(4.5)

Five-Year Total Return(%)	NA	Degree of Diversification	NA	Beta	NA	Bull (%)	NA	Bear (%)	(16.9)c

Objective: Seeks high current income. Capital appreciation is a secondary objective. Invests at least 65% of its assets in convertible bonds and preferred stocks. May invest 30% of fund's assets in issues rated BB or lower by Standard & Poor's.

Portfolio: (10/31/87) Convertible bonds 83%, convertible preferred stocks 16%. Largest holdings: capital goods—technology 26%, consumer growth staples 10%.

Distributions: Income: Quarterly   **Capital Gains:** Annually

12b-1: No

Minimum: Initial: $5,000   Subsequent: $500

Min IRA: Initial: $2,000   Subsequent: $500

Services: IRA, Keogh, Deduct, Withdraw

Tel Exchange: No

Registered: All states except: AL, AK, AR, ME, MS, ND, NH, SD, VT, WV, WY

CALIFORNIA INVESTMENT TRUST U.S. GOVERNMENT SECURITIES

Bond

CCM Partners
44 Montgomery Street
San Francisco, CA 94104
(800) 826-8166/(415) 398-2727
In California (800) 225-8778

	Years Ending 8/31					
	1982	**1983**	**1984**	**1985**	**1986** (9 mos.)	**1987**
Net Investment Income ($)	–	–	–	–	.59	.90
Dividends from Net Investment Income ($)	–	–	–	–	.50	.91
Net Gains (Losses) on Investments ($)	–	–	–	–	.17	(.63)
Distributions from Net Realized Capital Gains ($)	–	–	–	–	–	–
Net Asset Value End of Year ($)	–	–	–	–	10.26	9.62
Ratio of Expenses to Net Assets (%)	–	–	–	–	.04	.34
Portfolio Turnover Rate (%)	–	–	–	–	279	115
Total Assets: End of Year (Millions $)	–	–	–	–	.01	13.1
Annual Rate of Return (%) Years Ending 12/31	–	–	–	–	11.9	1.2

Five-Year Total Return(%)	NA	Degree of Diversification	NA	Beta	NA	Bull (%)	NA	Bear (%)	2.5A

Objective: Seeks safety from credit risk, liquidity, and as high a level of income as is consistent with these objectives by investing in full faith and credit obligations of the U.S. government and its agencies, primarily GNMAs.

Portfolio: (8/31/87) GNMAs 94%, U.S. Treasury notes 5%, other 1%.

Distributions: **Income:** Monthly   **Capital Gains:** Annually

12b-1: No

Minimum: **Initial:** $10,000   **Subsequent:** $250

Min IRA: **Initial:** None   **Subsequent:** None

Services: IRA, Keogh, Withdraw

Tel Exchange: Yes   **With MMF:** Yes

Registered: CA, NV, HI

CALVERT— EQUITY PORTFOLIO
Growth

Calvert Asset Management Co.
1700 Pennsylvania Ave., N.W.
Washington, DC 20006
(800) 368-2748/(301) 951-4820

	Years Ending 9/30					
	1982	1983	1984	1985	1986	1987
Net Investment Income ($)	–	.38	.44	.34	.17	.11
Dividends from Net Investment Income ($)	–	–	.37	.44	.34	.18
Net Gains (Losses) on Investments ($)	–	3.51	(1.98)	.14	5.35	4.80
Distributions from Net Realized Capital Gains ($)	–	–	.04	–	–	2.14
Net Asset Value End of Year ($)	–	18.89	16.94	16.98	22.16	24.75
Ratio of Expenses to Net Assets (%)	–	2.25	2.06	1.98	1.83	1.70
Portfolio Turnover Rate (%)	–	12	148	38	56	34
Total Assets: End of Year (Millions $)	–	8.6	6.8	5.9	7.6	9.7
Annual Rate of Return (%) Years Ending 12/31	–	9.0	(6.7)	23.6	12.1	(8.2)

Five-Year Total Return(%)	29.4E	Degree of Diversification	B	Beta	1.01	Bull (%)	92.3C	Bear (%)	(28.9)E

Objective: Seeks growth of capital through investment in equity securities considered neither speculative nor conservative. Chosen through analysis of cash flow, book value, dividend growth potential, management quality and current and future earnings.

Portfolio: (9/30/87) Common stocks 94%, convertible bonds 1%. Largest stock holdings: banking & financial services 19%; oil, gas & energy related 13%.

Distributions: Income: Annually   **Capital Gains:** Annually

12b-1: Yes   **Amount:** 0.75%

Minimum: Initial: $2,000   Subsequent: $250

Min IRA: Initial: $1,000   Subsequent: $250

Services: IRA, Keogh, 403(b), Withdraw, Deduct

Tel Exchange: Yes   **With MMF:** Yes

Registered: All states

CAPITAL PRESERVATION TREASURY NOTE TRUST

Bond

Benham Management Corp.
755 Page Mill Rd.
Palo Alto, CA 94304-1018
(800) 227-8380/(415) 858-3600

	Years Ending 3/31					
	1982	1983	1984	1985	1986	1987
Net Investment Income ($)	.91	1.01	.96	.99	.90	.71
Dividends from Net Investment Income ($)	.86	.91	1.03	.93	.83	1.69
Net Gains (Losses) on Investments ($)	.06	.42	(.15)	.16	1.55	(.08)
Distributions from Net Realized Capital Gains ($)	—	—	—	—	—	—
Net Asset Value End of Year ($)	9.83	10.35	10.13	10.35	11.97	10.91
Ratio of Expenses to Net Assets (%)	.88	1.00	1.00	1.00	1.00	.93
Portfolio Turnover Rate (%)	—	—	—	53	294	396
Total Assets: End of Year (Millions $)	7.1	11.1	9.2	12.5	28.5	43.2

Annual Rate of Return (%) Years Ending 12/31	17.1	7.4	12.0	17.6	13.1	(1.3)

Five-Year Total Return(%) 57.9ᴰ	Degree of Diversification ᴺᴬ	Beta .04	Bull (%) 39.8ᴱ	Bear (%) 3.4ᴬ

Objective: Seeks high current income consistent with safety of principal; at least 90% of the trust's portfolio invested in U.S. Treasury notes, and up to 10% in U.S. Treasury bills and repurchase agreements consisting of U.S. Treasury securities.

Portfolio: (9/30/87) U.S. Treasury notes 100%.

Distributions: Income: Monthly   **Capital Gains:** Dec

12b-1: No

Minimum: Initial: $1,000   Subsequent: $100

Min IRA: Initial: $100   Subsequent: None

Services: IRA, Keogh

Tel Exchange: Yes   **With MMF:** Yes

Registered: All states

CENTURY SHARES TRUST
Growth

Century Shares Trust
One Liberty Square
Boston, MA 02109
(800) 321-1928/(617) 482-3060

	Years Ending 12/31					
	1982	1983	1984	1985	1986	1987
Net Investment Income ($)	.60	.60	.55	.50	.50	.50
Dividends from Net Investment Income ($)	.64	.64	.60	.54	.51	.50
Net Gains (Losses) on Investments ($)	.61	1.86	1.36	5.15	1.20	(1.93)
Distributions from Net Realized Capital Gains ($)	.49	.45	.91	.91	1.11	1.61
Net Asset Value End of Year ($)	12.25	13.62	14.02	18.22	18.30	14.76
Ratio of Expenses to Net Assets (%)	1.13	.94	.95	.84	.77	.81
Portfolio Turnover Rate (%)	5	4	4	6	6	2
Total Assets: End of Year (Millions $)	68.0	74.4	76.8	123.2	141	109.4
Annual Rate of Return (%) Years Ending 12/31	11.0	21.2	15.6	42.6	9.4	(8.0)

Five-Year Total Return(%)	100.9ᴬ	Degree of Diversification	E	Beta	.80	Bull (%)	127.6ᴬ	Bear (%)	(20.2)ᴰ

Objective: Seeks long-term growth of capital and current income through investments exclusively in insurance and banking stocks and in bonds and obligations which are legal investments for savings banks in Massachusetts.

Portfolio: (12/31/87) Common stocks 99%, other 1%. Largest stock holdings: insurance 94%, banking 5%.

Distributions: Income: June, Dec   **Capital Gains:** Dec

12b-1: No

Minimum: Initial: $500   Subsequent: $25

Min IRA: Initial: $500   Subsequent: $25

Services: IRA

Tel Exchange: No

Registered: All states

COLUMBIA FIXED INCOME SECURITIES
Bond

Columbia Financial Center
1301 S.W. Fifth Ave.
P.O. Box 1350
Portland, OR 97207-1350
(800) 547-1037/(503) 222-3600

	Years Ending 12/31					
	1982	1983	1984	1985	1986	1987
Net Investment Income ($)	–	1.35	1.44	1.40	1.21	1.03
Dividends from Net Investment Income ($)	–	1.35	1.44	1.40	1.21	1.03
Net Gains (Losses) on Investments ($)	–	(.30)	(.07)	.91	.32	(.87)
Distributions from Net Realized Capital Gains ($)	–	–	–	–	–	.27
Net Asset Value End of Year ($)	–	12.21	12.14	13.05	13.37	12.23
Ratio of Expenses to Net Assets (%)	–	1.22	1.05	.88	.79	.82
Portfolio Turnover Rate (%)	–	46	98	94	97	114
Total Assets: End of Year (Millions $)	–	29.4	38.1	83.2	124.4	100.3

Annual Rate of Return (%) Years Ending 12/31	–	–	12.3	20.1	12.4	1.4

Five-Year Total Return(%)	NA	Degree of Diversification	NA	Beta	.01	Bull (%)	46.1E	Bear (%)	3.1A

Objective: Seeks high level of current income, consistent with conservation of capital, through investment in a broad range of investment grade fixed-income securities, amounting to 80% of its assets. Other 20% may be in lower grade debt securities as well as those of the U.S. government.

Portfolio: (12/31/87) U.S. government and agency obligations 58%, corporate bonds 38%, repos 3%, cash 1%. Largest bond holdings: industrial bonds 17%, financial bonds 15%.

Distributions: Income: Monthly   **Capital Gains:** Jan

12b-1: No

Minimum: Initial: $1,000   Subsequent: $100

Min IRA: Initial: $1,000   Subsequent: $100

Services: IRA, Keogh, SEP, Withdraw

Tel Exchange: Yes   ·With MMF: Yes

Registered: All states except AL, AR, DE, IN, KS, KY, LA, ME, MS, ND, NE, NH, NM, OK, RI, SC, SD, TN, UT, VT, WI, WV

COLUMBIA GROWTH
Growth

Columbia Financial Center
1301 S.W. Fifth Ave.
P.O. Box 1350
Portland, OR 97207-1350
(800) 547-1037/(503) 222-3600

	Years Ending 12/31					
	1982	1983	1984	1985	1986	1987
Net Investment Income ($)	.39	.37	.20	.29	.25	.32
Dividends from Net Investment Income ($)	.40	.12	.19	.33	.40	.61
Net Gains (Losses) on Investments ($)	6.82	4.20	(1.52)	6.53	1.49	2.93
Distributions from Net Realized Capital Gains ($)	4.14	2.42	2.41	—	6.48	5.33
Net Asset Value End of Year ($)	23.42	25.45	21.53	28.02	22.88	20.19
Ratio of Expenses to Net Assets (%)	1.15	1.10	1.18	1.06	1.00	1.04
Portfolio Turnover Rate (%)	160	95	90	93	131	197
Total Assets: End of Year (Millions $)	74.1	145.5	155.1	250.6	200.9	193.5
Annual Rate of Return (%) Years Ending 12/31	44.9	21.5	(5.1)	32.0	6.8	14.7

Five-Year Total Return(%)	86.4[B]	Degree of Diversification	A	Beta	.96	Bull (%)	121.0[B]	Bear (%)	(17.0)[C]

Objective: Seeks capital growth and preservation through selection of common stocks of large, established, dividend-paying companies on the basis of sales trends, earnings and profit margins, new products, industry environment, management and future orientation, all in the framework of the economy and market conditions. May adopt defensive posture in bonds or commercial paper.

Portfolio: (12/31/87) Common stocks 73%, repos 18%, commercial paper 10%. Largest stock holdings: technology 14%, machinery and capital spending 9%.

Distributions: Income: Jan   **Capital Gains:** Jan

12b-1: No

Minimum: Initial: $1,000   Subsequent: $100

Min IRA: Initial: $1,000   Subsequent: $100

Services: IRA, Keogh, SEP, Withdraw

Tel Exchange: Yes   **With MMF:** Yes

Registered: All states except NH

COLUMBIA SPECIAL
Aggressive Growth

Columbia Financial Center
1301 S.W. Fifth Avenue
P.O. Box 1350
Portland, OR 97207-1350
(800) 547-1037/(503) 222-3600

	Years Ending 12/31					
	1982	1983	1984	1985 (5 mos.)	1986	1987
Net Investment Income ($)	–	–	–	.03	(.13)	(.23)
Dividends from Net Investment Income ($)	–	–	–	–	–	–
Net Gains (Losses) on Investments ($)	–	–	–	5.43	3.88	1.05
Distributions from Net Realized Capital Gains ($)	–	–	–	–	.74	–
Net Asset Value End of Year ($)	–	–	–	23.96	26.97	27.79
Ratio of Expenses to Net Assets (%)	–	–	–	1.24	1.54	1.44
Portfolio Turnover Rate (%)	–	–	–	112	203	333
Total Assets: End of Year (Millions $)	–	–	–	3.1	20.4	20.6
Annual Rate of Return (%) Years Ending 12/31	–	–	–	–	15.8	3.0

Five-Year Total Return(%)	NA	Degree of Diversification	NA	Beta	NA	Bull (%)	NA	Bear (%)	(30.0)E

Objective: Seeks significant capital appreciation by investing in securities that are more aggressive and carry more risk than the market as a whole. Invests in small companies with capitalizations less than the average of those companies in the S&P 500.

Portfolio: (12/31/87) Common stocks 96%, repos 2%, cash 2%. Largest stock holdings: machinery & capital spending 19%, technology 19%.

Distributions: Income: Annually   **Capital Gains:** Annually

12b-1: No

Minimum: Initial: $2,000   Subsequent: $100

Min IRA: Initial: $2,000   Subsequent: $100

Services: IRA, Keogh, SEP, Withdraw

Tel Exchange: Yes   **With MMF:** Yes

Registered: All states except AL, AR, CA, DE, IN, KS, KY, LA, ME, MO, MS, ND, NE, NH, NM, OK, RI, SC, SD, TN, UT, VT, WI, WV

COPLEY
TAX-MANAGED
Growth

Copley Financial Services Corp.
109 Howe St.
P.O. Box 66
Fall River, MA 02724
(617) 674-8459

	Years Ending 2/28					
	1982	1983	1984	1985	1986	1987
Net Investment Income ($)	.30	.40	.52	.53	.59	.61
Dividends from Net Investment Income ($)	–	–	–	–	–	–
Net Gains (Losses) on Investments ($)	(.11)	.92	(.06)	1.01	1.77	1.10
Distributions from Net Realized Capital Gains ($)	–	–	–	–	–	–
Net Asset Value End of Year ($)	4.36	5.68	6.14	7.68	10.04	11.75
Ratio of Expenses to Net Assets (%)	2.75	2.23	1.40	1.50	1.47	1.43
Portfolio Turnover Rate (%)	9	56	39	29	19	16
Total Assets: End of Year (Millions $)	1.6	2.7	5.6	8.4	21.6	33.6

Annual Rate of Return (%) Years Ending 12/31	19.9	11.6	23.9	24.6	17.7	(8.3)

Five-Year Total Return(%)	86.2[B]	Degree of Diversification	E	Beta	.49	Bull (%)	86.7[C]	Bear (%)	(13.2)[C]

Objective: Seeks high income without concern for level of dividend income as it is tax-free. Set up as a corporation that is entitled to 85% exemption from federal income taxes on dividends received, and the 15% balance can be used as expenses to run the fund. Invests in highly visible companies with strong balance sheets that pay high dividends which have been increasing.

Portfolio: (8/31/87) Common and preferred stocks 94%, short-term securities 7%. Largest stock holdings: electric and gas 22%, electric power 21%.

Distributions: Income: NA   **Capital Gains:** NA
12b-1: No
Minimum: Initial: $1,000   Subsequent: $100
Min IRA: Initial: $100   Subsequent: $100
Services: IRA, Keogh, Withdraw
Tel Exchange: None
Registered: All states

CUMBERLAND GROWTH
Growth

Cumberland Advisors
614 Landis Avenue
Vineland, NJ 08360
(800) 257-7013/(609) 692-6690

	Years Ending 12/31					
	1982	1983*	1984	1985	1986*	1987*
Net Investment Income ($)	.19	.32	.21	.26	.15	.01
Dividends from Net Investment Income ($)	.30	.16	.24	.17	.17	.77
Net Gains (Losses) on Investments ($)	1.58	.78	(.79)	1.51	.33	(1.39)
Distributions from Net Realized Capital Gains ($)	–	–	.31	–	–	–
Net Asset Value End of Year ($)	8.55	9.74	8.61	10.21	10.73	8.87
Ratio of Expenses to Net Assets (%)	5.3	4.1	4.1	3.8	3.4	4.6
Portfolio Turnover Rate (%)	172	219	71	194	187	267
Total Assets: End of Year (Millions $)	.51	.91	.77	1.6	2.4	2.2
Annual Rate of Return (%) Years Ending 12/31	25.9	16.4	(6.0)	21.5	11.8	(15.0)

Five-Year Total Return(%)	26.2ᴱ	Degree of Diversification	D	Beta	.84	Bull (%)	67.8ᴰ	Bear (%)	(25.9)ᴱ

Per share data appear as reported in the fund's prospectus and annual report; figures for 1983, 1986 and 1987, however, do not balance.

Objective: Primary objective is capital appreciation; current income is a secondary consideration. Invests primarily in common stocks, but may invest in bonds rated BBB or lower by Standard & Poor's. Can leverage the fund through bank borrowings, and may also sell stock short.

Portfolio: (12/31/87) Common stocks 73%, corporate bonds 5%, convertible bonds 2%. Largest stock holdings: technology 10%, telecommunications 8%.

Distributions:	**Income:** Annually	**Capital Gains:** Annually
12b-1:	Yes	**Amount:** 0.50%
Minimum:	**Initial:** $1,000	**Subsequent:** $100
Min IRA:	**Initial:** $100	**Subsequent:** $100
Services:	IRA, Keogh	
Tel Exchange:	No	
Registered:	DE, NJ, NY, PA	

DELAWARE TREASURY RESERVES INVESTORS SERIES
Bond

Delaware Management Company
Ten Penn Center Plaza
Philadelphia, PA 19103
(800) 523-4640/(215) 988-1333

			Years Ending 12/31			
	1982	1983	1984	1985 (1 mo.)	1986	1987
Net Investment Income ($)	–	–	–	.06	.84	.70
Dividends from Net Investment Income ($)	–	–	–	.06	.84	.70
Net Gains (Losses) on Investments ($)	–	–	–	.04	(.06)	(.18)
Distributions from Net Realized Capital Gains ($)	–	–	–	–	–	–
Net Asset Value End of Year ($)	–	–	–	10.04	9.98	9.80
Ratio of Expenses to Net Assets (%)	–	–	–	–	1.02	1.06
Portfolio Turnover Rate (%)	–	–	–	–	39	304
Total Assets: End of Year (Millions $)	–	–	–	8.1	182.8	138.8

Annual Rate of Return (%) Years Ending 12/31		–	–	–	–	7.7	5.3

Five-Year Total Return(%)	NA	Degree of Diversification	NA	Beta	NA	Bull (%)	NA	Bear (%)	2.2ᴬ

Objective: Seeks high stable level of current income while attempting to minimize fluctuations in principal and provide maximum liquidity. Invests in short- and intermediate-term securities guaranteed by the U.S. government. Average maturity of the portfolio is no more than 5 years.

Portfolio: (12/25/87) U.S. government agency obligations 58%, U.S. Treasury obligations 44%.

Distributions: Income: Monthly   **Capital Gains:** Annually

12b-1: Yes   **Amount:** 0.30%

Minimum: Initial: $1,000   Subsequent: $25

Min IRA: Initial: $250   Subsequent: $25

Services: IRA, Keogh, Corp, SEP, 403(b), Withdraw, Deduct

Tel Exchange: Yes   **With MMF:** Yes

Registered: All states

DIVIDEND/GROWTH —DIVIDEND SERIES

Growth & Income

A.I.M. Management
107 N. Adams St.
Rockville, MD 20850
(800) 638-2042/(301) 251-1002

	Years Ending 12/31					
	1982*	1983	1984	1985	1986	1987
Net Investment Income ($)	1.54	.88	.88	.86	.66	.51
Dividends from Net Investment Income ($)	—	1.15	.87	.85	1.50	.55
Net Gains (Losses) on Investments ($)	.95	2.25	1.64	2.46	1.53	(.51)
Distributions from Net Realized Capital Gains ($)	—	—	—	1.70	1.68	2.13
Net Asset Value End of Year ($)	21.40	23.38	25.03	25.80	24.81	22.13
Ratio of Expenses to Net Assets (%)	3.10	2.43	2.00	2.00	2.00	1.99
Portfolio Turnover Rate (%)	150	67	56	34	43	34
Total Assets: End of Year (Millions $)	2.8	3.7	4.0	4.3	4.4	3.9

Annual Rate of Return (%) Years Ending 12/31	13.2	15.2	11.4	14.1	8.7	(0.2)

Five-Year Total Return(%) 58.9ᴰ	Degree of Diversification C	Beta .90	Bull (%) 85.0ᶜ	Bear (%) (22.0)ᴰ

Fund reorganized in 1982 and changed name.

Objective: Seeks income growth with secondary emphasis on growth of capital through investment in income-producing, large, well-established companies that are fundamentally sound. May take short positions, may use leverage and may write covered call options. May invest minor portion in new companies or in special situations.

Portfolio: (12/31/87) Common stocks 90%, short-term securities 6%, other assets 5%. Largest stock holdings: electric utilities 15%, computers & electronics 13%.

Distributions: Income: Feb, May, Aug, Nov   **Capital Gains:** Annually

12b-1: No

Minimum: Initial: $300   Subsequent: $50

Min IRA: Initial: $300   Subsequent: $50

Services: IRA, Keogh, SEP, Withdraw

Tel Exchange: Yes   **With MMF:** Yes

Registered: Call for availability

DODGE & COX BALANCED

Balanced

Dodge & Cox
One Post St., 35th Flr.
San Francisco, CA 94104
(415) 434-0311

	Years Ending 12/31					
	1982	1983	1984	1985	1986	1987
Net Investment Income ($)	1.68	1.71	1.72	1.71	1.62	1.67
Dividends from Net Investment Income ($)	1.67	1.72	1.73	1.70	1.62	1.70
Net Gains (Losses) on Investments ($)	3.65	2.45	(.57)	6.37	4.24	.80
Distributions from Net Realized Capital Gains ($)	.50	.31	.83	.37	3.55	2.67
Net Asset Value End of Year ($)	25.20	27.33	25.92	31.93	32.62	30.72
Ratio of Expenses to Net Assets (%)	.80	.76	.76	.75	.73	.72
Portfolio Turnover Rate (%)	7	10	7	26	14	15
Total Assets: End of Year (Millions $)	18.1	19.6	19.1	24.5	27.5	34.4

Annual Rate of Return (%) Years Ending 12/31	26.0	17.0	4.7	32.5	19.2	7.7

Five-Year Total Return(%)	108.2[A]	Degree of Diversification	NA	Beta	.63	Bull (%)	121.2[B]	Bear (%)	(13.4)[C]

Objective: To provide shareholders with regular income, conservation of principal and an opportunity for long-term growth of principal and income through investment (no more than 75%) in common stocks of dividend-paying, financially strong companies with sound economic backgrounds. Remaining 25% shall be invested in high grade bonds and preferred stocks.

Portfolio: (12/31/87) Common stocks 54%, bonds 36%, short-term securities 9%, other assets 1%. Largest stock holdings: finance 7%, public utilities 7%.

Distributions: Income: Mar, June, Sept, Dec   **Capital Gains:** Dec

12b-1: No

Minimum: Initial: $1,000   Subsequent: $100

Min IRA: Initial: $1,000   Subsequent: $100

Services: IRA, Withdraw

Tel Exchange: No

Registered: CA, CT, DC, GA, HI, NV, NY, OR, UT, WY

DODGE & COX STOCK

Growth & Income

Dodge & Cox
One Post St., 35th Flr.·
San Francisco, CA 94104
(415) 434-0311

	Years Ending 12/31					
	1982	1983	1984	1985	1986	1987
Net Investment Income ($)	.99	1.02	1.01	1.02	.94	.99
Dividends from Net Investment Income ($)	.99	1.00	1.02	1.01	.94	1.03
Net Gains (Losses) on Investments ($)	3.03	4.71	.15	7.72	4.61	2.90
Distributions from Net Realized Capital Gains ($)	.30	.77	1.88	1.23	3.90	1.58
Net Asset Value End of Year ($)	22.23	26.19	24.45	30.95	31.66	32.94
Ratio of Expenses to Net Assets (%)	.75	.70	.69	.68	.66	.65
Portfolio Turnover Rate (%)	17	17	14	22	10	12
Total Assets: End of Year (Millions $)	22.4	27.3	27.8	38.5	45.1	67.5
Annual Rate of Return (%) Years Ending 12/31	22.0	26.7	5.1	37.7	18.8	12.5

Five-Year Total Return(%)	145.0ᴬ	Degree of Diversification	A	Beta	.94	Bull (%)	165.1ᴬ	Bear (%)	(20.2)ᴰ

Objective: Seeks long-term growth of principal and income through investment in dividend-paying, financially strong companies with sound economic background. Must be from variety of industries and be traded readily. A secondary objective is to achieve some current income.

Portfolio: (12/31/87) Common stocks 96%, short-term securities 4%. Largest stock holdings: finance 14%, public utilities 12%.

Distributions: Income: Mar, June, Sept, Dec   **Capital Gains:** Dec

12b-1: No

Minimum: Initial: $1,000   Subsequent: $100

Min IRA: Initial: $1,000   Subsequent: $100

Services: IRA, Withdraw

Tel Exchange: No

Registered: CA, CT, DC, GA, HI, NV, NY, OR, UT, WY

DREYFUS
A BONDS PLUS
Bond

The Dreyfus Corp.
600 Madison Ave.
New York, NY 10022
(800) 645-6561/(718) 895-1206

	Years Ending 3/31					
	1982	**1983**	**1984**	**1985**	**1986**	**1987**
Net Investment Income ($)	1.62	1.57	1.50	1.50	1.45	1.32
Dividends from Net Investment Income ($)	1.61	1.57	1.52	1.48	1.42	1.30
Net Gains (Losses) on Investments ($)	(.48)	1.64	(1.03)	.27	2.19	.02
Distributions from Net Realized Capital Gains ($)	–	–	–	–	–	.25
Net Asset Value End of Year ($)	12.22	13.86	12.81	13.10	15.32	15.11
Ratio of Expenses to Net Assets (%)	1.04	.95	.93	.94	.87	.84
Portfolio Turnover Rate (%)	–	10	5	21	61	79
Total Assets: End of Year (Millions $)	27.2	97.6	105.5	123.3	222.9	319.6
Annual Rate of Return (%) Years Ending 12/31	26.0	7.6	12.4	23.1	13.9	(.4)

Five-Year Total Return(%) 68.9c	Degree of Diversification NA	Beta .08	Bull (%) 52.8D	Bear (%) 2.4A

Objective: Seeks maximization of current income with preservation of liquidity and capital. Invests 80% of assets in debt obligations rated A or better. The other components must be of high quality as well.

Portfolio: (9/30/87) Corporate bonds 96%, cash 3%, short-term securities 1%. Largest bond holdings: utilities 20%, banking 11%.

Distributions: Income: Monthly   **Capital Gains:** May

12b-1: No

Minimum: Initial: $2,500   Subsequent: $100

Min IRA: Initial: $750   Subsequent: None

Services: IRA, Keogh, Corp, SEP, 403(b), Withdraw, Deduct

Tel Exchange: Yes   **With MMF:** Yes

Registered: All states

DREYFUS CONVERTIBLE SECURITIES

Balanced

The Dreyfus Corp.
600 Madison Ave.
New York, NY 10022
(800) 645-6561/(718) 895-1206

	Years Ending 4/30					
	1982	1983	1984	1985	1986	1987
Net Investment Income ($)	.69	.65	.62	.57	.63	.49
Dividends from Net Investment Income ($)	.70	.67	.63	.60	.56	.51
Net Gains (Losses) on Investments ($)	(.85)	1.44	.13	.26	1.78	1.03
Distributions from Net Realized Capital Gains ($)	.29	.08	.04	.28	.24	.85
Net Asset Value End of Year ($)	6.35	7.69	7.77	7.72	9.33	9.49
Ratio of Expenses to Net Assets (%)	.87	.85	.85	.85	.85	.85
Portfolio Turnover Rate (%)	6	27	25	32	62	91
Total Assets: End of Year (Millions $)	61.3	83.2	92.2	101.1	143.4	250.1
Annual Rate of Return (%) Years Ending 12/31	17.1	21.0	7.6	23.5	23.7	(3.0)

Five-Year Total Return(%)	93.0[B]	Degree of Diversification	NA	Beta	.57	Bull (%)	103.8[B]	Bear (%)	(19.3)[D]

Objective:	Seeks to maximize current income. Invests primarily in bonds, debentures and preferred stocks and secondarily in common stocks with high current dividend and appreciation potential. May lend securities from its portfolio and write (sell) covered call options and invest in foreign securities.
Portfolio:	(7/31/87) Equity-related securities 83%, bonds and notes 14%, cash 2%, short-term securities 1%. Largest stock holdings: forest products 12%, aerospace 2%.
Distributions:	Income: Quarterly **Capital Gains:** May
12b-1:	No
Minimum:	Initial: $2,500 Subsequent: $100
Min IRA:	Initial: $750 Subsequent: None
Services:	IRA, Keogh, Corp, 403(b), SEP, Withdraw, Deduct
Tel Exchange:	Yes **With MMF:** Yes
Registered:	All states

DREYFUS GNMA
Bond

The Dreyfus Corp.
600 Madison Ave.
New York, NY 10022
(800) 645-6561/(718) 895-1206

	Years Ending 4/30					
	1982	1983	1984	1985	1986 (11 mos.)	1987
Net Investment Income ($)	–	–	–	–	1.44	1.38
Dividends from Net Investment Income ($)	–	–	–	–	1.32	1.39
Net Gains (Losses) on Investments ($)	–	–	–	–	1.19	(.69)
Distributions from Net Realized Capital Gains ($)	–	–	–	–	–	.03
Net Asset Value End of Year ($)	–	–	–	–	15.81	15.08
Ratio of Expenses to Net Assets (%)	–	–	–	–	.96	1.01
Portfolio Turnover Rate (%)	–	–	–	–	245	257
Total Assets: End of Year (Millions $)	–	–	–	–	1,739.5	2,396.6
Annual Rate of Return (%) Years Ending 12/31	–	–	–	–	9.5	2.5

Five-Year Total Return(%)	NA	Degree of Diversification	NA	Beta	NA	Bull (%)	NA	Bear (%)	2.1^

Objective: Seeks high current income consistent with capital preservation through investing at least 65% of its net assets in GNMAs. May also invest in other U.S. government-backed debt securities.

Portfolio: (10/31/87) GNMAs 91%, U.S. Treasury notes 13%, short-term securities 12%, U.S. Treasury bonds 1%.

Distributions: **Income:** Monthly   **Capital Gains:** Annually

12b-1: Yes   **Amount:** 0.20%

Minimum: Initial: $2,500   Subsequent: $100

Min IRA: Initial: $750   Subsequent: None

Services: IRA, Keogh, SEP, Corp, 403(b), Withdraw, Deduct

Tel Exchange: Yes   **With MMF:** Yes

Registered: All states

DREYFUS GROWTH OPPORTUNITY
Growth

The Dreyfus Corp.
600 Madison Ave.
New York, NY 10022
(800) 645-6561/(718) 895-1206

	Years Ending 2/28					
	1982	1983	1984	1985	1986	1987
Net Investment Income ($)	.33	.22	.17	.16	.23	.18
Dividends from Net Investment Income ($)	.14	.29	.25	.18	.21	.21
Net Gains (Losses) on Investments ($)	(2.98)	2.47	1.07	(.45)	2.64	2.61
Distributions from Net Realized Capital Gains ($)	.60	.81	.34	.88	.34	2.80
Net Asset Value End of Year ($)	9.00	10.59	11.24	9.89	12.21	11.99
Ratio of Expenses to Net Assets (%)	1.08	1.06	.99	1.02	.98	.95
Portfolio Turnover Rate (%)	35	68	60	44	56	73
Total Assets: End of Year (Millions $)	110.4	251.5	369.7	441.9	478.0	516.3

Annual Rate of Return (%) Years Ending 12/31	3.6	31.5	(12.1)	30.7	15.0	6.4

Five-Year Total Return(%)	84.6ᴮ	Degree of Diversification	E	Beta	.87	Bull (%)	108.2ᴮ	Bear (%)	(22.0)ᴰ

Objective: Primarily aims to promote growth of capital through investment in established companies. Up to 25% of portfolio may be in foreign companies. Income is secondary but in periods of market weakness the fund will emphasize investment in money market and other high-yielding securities.

Portfolio: (8/31/87) Common stocks 86%, preferred stocks 5%, short-term securities 5%, convertible bonds 4%. Largest stock holdings: mining and metals 9%, petroleum products 9%.

Distributions: Income: April   **Capital Gains:** April
12b-1: No
Minimum: Initial: $2,500   Subsequent: $100
Min IRA: Initial: $750   Subsequent: None
Services: IRA, Keogh, Corp, SEP, 403(b), Withdraw, Deduct
Tel Exchange: Yes   **With MMF:** Yes
Registered: All states

DREYFUS NEW LEADERS

Aggressive Growth

The Dreyfus Corp.
600 Madison Ave.
New York, NY 10022
(800) 645-6561/(516) 794-5210

	Years Ending 12/31					
	1982	1983	1984	1985 (11 mos.)	1986	1987
Net Investment Income ($)	–	–	–	.20	.15	.17
Dividends from Net Investment Income ($)	–	–	–	–	.01	.17
Net Gains (Losses) on Investments ($)	–	–	–	4.41	2.12	(1.20)
Distributions from Net Realized Capital Gains ($)	–	–	–	–	.01	–
Net Asset Value End of Year ($)	–	–	–	18.11	20.36	19.16
Ratio of Expenses to Net Assets (%)	–	–	–	1.46	1.30	1.41
Portfolio Turnover Rate (%)	–	–	–	81	195	177
Total Assets: End of Year (Millions $)	–	–	–	5.1	65.1	79.8
Annual Rate of Return (%) Years Ending 12/31	–	–	–	–	12.6	(5.3)

Five-Year Total Return(%)	NA	Degree of Diversification	NA	Beta	NA	Bull (%)	NA	Bear (%)	(28.5)E

Objective: The fund's goal is to maximize capital appreciation. Invests in small emerging growth stocks of both foreign and domestic issues. May invest up to 25% of assets in foreign stocks. May also buy and sell put and call options.

Portfolio: (12/31/87) Common stocks 79%, short-term securities 14%, cash 5%, convertible preferred stocks 1%. Largest stock holdings: basic industries 22%, technology 16%.

Distributions: Income: Annually   **Capital Gains:** Annually

12b-1: No

Minimum: Initial: $2,500   Subsequent: $100

Min IRA: Initial: $750   Subsequent: None

Services: IRA, Keogh, Corp, SEP, 403(b), Withdraw, Deduct

Tel Exchange: Yes   **With MMF:** Yes

Registered: All states

DREYFUS THIRD CENTURY
Growth & Income

The Dreyfus Corp.
600 Madison Ave.
New York, NY 10022
(800) 645-6561/(718) 895-1206

	Years Ending 5/31					
	1982	1983	1984	1985	1986	1987
Net Investment Income ($)	.33	.25	.20	.19	.30	.23
Dividends from Net Investment Income ($)	.21	.32	.26	.20	.21	.31
Net Gains (Losses) on Investments ($)	(2.24)	2.05	(.83)	1.54	1.13	.64
Distributions from Net Realized Capital Gains ($)	.48	.45	.55	.53	.51	.96
Net Asset Value End of Year ($)	6.33	7.86	6.42	7.42	8.13	7.73
Ratio of Expenses to Net Assets (%)	1.10	1.01	1.03	1.01	.97	.99
Portfolio Turnover Rate (%)	19	63	26	45	63	33
Total Assets: End of Year (Millions $)	91.8	151.5	114.4	174.3	176.7	170.0

Annual Rate of Return (%) Years Ending 12/31	4.8	20.2	1.6	29.5	4.6	2.5

Five-Year Total Return(%)	69.4[c]	Degree of Diversification	C	Beta	.80	Bull (%)	95.8[c]	Bear (%)	(20.1)[D]

Objective: Seeks capital growth through investment in the common stocks of companies that meet traditional investment standards and show evidence of contributing to the enhancement of the quality of life in the United States in four areas: protection and proper use of natural resources, occupational health and safety, consumer protection and equal employment opportunity.

Portfolio: (11/30/87) Common stocks 61%, short-term securities 34%, convertible preferred stocks 2%. Largest stock holdings: health 15%, natural gas pipeline and distributors 6%.

Distributions: Income: July   **Capital Gains:** July

12b-1: No

Minimum: Initial: $2,500   Subsequent: $100

Min IRA: Initial: $750   Subsequent: None

Services: IRA, Keogh, Corp, 403(b), SEP, Withdraw, Deduct

Tel Exchange: Yes   **With MMF:** Yes

Registered: All states

ENERGY
Growth & Income

Neuberger & Berman Mgmt.
342 Madison Ave.
New York, NY 10173
(800) 367-0770/(212) 850-8300

| | Years Ending 9/30 | | | | | |
	1982	1983	1984	1985	1986	1987
Net Investment Income ($)	1.08	.97	.87	.89	.83	.48
Dividends from Net Investment Income ($)	1.00	1.01	.86	.92	.88	.49
Net Gains (Losses) on Investments ($)	(1.62)	4.31	.08	.95	2.21	5.46
Distributions from Net Realized Capital Gains ($)	.51	.79	.66	.93	1.66	3.31
Net Asset Value End of Year ($)	14.56	18.04	17.47	17.46	17.96	20.10
Ratio of Expenses to Net Assets (%)	.88	.83	.88	.89	.88	.86
Portfolio Turnover Rate (%)	18	32	22	18	28	88
Total Assets: End of Year (Millions $)	300.2	334.6	337.9	333.9	376.5	481.2

Annual Rate of Return (%) Years Ending 12/31	1.0	22.1	4.8	22.6	10.1	0.6

Five-Year Total Return(%)	73.9[C]	Degree of Diversification	C	Beta	.84	Bull (%)	97.2[C]	Bear (%)	(23.8)[D]

Objective: Seeks long-term capital growth by investing in companies whose activities are related to the field of energy—two-thirds directly related and the remainder indirectly related. Familiar energy sources as well as newer sources and transformed energy are all possibilities. Up to 20% of portfolio may be unrelated to energy. May invest in foreign securities, write covered call options and loan its securities.

Portfolio: (9/30/87) Common stocks 90%, short-term corporate notes 6%, U.S. government obligations 4%, repos 3%. Largest stock holdings: oil 26%, gas 10%.

Distributions: Income: Sept   **Capital Gains:** Sept
12b-1: No
Minimum: Initial: $500   **Subsequent:** $50
Min IRA: Initial: $250   **Subsequent:** $50
Services: IRA, Keogh, Withdraw, Deduct
Tel Exchange: Yes   **With MMF:** Yes
Registered: All states except NH

EVERGREEN
Aggressive Growth

Saxon Woods Asset Mgmt. Corp.
550 Mamaroneck Ave.
Harrison, NY 10528
(800) 235-0064/(914) 698-5711/
(800) 262-4471

	Years Ending 9/30					
	1982	1983	1984	1985	1986	1987
Net Investment Income ($)	.20	.17	.15	.16	.14	.17
Dividends from Net Investment Income ($)	.15	.19	.17	.16	.14	.13
Net Gains (Losses) on Investments ($)	.49	4.23	(.51)	1.66	3.18	2.65
Distributions from Net Realized Capital Gains ($)	1.08	.05	1.20	.41	.66	1.12
Net Asset Value End of Year ($)	7.35	11.51	9.78	11.03	13.55	15.12
Ratio of Expenses to Net Assets (%)	1.13	1.11	1.10	1.08	1.04	1.03
Portfolio Turnover Rate (%)	86	78	53	59	48	46
Total Assets: End of Year (Millions $)	112.6	210.4	240.0	334.2	638.6	808.3
Annual Rate of Return (%) Years Ending 12/31	20.3	29.1	0.6	34.6	12.9	(3.5)

Five-Year Total Return(%)	90.3ᴮ	Degree of Diversification	B	Beta	.91	Bull (%)	116.7ᴮ	Bear (%)	(24.7)ᴰ

Objective: Achieve capital appreciation by investing principally in securities of little-known companies, relatively small companies and companies undergoing changes that are believed favorable.

Portfolio: (9/30/87) Common stocks 86%, short-term securities 14%. Largest stock holdings: banks 17%, retailing 12%.

Distributions: Income: Annually   **Capital Gains:** Annually

12b-1: No

Minimum: Initial: $2,000   Subsequent: None

Min IRA: Initial: None   Subsequent: None

Services: IRA, Keogh, SEP, Withdraw

Tel Exchange: Yes   **With MMF:** Yes

Registered: All states

EVERGREEN
TOTAL RETURN
Balanced

Saxon Woods Asset Mgmt. Corp.
550 Mamaroneck Ave.
Harrison, NY 10528
(800) 235-0064/(914) 698-5711

	Years Ending 3/31					
	1982	1983	1984	1985	1986	1987
Net Investment Income ($)	.74	.83	.90	.87	1.03	1.14
Dividends from Net Investment Income ($)	.76	.79	.86	.96	1.22	1.14
Net Gains (Losses) on Investments ($)	(.83)	3.99	1.12	2.83	4.26	1.76
Distributions from Net Realized Capital Gains ($)	.99	.81	.73	1.32	.98	1.11
Net Asset Value End of Year ($)	11.56	14.78	15.21	16.63	19.72	20.37
Ratio of Expenses to Net Assets (%)	1.37	1.29	1.09	1.31	1.11	1.02
Portfolio Turnover Rate (%)	100	113	67	82	65	44
Total Assets: End of Year (Millions $)	17.1	32.9	47.4	83.7	408.4	1,635.7

Annual Rate of Return (%) Years Ending 12/31	25.5	30.3	14.4	31.5	20.3	(8.9)

Five-Year Total Return(%) 114.6^	Degree of Diversification NA	Beta .56	Bull (%) 100.2^c	Bear (%) (16.3)^c

Objective: The fund invests primarily in common and preferred stocks and fixed-income securities that are established and income-producing, with the objective of obtaining current income and capital appreciation. May write covered call options. Portfolio usually 75% in equity securities and 25% in debt securities.

Portfolio: (9/30/87) Common stocks 58%, convertible debentures 21%, convertible preferred stocks 13%, short-term securities 6%. Largest stock holdings: electric utilities 15%, banks 10%.

Distributions: Income: Jan, April, July, Oct   **Capital Gains:** April
12b-1: No
Minimum: Initial: $2,000   **Subsequent:** None
Min IRA: Initial: None   **Subsequent:** None
Services: IRA, Keogh, SEP, Withdraw
Tel Exchange: Yes   **With MMF:** Yes
Registered: All states

THE FAIRMONT
Aggressive Growth

Morton H. Sachs & Co.
1346 S. Third St.
Louisville, KY 40208
(502) 636-5633

			2/28			12/31	
	1982	1983	1984	1985	1986	1986* (10 mos.)	1987
Net Investment Income ($)	.90	1.13	.94	.60	.62	.33	.51
Dividends from Net Investment Income ($)	–	1.13	.94	.60	.62	.33	.51
Net Gains (Losses) on Investments ($)	.67	13.64	6.90	8.78	16.00	2.06	(4.40)
Distributions from Net Realized Capital Gains ($)	–	3.82	1.93	3.28	7.42	6.20	.23
Net Asset Value End of Year ($)	24.77	34.59	39.56	45.06	53.64	49.50	44.87
Ratio of Expenses to Net Assets (%)	1.88	1.99	2.15	2.05	1.48	1.26	1.18
Portfolio Turnover Rate (%)	44	135	103	123	129	124	145
Total Assets: End of Year (Millions $)	1.5	5.7	14.7	24.5	60.7	79.6	79.0

Annual Rate of Return (%) Years Ending 12/31	35.0	35.9	10.8	32.1	14.0	*	(7.6)

Five-Year Total Return(%) 109.6[A]	Degree of Diversification C	Beta 1.08	Bull (%) 117.4[B]	Bear (%) (26.2)[E]

Fiscal year-end changed from 2/28 to 12/31. All annual return figures are for full years ending 12/31.

Objective: Seeks capital appreciation through investment in common stocks chosen on the basis of economic projections, technical analysis and earnings projections. Market timing is also used. May invest in foreign securities and enter into repos. May convert to cash or U.S. government securities for defensive purposes.

Portfolio: (12/31/87) Common stocks 96%, repos 4%. Largest stock holdings: electronic 18%, financial services 12%.

Distributions: Income: Feb, Aug   **Capital Gains:** Feb

12b-1: No

Minimum: Initial: $10,000   Subsequent: $1,000

Min IRA: Initial: $10,000   Subsequent: $1,000

Services: IRA, Keogh, Corp, 403(b)

Tel Exchange: No

Registered: All states except ME, NH, VT

FIDELITY CONTRAFUND

Growth

Fidelity Investments Co.
82 Devonshire St.
Boston, MA 02109
(800) 544-6666/(617) 523-1919

	Years Ending 12/31					
	1982	1983	1984	1985	1986	1987
Net Investment Income ($)	.55	.45	.27	.43	.05	.17
Dividends from Net Investment Income ($)	.50	.45	.29	.25	.25	–
Net Gains (Losses) on Investments ($)	1.07	2.05	(1.25)	2.21	1.48	(.31)
Distributions from Net Realized Capital Gains ($)	1.23	.38	1.69	–	2.15	.43
Net Asset Value End of Year ($)	11.06	12.73	9.77	12.16	11.29	10.72
Ratio of Expenses to Net Assets (%)	1.01	.96	.99	.95	.88	.92
Portfolio Turnover Rate (%)	220	452	234	135	190	196
Total Assets: End of Year (Millions $)	72.7	86.2	80.8	86.7	84.0	86.7

Annual Rate of Return (%) Years Ending 12/31	16.6	23.2	(8.3)	27.0	12.8	(2.1)

Five-Year Total Return(%)	58.5[D]	Degree of Diversification	B	Beta	1.09	Bull (%)	132.8[A]	Bear (%)	(30.3)[E]

Objective: Seeks capital growth through investment in securities believed to be undervalued due to an overly pessimistic appraisal by the public. Income received from investments is incidental to the objective.

Portfolio: (12/31/87) Common stocks 85%, short-term obligations 11%, corporate bonds 2%, convertible preferred stocks 2%, foreign government agency obligations 1%, units 1%. Largest stock holdings: utilities 18%, finance 13%.

Distributions:	**Income:** Annually	**Capital Gains:** Annually
12b-1:	Yes	**Amount:** Pd. by Advisor
Minimum:	**Initial:** $1,000	**Subsequent:** $250
Min IRA:	**Initial:** $500	**Subsequent:** $250
Services:	IRA, Keogh, Corp, SEP, 403(b), Withdraw, Deduct	
Tel Exchange:	Yes	**With MMF:** Yes
Registered:	All states	

FIDELITY
FLEXIBLE BOND
Bond

Fidelity Investments Co.
82 Devonshire St.
Boston, MA 02109
(800) 544-6666/(617) 523-1919

	Years Ending 4/30					
	1982	1983	1984	1985	1986	1987
Net Investment Income ($)	.86	.80	.76	.79	.74	.67
Dividends from Net Investment Income ($)	.86	.80	.76	.79	.74	.67
Net Gains (Losses) on Investments ($)	.05	1.07	(.95)	.26	.86	(.46)
Distributions from Net Realized Capital Gains ($)	—	—	—	—	—	—
Net Asset Value End of Year ($)	6.22	7.29	6.34	6.60	7.46	7.00
Ratio of Expenses to Net Assets (%)	.81	.81	.77	.79	.67	.69
Portfolio Turnover Rate (%)	204	378	164	164	243	127
Total Assets: End of Year (Millions $)	112.7	169.2	134.6	166.5	250.5	383.5

Annual Rate of Return (%) Years Ending 12/31	30.1	6.6	11.8	21.1	13.5	.1

Five-Year Total Return(%)	63.9ᶜ	Degree of Diversification	NA	Beta	.05	Bull (%)	48.8ᴰ	Bear (%)	2.6ᴬ

Objective: Seeks current income and security of shareholders' capital. At least 80% of assets are in investment grade (BBB or higher) debt securities.

Portfolio: (10/31/87) Corporate bonds 37%, U.S. government obligations 33%, Canadian obligations 13%, short-term obligations 10%, supranational obligations 5%, foreign obligations 2%.

Distributions: **Income:** Monthly   **Capital Gains:** Annually

12b-1: Yes   **Amount:** Pd. by Advisor

Minimum: **Initial:** $2,500   **Subsequent:** $250

Min IRA: **Initial:** $500   **Subsequent:** $250

Services: IRA, Keogh, Corp, SEP, 403(b), Withdraw, Deduct

Tel Exchange: Yes   **With MMF:** Yes

Registered: All states

FIDELITY FREEDOM

Aggressive Growth

Fidelity Investments Co.
82 Devonshire St.
Boston, MA 02109
(800) 544-6666/(617) 523-1919

	Years Ending 11/30					
	1982	**1983** (8 mos.)	**1984**	**1985**	**1986**	**1987**
Net Investment Income ($)	–	.07	.24	.37	.16	.19
Dividends from Net Investment Income ($)	–	–	.04	.24	.35	.14
Net Gains (Losses) on Investments ($)	–	2.61	(.31)	2.75	3.22	(.54)
Distributions from Net Realized Capital Gains ($)	–	–	.42	.15	.98	3.50
Net Asset Value End of Year ($)	–	12.68	12.15	14.88	16.93	12.94
Ratio of Expenses to Net Assets (%)	–	1.26	1.13	1.14	1.07	.97
Portfolio Turnover Rate (%)	–	116	97	100	161	171
Total Assets: End of Year (Millions $)	–	141.3	388.3	600.5	916.0	993.0
Annual Rate of Return (%) Years Ending 12/31	–	–	3.4	28.5	13.7	8.9

Five-Year Total Return(%) NA	Degree of Diversification A	Beta 1.12	Bull (%) 143.9[A]	Bear (%) (25.5)[E]

Objective: Seeks long- and short-term capital gains by investing in common stocks of well-known and established companies as well as small companies. Best suited to retirement plans where the tax status of distributions is immaterial.

Portfolio: (11/30/87) Common stocks 91%, short-term obligations 9%. Largest stock holdings: oil and gas 14%, insurance 7%.

Distributions: **Income:** Jan **Capital Gains:** Jan

12b-1: Yes **Amount:** Pd. by Advisor

Minimum: **Initial:** $500 **Subsequent:** $250

Min IRA: **Initial:** $500 **Subsequent:** $250

Services: IRA, Keogh, Corp, SEP, 403(b), Withdraw, Deduct

Tel Exchange: Yes **With MMF:** Yes

Registered: All states

FIDELITY FUND
Growth & Income

Fidelity Investments Co.
82 Devonshire St.
Boston, MA 02109
(800) 544-6666/(617) 523-1919

	Years Ending 12/31					
	1982	1983	1984	1985	1986	1987
Net Investment Income ($)	.89	.84	.74	.70	.63	.45
Dividends from Net Investment Income ($)	.89	.84	.71	.72	.66	.48
Net Gains (Losses) on Investments ($)	3.89	2.96	(.70)	3.33	2.08	.28
Distributions from Net Realized Capital Gains ($)	3.00	1.97	4.40	.05	4.08	2.72
Net Asset Value End of Year ($)	18.90	19.89	14.82	18.08	16.05	13.58
Ratio of Expenses to Net Assets (%)	.73	.71	.66	.66	.60	.67
Portfolio Turnover Rate (%)	165	210	200	215	214	211
Total Assets: End of Year (Millions $)	588.2	668.9	617.6	761.5	780.7	869.8
Annual Rate of Return (%) Years Ending 12/31	33.3	22.4	1.4	28.0	15.4	3.1

Five-Year Total Return(%)	89.1B	Degree of Diversification	A	Beta	.99	Bull (%)	124.5A	Bear (%)	(23.2)D

Objective: Seeks long-term capital growth. In order to provide a reasonable current return, invests in securities selected for their current income characteristics. Companies are well-established, dividend-paying and from variety of industries that show potential for stability and reliability of earnings.

Portfolio: (12/31/87) Common stocks 87%, U.S. government obligations 4%, corporate bonds 4%, convertible preferred stocks 3%, short-term obligations 2%. Largest stock holdings: basic industries 17%, technology 15%.

Distributions: Income: Mar, June, Sept, Dec   **Capital Gains:** Dec

12b-1: Yes   **Amount:** Pd. by Advisor

Minimum: Initial: $1,000   **Subsequent:** $250

Min IRA: Initial: $500   **Subsequent:** $250

Services: IRA, Keogh, Corp, SEP, 403(b), Withdraw, Deduct

Tel Exchange: Yes   **With MMF:** Yes

Registered: All states

FIDELITY GINNIE MAE
Bond

Fidelity Investments Co.
82 Devonshire St.
Boston, MA 02109
(800) 544-6666/(617) 523-1919

	Years Ending 7/31					
	1982	1983	1984	1985	1986 (9 mos.)	1987
Net Investment Income ($)	–	–	–	–	.72	.87
Dividends from Net Investment Income ($)	–	–	–	–	.72	.87
Net Gains (Losses) on Investments ($)	–	–	–	–	.58	(.34)
Distributions from Net Realized Capital Gains ($)	–	–	–	–	–	.01
Net Asset Value End of Year ($)	–	–	–	–	10.58	10.23
Ratio of Expenses to Net Assets (%)	–	–	–	–	.75	.79
Portfolio Turnover Rate (%)	–	–	–	–	106	177
Total Assets: End of Year (Millions $)	–	–	–	–	652.9	868.9

Annual Rate of Return (%) Years Ending 12/31	–	–	–	–	13.0	1.2

Five-Year Total Return(%)	NA	Degree of Diversification	NA	Beta	NA	Bull (%)	NA	Bear (%)	2.5^

Objective: Seeks high level of current income through investment primarily in GNMAs and other debt securities guaranteed by the U.S. government. May hedge the portfolio with futures contracts and put options.

Portfolio: (7/31/87) GNMAs 68%, U.S. Treasury notes 25%, short-term securities 7%.

Distributions: **Income:** Monthly   **Capital Gains:** Annually

12b-1: Yes   **Amount:** Pd. by Advisor

Minimum: **Initial:** $1,000   **Subsequent:** $250

Min IRA: **Initial:** $500   **Subsequent:** $250

Services: IRA, Keogh, Corp, SEP, 403(b), Withdraw, Deduct

Tel Exchange: Yes   **With MMF:** Yes

Registered: All states

FIDELITY GOVERNMENT SECURITIES

Bond

Fidelity Investments Co.
82 Devonshire St.
Boston, MA 02109
(800) 544-6666/(617) 523-1919

	Years Ending 12/31					
	1982	1983	1984	1985	1986	1987
Net Investment Income ($)	1.14	.94	1.01	.98	.90	.85
Dividends from Net Investment Income ($)	1.14	.94	1.01	.98	.90	.85
Net Gains (Losses) on Investments ($)	1.03	(.38)	(.04)	.56	.48	(.76)
Distributions from Net Realized Capital Gains ($)	–	.28	–	–	–	–
Net Asset Value End of Year ($)	9.94	9.28	9.24	9.80	10.28	9.52
Ratio of Expenses to Net Assets (%)	.91	.88	.85	.81	.84	.87
Portfolio Turnover Rate (%)	NA	NA	NA	137	138	253
Total Assets: End of Year (Millions $)	89.2	85.6	89.2	269.6	751.7	682.7

Annual Rate of Return (%) Years Ending 12/31	26.2	6.0	11.3	17.6	14.7	1.0

Five-Year Total Return(%)	60.9ᴰ	Degree of Diversification	NA	Beta	.05	Bull (%)	45.5ᴱ	Bear (%)	2.6ᴬ

Objective: Seeks income from investment in U.S. government obligations. Income is exempt from state and local income taxes in all states.

Portfolio: (12/31/87) U.S. government and agency obligations 100%.

Distributions: Income: Monthly   **Capital Gains:** Dec
12b-1: Yes   **Amount:** Pd. by Advisor
Minimum: Initial: $1,000   **Subsequent:** $250
Min IRA: Initial: NA*   **Subsequent:** NA
Services: Withdraw, Deduct
Tel Exchange: Yes   **With MMF:** Yes
Registered: All states

Fund is structured as a limited partnership.

FIDELITY HIGH INCOME
Bond

Fidelity Investments Co.
82 Devonshire St.
Boston, MA 02109
(800) 544-6666/(617) 523-1919

	Years Ending 11/30					4/30
	1982	1983	1984	1985	1986	1987* (5 mos.)
Net Investment Income ($)	1.15	1.10	1.16	1.15	1.10	.45
Dividends from Net Investment Income ($)	1.15	1.10	1.16	1.15	1.10	.45
Net Gains (Losses) on Investments ($)	.78	.59	(.33)	.56	.83	(.06)
Distributions from Net Realized Capital Gains ($)	–	–	–	–	.13	.26
Net Asset Value End of Year ($)	8.42	9.01	8.68	9.24	9.94	9.62
Ratio of Expenses to Net Assets (%)	.83	.87	.85	.83	.80	.78
Portfolio Turnover Rate (%)	90	129	71	157	104	116
Total Assets: End of Year (Millions $)	177.2	261.1	395.9	782.9	1,645.7	1,720.2

Annual Rate of Return (%) Years Ending 12/31	35.7	18.5	10.5	25.5	18.0	1.2

Five-Year Total Return(%)	96.4ᴬ	Degree of Diversification	NA	Beta	.21	Bull (%)	72.8ᶜ	Bear (%)	(4.0)ᶜ

Fiscal year changed from 11/30 to 4/30.

Objective: Seeks high current income through investments in high-yielding, fixed-income corporate securities that are rated Baa (BBB) or lower and securities unrated by rating services and further screened for future potential financial strength of the issuing company.

Portfolio: (10/31/87) Corporate bonds 84%, short-term obligations 11%, U.S. government obligations 5%, preferred stocks 1%. Largest bond holdings: media and leisure 21%, retail and wholesale 10%.

Distributions: Income: Monthly   **Capital Gains:** Annually
12b-1: Yes   **Amount:** Pd. by Advisor
Minimum: Initial: $2,500   **Subsequent:** $250
Min IRA: Initial: $500   **Subsequent:** $250
Services: IRA, Keogh, Corp, SEP, 403(b), Withdraw, Deduct
Tel Exchange: Yes   **With MMF:** Yes
Registered: All states

FIDELITY INTERMEDIATE BOND
(formerly FIDELITY THRIFT)
Bond

Fidelity Investments Co.
82 Devonshire St.
Boston, MA 02109
(800) 544-6666/(617) 523-1919

	Years Ending 12/31					
	1982	1983	1984	1985	1986	1987
Net Investment Income ($)	1.21	1.03	1.10	1.08	.92	1.00
Dividends from Net Investment Income ($)	1.21	1.03	1.10	.74	.66	1.61
Net Gains (Losses) on Investments ($)	.82	(.14)	.11	.84	.50	(.80)
Distributions from Net Realized Capital Gains ($)	—	—	—	—	.22	.10
Net Asset Value End of Year ($)	9.86	9.72	9.83	11.01	11.55	10.04
Ratio of Expenses to Net Assets (%)	.70	.69	.73	.79	.75	.86
Portfolio Turnover Rate (%)	180	238	80	68	101	67
Total Assets: End of Year (Millions $)	88.0	114.2	151.7	244.1	367.9	370.4

Annual Rate of Return (%) Years Ending 12/31	24.1	9.4	13.5	20.9	13.1	2.1

Five-Year Total Return(%)	73.4ᶜ	Degree of Diversification	NA	Beta	.06	Bull (%)	51.4ᴰ	Bear (%)	2.7ᴬ

Objective: Seeks current income through investment in corporate bonds rated A or better, government securities and money market instruments. Average maturity is less than 10 years.

Portfolio: (12/31/87) U.S. government and agency obligations 42%, corporate bonds 37%, Canadian obligations 10%, short-term obligations 7%, supranational obligations 4%.

Distributions: Income: Monthly   **Capital Gains:** Annually
12b-1: Yes   **Amount:** Pd. by Advisor
Minimum: Initial: $1,000   Subsequent: $250
Min IRA: Initial: $500   Subsequent: $250
Services: IRA, Keogh, Corp, SEP, 403(b), Withdraw, Deduct
Tel Exchange: Yes   **With MMF:** Yes
Registered: All states

FIDELITY MORTGAGE SECURITIES
Bond

Fidelity Investments Co.
82 Devonshire St.
Boston, MA 02109
(800) 544-6666/(617) 523-1919

	Years Ending 7/31					
	1982	1983	1984	1985 (7 mos.)	1986	1987
Net Investment Income ($)	–	–	–	.70	1.06	.91
Dividends from Net Investment Income ($)	–	–	–	.70	1.06	.91
Net Gains (Losses) on Investments ($)	–	–	–	.29	.39	(.36)
Distributions from Net Realized Capital Gains ($)	–	–	–	–	–	.03
Net Asset Value End of Year ($)	–	–	–	10.10	10.49	10.10
Ratio of Expenses to Net Assets (%)	–	–	–	.75	.75	.80
Portfolio Turnover Rate (%)	–	–	–	72	59	160
Total Assets: End of Year (Millions $)	–	–	–	140.6	642.3	603.4
Annual Rate of Return (%) Years Ending 12/31	–	–	–	19.6	11.5	2.6

Five-Year Total Return(%)	NA	Degree of Diversification	NA	Beta	.01	Bull (%)	NA	Bear (%)	2.6^A

Objective: Seeks high current income through investment in mortgage-related securities such as GNMAs, FNMAs, FHLMCs and CMOs comprising 65% of the portfolio. Other 35% can be long- or short-term debt.

Portfolio: (7/31/87) Mortgage-related securities 69%, U.S. Treasury notes 17%, Federal Farm Credit Bank notes 10%, short-term securities 4%.

Distributions: Income: Monthly   **Capital Gains:** Annually
12b-1: Yes   **Amount:** Pd. by Advisor
Minimum: Initial: $1,000   Subsequent: $250
Min IRA: Initial: $500   Subsequent: $250
Services: IRA, Keogh, Corp, SEP, 403(b), Withdraw, Deduct
Tel Exchange: Yes   **With MMF:** Yes
Registered: All states

FIDELITY SHORT-TERM BOND
Bond

Fidelity Investments'Co.
82 Devonshire St.
Boston, MA 02109
(800) 544-6666/(617) 523-1919

	Years Ending 4/30					
	1982	1983	1984	1985	1986	1987 (7 mos.)
Net Investment Income ($)	–	–	–	–	–	.48
Dividends from Net Investment Income ($)	–	–	–	–	–	.48
Net Gains (Losses) on Investments ($)	–	–	–	–	–	(.33)
Distributions from Net Realized Capital Gains ($)	–	–	–	–	–	–
Net Asset Value End of Year ($)	–	–	–	–	–	9.67
Ratio of Expenses to Net Assets (%)	–	–	–	–	–	.90
Portfolio Turnover Rate (%)	–	–	–	–	–	149
Total Assets: End of Year (Millions $)	–	–	–	–	–	137.1
Annual Rate of Return (%) Years Ending 12/31	–	–	–	–	–	3.9

Five-Year Total Return(%)	NA	Degree of Diversification	NA	Beta	NA	Bull (%)	NA	Bear (%)	2.3^

Objective: Seeks high level of current income consistent with preservation of capital. Average maturity of portfolio cannot exceed three years. Invests in investment-grade fixed-income securities rated BBB or higher by Standard & Poor's—including government notes, commercial paper and bankers' acceptances.

Portfolio: (10/31/87) Corporate bonds 47%, U.S. government obligations 16%, short-term obligations 13%, foreign obligations 12%, Canadian obligations 7%, supranational obligations 5%, municipal obligations 1%.

Distributions: Income: Monthly   **Capital Gains:** Annually

12b-1: Yes   **Amount:** Pd. by Advisor

Minimum: Initial: $1,000   **Subsequent:** $250

Min IRA: Initial: $500   **Subsequent:** $250

Services: IRA, Keogh, Corp, SEP, 403(b), Withdraw, Deduct

Tel Exchange: Yes   **With MMF:** Yes

Registered: All states except AZ, WI

FIDELITY TREND
Growth

Fidelity Investments Co.
82 Devonshire St.
Boston, MA 02109
(800) 544-6666/(617) 523-1919

	Years Ending 12/31					
	1982	1983	1984	1985	1986	1987
Net Investment Income ($)	1.19	.96	1.04	.98	.96	.67
Dividends from Net Investment Income ($)	.79	.78	.83	.79	.61	.44
Net Gains (Losses) on Investments ($)	2.76	7.31	(1.91)	9.22	5.10	(2.46)
Distributions from Net Realized Capital Gains ($)	1.49	–	–	1.25	10.64	6.20
Net Asset Value End of Year ($)	31.07	38.56	36.86	45.02	39.83	31.40
Ratio of Expenses to Net Assets (%)	.78	.66	.56	.52	.52	.49
Portfolio Turnover Rate (%)	129	71	57	62	71	128
Total Assets: End of Year (Millions $)	553.6	637.6	602.4	712.7	669.1	599.0

Annual Rate of Return (%) Years Ending 12/31	19.0	25.2	(2.2)	28.2	13.5	(4.2)

Five-Year Total Return(%) 70.7ᶜ	Degree of Diversification	B	Beta 1.16	Bull (%) 119.4ᴮ	Bear (%) (28.4)ᴱ

Objective: Seeks growth of capital through investment in securities of both well-established companies and smaller firms. Decisions based on studies of momentum in trends of earnings and security prices of individual companies, industries and the market. May loan its portfolio securities, use leverage and engage in repos. Income return is incidental to the objective of capital growth.

Portfolio: (12/31/87) Common stocks 95%, short-term obligations 4%, convertible preferred stocks 1%, convertible corporate bonds 1%. Largest stock holdings: basic industries 19%, utilities 14%.

Distributions: Income: Annually   **Capital Gains:** Annually

12b-1: Yes   **Amount:** Pd. by Advisor

Minimum: Initial: $1,000   Subsequent: $250

Min IRA: Initial: $500   Subsequent: $250

Services: IRA, Keogh, Corp, SEP, 403(b), Withdraw, Deduct

Tel Exchange: Yes   With MMF: Yes

Registered: All states

FIDELITY VALUE
Growth

Fidelity Investments Co.
82 Devonshire St.
Boston, MA 02109
(800) 544-6666/(617) 523-1919

	Years Ending 10/31					
	1982	1983	1984	1985	1986	1987
Net Investment Income ($)	.72	.75	.94	.69	.59	.26
Dividends from Net Investment Income ($)	.19	–	.27	.49	.42	.15
Net Gains (Losses) on Investments ($)	2.85	5.28	(1.55)	1.56	6.03	(3.23)
Distributions from Net Realized Capital Gains ($)	1.31	–	3.63	–	–	2.36
Net Asset Value End of Year ($)	17.01	23.04	18.53	20.29	26.49	21.01
Ratio of Expenses to Net Assets (%)	1.10	.88	1.26	1.13	1.07	1.07
Portfolio Turnover Rate (%)	105	353	389	246	281	442
Total Assets: End of Year (Millions $)	41.5	96.9	114.0	100.8	142.8	92.0
Annual Rate of Return (%) Years Ending 12/31	35.2	31.9	(8.7)	22.1	15.1	(8.6)

Five-Year Total Return(%)	54.7[D]	Degree of Diversification	C	Beta	.92	Bull (%)	95.4[C]	Bear (%)	(26.2)[E]

Objective: Seeks capital growth through investment in securities of companies that possess valuable fixed assets, or that fund management believes to be undervalued in the marketplace because of changes in the company, the economy, or the industry. May loan its portfolio securities and engage in repos.

Portfolio: (10/31/87) Common stocks 88%, short-term obligations 12%. Largest stock holdings: utilities 29%, media and leisure 17%.

Distributions: Income: Dec **Capital Gains:** Dec
12b-1: Yes Amount: Pd. by Advisor
Minimum: Initial: $1,000 Subsequent: $250
Min IRA: Initial: $500 Subsequent: $250
Services: IRA, Keogh, Corp, SEP, 403(b), Withdraw, Deduct
Tel Exchange: Yes With MMF: Yes
Registered: All states

FIDUCIARY CAPITAL GROWTH

Aggressive Growth

Fiduciary Management, Inc.
222 E. Mason St.
Milwaukee, WI 53202
(414) 271-6666

	Years Ending 9/30					
	1982 (9 mos.)	1983	1984	1985	1986	1987
Net Investment Income ($)	.25	.18	.29	.20	.09	.12
Dividends from Net Investment Income ($)	–	.25	.16	.31	.19	.10
Net Gains (Losses) on Investments ($)	1.61	7.61	(1.29)	1.47	3.54	3.11
Distributions from Net Realized Capital Gains ($)	–	–	.30	.20	.03	3.68
Net Asset Value End of Year ($)	11.86	19.40	17.94	19.10	22.51	21.96
Ratio of Expenses to Net Assets (%)	2.00	1.80	1.50	1.30	1.2	1.1
Portfolio Turnover Rate (%)	36	30	26	38	57	83
Total Assets: End of Year (Millions $)	2.5	20.8	28.5	41.5	51.9	55.2

Annual Rate of Return (%) Years Ending 12/31	45.1	29.0	(4.2)	29.8	(.4)	(9.0)

Five-Year Total Return(%)	45.4[E]	Degree of Diversification	C	Beta	1.02	Bull (%)	70.4[D]	Bear (%)	(27.0)[E]

Objective: Seeks long-term capital appreciation principally through investing in common stocks underpriced relative to growth prospects, unseasoned companies and those in special situations such as mergers. May invest in foreign securities.

Portfolio: (9/30/87) Common stocks 87%, short-term securities 10%, corporate bonds 3%, convertible debentures 1%. Largest stock holdings: computer software/design automation 8%, banks and savings & loans 7%.

Distributions: Income: Oct, Dec   **Capital Gains:** Oct, Dec
12b-1: No
Minimum: Initial: $1,000   Subsequent: $100
Min IRA: Initial: $1,000   Subsequent: $100
Services: IRA, Keogh, Withdraw
Tel Exchange: No
Registered: All states except AK, AR, ID, ME, MS, MT, NC, ND, NE, NH, SD, VT, WV, WY

FINANCIAL BOND SHARES—HIGH YIELD PORTFOLIO
Bond

Financial Programs, Inc.
P.O. Box 2040
Denver, CO 80201
(800) 525-8085/(303) 779-1233

	Years Ending 12/31					
	1982	1983	1984 (10 mos.)	1985	1986	1987
Net Investment Income ($)	–	–	.81	1.03	1.00	.94
Dividends from Net Investment Income ($)	–	–	.81	1.03	1.01	.94
Net Gains (Losses) on Investments ($)	–	–	–	.86	.19	(.63)
Distributions from Net Realized Capital Gains ($)	–	–	–	–	.17	–
Net Asset Value End of Year ($)	–	–	7.51	8.37	8.38	7.75
Ratio of Expenses to Net Assets (%)	–	–	.43	.93	.76	.86
Portfolio Turnover Rate (%)	–	–	35	96	134	89
Total Assets: End of Year (Millions $)	–	–	3.8	18.3	46.6	37.9
Annual Rate of Return (%) Years Ending 12/31	–	–	–	26.6	14.5	3.6

Five-Year Total Return(%)	NA	Degree of Diversification	NA	Beta	.19	Bull (%)	NA	Bear (%)	(2.3)B

Objective: Seeks high current income through investment in bonds and other debt securities and preferred stock rated low and medium (BBB/Baa or lower). More than 25% of its assets may be concentrated in the public utility industry.

Portfolio: (12/31/87) Corporate bonds 92%, U.S. government obligations 4%, corporate short-term notes 3%, preferred stocks 1%. Largest bond holdings: manufacturing 13%, retail 12%.

Distributions: Income: Monthly   **Capital Gains:** Annually

12b-1: No

Minimum: Initial: $250   Subsequent: $50

Min IRA: Initial: $250   Subsequent: $50

Services: IRA, Keogh, Corp, SEP, 403(b), Withdraw, Deduct

Tel Exchange: Yes   **With MMF:** Yes

Registered: All states

FINANCIAL BOND SHARES—SELECT INCOME PORTFOLIO
Bond

Financial Programs, Inc.
P.O. Box 2040
Denver, CO 80201
(800) 525-8085/(303) 779-1233

	Years Ending 12/31					
	1982	1983	1984	1985	1986	1987
Net Investment Income ($)	.82	.78	.74	.72	.67	.64
Dividends from Net Investment Income ($)	.81	.78	.73	.72	.68	.64
Net Gains (Losses) on Investments ($)	.95	(.42)	(.44)	.62	.60	(.75)
Distributions from Net Realized Capital Gains ($)	—	.05	—	—	.32	—
Net Asset Value End of Year ($)	7.12	6.65	6.22	6.84	7.10	6.36
Ratio of Expenses to Net Assets (%)	0	0	.23	.97	.85	.99
Portfolio Turnover Rate (%)	36	33	188	146	153	131
Total Assets: End of Year (Millions $)	7.3	8.5	8.1	15.1	24.7	19.8
Annual Rate of Return (%) Years Ending 12/31	30.5	5.1	5.2	22.7	18.8	(1.5)

Five-Year Total Return(%)	58.9ᴅ	Degree of Diversification	NA	Beta	.15	Bull (%)	57.0ᴅ	Bear (%)	0.5ᴮ

Objective: Seeks a high level of current income through investment in bonds and other debt securities of established companies and of government and municipal issues. 50% of assets invested in investment grade securities (Baa/BBB or higher). Remaining 50% invested in lower grade or unrated securities.

Portfolio: (12/31/87) Corporate bonds 60%, U.S. government obligations 32%, corporate short-term notes 4%, municipal bonds 4%. Largest bond holdings: utilities 14%, food products & beverages 7%.

Distributions: Income: Monthly   **Capital Gains:** Annually
12b-1: No
Minimum: Initial: $250   Subsequent: $50
Min IRA: Initial: $250   Subsequent: $50
Services: IRA, Keogh, Corp, SEP, 403(b), Withdraw, Deduct
Tel Exchange: Yes   **With MMF:** Yes
Registered: All states

FINANCIAL BOND SHARES— U.S. GOVERNMENT
Bond

Financial Programs, Inc.
P.O. Box 2040
Denver, CO 80201
(800) 525-8085/(303) 779-1233

		Years Ending 12/31				
	1982	1983	1984	1985	1986	1987
Net Investment Income ($)	–	–	–	–	.61	.53
Dividends from Net Investment Income ($)	–	–	–	–	.61	.53
Net Gains (Losses) on Investments ($)	–	–	–	–	.43	(.92)
Distributions from Net Realized Capital Gains ($)	–	–	–	–	.03	–
Net Asset Value End of Year ($)	–	–	–	–	7.90	6.98
Ratio of Expenses to Net Assets (%)	–	–	–	–	.74	1.29
Portfolio Turnover Rate (%)	–	–	–	–	61	284
Total Assets: End of Year (Millions $)	–	–	–	–	7.2	7.9

Annual Rate of Return (%) Years Ending 12/31	–	–	–	–	–	(5.1)

Five-Year Total Return(%)	NA	Degree of Diversification	NA	Beta	NA	Bull (%)	NA	Bear (%)	(0.3)B

Objective:	Seeks high level of current income by investing in U.S. government and government agency debt obligations. These include bills, notes, bonds, and GNMA mortgage-backed securities. May also buy and sell interest rate futures contracts to hedge the portfolio.
Portfolio:	(12/31/87) U.S. government obligations 95%, repos 5%.
Distributions:	**Income:** Monthly **Capital Gains:** Annually
12b-1:	No
Minimum:	**Initial:** $250 **Subsequent:** $50
Min IRA:	**Initial:** $250 **Subsequent:** $50
Services:	IRA, Keogh, Corp, SEP, 403(b), Withdraw, Deduct
Tel Exchange:	Yes **With MMF:** Yes
Registered:	All states

FINANCIAL DYNAMICS
Aggressive Growth

Financial Programs, Inc.
P.O. Box 2040
Denver, CO 80201
(800) 525-8085/(303) 779-1233

	Years Ending 4/30					
	1982	1983	1984	1985	1986	1987
Net Investment Income ($)	.28	.17	.15	.09	.06	.02
Dividends from Net Investment Income ($)	.28	.18	.15	.09	.06	.02
Net Gains (Losses) on Investments ($)	(.42)	3.95	(1.77)	.41	2.56	1.58
Distributions from Net Realized Capital Gains ($)	–	.99	1.38	–	1.24	1.75
Net Asset Value End of Year ($)	7.07	10.02	6.87	7.28	8.59	8.42
Ratio of Expenses to Net Assets (%)	.69	.66	.66	.78	.90	.92
Portfolio Turnover Rate (%)	101	114	56	152	246	234
Total Assets: End of Year (Millions $)	62.5	94.5	66.6	73.8	87.7	91.0
Annual Rate of Return (%) Years Ending 12/31	36.9	13.1	(13.8)	29.1	6.4	3.7

Five-Year Total Return(%)	39.0ᴱ	Degree of Diversification	C	Beta 1.32	Bull (%) 116.5ᴮ	Bear (%) (30.3)ᴱ

Objective: Seeks capital growth through aggressive investment policies. Invests primarily in common stocks appearing to be in an early stage of growth, and gives no consideration to immediate income return. Stocks are chosen by fundamental analysis techniques. May use leverage.

Portfolio: (10/31/87) Common stocks 91%, fixed-income securities 4%, corporate short-term notes 4%. Largest stock holdings: computer related 23%, oil & gas related 14%.

Distributions: Income: April   **Capital Gains:** April
12b-1: No
Minimum: Initial: $250   Subsequent: $50
Min IRA: Initial: $250   Subsequent: $50
Services: IRA, Keogh, Corp, 403(b), SEP, Withdraw, Deduct
Tel Exchange: Yes   **With MMF:** Yes
Registered: All states

FINANCIAL
INDUSTRIAL
Growth

Financial Programs, Inc.
P.O. Box 2040
Denver, CO 80201
(800) 525-8085/(303) 779-1233

	Years Ending 8/31					
	1982	1983	1984	1985	1986	1987
Net Investment Income ($)	.30	.17	.16	.14	.10	.07
Dividends from Net Investment Income ($)	.29	.20	.16	.14	.12	.08
Net Gains (Losses) on Investments ($)	.31	1.37	(.36)	.46	1.09	1.14
Distributions from Net Realized Capital Gains ($)	–	.89	.04	.46	1.02	.64
Net Asset Value End of Year ($)	4.04	4.49	4.09	4.09	4.14	4.64
Ratio of Expenses to Net Assets (%)	.64	.63	.64	.72	.74	.77
Portfolio Turnover Rate (%)	122	88	80	133	227	250
Total Assets: End of Year (Millions $)	297.2	363.8	336.2	342.3	397.1	480.5
Annual Rate of Return (%) Years Ending 12/31	36.3	15.3	(1.2)	28.2	8.4	0.0

Five-Year Total Return(%)	58.2[D]	Degree of Diversification	A	Beta	1.06	Bull (%)	112.3[B]	Bear (%)	(25.9)[E]

Objective: Seeks long-term capital growth and a reasonable degree of current income through investment in well-established, dividend-paying companies from major fields of business and industrial activity.

Portfolio: (8/31/87) Common stocks 96%, fixed-income securities 4%. Largest stock holdings: pharmaceuticals 16%, oil & gas related 12%.

Distributions: Income: Feb, May, Aug, Nov   **Capital Gains:** Aug

12b-1: No

Minimum: Initial: $250   Subsequent: $50

Min IRA: Initial: $250   Subsequent: $50

Services: IRA, Keogh, Corp, 403(b), SEP, Withdraw, Deduct

Tel Exchange: Yes   **With MMF:** Yes

Registered: All states

FINANCIAL INDUSTRIAL INCOME
Balanced

Financial Programs, Inc.
P.O. Box 2040
Denver, CO 80201
(800) 525-8085/(303) 779-1233

	Years Ending 6/30					
	1982	1983	1984	1985	1986	1987
Net Investment Income ($)	.61	.44	.53	.46	.45	.34
Dividends from Net Investment Income ($)	.58	.48	.54	.48	.48	.36
Net Gains (Losses) on Investments ($)	(.50)	2.99	(.69)	1.81	2.61	.83
Distributions from Net Realized Capital Gains ($)	–	.56	.96	.66	1.89	1.06
Net Asset Value End of Year ($)	6.58	8.97	7.30	8.42	9.10	8.85
Ratio of Expenses to Net Assets (%)	.65	.63	.64	.68	.71	.74
Portfolio Turnover Rate (%)	72	57	54	54	160	195
Total Assets: End of Year (Millions $)	148.4	222.7	182.7	249.3	341.7	451.1

Annual Rate of Return (%) Years Ending 12/31	30.9	23.5	9.7	30.8	14.6	4.8

Five-Year Total Return(%)	113.0[A]	Degree of Diversification	NA	Beta	.80	Bull (%)	120.8[B]	Bear (%)	(17.9)[C]

Objective: Seeks current income through investment in common and preferred stocks and convertible bonds of well-established, dividend-paying companies as well as debt securities with high payments.

Portfolio: (9/30/87) Common stocks 70%, fixed-income securities 20%, short-term corporate notes 9%, preferred stocks 3%. Largest stock holdings: chemicals & plastic products 9%, utilities 9%.

Distributions: Income: Mar, June, Sept, Dec   **Capital Gains:** June

12b-1: No

Minimum: Initial: $250   Subsequent: $50

Min IRA: Initial: $250   Subsequent: $50

Services: IRA, Keogh, Corp, SEP, 403(b), Withdraw, Deduct

Tel Exchange: Yes   **With MMF:** Yes

Registered: All states

FINANCIAL STRATEGIC PORTFOLIO— ENERGY
Aggressive Growth

Financial Programs, Inc.
P.O. Box 2040
Denver, CO 80201
(800) 525-8085/(303) 779-1233

	Years Ending 10/31					
	1982	1983	1984 (9 mos.)	1985	1986	1987
Net Investment Income ($)	–	–	.14	.15	.14	.11
Dividends from Net Investment Income ($)	–	–	.13	.16	.14	.11
Net Gains (Losses) on Investments ($)	–	–	(.52)	.81	.21	.41
Distributions from Net Realized Capital Gains ($)	–	–	–	–	.17	.53
Net Asset Value End of Year ($)	–	–	7.49	8.29	8.33	8.22
Ratio of Expenses to Net Assets (%)	–	–	1.17	1.50	1.50	1.30
Portfolio Turnover Rate (%)	–	–	28	235	629	452
Total Assets: End of Year (Millions $)	–	–	.3	.5	1.7	12.0

Annual Rate of Return (%) Years Ending 12/31	–	–	–	13.6	7.2	4.9

Five-Year Total Return(%)	NA	Degree of Diversification	E	Beta	.88	Bull (%)	102.5ᴮ	Bear (%)	(28.2)ᴱ

Objective: Seeks capital appreciation through investment in energy-related stocks. These include companies that explore, develop, produce or distribute known sources of energy such as oil, gas, coal, uranium, geothermal or solar.

Portfolio: (10/31/87) Common stocks 100%. Largest stock holdings: oil & gas—domestic 45%, natural gas 14%.

Distributions: Income: Annually   **Capital Gains:** Annually

12b-1: No

Minimum: Initial: $250   Subsequent: $50

Min IRA: Initial: $250   Subsequent: $50

Services: IRA, Keogh, Corp, SEP, 403(b), Withdraw, Deduct

Tel Exchange: Yes   **With MMF:** Yes

Registered: All states

FINANCIAL STRATEGIC PORTFOLIO— EUROPEAN

International

Financial Programs, Inc.
P.O. Box 2040
Denver, CO 80201
(800) 525-8085/(303) 779-1233

	Years Ending 10/31					
	1982	1983	1984	1985	1986 (5 mos.)	1987
Net Investment Income ($)	–	–	–	–	.01	.05
Dividends from Net Investment Income ($)	–	–	–	–	.01	.05
Net Gains (Losses) on Investments ($)	–	–	–	–	.31	(.32)
Distributions from Net Realized Capital Gains ($)	–	–	–	–	–	.01
Net Asset Value End of Year ($)	–	–	–	–	8.31	7.98
Ratio of Expenses to Net Assets (%)	–	–	–	–	.63	1.50
Portfolio Turnover Rate (%)	–	–	–	–	4	131
Total Assets: End of Year (Millions $)	–	–	–	–	.8	9.5

Annual Rate of Return (%) Years Ending 12/31	–	–	–	–	–	(4.6)

Five-Year Total Return(%)	NA	Degree of Diversification	NA	Beta	NA	Bull (%)	NA	Bear (%)	(20.3)D

Objective: Seeks capital appreciation through investment in foreign securities located on principal exchanges in Europe—including England, France, West Germany and Italy. May enter into forward foreign currency contracts to hedge against exchange rate fluctuations.

Portfolio: (10/31/87) Common stocks 88%, corporate short-term notes 12%. Largest stock holdings: diversified companies 9%, chemicals & plastic products 8%.

Distributions: Income: Annually   **Capital Gains:** Annually

12b-1: No

Minimum: Initial: $250   Subsequent: $50

Min IRA: Initial: $250   Subsequent: $50

Services: IRA, Keogh, Corp, SEP, 403(b), Withdraw, Deduct

Tel Exchange: Yes   **With MMF:** Yes

Registered: All states

FINANCIAL STRATEGIC PORTFOLIO-FINANCIAL SERVICES
Aggressive Growth

Financial Programs, Inc.
P.O. Box 2040
Denver, CO 80201
(800) 525-8085/(303) 779-1233

	Years Ending 10/31					
	1982	1983	1984	1985	1986 (5 mos.)	1987
Net Investment Income ($)	–	–	–	–	.03	.07
Dividends from Net Investment Income ($)	–	–	–	–	.03	.06
Net Gains (Losses) on Investments ($)	–	–	–	–	(.26)	(1.25)
Distributions from Net Realized Capital Gains ($)	–	–	–	–	–	.12
Net Asset Value End of Year ($)	–	–	–	–	7.74	6.37
Ratio of Expenses to Net Assets (%)	–	–	–	–	.63	1.50
Portfolio Turnover Rate (%)	–	–	–	–	76	284
Total Assets: End of Year (Millions $)	–	–	–	–	.5	1.2

Annual Rate of Return (%) Years Ending 12/31	–	–	–	–	–	(11.0)

Five-Year Total Return(%)	NA	Degree of Diversification	NA	Beta	NA	Bull (%)	NA	Bear (%)	(18.4)c

Objective: Seeks capital appreciation through investment in companies in the financial services industry. These include banks, savings and loans, securities brokers and insurance companies.

Portfolio: (10/31/87) Common stocks 95%, fixed-income securities 5%. Largest stock holdings: banking 39%, insurance 35%.

Distributions: Income: Annually   Capital Gains: Annually

12b-1: No

Minimum: Initial: $250   Subsequent: $50

Min IRA: Initial: $250   Subsequent: $50

Services: IRA, Keogh, Corp, SEP, 403(b), Withdraw, Deduct

Tel Exchange: Yes   With MMF: Yes

Registered: All states

FINANCIAL STRATEGIC PORTFOLIO— GOLD

Aggressive Growth

Financial Programs, Inc.
P.O. Box 2040
Denver, CO 80201
(800) 525-8085/(303) 779-1233

	Years Ending 10/31					
	1982	1983	1984 (9 mos.)	1985	1986	1987
Net Investment Income ($)	–	–	.07	.10	.08	.06
Dividends from Net Investment Income ($)	–	–	.06	.11	.08	.06
Net Gains (Losses) on Investments ($)	–	–	(3.10)	(.91)	1.13	.57
Distributions from Net Realized Capital Gains ($)	–	–	–	–	.05	.04
Net Asset Value End of Year ($)	–	–	4.91	3.99	5.08	5.60
Ratio of Expenses to Net Assets (%)	–	–	1.17	1.50	1.50	1.21
Portfolio Turnover Rate (%)	–	–	110	46	232	124
Total Assets: End of Year (Millions $)	–	–	1.2	2.4	5.2	37.8

Annual Rate of Return (%) Years Ending 12/31	–	–	–	(4.4)	38.7	16.0

Five-Year Total Return(%)	NA	Degree of Diversification	E	Beta	.65	Bull (%)	95.2[c]	Bear (%)	(31.3)[E]

Objective: Seeks capital appreciation through investment in companies involved in the gold industry. These include companies engaged in mining, exploration, processing, dealing or investing in gold.

Portfolio: (10/31/87) Common stocks 100%. Largest stock holdings: exploration & mining 100%.

Distributions: Income: Annually   **Capital Gains:** Annually

12b-1: No

Minimum: Initial: $250   Subsequent: $50

Min IRA: Initial: $250   Subsequent: $50

Services: IRA, Keogh, Corp, SEP, 403(b), Withdraw, Deduct

Tel Exchange: Yes   **With MMF:** Yes

Registered: All states

FINANCIAL STRATEGIC PORTFOLIO— HEALTH SCIENCES

Aggressive Growth

Financial Programs, Inc.
P.O. Box 2040
Denver, CO 80201
(800) 525-8085/(303) 779-1233

	1982	1983	1984 (9 mos.)	1985	1986	1987
Net Investment Income ($)	–	–	.03	.01	(.03)	(.01)
Dividends from Net Investment Income ($)	–	–	.03	.01	–	–
Net Gains (Losses) on Investments ($)	–	–	.13	1.62	4.42	(.19)
Distributions from Net Realized Capital Gains ($)	–	–	–	–	1.37	.90
Net Asset Value End of Year ($)	–	–	8.13	9.75	12.78	11.69
Ratio of Expenses to Net Assets (%)	–	–	1.17	1.50	1.50	1.40
Portfolio Turnover Rate (%)	–	–	101	203	479	364
Total Assets: End of Year (Millions $)	–	–	.3	1.4	4.1	10.4

Years Ending 10/31

Annual Rate of Return (%) Years Ending 12/31	–	–	–	31.5	29.5	7.1

Five-Year Total Return(%)	NA	Degree of Diversification	D	Beta 1.26	Bull (%) 166.4^	Bear (%) (24.9)ᴱ

Objective: Primary objective is capital appreciation through investment in companies engaged in the development, production or distribution of products or services related to the health sciences industry, including pharmaceutical companies, R&D companies and hospital chains.

Portfolio: (10/31/87) Common stocks 86%, corporate short-term notes 14%. Largest stock holdings: pharmaceuticals 32%, biotechnology 31%.

Distributions: Income: Annually   **Capital Gains:** Annually

12b-1: No

Minimum: Initial: $250   Subsequent: $50

Min IRA: Initial: $250   Subsequent: $50

Services: IRA, Keogh, Corp, SEP, 403(b), Withdraw, Deduct

Tel Exchange: Yes   **With MMF:** Yes

Registered: All states

FINANCIAL STRATEGIC PORTFOLIO— LEISURE

Aggressive Growth

Financial Programs, Inc.
P.O. Box 2040
Denver, CO 80201
(800) 525-8085/(303) 779-1233

			Years Ending 10/31			
	1982	1983	1984 (9 mos.)	1985	1986	1987
Net Investment Income ($)	–	–	.07	.04	(.01)	(.05)
Dividends from Net Investment Income ($)	–	–	.06	.04	–	–
Net Gains (Losses) on Investments ($)	–	–	.46	1.56	4.13	(.90)
Distributions from Net Realized Capital Gains ($)	–	–	–	–	2.76	1.43
Net Asset Value End of Year ($)	–	–	8.47	10.03	11.38	9.00
Ratio of Expenses to Net Assets (%)	–	–	1.17	1.50	1.50	1.50
Portfolio Turnover Rate (%)	–	–	23	160	458	376
Total Assets: End of Year (Millions $)	–	–	.3	1.2	2.8	2.7

Annual Rate of Return (%) Years Ending 12/31	–	–	–	32.3	18.8	0.7

Five-Year Total Return(%)	NA	Degree of Diversification	D	Beta	1.11	Bull (%)	127.7[A]	Bear (%)	(25.0)[E]

Objective: Seeks capital appreciation through investment in companies engaged in the design, production or distribution of products or services related to the leisure-time activities of individuals, including companies in the motion picture, casino, and recreation industries.

Portfolio: (10/31/87) Common stocks 100%. Largest stock holdings: broadcasting 23%, retail 16%.

Distributions: **Income:** Annually   **Capital Gains:** Annually

12b-1: No

Minimum: **Initial:** $250   **Subsequent:** $50

Min IRA: **Initial:** $250   **Subsequent:** $50

Services: IRA, Keogh, Corp, SEP, 403(b), Withdraw, Deduct

Tel Exchange: Yes   **With MMF:** Yes

Registered: All states

FINANCIAL STRATEGIC PORTFOLIO— PACIFIC BASIN
International

Financial Programs, Inc.
P.O. Box 2040
Denver, CO 80201
(800) 525-8085/(303) 779-1233

			Years Ending 10/31			
	1982	**1983**	**1984** (9 mos.)	**1985**	**1986**	**1987**
Net Investment Income ($)	–	–	.09	.04	.03	.07
Dividends from Net Investment Income ($)	–	–	.09	.04	.04	.07
Net Gains (Losses) on Investments ($)	–	–	(.95)	1.34	4.85	1.27
Distributions from Net Realized Capital Gains ($)	–	–	–	–	1.73	3.12
Net Asset Value End of Year ($)	–	–	7.05	8.39	11.52	9.68
Ratio of Expenses to Net Assets (%)	–	–	1.17	1.50	1.47	1.26
Portfolio Turnover Rate (%)	–	–	99	161	199	155
Total Assets: End of Year (Millions $)	–	–	.8	2.9	8.5	36.0
Annual Rate of Return (%) Years Ending 12/31	–	–	–	27.3	71.8	9.8

Five-Year Total Return(%)	NA	Degree of Diversification	E	Beta	.68	Bull (%)	252.3[A]	Bear (%)	(27.9)[E]

Objective: Seeks capital appreciation through investment in companies domiciled in Far Eastern or Western Pacific countries, including Japan, Australia, Hong Kong, Singapore and the Philippines. May use currency futures to hedge the portfolio.

Portfolio: (10/31/87) Common stocks 100%. Largest stock holdings: diversified companies 15%, electrical equipment 13%.

Distributions: Income: Annually   **Capital Gains:** Annually

12b-1: No

Minimum: Initial: $250   Subsequent: $50

Min IRA: Initial: $250   Subsequent: $50

Services: IRA, Keogh, Corp, SEP, 403(b), Withdraw, Deduct

Tel Exchange: Yes   **With MMF:** Yes

Registered: All states

FINANCIAL STRATEGIC PORTFOLIO— TECHNOLOGY

Aggressive Growth

Financial Programs, Inc.
P.O. Box 2040
Denver, CO 80201
(800) 525-8085/(303) 779-1233

			Years Ending 10/31			
	1982	**1983**	**1984** (9 mos.)	**1985**	**1986**	**1987**
Net Investment Income ($)	–	–	.02	–	(.04)	(.11)
Dividends from Net Investment Income ($)	–	–	.02	–	–	–
Net Gains (Losses) on Investments ($)	–	–	(.89)	.48	2.82	(.69)
Distributions from Net Realized Capital Gains ($)	–	–	–	–	1.07	.01
Net Asset Value End of Year ($)	–	–	7.11	7.59	9.29	8.49
Ratio of Expenses to Net Assets (%)	–	–	1.17	1.50	1.50	1.47
Portfolio Turnover Rate (%)	–	–	91	175	368	556
Total Assets: End of Year (Millions $)	–	–	1.0	2.5	4.7	9.3

Annual Rate of Return (%) Years Ending 12/31	–	–	–	27.3	22.0	(5.3)

Five-Year Total Return(%)	NA	Degree of Diversification	E	Beta	1.34	Bull (%) 114.9[B]	Bear (%) (30.4)[E]

Objective: Primary objective is capital appreciation through investment in companies in the technology industries. These companies derive at least 25% of their sales from technology-related areas such as computers, communications, video, electronics and robotics.

Portfolio: (10/31/87) Common stocks 82%, corporate short-term notes 16%, fixed-income securities 2%. Largest stock holdings: computer software 23%, computer systems 13%.

Distributions: Income: Annually   **Capital Gains:** Annually
12b-1: No
Minimum: Initial: $250   Subsequent: $50
Min IRA: Initial: $250   Subsequent: $50
Services: IRA, Keogh, Corp, SEP, 403(b), Withdraw, Deduct
Tel Exchange: Yes   **With MMF:** Yes
Registered: All states

FINANCIAL STRATEGIC PORTFOLIO-UTILITIES
Aggressive Growth

Financial Programs, Inc.
P.O. Box 2040
Denver, CO 80201
(800) 525-8085/(303) 779-1233

	Years Ending 10/31					
	1982	1983	1984	1985	1986 (5 mos.)	1987
Net Investment Income ($)	–	–	–	–	.06	.40
Dividends from Net Investment Income ($)	–	–	–	–	.06	.40
Net Gains (Losses) on Investments ($)	–	–	–	–	.75	(.68)
Distributions from Net Realized Capital Gains ($)	–	–	–	–	.01	.01
Net Asset Value End of Year ($)	–	–	–	–	8.74	8.05
Ratio of Expenses to Net Assets (%)	–	–	–	–	.63	1.39
Portfolio Turnover Rate (%)	–	–	–	–	69	84
Total Assets: End of Year (Millions $)	–	–	–	–	7.5	16.1

Annual Rate of Return (%) Years Ending 12/31	–	–	–	–	–	(4.9)

Five-Year Total Return(%)	NA	Degree of Diversification	NA	Beta	NA	Bull (%)	NA	Bear (%)	(11.0)c

Objective: Seeks capital appreciation through investment in public utility companies. These include companies that manufacture, produce, generate, transmit or sell gas or electric energy. Also invests in telephone and other communication utilities.

Portfolio: (10/31/87) Common stocks 94%, corporate short-term notes 6%. Largest stock holdings: power 79%, telephone 15%.

Distributions: Income: Jan, April, July, Oct   **Capital Gains:** Annually

12b-1: No

Minimum: Initial: $250   Subsequent: $50

Min IRA: Initial: $250   Subsequent: $50

Services: IRA, Keogh, Corp, SEP, 403(b), Withdraw, Deduct

Tel Exchange: Yes   **With MMF:** Yes

Registered: All states

FLEX BOND
Bond

R. Meeder & Associates
6000 Memorial Drive
P.O. Box 7177
Dublin, OH 43017
(800) 325-3539/(614) 766-7000

	Years Ending 12/31					
	1982	**1983**	**1984**	**1985** (8 mos.)	**1986**	**1987**
Net Investment Income ($)	–	–	–	1.21	1.83	1.66
Dividends from Net Investment Income ($)	–	–	–	1.21	1.83	1.66
Net Gains (Losses) on Investments ($)	–	–	–	.84	.64	(1.78)
Distributions from Net Realized Capital Gains ($)	–	–	–	–	.17	.31
Net Asset Value End of Year ($)	–	–	–	20.84	21.31	19.22
Ratio of Expenses to Net Assets (%)	–	–	–	1.05	.78	.75
Portfolio Turnover Rate (%)	–	–	–	239	150	258
Total Assets: End of Year (Millions $)	–	–	–	4.2	13.6	13.4

Annual Rate of Return (%) Years Ending 12/31	–	–	–	–	12.5	(0.7)

Five-Year Total Return(%)	NA	Degree of Diversification	NA	Beta	NA	Bull (%)	NA	Bear (%)	(0.3)[B]

Objective: Seeks to maximize current income through investment in fixed-income securities. Investments will be limited to debt obligations of the U.S. government and its agencies and high grade corporate bonds rated A or better by Standard & Poor's. For defensive purposes the fund can invest in money market securities.

Portfolio: (12/31/87) U.S. government and agency obligations 85%, repos 12%, commercial paper 2%, options on futures 1%.

Distributions: Income: Monthly   **Capital Gains:** Annually

12b-1: Yes   **Amount:** 0.20%

Minimum: Initial: $2,500   **Subsequent:** $100

Min IRA: Initial: $500   **Subsequent:** $100

Services: IRA, Keogh, Corp, SEP, Withdraw

Tel Exchange: Yes   **With MMF:** Yes

Registered: AL, AZ, CA, CO, DC, FL, GA, HI, IL IN, MA, MD, MI, MN, MO, NC, NJ, NV, NY, OH, PA, SC, TN, TX, VA, WA

FLEX GROWTH
Growth

R. Meeder & Associates, Inc.
6000 Memorial Drive
P.O. Box 7177
Dublin, OH 43017
(800) 325-3539/(614) 766-7000

	Years Ending 12/31					
	1982	1983	1984	1985 (9 mos.)	1986	1987
Net Investment Income ($)	–	–	–	.30	.20	.21
Dividends from Net Investment Income ($)	–	–	–	–	.28	.05
Net Gains (Losses) on Investments ($)	–	–	–	.39	1.06	.59
Distributions from Net Realized Capital Gains ($)	–	–	–	–	1.15	–
Net Asset Value End of Year ($)	–	–	–	10.69	10.52	11.27
Ratio of Expenses to Net Assets (%)	–	–	–	1.62	1.49	1.51
Portfolio Turnover Rate (%)	–	–	–	218	152	326
Total Assets: End of Year (Millions $)	–	–	–	6.9	10.2	12.8
Annual Rate of Return (%) Years Ending 12/31	–	–	–	–	10.6	7.6

Five-Year Total Return(%)	NA	Degree of Diversification	NA	Beta	NA	Bull (%)	NA	Bear (%)	(13.4)c

Objective: Seeks capital appreciation through investment in common stocks of smaller companies that have above normal prospects for growth and earnings. Primarily buys the securities of companies listed on the New York Stock Exchange. For defensive purposes the fund can invest in debt obligations or money market securities.

Portfolio: (12/31/87) Short term investments 58%, common stocks 44%. Largest stock holdings: food processing 6%, electrical equipment 4%.

Distributions: Income: Annually   **Capital Gains:** Annually

12b-1: Yes   **Amount:** 0.20%

Minimum: Initial: $2,500   Subsequent: $100

Min IRA: Initial: $500   Subsequent: $100

Services: IRA, Keogh, Corp, SEP, Withdraw

Tel Exchange: Yes   **With MMF:** Yes

Registered: AL, AZ, CA, CO, DC, FL, GA, HI, IL, IN, MA, MD, MI, MN, MO, NC, NJ, NV, NY, OH, PA, SC, TN, TX, VA, WA

FLEX INCOME AND GROWTH
Growth & Income

R. Meeder & Associates, Inc.
6000 Memorial Drive
P.O. Box 7177
Dublin, OH 43017
(800) 325-3539/(614) 766-7000

	Years Ending 12/31					
	1982	1983	1984	1985 (1mo.)	1986	1987
Net Investment Income ($)	–	–	–	.12	1.05	1.38
Dividends from Net Investment Income ($)	–	–	–	–	1.04	1.51
Net Gains (Losses) on Investments ($)	–	–	–	.32	2.29	(3.02)
Distributions from Net Realized Capital Gains ($)	–	–	–	–	.74	–
Net Asset Value End of Year ($)	–	–	–	20.44	22.00	18.85
Ratio of Expenses to Net Assets (%)	–	–	–	1.74	1.01	1.64
Portfolio Turnover Rate (%)	–	–	–	0	219	259
Total Assets: End of Year (Millions $)	–	–	–	2.2	7.9	3.6

Annual Rate of Return (%) Years Ending 12/31	–	–	–	–	16.7	(7.6)

Five-Year Total Return(%)	NA	Degree of Diversification	NA	Beta	NA	Bull (%)	NA	Bear (%)	(10.6)c

Objective: Seeks current dividend income and long-term growth of capital through investment in high yielding common and preferred stocks. May also invest in bonds and money market instruments for defensive purposes.

Portfolio: (12/31/87) Short-term investments 44%, common stocks 28%. Largest stock holdings: telecommunication services 10%, auto and truck 4%.

Distributions: Income: Monthly   **Capital Gains:** Annually

12b-1: Yes   **Amount:** 0.20%

Minimum: Initial: $2,500   Subsequent: $100

Min IRA: Initial: $500   Subsequent: $100

Services: IRA, Keogh, Corp, SEP, Withdraw

Tel Exchange: Yes   **With MMF:** Yes

Registered: AL, AZ, CA, CO, DC, FL, GA, HI, IL, IN, MA, MD, MI, MN, MO, NC, NJ, NV, NY, OH, PA, SC, TN, TX, VA, WA

FLEX RETIREMENT GROWTH
Growth

R. Meeder & Associates
6000 Memorial Drive
P.O. Box 7177
Dublin, OH 43017
(800) 325-3539/(614) 766-7000

	Years Ending 12/31					
	1982 (6 mos.)	1983	1984	1985	1986	1987
Net Investment Income ($)	.09	.54	.62	.43	.26	.27
Dividends from Net Investment Income ($)	–	.05	.41	.52	.42	.07
Net Gains (Losses) on Investments ($)	.19	1.37	(.81)	1.06	.89	.83
Distributions from Net Realized Capital Gains ($)	–	–	1.06	–	1.27	–
Net Asset Value End of Year ($)	10.28	12.14	10.48	11.45	10.91	11.94
Ratio of Expenses to Net Assets (%)	3.40	1.51	1.48	1.50	1.44	1.34
Portfolio Turnover Rate (%)	124	201	143	244	141	274
Total Assets: End of Year (Millions $)	16.8	39.6	52.7	48.4	59.0	89.4
Annual Rate of Return (%) Years Ending 12/31	–	18.6	(1.2)	14.1	10.2	10.1

Five-Year Total Return(%)	62.2D	Degree of Diversification	D	Beta	.67	Bull (%)	59.3D	Bear (%)	(14.0)C

Objective: Seeks capital appreciation through investment in common stocks of companies with market value above $100 million and records of financial strength and strong earnings. Intended for retirement accounts, so will not avoid ordinary income or short-term capital gains. May convert entire portfolio to cash during down markets.

Portfolio: (12/31/87) Short-term securities: commercial paper 86%, repos 7%, time deposits 5%, CDs 2%, U.S. government and agency obligations 1%.

Distributions: Income: Annually   **Capital Gains:** Annually

12b-1: Yes   **Amount:** 0.20%

Minimum: Initial: $2,500   Subsequent: $100

Min IRA: Initial: $500   Subsequent: $100

Services: IRA, Keogh, Corp, SEP, Withdraw

Tel Exchange: Yes   **With MMF:** Yes

Registered: AL, AZ, CA, CO, DC, FL, GA, HI, IL, IN, MA, MD, MI, MN, MO, NC, NJ, NV, NY, OH, PA, SC, TN, TX, VA, WA

44 WALL STREET
Aggressive

Forty-Four Management Ltd.
1 State St. Plaza
New York, NY 10004
(800) 221-7836/(212) 808-5220

	Years Ending 6/30					
	1982	1983	1984	1985	1986	1987
Net Investment Income ($)	(.28)	(.06)	(.52)	(.23)	(.22)	(.18)
Dividends from Net Investment Income ($)	–	–	–	–	–	–
Net Gains (Losses) on Investments ($)	(8.43)	11.28	(10.01)	(2.82)	.50	(.22)
Distributions from Net Realized Capital Gains ($)	3.18	1.09	4.02	.58	–	–
Net Asset Value End of Year ($)	11.98	22.11	7.56	3.93	4.21	3.81
Ratio of Expenses to Net Assets (%)	1.19	.93	1.16	1.38	3.26	5.06
Portfolio Turnover Rate (%)	40	113	95	163	104	57
Total Assets: End of Year (Millions $)	98.7	248.5	82.0	55.4	34.3	19.2

Annual Rate of Return (%) Years Ending 12/31	7.7	9.7	(58.6)	(20.1)	(16.3)	(34.6)

Five-Year Total Return(%) (80.1)E	Degree of Diversification	E	Beta 1.66	Bull (%) (37.1)E	Bear (%) (42.1)E

Objective:	The fund does not have a current prospectus and is not accepting new money.
Portfolio:	NA
Distributions:	Income: NA **Capital Gains:** NA
12b-1:	NA
Minimum:	Initial: NA Subsequent: NA
Min IRA:	Initial: NA Subsequent: NA
Services:	NA
Tel Exchange:	NA **With MMF:** NA
Registered:	NA

FOUNDERS BLUE CHIP†
(formerly FOUNDERS MUTUAL)
Growth & Income

Founders Mutual Depositor Corp.
3033 E. First Ave., #810
Denver, CO 80206
(800) 525-2440/(303) 394-4404

	Years Ending 9/30						12/31
	1982	**1983**	**1984**	**1985**	**1986**	**1987**	**1987*** (3 mos.)
Net Investment Income ($)	.43	.41	.41	.36	.28	.20	.06
Dividends from Net Investment Income ($)	.44	.40	.31	.38	.32	.26	.05
Net Gains (Losses) on Investments ($)	.19	3.41	(.30)	.72	2.56	2.58	(2.14)
Distributions from Net Realized Capital Gains ($)	.03	.71	—	1.17	1.85	3.22	1.71
Net Asset Value End of Year ($)	7.97	10.68	10.48	10.01	10.68	9.98	6.14
Ratio of Expenses to Net Assets (%)	.47	.42	.74	.70	.74	.87	.98
Portfolio Turnover Rate (%)	—	—	16	18	42	56	31
Total Assets: End of Year (Millions $)	112.0	143.6	134.9	138.8	175.0	239.7	174.6
Annual Rate of Return (%) Years Ending 12/31	24.4	25.0	1.6	31.3	16.8	2.4	*

Five-Year Total Return(%)	99.4ᴬ	Degree of Diversification	A	Beta	.96	Bull (%)	128.5ᴬ	Bear (%)	(23.1)ᴰ

*Fiscal year end changed from 9/30 to 12/31. All annual return figures are for full years ending 12/31.

Objective: Seeks long-term growth of income and capital through investment in common stocks of companies that have at least $500 million in revenues, have proven earnings records and are in sound financial condition. May invest in foreign securities.

Portfolio: (9/30/87) Common stocks 97%, corporate short-term notes 3%, cash 1%. Largest stock holdings: consumer non-durable products 15%, data processing equipment 12%.

Distributions: Income: Mar, June, Sept, Dec   **Capital Gains:** Dec
12b-1: Yes   **Amount:** 0.25%
Minimum: Initial: $1,000   **Subsequent:** $100
Min IRA: Initial: $500   **Subsequent:** $100
Services: IRA, Keogh, Corp, SEP, 403(b), Withdraw, Deduct
Tel Exchange: Yes   **With MMF:** Yes
Registered: All states except NH

†Fund was a unit investment trust prior to December 1, 1983.

FOUNDERS EQUITY INCOME

Balanced

Founders Mutual Depositor Corp.
3033 E. First Ave., #810
Denver, CO 80206
(800) 525-2440/(303) 394-4404

	Years Ending 9/30						12/31
	1982	1983	1984	1985	1986	1987	1987* (3 mos.)
Net Investment Income ($)	.92	.42	.46	.37	.32	.32	.09
Dividends from Net Investment Income ($)	.92	.29	.50	.46	.37	.42	.08
Net Gains (Losses) on Investments ($)	.49	1.16	0	.48	.83	1.37	(1.29)
Distributions from Net Realized Capital Gains ($)	–	–	.25	.32	.15	.44	.87
Net Asset Value End of Year ($)	12.38	7.48	7.19	7.26	7.89	8.72	6.55
Ratio of Expenses to Net Assets (%)	1.50	1.50	1.50	1.50	1.59	1.66	1.84
Portfolio Turnover Rate (%)	180	159	145	126	178	133	141
Total Assets: End of Year (Millions $)	6.0	7.3	7.3	10.0	12.1	16.9	13.2

Annual Rate of Return (%) Years Ending 12/31	13.0	15.4	11.5	12.7	14.5	1.9	*

Five-Year Total Return(%) 69.1C	Degree of Diversification NA	Beta .53	Bull (%) 69.3D	Bear (%) (13.9)C

Fiscal year end changed from 9/30 to 12/31. All annual return figures are for full years ending 12/31.

Objective: Intends to provide as high income as is consistent with investment quality of companies that are well established and pay dividends. Debt investments will yield interest income. May invest in foreign securities.

Portfolio: (9/30/87) Common stocks 67%, corporate short-term notes 17%, other bonds 12%, U.S. Treasury obligations 7%. Largest stock holdings: telecommunications 20%, chemicals 13%.

Distributions: Income: Mar, June, Sept, Dec   **Capital Gains:** Dec

12b-1: Yes   **Amount:** 0.25%

Minimum: Initial: $1,000   Subsequent: $100

Min IRA: Initial: $500   Subsequent: $100

Services: IRA, Keogh, 403(b), Corp, SEP, Withdraw, Deduct

Tel Exchange: Yes   **With MMF:** Yes

Registered: All states except NH

FOUNDERS GROWTH
Growth

Founders Mutual Depositor Corp.
3033 E. First Ave., #810
Denver, CO 80206
(800) 525-2440/(303) 394-4404

	Years Ending 10/31						12/31
	1982	1983	1984	1985	1986	1987	1987* (2 mos.)
Net Investment Income ($)	.29	.17	.17	.20	.10	.11	.02
Dividends from Net Investment Income ($)	.26	.29	.16	.18	.17	.11	.13
Net Gains (Losses) on Investments ($)	.72	2.06	(.99)	.86	2.47	.38	.22
Distributions from Net Realized Capital Gains ($)	1.44	.34	2.51	—	—	1.34	1.61
Net Asset Value End of Year ($)	8.48	10.08	6.59	7.47	9.87	8.91	7.41
Ratio of Expenses to Net Assets (%)	1.37	1.24	1.22	1.17	1.27	1.25	1.54
Portfolio Turnover Rate (%)		150	203	186	142	147	20
Total Assets: End of Year (Millions $)	37.7	46.6	41.3	42.7	61.6	58.3	69.0

Annual Rate of Return (%) Years Ending 12/31	21.4	18.9	(11.1)	28.8	19.3	10.2	*

Five-Year Total Return(%)	79.2ᴮ	Degree of Diversification	B	Beta 1.01	Bull (%) 131.7ᴬ	Bear (%) (21.4)ᴰ

Fiscal year changed from 10/31 to 12/31. All annual return figures are for full years ending 12/31.

Objective: Seeks capital appreciation by investing in common stocks of established companies. Current dividends are considered but are not a major factor in stock selection. Engages in short-term trading so that portfolio turnover usually exceeds 100% and brokerage commission expenses are correspondingly high.

Portfolio: (10/31/87) Common stocks 62%, repos 38%, corporate short-term notes 10%. Largest stock holdings: chemicals 12%, data processing equipment 9%.

Distributions: Income: Dec   **Capital Gains:** Dec

12b-1: Yes   **Amount:** 0.25%

Minimum: Initial: $1,000   Subsequent: $100

Min IRA: Initial: $500   Subsequent: $100

Services: IRA, Keogh, Corp, SEP, 403(b), Withdraw, Deduct

Tel Exchange: Yes   **With MMF:** Yes

Registered: All states except NH

FOUNDERS SPECIAL
Aggressive Growth

Founders Mutual Depositor Corp.
3033 E. First Ave., #810
Denver, CO 80206
(800) 525-2440/(303) 394-4404

	Years Ending 12/31					
	1982*	1983*	1984*	1985*	1986*	1987
Net Investment Income ($)	.09	.06	.11	.05	.04	.03
Dividends from Net Investment Income ($)	.08	.05	.11	.05	.06	.03
Net Gains (Losses) on Investments ($)	1.08	1.10	(.78)	.66	.97	.26
Distributions from Net Realized Capital Gains ($)	—	.61	—	—	.69	.72
Net Asset Value End of Year ($)	4.96	5.46	4.68	5.34	5.60	5.14
Ratio of Expenses to Net Assets (%)	1.42	1.20	1.11	1.02	1.06	1.14
Portfolio Turnover Rate (%)	214	141	191	192	138	210
Total Assets: End of Year (Millions $)	45.9	94.5	81.3	95.4	70.2	66.8

Annual Rate of Return (%) Years Ending 12/31	30.2	23.4	(12.2)	15.2	18.9	5.3

Five-Year Total Return(%) 56.3[D]	Degree of Diversification C	Beta 1.09	Bull (%) 102.4[B]	Bear (%) (24.2)[D]

Prices reflect an adjustment for a 5-for-1 stock split on 8/31/87.

Objective: Seeks above-average capital growth by investing in common stocks of smaller companies that are rapidly growing. Dividends play a minor role in the fund's strategy.

Portfolio: (12/31/87) Common stocks 78%, corporate short-term notes 25%. Largest stock holdings: cable television 8%, pharmaceuticals 7%.

Distributions: Income: Dec   **Capital Gains:** Dec

12b-1: No

Minimum: Initial: $1,000   Subsequent: $100

Min IRA: Initial: $500   Subsequent: $100

Services: IRA, Keogh, Corp, SEP, 403(b), Withdraw, Deduct

Tel Exchange: Yes   **With MMF:** Yes

Registered: All states except ME, NH

FUND TRUST AGGRESSIVE GROWTH*

Aggressive Growth

Furman Selz Mager Dietz &
Birney, Inc.
230 Park Ave.
New York, NY 10169
(800) 845-8406/(212) 309-8400

	Years Ending 9/30					
	1982	1983	1984	1985 (11 mos.)	1986	1987
Net Investment Income ($)	–	–	–	.34	0	.06
Dividends from Net Investment Income ($)	–	–	–	.22	.25	.02
Net Gains (Losses) on Investments ($)	–	–	–	.96	2.39	3.82
Distributions from Net Realized Capital Gains ($)	–	–	–	–	.09	.37
Net Asset Value End of Year ($)	–	–	–	11.08	13.13	16.62
Ratio of Expenses to Net Assets (%)	–	–	–	1.50	1.50	1.50
Portfolio Turnover Rate (%)	–	–	–	16	133	64
Total Assets: End of Year (Millions $)	–	–	–	4.8	42.3	49.6
Annual Rate of Return (%) Years Ending 12/31	–	–	–	25.7	11.7	(1.4)

Five-Year Total Return(%)	NA	Degree of Diversification	D	Beta	.79	Bull (%)	NA	Bear (%)	(22.1)ᴰ

Objective: Seeks capital appreciation without regard to current income through investment in other mutual funds. Invests primarily in aggressive growth funds. May also invest in bond and money market funds for defensive purposes.

Portfolio: (9/30/87) Capital appreciation funds 96%, short-term funds 3%. Largest holdings: Manhattan Fund 18%, Pennsylvania Mutual Fund 14%.

Distributions: Income: Semiannually   **Capital Gains:** Annually

12b-1: Yes   **Amount:** 0.50%

Minimum: Initial: $1,000   Subsequent: $100

Min IRA: Initial: $250   Subsequent: $100

Services: IRA, Keogh, Corp, 403(b), Withdraw

Tel Exchange: Yes   **With MMF:** Yes

Registered: All states

Instituted a 1½% front-end load 2/88.

FUND TRUST GROWTH*

Growth

Furman Selz Mager Dietz & Birney, Inc.
230 Park Ave.
New York, NY 10169
(800) 845-8406/(212) 309-8400

	Years Ending 9/30					
	1982	1983	1984	1985 (11 mos.)	1986	1987
Net Investment Income ($)	–	–	–	.42	.20	.22
Dividends from Net Investment Income ($)	–	–	–	.24	.39	.14
Net Gains (Losses) on Investments ($)	–	–	–	.86	2.08	3.05
Distributions from Net Realized Capital Gains ($)	–	–	–	–	.11	.24
Net Asset Value End of Year ($)	–	–	–	11.04	12.82	15.71
Ratio of Expenses to Net Assets (%)	–	–	–	1.50	1.60	1.50
Portfolio Turnover Rate (%)	–	–	–	50	107	65
Total Assets: End of Year (Millions $)	–	–	–	3.7	31.2	48.6

Annual Rate of Return (%) Years Ending 12/31	–	–	–	25.0	13.3	(1.1)

Five-Year Total Return(%)	NA	Degree of Diversification	B	Beta	.73	Bull (%)	NA	Bear (%)	(19.4)D

Objective: Seeks long-term capital appreciation through investment in other growth-oriented mutual funds. Income is a secondary consideration. May also invest in funds that invest in bonds and money market instruments.

Portfolio: (9/30/87) Long-term capital appreciation funds 97%, short-term funds 3%. Largest holdings: Affiliated Fund 16%, Franklin Equity Fund 15%.

Distributions: Income: Semiannually   **Capital Gains:** Annually

12b-1: Yes   **Amount:** 0.50%

Minimum: Initial: $1,000   Subsequent: $100

Min IRA: Initial: $250   Subsequent: $100

Services: IRA, Keogh, Corp, 403(b), Withdraw

Tel Exchange: Yes   **With MMF:** Yes

Registered: All states

Instituted a 1½% front-end load 2/88.

FUND TRUST GROWTH AND INCOME*

Growth & Income

Furman Selz Mager Dietz &
  Birney, Inc.
230 Park Ave.
New York, NY 10169
(800) 845-8406/(212) 309-8400

	Years Ending 9/30					
	1982	1983	1984	1985 (11 mos.)	1986	1987
Net Investment Income ($)	—	—	—	.46	.45	.45
Dividends from Net Investment Income ($)	—	—	—	.24	.40	.43
Net Gains (Losses) on Investments ($)	—	—	—	.88	1.86	2.00
Distributions from Net Realized Capital Gains ($)	—	—	—	—	.15	.36
Net Asset Value End of Year ($)	—	—	—	11.10	12.86	14.52
Ratio of Expenses to Net Assets (%)	—	—	—	1.50	1.50	1.4
Portfolio Turnover Rate (%)	—	—	—	22	87	20
Total Assets: End of Year (Millions $)	—	—	—	3.9	47.7	91.7
Annual Rate of Return (%) Years Ending 12/31	—	—	—	23.7	14.2	(4.5)

Five-Year Total Return(%)	NA	Degree of Diversification	C	Beta	.66	Bull (%)	NA	Bear (%)	(18.6)[c]

Objective: Seeks high total return from both capital appreciation and current income by investing in other growth and income oriented mutual funds. May also invest in funds that invest in bonds and money market instruments.

Portfolio: (9/30/87) Common stock and bond funds 98%, short-term funds 1%. Largest holdings: Putnam Fund for Growth & Income 13%, Financial Industrial Income Fund 12%.

Distributions: Income: Quarterly   **Capital Gains:** Annually
12b-1: Yes   **Amount:** 0.50%
Minimum: Initial: $1,000   Subsequent: $100
Min IRA: Initial: $250   Subsequent: $100
Services: IRA, Keogh, Corp, 403(b), Withdraw
Tel Exchange: Yes   **With MMF:** Yes
Registered: All states

Instituted a 1½% front-end load 2/88.

FUND TRUST INCOME*

Bond

Furman Selz Mager Dietz &
  Birney, Inc.
230 Park Ave.
New York, NY 10169
(800) 845-8406/(212) 309-8400

| | \multicolumn{6}{c}{Years Ending 9/30} | | | | | |
	1982	1983	1984	1985 (11 mos.)	1986	1987
Net Investment Income ($)	–	–	–	.84	.93	.90
Dividends from Net Investment Income ($)	–	–	–	.52	1.17	.92
Net Gains (Losses) on Investments ($)	–	–	–	.34	.27	(.71)
Distributions from Net Realized Capital Gains ($)	–	–	–	–	.01	.05
Net Asset Value End of Year ($)	–	–	–	10.66	10.68	9.90
Ratio of Expenses to Net Assets (%)	–	–	–	1.50	1.70	1.60
Portfolio Turnover Rate (%)	–	–	–	83	125	27
Total Assets: End of Year (Millions $)	–	–	–	1.8	33.6	53.5

| Annual Rate of Return (%) Years Ending 12/31 | – | – | – | 16.8 | 9.5 | 0.4 |

| Five-Year Total Return(%) | NA | Degree of Diversification | NA | Beta | .15 | Bull (%) | NA | Bear (%) | (2.0)B |

Objective: Seeks high level of current income through investment in other bond mutual funds. These funds will invest in both investment grade and lower grade bonds. They may also use futures contracts and options.

Portfolio: (9/30/87) Fixed-income funds 99%. Largest holdings: IDS Bond Fund 21%, Vanguard Fixed Income High Yield Fund 15%.

Distributions: Income: Monthly   **Capital Gains:** Annually

12b-1: Yes   Amount: 0.50%

Minimum: Initial: $1,000   Subsequent: $100

Min IRA: Initial: $250   Subsequent: $100

Services: IRA, Keogh, Corp, 403(b), Withdraw

Tel Exchange: Yes   **With MMF:** Yes

Registered: All states

Instituted a 1½% front-end load 2/88.

GATEWAY
GROWTH PLUS
Growth

Gateway Investment Advisors
P.O. Box 458167
Cincinnati, OH 45245
(800) 354-6339/(513) 248-2700

	Years Ending 12/31					
	1982	1983	1984	1985	1986 (8 mos.)	1987
Net Investment Income ($)	–	–	–	–	.09	.03
Dividends from Net Investment Income ($)	–	–	–	–	–	.11
Net Gains (Losses) on Investments ($)	–	–	–	–	(.09)	.05
Distributions from Net Realized Capital Gains ($)	–	–	–	–	–	.01
Net Asset Value End of Year ($)	–	–	–	–	10.00	9.96
Ratio of Expenses to Net Assets (%)	–	–	–	–	1.47	1.49
Portfolio Turnover Rate (%)	–	–	–	–	96	157
Total Assets: End of Year (Millions $)	–	–	–	–	3.2	4.4

Annual Rate of Return (%) Years Ending 12/31	–	–	–	–	–	0.7

Five-Year Total Return(%)	NA	Degree of Diversification	NA	Beta	NA	Bull (%)	NA	Bear (%)	(22.8)ᴰ

Objective: Seeks long-term growth of capital with secondary objective of conserving capital. Normally will invest in New York or American Stock Exchange-listed issues which have market capitalizations above $50 million and revenues exceeding $100 million. Can also invest in index options.

Portfolio: (12/31/87) Common stock 88%, repos 15%, put options 2%. Largest stock holdings: capital goods—information processing 23%, consumer growth—health 14%.

Distributions: Income: Annually   **Capital Gains:** Annually

12b-1: No

Minimum: Initial: $500   Subsequent: $100

Min IRA: Initial: $500   Subsequent: $100

Services: IRA, SEP, Withdraw

Tel Exchange: Yes   With MMF: No

Registered: AZ, CA, DE, FL, GA, HI, IA, IL, IN, KS, ME, MI, MN, MO, NJ, NY, OH, OR, SC, TN, WI, WV, WY

GATEWAY OPTION INDEX
(formerly GATEWAY OPTION INCOME)

Growth & Income

Gateway Investment Advisors
P.O. Box 458167
Cincinnati, OH 45245
(800) 354-6339/(513) 248-2700

	Years Ending 12/31					
	1982	1983	1984	1985*	1986	1987
Net Investment Income ($)	.61	.52	.53	.40	.33	.27
Dividends from Net Investment Income ($)	.64	.55	.57	.46	.34	.33
Net Gains (Losses) on Investments ($)	.64	1.57	.01	1.74	1.41	(1.05)
Distributions from Net Realized Capital Gains ($)	.62	1.31	.65	1.22	1.46	1.92
Net Asset Value End of Year ($)	14.68	14.91	14.23	14.69	14.63	11.60
Ratio of Expenses to Net Assets (%)	1.45	1.41	1.45	1.50	1.49	1.48
Portfolio Turnover Rate (%)	115	170	103	96	85	175
Total Assets: End of Year (Millions $)	20.7	26.9	21.6	28.4	45.3	27.4

Annual Rate of Return (%) Years Ending 12/31	9.5	14.9	4.0	16.0	12.6	(5.7)

Five-Year Total Return(%)	47.1ᴱ	Degree of Diversification	D	Beta	.53	Bull (%)	61.1ᴰ	Bear (%)	(16.5)ᶜ

Changed objective March 1985.

Objective: Seeks a high current return at a reduced level of risk, primarily by investing in the common stocks listed in the S&P 100 index and selling call options on that index. May engage in repos as well.

Portfolio: (12/31/87) Common stocks 105%. Largest stock holdings: consumer growth 16%, capital goods: information processing 16%.

Distributions: Income: Mar, June, Sept, Dec   **Capital Gains:** Dec

12b-1: No

Minimum: Initial: $500   Subsequent: $100

Min IRA: Initial: $500   Subsequent: $100

Services: IRA, SEP, Withdraw

Tel Exchange: Yes   **With MMF:** No

Registered: AZ, CA, DE, FL, GA, HI, IA, IL, IN, KS, ME, MI, MN, MO, NJ, NY, OH, OR, SC, TN, WI, WV, WY

GENERAL SECURITIES
Growth & Income

Craig-Hallum, Inc.
701 Fourth Ave. South
Minneapolis, MN 55415
(612) 332-1212

	Years Ending 11/30					
	1982	**1983**	**1984**	**1985**	**1986**	**1987**
Net Investment Income ($)	.46	.63	.44	.31	.66	.34
Dividends from Net Investment Income ($)	.48	.58	.51	.30	.38	.70
Net Gains (Losses) on Investments ($)	1.77	1.26	(.98)	2.91	1.72	(.99)
Distributions from Net Realized Capital Gains ($)	.52	1.50	.87	1.25	2.13	.31
Net Asset Value End of Year ($)	12.28	12.09	10.17	11.84	11.71	10.05
Ratio of Expenses to Net Assets (%)	1.50	1.50	1.50	1.50	1.45	1.49
Portfolio Turnover Rate (%)	46	13	70	76	68	77
Total Assets: End of Year (Millions $)	11.8	11.6	10.9	13.6	14.2	14.4

Annual Rate of Return (%) Years Ending 12/31	28.1	8.9	(0.9)	38.6	9.0	2.0

Five-Year Total Return(%)	66.4c	Degree of Diversification	E	Beta	.56	Bull (%)	87.9c	Bear (%)	(9.0)c

Objective: Seeks long-term capital appreciation and security of principal by investing primarily in common stocks of large, seasoned companies. May write covered call options. May adopt defensive posture in debt securities.

Portfolio: (11/30/87) Common stocks 65%, U.S. Treasury bills 28%, cash 10%. Largest stock holdings: health care 20%, retail and wholesale 11%.

Distributions: Income: Feb, May, Aug, Nov   **Capital Gains:** Nov

12b-1: No

Minimum: Initial: $100   Subsequent: $10

Min IRA: Initial: $100   Subsequent: $10

Services: IRA, Keogh, Corp, SEP, Withdraw

Tel Exchange: No

Registered: All states except AL, AR, FL, HI, KY, LA, MA, MO, MS, MT, ND, SC, TN, TX, WI

GINTEL CAPITAL APPRECIATION
Aggressive Growth

Gintel Equity Management, Inc.
Greenwich Office Park OP-6
Greenwich, CT 06830
(800) 243-5808/(203) 622-6400

			Years Ending 12/31			
	1982	1983	1984	1985	1986 (12 mos.)	1987
Net Investment Income ($)	–	–	–	–	.16	.12
Dividends from Net Investment Income ($)	–	–	–	–	–	.23
Net Gains (Losses) on Investments ($)	–	–	–	–	1.82	(.95)
Distributions from Net Realized Capital Gains ($)	–	–	–	–	.91	.01
Net Asset Value End of Year ($)	–	–	–	–	11.07	10.00
Ratio of Expenses to Net Assets (%)	–	–	–	–	1.9	1.8
Portfolio Turnover Rate (%)	–	–	–	–	119	125
Total Assets: End of Year (Millions $)	–	–	–	–	21.8	21.6

Annual Rate of Return (%) Years Ending 12/31	–	–	–	–	19.1	(7.1)

Five-Year Total Return(%)	NA	Degree of Diversification	NA	Beta	NA	Bull (%)	NA	Bear (%)	(21.4)[D]

Objective: Seeks capital appreciation through investment in common stocks of major companies listed on the NYSE or Amex and up to 25% of total assets in the OTC. May concentrate investments in 12 issues or four industry groups; and may invest in foreign securities, employ leverage, lend its securities and make short sales of securities it holds.

Portfolio: (12/31/87) Common stocks 74%, cash equivalents 29%. Largest stock holdings: banking 11%, mortgage investments 10%.

Distributions: Income: Annually   Capital Gains: Annually
12b-1: Yes   Amount: 0.50%
Minimum: Initial: $5,000   Subsequent: None
Min IRA: Initial: $2,000   Subsequent: None
Services: IRA, Keogh, Corp, SEP, 403(b), Withdraw
Tel Exchange: Yes   With MMF: Yes
Registered: Call for availability

GINTEL ERISA
Growth & Income

Gintel Equity Management, Inc.
Greenwich Office Park OP-6
Greenwich, CT 06830
(800) 243-5808/(203) 622-6400

	Years Ending 12/31					
	1982	**1983**	**1984**	**1985**	**1986**	**1987**
Net Investment Income ($)	2.02	1.38	1.43	1.11	.66	1.47
Dividends from Net Investment Income ($)	–	1.43	.85	1.10	1.08	1.99
Net Gains (Losses) on Investments ($)	4.95	6.84	(.70)	6.65	7.70	(1.57)
Distributions from Net Realized Capital Gains ($)	–	1.19	2.75	1.88	1.47	13.41
Net Asset Value End of Year ($)	31.97	37.57	34.70	39.48	45.29	29.79
Ratio of Expenses to Net Assets (%)	1.50	1.40	1.40	1.30	1.30	1.20
Portfolio Turnover Rate (%)	1	59	109	100	69	109
Total Assets: End of Year (Millions $)	27.7	54.3	71.9	85.4	88.6	75.0

Annual Rate of Return (%) Years Ending 12/31	–	27.5	2.6	23.9	21.8	(1.1)

Five-Year Total Return(%)	95.1ᴮ	Degree of Diversification	E	Beta	.78	Bull (%)	97.7ᶜ	Bear (%)	(18.4)ᶜ

Objective: An investment vehicle exclusively for tax-exempt investors or retirement plans. The fund seeks long-term capital growth, investment income, and short-term capital gains by investing in common stocks of major corporations listed on the NYSE or Amex, or traded in the OTC and having at least three years of continuous operation.

Portfolio: (12/31/87) Common and preferred stocks 73%, cash equivalents 26%, other assets 1%. Largest stock holdings: supermarkets 15%, savings and loan 13%.

Distributions: Income: Dec   **Capital Gains:** Dec

12b-1: Yes   **Amount:** 0.20% fund, 0.20% Advisor

Minimum: Initial: $10,000   **Subsequent:** None

Min IRA: Initial: $2,000   **Subsequent:** None

Services: IRA, Keogh, Corp, SEP, 403(b), Withdraw

Tel Exchange: No

Registered: All states except OH

GIT EQUITY SPECIAL GROWTH

Aggressive Growth

Bankers Finance Investment
Mgmt. Corp.
1655 North Ft. Myer Drive
Arlington, VA 22209
(800) 336-3063/(703) 528-6500

	Years Ending 3/31					
	1982	1983	1984 (10 mos.)	1985	1986	1987
Net Investment Income ($)	–	–	.20	.09	.12	.14
Dividends from Net Investment Income ($)	–	–	.20	.09	.12	.14
Net Gains (Losses) on Investments ($)	–	–	(.79)	2.27	5.22	1.71
Distributions from Net Realized Capital Gains ($)	–	–	–	–	.25	.13
Net Asset Value End of Year ($)	–	–	9.21	11.47	16.44	18.02
Ratio of Expenses to Net Assets (%)	–	–	.36	1.09	1.35	1.50
Portfolio Turnover Rate (%)	–	–	18	30	35	8
Total Assets: End of Year (Millions $)	–	–	.64	2.5	10.7	19.6

Annual Rate of Return (%) Years Ending 12/31	–	–	(1.2)	47.2	15.1	(1.4)

Five-Year Total Return(%)	NA	Degree of Diversification	D	Beta	.98	Bull (%)	119.6[B]	Bear (%)	(20.0)[D]

Objective: Seeks maximum capital appreciation through investment in small growth companies. Current income is not a consideration. Designed for investors who can assume an above-average level of risk from investment in common stock.

Portfolio: (9/30/87) Common stocks 84%, repurchase agreements 13%, convertible bonds 3%. Largest stock holdings: automotive 10%, merchandising 7%.

Distributions: Income: Annually   **Capital Gains:** Annually

12b-1: Yes   **Amount:** 1.00%

Minimum: Initial: $1,000   **Subsequent:** None

Min IRA: Initial: $500   **Subsequent:** None

Services: IRA, Keogh, Withdraw

Tel Exchange: Yes   **With MMF:** Yes

Registered: All states except: AK, MT, ND, OK, SD, UT

GIT INCOME– A-RATED

Bond

Bankers Finance Investment
Management Corp.
1655 N. Ft. Myer Dr.
Arlington, VA 22209
(800) 336-3063/(703) 528-6500

	1982	1983	1984 (11 mos.)	1985	1986	1987
Years Ending 3/31						
Net Investment Income ($)	–	–	.84	1.11	1.04	.91
Dividends from Net Investment Income ($)	–	–	.84	1.11	1.04	.91
Net Gains (Losses) on Investments ($)	–	–	(.79)	.34	1.94	(.10)
Distributions from Net Realized Capital Gains ($)	–	–	–	–	–	–
Net Asset Value End of Year ($)	–	–	9.21	9.55	11.49	11.39
Ratio of Expenses to Net Assets (%)	–	–	–	.89	1.12	1.41
Portfolio Turnover Rate (%)	–	–	–	63	26	31
Total Assets: End of Year (Millions $)	–	–	2.9	4.4	7.8	9.3
Annual Rate of Return (%) Years Ending 12/31	–	–	14.7	24.9	13.6	(1.1)

Five-Year Total Return(%)	NA	Degree of Diversification	NA	Beta	.06	Bull (%)	55.9D	Bear (%)	2.7A

Objective: Seeks to obtain high current income through investment in bonds rated A or above by Standard & Poor's. Cannot invest more than 25% of fund assets in the securities of issuers in a single industry.

Portfolio: (9/30/87) Corporate bonds 47%, U.S. government and agency obligations 44%, repos 9%. Largest bond holdings: electric utilities 16%, telephone utilities 12%.

Distributions: Income: Monthly   **Capital Gains:** Annually

12b-1: Yes   **Amount:** 1.00%

Minimum: Initial: $1,000   Subsequent: None

Min IRA: Initial: $500   Subsequent: None

Services: IRA, Keogh, Withdraw

Tel Exchange: Yes   **With MMF:** Yes

Registered: All states except ND, NE, UT

GIT INCOME– MAXIMUM
Bond

Bankers Finance Investment
Mgmt. Corp.
1655 N. Fort Myer Dr.
Arlington, VA 22209
(800) 336-3063/(703) 528-6500

			Years Ending 3/31			
	1982	1983	1984	1985	1986	1987
Net Investment Income ($)	–	–	.91	1.23	1.16	1.06
Dividends from Net Investment Income ($)	–	–	.91	1.23	1.16	1.06
Net Gains (Losses) on Investments ($)	–	–	(.91)	(.11)	.98	(.31)
Distributions from Net Realized Capital Gains ($)	–	–	–	–	–	–
Net Asset Value End of Year ($)	–	–	9.09	8.99	9.97	9.66
Ratio of Expenses to Net Assets (%)	–	–	–	.93	1.10	1.39
Portfolio Turnover Rate (%)	–	–	16	66	47	127
Total Assets: End of Year (Millions $)	–	–	3.3	7.3	12.9	16.7
Annual Rate of Return (%) Years Ending 12/31	–	–	9.6	22.0	10.6	(2.8)

Five-Year Total Return(%)	NA	Degree of Diversification	NA	Beta	.19	Bull (%)	52.9D	Bear (%)	(5.9)C

Objective: Seeks high current income through investment in long-term lower medium-grade (BB) and low-grade (Caa/CCC) debt securities of U.S. government, corporations and foreign governments. May enter into repos and may temporarily hold short-term debt securities and cash for defensive purposes.

Portfolio: (9/30/87) Corporate bonds 96%, repos 4%. Largest bond holdings: manufacturing 19%, retail 16%.

Distributions:	Income: Monthly	**Capital Gains:** Annually	
12b-1:	Yes	**Amount:** 1.00%	
Minimum:	Initial: $1,000	Subsequent: None	
Min IRA:	Initial: $500	Subsequent: None	
Services:	IRA, Keogh, Withdraw		
Tel Exchange:	Yes	**With MMF:** Yes	
Registered:	All states except ND, NE, SC, UT		

GRADISON ESTABLISHED GROWTH

Growth

Gradison & Co.
The 580 Building, 6th & Walnut
Cincinnati, OH 45202-3198
(800) 543-1818/(513) 579-5700

	1982	1983	1984 (8 mos.)	1985	1986	1987
Years Ending 4/30						
Net Investment Income ($)	–	–	.19	.25	.31	.37
Dividends from Net Investment Income ($)	–	–	.10	.26	.30	.34
Net Gains (Losses) on Investments ($)	–	–	.09	1.49	3.38	3.79
Distributions from Net Realized Capital Gains ($)	–	–	–	–	–	1.18
Net Asset Value End of Year ($)	–	–	10.17	11.66	15.04	17.69
Ratio of Expenses to Net Assets (%)	–	–	2.00	2.00	1.72	1.61
Portfolio Turnover Rate (%)	–	–	20	71	80	76
Total Assets: End of Year (Millions $)	–	–	6.7	12.6	30.7	53.8
Annual Rate of Return (%) Years Ending 12/31	–	–	4.5	28.8	22.0	12.4

Five-Year Total Return(%)	NA	Degree of Diversification	B	Beta	.84	Bull (%)	134.9[A]	Bear (%)	(13.1)[C]

Objective: Seeks long-term growth of capital by investing in common stocks of established companies in the S&P 500 stock index. Employs computer model to screen companies on basis of earnings, P/E ratios, rate of return, etc.

Portfolio: (10/31/87) Common stocks 77%, repos 23%. Largest stock holdings: forest/paper products 13%, utilities 10%.

Distributions: Income: Nov, Feb, May, Aug　　**Capital Gains:** May

12b-1: Yes　　Amount: 0.50%

Minimum: Initial: $1,000　　Subsequent: $50

Min IRA: Initial: $1,000　　Subsequent: $50

Services: IRA, Withdraw

Tel Exchange: Yes　　**With MMF:** Yes

Registered: AZ, CA, CO, CT, FL, GA, IL, IN, KY, MA, MD, MI, NJ, NY, OH, PA, SC, TX, VA, WA

GRADISON OPPORTUNITY GROWTH

Aggressive Growth

Gradison & Co.
The 580 Building, 6th & Walnut
Cincinnati, OH 45202-3198
(800) 543-1818/(513) 579-5700

	Years Ending 4/30					
	1982	1983	1984 (8 mos.)	1985	1986	1987
Net Investment Income ($)	–	–	.01	.02	.02	.11
Dividends from Net Investment Income ($)	–	–	.01	Nil	.03	.04
Net Gains (Losses) on Investments ($)	–	–	(1.97)	1.24	3.87	.81
Distributions from Net Realized Capital Gains ($)	–	–	–	–	–	.80
Net Asset Value End of Year ($)	–	–	8.04	9.30	13.16	13.23
Ratio of Expenses to Net Assets (%)	–	–	2.00	2.00	2.00	1.73
Portfolio Turnover Rate (%)	–	–	108	99	83	65
Total Assets: End of Year (Millions $)	–	–	3.9	4.8	14.4	20.3
Annual Rate of Return (%) Years Ending 12/31	–	–	(3.2)	28.1	13.0	(5.4)

Five-Year Total Return(%)	NA	Degree of Diversification	D	Beta	.89	Bull (%)	93.4[c]	Bear (%)	(22.0)[D]

Objective: Seeks long-term capital growth through investment in common stocks of smaller companies (under $350 million) that show dynamic growth potential.

Portfolio: (10/31/87) Common stocks 76%, repos 24%. Largest stock holdings: business/industrial products & services 11%, construction & building materials 10%.

Distributions: Income: May, Nov   **Capital Gains:** Nov
12b-1: Yes   Amount: 0.50%
Minimum: Initial: $1,000   Subsequent: $50
Min IRA: Initial: $1,000   Subsequent: $50
Services: IRA, Withdraw
Tel Exchange: Yes   With MMF: Yes
Registered: AZ, CA, CO, CT, FL, GA, IL, IN, KY, MA, MD, MI, NJ, NY, OH, PA, SC, TX, VA, WA

GROWTH INDUSTRY SHARES
Growth

William Blair and Co.
135 S. LaSalle St.
Chicago, IL 60603
(312) 346-4830

	Years Ending 12/31					
	1982	1983	1984	1985	1986	1987
Net Investment Income ($)	.17	.21	.21	.21	.18	.15
Dividends from Net Investment Income ($)	.17	.19	.19	.23	.22	.14
Net Gains (Losses) on Investments ($)	2.16	1.21	(.73)	2.11	.84	.47
Distributions from Net Realized Capital Gains ($)	.33	.34	.70	.57	3.52	1.37
Net Asset Value End of Year ($)	10.81	11.69	10.29	11.82	9.10	8.21
Ratio of Expenses to Net Assets (%)	.94	.87	.92	.95	.90	.87
Portfolio Turnover Rate (%)	10	10	13	43	26	22
Total Assets: End of Year (Millions $)	54.1	63.5	58.4	72.2	68.6	66.3

Annual Rate of Return (%) Years Ending 12/31	27.7	13.5	(4.1)	23.3	9.2	6.6

Five-Year Total Return(%)	56.3ᴰ	Degree of Diversification	B	Beta	.94	Bull (%)	85.4ᶜ	Bear (%)	(18.5)ᶜ

Objective:	Seeks long-term capital growth by investing in well-managed companies in growth industries. Secondary objective is growth of income. Companies chosen on eight criteria: leader in field, unique or specialty company, quality products, outstanding marketing, value-based pricing, competitive internationally, above-average return on equity, sound financial practices.
Portfolio:	(12/31/87) Common stocks 88%, temporary investments 12%. Largest stock holdings: industrial technology 18%, consumer services and products 18%.
Distributions:	**Income:** May, Aug, Nov, Dec **Capital Gains:** Dec
12b-1:	No
Minimum:	**Initial:** $1,000 **Subsequent:** $250
Min IRA:	**Initial:** $1,000 **Subsequent:** $250
Services:	IRA, Keogh, SEP, Withdraw, Deduct
Tel Exchange:	No
Registered:	All states except NH

GUARDIAN MUTUAL
Growth & Income

Neuberger and Berman
Management Inc.
342 Madison Ave.
New York, NY 10173
(800) 367-0770/(212) 850-8300

	Years Ending 10/31					
	1982	1983	1984	1985	1986	1987
Net Investment Income ($)	1.61	1.51	1.40	1.90	1.49	1.21
Dividends from Net Investment Income ($)	1.58	1.45	1.43	1.76	1.51	1.24
Net Gains (Losses) on Investments ($)	5.25	7.22	1.82	5.25	7.50	(2.30)
Distributions from Net Realized Capital Gains ($)	.82	2.38	1.12	6.44	4.50	3.94
Net Asset Value End of Year ($)	32.02	36.92	37.59	36.54	39.52	33.25
Ratio of Expenses to Net Assets (%)	.76	.67	.77	.76	.73	.74
Portfolio Turnover Rate (%)	68	50	32	57	70	91
Total Assets: End of Year (Millions $)	209.5	276.1	344.9	388.5	531.8	461.1

Annual Rate of Return (%) Years Ending 12/31	28.7	25.3	7.5	25.3	11.9	(1.0)

Five-Year Total Return(%)	86.9[B]	Degree of Diversification	A	Beta	.92	Bull (%)	121.0[B]	Bear (%) (26.2)[E]

Objective: Seeks capital appreciation through investment in common stocks of dividend-paying, seasoned companies. Current income is a secondary objective. May invest in foreign securities, lend its securities, engage in repos, and write covered call options.

Portfolio: (10/31/87) Common stocks 90%, U.S. government obligations 6%, cash 4%. Largest stock holdings: telephone utilities 12%, retail 12%.

Distributions: Income: Jan, April, July, Oct   **Capital Gains:** Oct

12b-1: No

Minimum: Initial: $1,000   Subsequent: $100

Min IRA: Initial: $250   Subsequent: $50

Services: IRA, Keogh, Withdraw, Deduct

Tel Exchange: Yes   **With MMF:** Yes

Registered: All states except NH

HARBOR GROWTH
Growth

Harbor Capital Advisors, Inc.
One SeaGate
Toledo, OH 43666
(419) 247-1940

	Years Ending 10/31					
	1982	**1983**	**1984**	**1985**	**1986**	**1987** (11 mos.)
Net Investment Income ($)	–	–	–	–	–	.07
Dividends from Net Investment Income ($)	–	–	–	–	–	–
Net Gains (Losses) on Investments ($)	–	–	–	–	–	.44
Distributions from Net Realized Capital Gains ($)	–	–	–	–	–	.26
Net Asset Value End of Year ($)	–	–	–	–	–	10.25
Ratio of Expenses to Net Assets (%)	–	–	–	–	–	1.33
Portfolio Turnover Rate (%)	–	–	–	–	–	56
Total Assets: End of Year (Millions $)	–	–	–	–	–	98.7
Annual Rate of Return (%) Years Ending 12/31	–	–	–	–	–	2.9

Five-Year Total Return(%)	NA	Degree of Diversification	NA	Beta	NA	Bull (%)	NA	Bear (%)	(25.2)ᴱ

Objective: Primary objective is to achieve long-term growth of capital through investment in common stocks. Uses computer-generated forecasts of earnings and return-on-investment to select above-average growth companies.

Portfolio: (10/31/87) Common stocks 100%. Largest stock holdings: drugs & medical 9%, chemicals 5%.

Distributions: Income: Quarterly   **Capital Gains:** Annually

12b-1: No

Minimum: Initial: $2,000   Subsequent: $500

Min IRA: Initial: $2,000   Subsequent: $500

Services: IRA, Withdraw

Tel Exchange: No

Registered: All states except HI, MO, NE

IAI APOLLO
(formerly NORTH STAR APOLLO)
Growth

Investment Advisers, Inc.
1100 Dain Tower
P.O. Box 357
Minneapolis, MN 55440
(612) 371-2884

| | \multicolumn{6}{c}{Years Ending 3/31} |
	1982	1983	1984 (10 mos.)	1985	1986	1987
Net Investment Income ($)	–	–	.23	.22	.20	.15
Dividends from Net Investment Income ($)	–	–	–	.22	.20	.18
Net Gains (Losses) on Investments ($)	–	–	(.02)	–	1.59	1.42
Distributions from Net Realized Capital Gains ($)	–	–	–	.14	.20	.34
Net Asset Value End of Year ($)	–	–	10.21	10.07	11.46	12.51
Ratio of Expenses to Net Assets (%)	–	–	1.00	1.00	1.00	1.00
Portfolio Turnover Rate (%)	–	–	20	36	85	86
Total Assets: End of Year (Millions $)	–	–	12.9	18.2	24.7	22.3
Annual Rate of Return (%) Years Ending 12/31	–	–	–	12.7	2.0	13.9

Five-Year Total Return(%)	NA	Degree of Diversification	D	Beta	.95	Bull (%)	NA	Bear (%)	(20.3)ᴰ

Objective: Seeks long-term capital appreciation through investment in common stocks of companies that are unpopular, undervalued or in severe financial difficulties. A minor portion of portfolio may be invested in Ba (BB) or lower-rated debt securities. May enter into repos, invest in venture capital limited partnerships, restricted securities and foreign securities.

Portfolio: (9/30/87) Common stocks 77%, restricted securities 13%, short-term securities 10%. Largest stock holdings: office equipment 10%, building and home furnishing 9%.

Distributions: Income: June, Dec   **Capital Gains:** June

12b-1: No

Minimum: Initial: $2,500   Subsequent: $100

Min IRA: Initial: $100   Subsequent: $100

Services: IRA, Keogh, Corp, 403(b), Withdraw

Tel Exchange: No

Registered: AZ, CA, CO, IA, IL, MD, MI, MN, MO, MT, ND, NE, NY, PA, SD, TN, TX, WA, WI

IAI BOND
(formerly NORTH STAR BOND)
Bond

Investment Advisers, Inc.
1100 Dain Tower
P.O. Box 357
Minneapolis, MN 55440
(612) 371-2884

	Years Ending 3/31					
	1982	1983	1984	1985	1986	1987
Net Investment Income ($)	.95	.98	.91	1.01	.95	.85
Dividends from Net Investment Income ($)	.92	1.00	.91	1.00	.95	.89
Net Gains (Losses) on Investments ($)	(.42)	1.51	(.58)	.41	1.31	(.11)
Distributions from Net Realized Capital Gains ($)	—	—	—	—	—	.28
Net Asset Value End of Year ($)	8.08	9.57	8.99	9.41	10.72	10.29
Ratio of Expenses to Net Assets (%)	1.00	.90	.80	.70	.70	.70
Portfolio Turnover Rate (%)	23	83	40	22	76	35
Total Assets: End of Year (Millions $)	8.0	11.2	16.8	22.8	31.5	46.1
Annual Rate of Return (%) Years Ending 12/31	32.1	8.0	15.5	20.1	12.1	2.1

Five-Year Total Return(%)	71.4[C]	Degree of Diversification	NA	Beta	.03	Bull (%)	52.3[D]	Bear (%)	3.0[A]

Objective: Seeks high level of current income and preservation of capital through investment in a diversified portfolio of investment grade bonds and other debt securities of similar quality. May enter into repos and invest in foreign securities.

Portfolio: (9/30/87) Long-term government and corporate bonds 96%, short-term securities 1%. Largest bond holdings: finance & credit 10%, industrial 8%.

Distributions: Income: Mar, June, Sept, Dec   **Capital Gains:** June

12b-1: No

Minimum: Initial: $1,000   Subsequent: $100

Min IRA: Initial: $100   Subsequent: $100

Services: IRA, Keogh, Corp, 403(b), Withdraw

Tel Exchange: No

Registered: AZ, CA, CO, IA, IL, MD, MI, MN, MO, MT, ND, NE, NY, PA, SD, TN, TX, WA, WI

IAI REGIONAL
(formerly NORTH STAR REGIONAL)
Growth

Investment Advisers, Inc.
1100 Dain Tower
P.O. Box 357
Minneapolis, MN 55440
(612) 371-2884

	Years Ending 3/31					
	1982	1983	1984	1985	1986	1987
Net Investment Income ($)	.57	.39	.43	.46	.41	.36
Dividends from Net Investment Income ($)	.51	.45	.40	.48	.43	.42
Net Gains (Losses) on Investments ($)	(1.18)	6.48	(.53)	1.81	6.57	4.26
Distributions from Net Realized Capital Gains ($)	.15	.03	1.19	1.11	.40	6.45
Net Asset Value End of Year ($)	11.91	18.30	16.61	17.29	23.44	21.19
Ratio of Expenses to Net Assets (%)	1.00	1.00	.90	.80	.80	.80
Portfolio Turnover Rate (%)	84	116	77	80	112	133
Total Assets: End of Year (Millions $)	14.1	38.4	44.9	56.5	77.8	101.9

Annual Rate of Return (%) Years Ending 12/31	41.4	13.1	(2.1)	38.4	22.8	5.0

Five-Year Total Return(%)	97.5[A]	Degree of Diversification	B	Beta	.89	Bull (%)	139.2[A]	Bear (%)	(18.1)[C]

Objective: Seeks capital appreciation through investment of at least 80% of its equity investments in companies headquartered in MN, WI, IA, NE, MT, ND or SD. For defensive purposes, may convert entire portfolio to debt securities. May enter into repos, invest in restricted securities, venture capital, limited partnerships and foreign securities.

Portfolio: (9/30/87) Common stocks 75%, short-term securities 18%, restricted securities 6%. Largest stock holdings: food, sugar, tobacco 9%; miscellaneous consumer cyclicals 9%.

Distributions: Income: June, Dec   **Capital Gains:** June

12b-1: No

Minimum: Initial: $2,500   Subsequent: $100

Min IRA: Initial: $100   Subsequent: $100

Services: IRA, Keogh, Corp, 403(b), Withdraw

Tel Exchange: No

Registered: AZ, CA, CO, IA, IL, MD, MI, MN, MO, MT, ND, NE, NY, PA, SD, TN, TX, WA, WI

IAI RESERVE FUND

Bond

Investment Advisers, Inc.
1100 Dain Tower
P.O. Box 357
Minneapolis, MN 55440
(612) 371-2884

	Years Ending 3/31					
	1982	**1983**	**1984**	**1985**	**1986** **(2 mos.)**	**1987**
Net Investment Income ($)						
Net Investment Income ($)	–	–	–	–	.06	.54
Dividends from Net Investment Income ($)	–	–	–	–	–	.47
Net Gains (Losses) on Investments ($)	–	–	–	–	.04	.02
Distributions from Net Realized Capital Gains ($)	–	–	–	–	–	–
Net Asset Value End of Year ($)	–	–	–	–	10.10	10.19
Ratio of Expenses to Net Assets (%)	–	–	–	–	.9	.8
Portfolio Turnover Rate (%)	–	–	–	–	–	30
Total Assets: End of Year (Millions $)	–	–	–	–	25.5	35.0
Annual Rate of Return (%) Years Ending 12/31	–	–	–	–	–	5.9

Five-Year Total Return(%)	NA	Degree of Diversification	NA	Beta NA	Bull (%) NA	Bear (%) 2.1^

Objective: Seeks a high level of capital stability and liquidity, with a secondary objective of high current income. Invests in investment-grade government and commercial paper. Will not purchase securities with a maturity date more than 25 months from the date of acquisition.

Portfolio: (9/30/87) Short-term securities 90%, corporate bonds 10%.

Distributions: Income: Mar, June, Sept, Dec **Capital Gains:** June

12b-1: No

Minimum: Initial: $2,500 Subsequent: $100

Min IRA: Initial: $100 Subsequent: $100

Services: IRA, Keogh, Corp, 403(b), Withdraw

Tel Exchange: No

Registered: AZ, CO, IA, IL, MD, MI, MN, MO, MT, ND, NY, PA, SD, TN, WA, WI

IAI STOCK
(formerly NORTH STAR STOCK)
Growth

Investment Advisers, Inc.
1100 Dain Tower
P.O. Box 357
Minneapolis, MN 55440
(612) 371-2884

	Years Ending 3/31					
	1982	1983	1984	1985	1986	1987
Net Investment Income ($)	.54	.40	.37	.45	.42	.33
Dividends from Net Investment Income ($)	.52	.48	.35	.41	.48	.37
Net Gains (Losses) on Investments ($)	(1.30)	4.38	.27	1.07	3.36	3.07
Distributions from Net Realized Capital Gains ($)	1.05	.64	.62	1.39	.46	1.80
Net Asset Value End of Year ($)	10.20	13.86	13.53	13.25	16.09	17.32
Ratio of Expenses to Net Assets (%)	.80	.80	.70	.70	.70	.80
Portfolio Turnover Rate (%)	76	81	69	62	50	68
Total Assets: End of Year (Millions $)	16.9	35.3	48.7	60.2	69.1	83.7
Annual Rate of Return (%) Years Ending 12/31	33.9	19.4	3.7	23.2	12.9	15.4

Five-Year Total Return(%)	98.8[A]	Degree of Diversification	A	Beta	.87	Bull (%)	121.0[B]	Bear (%)	(18.3)[C]

Objective:	Seeks capital appreciation and income secondarily through investment in common stocks of primarily widely-known companies and some not so well-known. May enter into repos, invest in restricted securities, REITS and venture capital limited partnerships.
Portfolio:	(9/30/87) Common stocks 75%, short-term securities 15%, restricted securities 9%, corporate bonds 1%. Largest stock holdings: office equipment 15%, energy 5%.
Distributions:	Income: June, Dec **Capital Gains:** June
12b-1:	No
Minimum:	**Initial:** $1,000 **Subsequent:** $100
Min IRA:	**Initial:** $100 **Subsequent:** $100
Services:	IRA, Keogh, Corp, 403(b), Withdraw
Tel Exchange:	No
Registered:	AZ, CA, CO, IA, IL, MD, MI, MN, MO, MT, ND, NE, NY, PA, SD, TN, TX, WA, WI

INTERNATIONAL EQUITY TRUST
International

Furman Selz
230 Park Ave.
New York, NY 10169
(800) 845-8406/(212) 309-8400

			Years Ending 9/30			
	1982	1983	1984	1985	1986 (9 mos.)	1987
Net Investment Income ($)	–	–	–	–	.02	(.07)
Dividends from Net Investment Income ($)	–	–	–	–	–	.02
Net Gains (Losses) on Investments ($)	–	–	–	–	4.05	4.71
Distributions from Net Realized Capital Gains ($)	–	–	–	–	–	.67
Net Asset Value End of Year ($)	–	–	–	–	14.07	18.02
Ratio of Expenses to Net Assets (%)	–	–	–	–	2.47	1.64
Portfolio Turnover Rate (%)	–	–	–	–	78	85
Total Assets: End of Year (Millions $)	–	–	–	–	9.2	32.6
Annual Rate of Return (%) Years Ending 12/31	–	–	–	–	49.6	3.3

Five-Year Total Return(%)	NA	Degree of Diversification	NA	Beta	NA	Bull (%)	NA	Bear (%)	(18.1)c

Objective: Seeks long-term capital appreciation through investment in securities markets outside the United States. The fund will normally have 65% of its assets invested in foreign equity securities. May also invest in foreign debt obligations and use currency futures to hedge the portfolio.

Portfolio: (9/30/87) Common stocks 100%. Largest country holdings: Japan 36%, United Kingdom 26%.

Distributions: Income: Semiannually   **Capital Gains:** Annually

12b-1: Yes   **Amount:** 0.50%

Minimum: Initial: $2,500   Subsequent: $100

Min IRA: Initial: $250   Subsequent: $100

Services: IRA, Keogh, Corp, 403(b), Withdraw

Tel Exchange: No

Registered: All states except AR, NH

ISTEL (LEPERCQ)
Growth & Income

Lepercq, de Neuflize & Co.
345 Park Ave.
New York, NY 10154
(800) 548-7878/(212) 702-0174

	Years Ending 12/31					
	1982	1983	1984	1985	1986	1987
Net Investment Income ($)	.85	.61	.53	.63	.40	.40
Dividends from Net Investment Income ($)	.93	.95	.60	.74	.64	.57
Net Gains (Losses) on Investments ($)	(.52)	1.71	(1.31)	1.89	.72	(.04)
Distributions from Net Realized Capital Gains ($)	.41	—	.73	1.47	1.08	.85
Net Asset Value End of Year ($)	14.32	15.69	13.58	13.89	13.29	12.23
Ratio of Expenses to Net Assets (%)	1.06	1.02	1.04	1.12	1.67	1.44
Portfolio Turnover Rate (%)	6	27	26	28	45	67
Total Assets: End of Year (Millions $)	111.9	111.1	91.9	28.7	23.6	22.3

Annual Rate of Return (%) Years Ending 12/31	3.6	17.1	(5.1)	20.0	8.2	2.3

Five-Year Total Return(%)	47.5[E]	Degree of Diversification	B	Beta	.71	Bull (%)	74.9[C]	Bear (%)	(17.1)[C]

Objective: Seeks long-term growth of capital and reasonable current income from investment in securities of companies that through fundamental analysis show potential for growth and value. Fund chooses a few from each industry group that show promise in prevailing industrial and economic environment. Looks for promising geographical regions. May invest in international securities. May write covered call options.

Portfolio: (12/31/87) Common stocks 51%, U.S. gov't. obligations 28%, short-term securities 21%. Largest stock holdings: financial/interest-rate sensitive 15%, energy 14%.

Distributions: Income: July, Dec   **Capital Gains:** Dec

12b-1: Yes   **Amount:** 1.00%

Minimum: Initial: $500   **Subsequent:** 1 full share

Min IRA: Initial: $500   **Subsequent:** 1 full share

Services: IRA, Withdraw

Tel Exchange: Yes   **With MMF:** No

Registered: All states

IVY GROWTH
Growth & Income

Hingham Management Inc.
South Shore Park
40 Industrial Park Rd.
Hingham, MA 02043
(800) 235-3322/(617) 749-1416

	Years Ending 12/31					
	1982	1983	1984	1985	1986	1987
Net Investment Income ($)	.75	.77	.89	.51	.61	.32
Dividends from Net Investment Income ($)	.59	.74	.78	.96	.46	.91
Net Gains (Losses) on Investments ($)	2.45	2.85	.06	3.23	1.87	(.46)
Distributions from Net Realized Capital Gains ($)	—	.38	1.78	.76	4.48	.30
Net Asset Value End of Year ($)	12.99	15.49	13.88	15.90	13.44	12.09
Ratio of Expenses to Net Assets (%)	1.28	1.22	1.29	1.27	1.29	1.27
Portfolio Turnover Rate (%)	86	59	97	132	95	74
Total Assets: End of Year (Millions $)	76.7	114.4	63.5*	136.7	158.1	173.1

Annual Rate of Return (%) Years Ending 12/31	32.9	30.1	7.9	29.4	16.8	(1.8)

Five-Year Total Return(%)	108.2[A]	Degree of Diversification	B	Beta	.74	Bull (%)	117.4[B]	Bear (%)	(21.7)[D]

Change in size reflects halving of total assets in the forming of the other fund in this series, Ivy Institutional Investors Fund.

Objective: Seeks long-term growth of capital primarily through investment in equity securities of large, well-established companies. May write covered call options and may convert portfolio to debt investments as a defensive posture.

Portfolio: (12/31/87) Common stocks 54%, short-term notes 45%, U.S. government securities 5%, preferred stocks 1%. Largest stock holdings: drugs and hospital supply 6%, banking and credit 6%.

Distributions: Income: Annually   **Capital Gains:** Annually

12b-1: No

Minimum: Initial: $1,000   Subsequent: None

Min IRA: Initial: None   Subsequent: None

Services: IRA, Keogh, Corp, SEP, Withdraw

Tel Exchange: Yes   **With MMF:** Yes

Registered: All states

IVY INTERNATIONAL
International

Hingham Management Inc.
South Shore Park
40 Industrial Park Rd.
Hingham, MA 02043
(800) 235-3322/(617) 749-1416

	Years Ending 12/31					
	1982	1983	1984	1985	1986	1987
Net Investment Income ($)	–	–	–	–	.03	.04
Dividends from Net Investment Income ($)	–	–	–	–	.07	.05
Net Gains (Losses) on Investments ($)	–	–	–	–	2.37	2.38
Distributions from Net Realized Capital Gains ($)	–	–	–	–	–	1.87
Net Asset Value End of Year ($)	–	–	–	–	12.40	12.90
Ratio of Expenses to Net Assets (%)	–	–	–	–	2.00	1.90
Portfolio Turnover Rate (%)	–	–	–	–	20	47
Total Assets: End of Year (Millions $)	–	–	–	–	9.6	21.1

Annual Rate of Return (%) Years Ending 12/31	–	–	–	–	–	19.6

Five-Year Total Return(%)	NA	Degree of Diversification	NA	Beta	NA	Bull (%)	NA	Bear (%)	(21.6)ᴰ

Objective: Seeks long-term capital appreciation through investment in foreign equity securities, primarily those traded in European and Pacific Basin markets. For defensive purposes the fund may invest in U.S. equity securities. Current income is a secondary objective.

Portfolio: (12/31/87) Common stocks 91%, short-term securities 5%, corporate bonds 4%. Largest stock holdings: miscellaneous 18%, insurance 10%.

Distributions: Income: Annually   **Capital Gains:** Annually

12b-1: No

Minimum: Initial: $1,000   Subsequent: None

Min IRA: Initial: None   Subsequent: None

Services: IRA, Keogh, Corp, SEP, Withdraw

Tel Exchange: Yes   **With MMF:** Yes

Registered: All states

JANUS FUND
Growth

Janus Capital Corp.
100 Fillmore Street, Suite 300
Denver, CO 80206-4923
(800) 525-3713/(303) 333-3863

	Years Ending 10/31					
	1982	1983	1984	1985	1986	1987
Net Investment Income ($)	.31	.15	.45	.48	.42	.19
Dividends from Net Investment Income ($)	.16	.25	.14	.48	.47	.38
Net Gains (Losses) on Investments ($)	1.41	3.42	(.20)	1.23	2.20	.30
Distributions from Net Realized Capital Gains ($)	1.91	.14	1.03	—	.80	2.49
Net Asset Value End of Year ($)	9.93	13.11	12.19	13.42	14.77	12.39
Ratio of Expenses to Net Assets (%)	1.31	1.11	1.06	1.03	1.00	1.01
Portfolio Turnover Rate (%)	106	94	162	163	254	214
Total Assets: End of Year (Millions $)	76.5	264.7	319.1	410.7	474.4	387.5

Annual Rate of Return (%) Years Ending 12/31	30.6	26.1	(0.1)	24.5	11.2	3.9

Five-Year Total Return(%)	81.3ᴮ	Degree of Diversification	C	Beta	.68	Bull (%)	85.1ᶜ	Bear (%)	(17.1)ᶜ

Objective:	Seeks long-term capital growth by investing in securities selected solely for their capital appreciation. Emphasizes companies, their divisions, or new products in early growth stage. Companies may be quite new or small. May convert portfolio to debt securities as a defensive posture.
Portfolio:	(10/31/87) Corporate short-term notes 57%, common stocks 33%, cash and other assets 10%. Largest stock holdings: communications 8%, financial services 5%.
Distributions:	Income: Dec **Capital Gains:** Dec
12b-1:	Yes **Amount:** Pd. by Advisor
Minimum:	Initial: $1,000 Subsequent: $50
Min IRA:	Initial: $500 Subsequent: $50
Services:	IRA, Keogh, Withdraw, Deduct
Tel Exchange:	Yes **With MMF:** Yes
Registered:	All states

JANUS VALUE
Growth

Janus Capital Corp.
100 Fillmore Street, Suite 300
Denver, CO 80206-4923
(800) 525-3713/(303) 333-3863

	1982	1983	1984	1985 (7 mos.)	1986	1987
Years Ending 5/31						
Net Investment Income ($)	–	–	–	.36	.19	.30
Dividends from Net Investment Income ($)	–	–	–	–	.23	.25
Net Gains (Losses) on Investments ($)	–	–	–	1.21	3.05	.74
Distributions from Net Realized Capital Gains ($)	–	–	–	–	.31	1.37
Net Asset Value End of Year ($)	–	–	–	11.57	14.27	13.69
Ratio of Expenses to Net Assets (%)	–	–	–	1.99	2.00	1.79
Portfolio Turnover Rate (%)	–	–	–	68	152	202
Total Assets: End of Year (Millions $)	–	–	–	2.5	10.1	18.9

Annual Rate of Return (%) Years Ending 12/31			–	–	–	–	11.5	(11.7)
Five-Year Total Return(%)	NA	Degree of Diversification	NA	Beta	NA	Bull (%)	NA	Bear (%) (26.1)ᴱ

Objective: Seeks capital appreciation through investment in common stocks chosen primarily from a "contrarian" viewpoint, including those with a strong financial position and low P/E. May invest 25% of assets in ADRs of foreign issues.

Portfolio: (11/30/87) Short-term corporate notes 53%, common stocks 46%, cash 1%. Largest stock holdings: communications 15%, steel 10%.

Distributions: Income: Dec   **Capital Gains:** Dec
12b-1: Yes   **Amount:** Pd. by Advisor
Minimum: Initial: $1,000   Subsequent: $50
Min IRA: Initial: $500   Subsequent: $50
Services: IRA, Keogh, Withdraw, Deduct
Tel Exchange: Yes   **With MMF:** Yes
Registered: All states except NH

JANUS VENTURE
Aggressive Growth

Janus Capital Corp.
100 Fillmore Street, Suite 300
Denver, CO 80206
(800) 525-3713/(303) 333-3863

			Years Ending 7/31			
	1982	1983	1984	1985 (3 mos.)	1986	1987
Net Investment Income ($)	–	–	–	.26	.11	.12
Dividends from Net Investment Income ($)	–	–	–	–	.18	.19
Net Gains (Losses) on Investments ($)	–	–	–	3.91	7.88	6.25
Distributions from Net Realized Capital Gains ($)	–	–	–	–	1.20	2.33
Net Asset Value End of Year ($)	–	–	–	24.17	30.78	34.63
Ratio of Expenses to Net Assets (%)	–	–	–	2.00	1.90	1.44
Portfolio Turnover Rate (%)	–	–	–	293	248	250
Total Assets: End of Year (Millions $)	–	–	–	4.1	30.9	46.3
Annual Rate of Return (%) Years Ending 12/31	–	–	–	–	20.2	5.1

Five-Year Total Return(%)	NA	Degree of Diversification	NA	Beta	NA	Bull (%)	NA	Bear (%)	(17.3)C

Objective: Seeks capital appreciation through investment primarily in common stocks of small companies with less than $250 million in annual revenues. May also invest in larger companies with strong growth potential and in foreign companies through ADRs.

Portfolio: (7/31/87) Common stocks 70%, short-term corporate notes 24%, cash and other 6%. Largest stock holdings: environmental services 13%, entertainment 13%.

Distributions: Income: Dec   **Capital Gains:** Dec

12b-1: Yes   **Amount:** Pd. by Advisor

Minimum: Initial: $1,000   **Subsequent:** $50

Min IRA: Initial: $500   **Subsequent:** $50

Services: IRA, Keogh, Withdraw, Deduct

Tel Exchange: Yes   **With MMF:** Yes

Registered: All states except NH

LEGG MASON
SPECIAL
INVESTMENT TRUST
Aggressive Growth

Legg Mason Wood Walker
7 E. Redwood Street
Baltimore, MD 21202
(800) 822-5544/(301) 539-3400

	1982	1983	1984	1985	1986 (3 mos.)	1987
Net Investment Income ($)	–	–	–	–	.04	.00
Dividends from Net Investment Income ($)	–	–	–	–	–	.02
Net Gains (Losses) on Investments ($)	–	–	–	–	1.49	1.51
Distributions from Net Realized Capital Gains ($)	–	–	–	–	–	.22
Net Asset Value End of Year ($)	–	–	–	–	11.53	12.80
Ratio of Expenses to Net Assets (%)	–	–	–	–	2.5	2.5
Portfolio Turnover Rate (%)	–	–	–	–	41	77
Total Assets: End of Year (Millions $)	–	–	–	–	34.3	55.8

Years Ending 3/31

Annual Rate of Return (%) Years Ending 12/31	–	–	–	–	7.5	(10.6)

Five-Year Total Return(%)	NA	Degree of Diversification	NA	Beta	NA	Bull (%)	NA	Bear (%)	(29.8)E

Objective: Seeks capital appreciation through investment in equity securities of out-of-favor companies, not closely followed by analysts. Current income is not a consideration. Also invests in companies involved in reorganization or restructuring.

Portfolio: (9/30/87) Common stocks 83%, corporate bonds 9%, repos 9%. Largest stock holdings: insurance 12%, technology 11%.

Distributions: Income: Annually   **Capital Gains:** Annually

12b-1: Yes   **Amount:** 1.00%

Minimum: Initial: $1,000   Subsequent: $500

Min IRA: Initial: $1,000   Subsequent: $500

Services: IRA, Keogh, Corp, SEP, 403(b), Withdraw, Deduct

Tel Exchange: Yes   **With MMF:** Yes

Registered: All states except AK, CA, MO

LEGG MASON TOTAL RETURN TRUST

Growth & Income

Legg Mason Wood Walker
7 E. Redwood St.
Baltimore, MD 21202
(800) 822-5544/(301) 539-3400

	Years Ending 3/31					
	1982	1983	1984	1985	1986 (4 mos.)	1987
Net Investment Income ($)	–	–	–	–	.13	.18
Dividends from Net Investment Income ($)	–	–	–	–	–	.19
Net Gains (Losses) on Investments ($)	–	–	–	–	.65	.90
Distributions from Net Realized Capital Gains ($)	–	–	–	–	–	.04
Net Asset Value End of Year ($)	–	–	–	–	10.78	11.63
Ratio of Expenses to Net Assets (%)	–	–	–	–	2.2	2.4
Portfolio Turnover Rate (%)	–	–	–	–	40	83
Total Assets: End of Year (Millions $)	–	–	–	–	44.3	47.0

Annual Rate of Return (%) Years Ending 12/31	–	–	–	–	1.4	(7.5)

Five-Year Total Return(%)	NA	Degree of Diversification	NA	Beta	NA	Bull (%)	NA	Bear (%)	(24.6)ᴰ

Objective: To obtain capital appreciation and current income in order to achieve an attractive total return consistent with reasonable risk. Invests primarily in dividend-paying common stocks, convertible securities and bonds. Will invest no more than 25% of assets in bonds rated BBB or less.

Portfolio: (9/30/87) Common stocks 80%, corporate bonds 10%, repos 9%, preferred stocks 2%. Largest stock holdings: banking 24%, savings & loan 17%.

Distributions: Income: Jan, May, July, Oct   **Capital Gains:** May

12b-1: Yes   **Amount:** 1.00%

Minimum: Initial: $1,000   Subsequent: $500

Min IRA: Initial: $1,000   Subsequent: $500

Services: IRA, Keogh, Corp, SEP, 403(b), Withdraw, Deduct

Tel Exchange: Yes   **With MMF:** Yes

Registered: All states except AK, MO

LEGG MASON VALUE TRUST
Growth

Legg Mason Wood Walker
7 E. Redwood St.
Baltimore, MD 21202
(800) 822-5544/(301) 539-3400

	Years Ending 3/31					
	1982	1983 (13 mos.)	1984	1985	1986	1987
Net Investment Income ($)	–	.54	.46	.46	.50	.42
Dividends from Net Investment Income ($)	–	.20	.27	.34	.36	.40
Net Gains (Losses) on Investments ($)	–	5.82	2.52	4.49	8.31	2.22
Distributions from Net Realized Capital Gains ($)	–	–	.05	.34	.86	2.78
Net Asset Value End of Year ($)	–	16.16	18.82	23.09	30.68	30.14
Ratio of Expenses to Net Assets (%)	–	2.50	2.50	2.41	2.07	2.00
Portfolio Turnover Rate (%)	–	6	18	38	33	43
Total Assets: End of Year (Millions $)	–	15.1	61.1	163.4	599.1	819.3
Annual Rate of Return (%) Years Ending 12/31	–	42.8	12.0	31.7	9.4	(7.2)

Five-Year Total Return(%)	113.8[A]	Degree of Diversification	B	Beta	.95	Bull (%)	116.2[B]	Bear (%)	(26.4)[E]

Objective: Seeks long-term capital growth through investment in undervalued companies, temporarily depressed due to any of a variety of factors, but deemed to have potential for superior performance.

Portfolio: (9/30/87) Common stocks 85%, short-term securities 14%, corporate bonds 1%. Largest stock holdings: banking 19%, savings & loan 10%.

Distributions: Income: Jan, May, July, Oct   **Capital Gains:** May

12b-1: Yes   **Amount:** 1.00%

Minimum: Initial: $1,000   **Subsequent:** $500

Min IRA: Initial: $1,000   **Subsequent:** $500

Services: IRA, Keogh, Corp, SEP, 403(b), Withdraw, Deduct

Tel Exchange: Yes   **With MMF:** Yes

Registered: All states except AK, MO

LEHMAN OPPORTUNITY
Aggressive Growth

Lehman Management Co.
55 Water St.
New York, NY 10041
(800) 221-5350/(212) 668-8578

	Years Ending 8/31					
	1982	1983	1984	1985	1986	1987
Net Investment Income ($)	.48	.42	.41	.52	.53	.54
Dividends from Net Investment Income ($)	.47	.48	.43	.41	.48	.59
Net Gains (Losses) on Investments ($)	(.74)	7.56	1.92	4.69	5.48	4.49
Distributions from Net Realized Capital Gains ($)	.79	—	1.39	1.37	1.40	2.79
Net Asset Value End of Year ($)	12.28	19.78	20.30	23.73	27.87	29.53
Ratio of Expenses to Net Assets (%)	1.33	1.30	1.23	1.23	1.16	1.16
Portfolio Turnover Rate (%)	27	46	32	24	28	25
Total Assets: End of Year (Millions $)	20.3	38.7	48.5	71.2	110.1	113.6
Annual Rate of Return (%) Years Ending 12/31	29.0	38.9	11.1	32.8	6.4	4.5

Five-Year Total Return(%)	128.0[A]	Degree of Diversification	B	Beta	.80	Bull (%)	114.2[B]	Bear (%)	(20.0)[D]

Objective: Seeks above-average long-term capital appreciation by investing principally in common stocks and convertible securities of both seasoned, established companies and small, new companies. May invest up to 5% of its assets in foreign securities and foreign bank acceptances, and may use leverage.

Portfolio: (8/31/87) Common stocks 88%, short-term notes 11%, preferred stocks 1%. Largest stock holdings: finance 20%, insurance 19%.

Distributions: Income: Annually   **Capital Gains:** Annually

12b-1: No

Minimum: Initial: $1,000   Subsequent: $100

Min IRA: Initial: $250   Subsequent: $50

Services: IRA, Keogh, Withdraw

Tel Exchange: Yes   **With MMF:** Yes

Registered: All states

LEVERAGE FUND OF BOSTON

Aggressive Growth

Eaton Vance Management
24 Federal St.
Boston, MA 02110
(800) 225-6265/(617) 482-8260

	Years Ending 12/31					
	1982*	1983	1984	1985	1986	1987
Net Investment Income ($)	.36	(.06)	(.18)	—	(.15)	(.11)
Dividends from Net Investment Income ($)	.36	—	—	—	—	—
Net Gains (Losses) on Investments ($)	2.92	1.63	(.91)	2.14	.10	(.24)
Distributions from Net Realized Capital Gains ($)	2.30	3.04	.50	—	1.53	1.50
Net Asset Value End of Year ($)	9.76	8.29	6.70	8.84	7.26	5.41
Ratio of Expenses to Net Assets (%)	1.26	3.47	4.30	2.73	2.76	2.50
Portfolio Turnover Rate (%)	82	75	48	78	53	115
Total Assets: End of Year (Millions $)	39.9	41.5	28.9	33.2	23.4	18.8

Annual Rate of Return (%) Years Ending 12/31	—	16.1	(13.1)	32.1	(0.7)	(4.0)

Five-Year Total Return(%)	27.0ᴱ	Degree of Diversification	C	Beta	1.38	Bull (%)	126.8ᴬ	Bear (%)	(34.9)ᴱ

Was closed-end fund prior to 1/4/82.

Objective: Seeks growth of capital primarily through investment in equity securities of large and small companies that show growth promise because of new products, other changes or special situations. May employ leverage by borrowing money to purchase securities but must have assets representing three times borrowings. May invest in foreign securities and engage in repos.

Portfolio: (12/31/87) Common stocks 100%. Largest stock holdings: computer products/services 21%, drugs and medical 11%.

Distributions: **Income:** Semiannually   **Capital Gains:** Annually

12b-1: No

Minimum: Initial: $1,000   Subsequent: $50

Min IRA: Initial: $1,000   Subsequent: $50

Services: IRA, Keogh, Corp, 403(b), Withdraw, Deduct

Tel Exchange: Yes   **With MMF:** Yes

Registered: All states

LEXINGTON
GNMA INCOME
Bond

Lexington Management Corp.
P.O. Box 1515
Park 80 W. Plaza 2
Saddle Brook, NJ 07662
(800) 526-0056

	Years Ending 12/31					
	1982	1983	1984	1985	1986	1987
Net Investment Income ($)	.83	.74	.87	.76	.74	.71
Dividends from Net Investment Income ($)	.88	.80	.82	.93	.75	.73
Net Gains (Losses) on Investments ($)	.90	(.17)	(.03)	.49	.17	(.59)
Distributions from Net Realized Capital Gains ($)	—	—	—	—	—	.03
Net Asset Value End of Year ($)	7.95	7.72	7.74	8.06	8.22	7.58
Ratio of Expenses to Net Assets (%)	1.59	1.47	1.22	1.01	.86	.98
Portfolio Turnover Rate (%)	95	207	133	168	300	89
Total Assets: End of Year (Millions $)	9.2	22.4	25.4	87.4	141.4	107.6

Annual Rate of Return (%) Years Ending 12/31	26.1	7.6	11.9	18.3	11.7	0.8

Five-Year Total Return(%) 60.4[D]	Degree of Diversification NA	Beta −.02	Bull (%) 45.6[E]	Bear (%) 1.7[A]

Objective:	Seeks high level of current income, retaining liquidity and safety of principal. At least 80% of assets invested in GNMA certificates and balance in other U.S. government securities. May buy repos.
Portfolio:	(12/31/87) GNMA 96%, U.S. government obligations 2%, repos 2%.
Distributions:	Income: Monthly **Capital Gains:** Annually
12b-1:	Yes **Amount:** 0.25%
Minimum:	Initial: $1,000 **Subsequent:** $50
Min IRA:	Initial: $250 **Subsequent:** $50
Services:	IRA, Keogh, SEP, Corp, 403(b), Withdraw, Deduct
Tel Exchange:	Yes **With MMF:** Yes
Registered:	All states

LEXINGTON GOLDFUND
Precious Metals

Lexington Management Corp.
P.O. Box 1515
Park 80 W. Plaza 2
Saddle Brook, NJ 07662
(800) 526-0056

	3/31		Years Ending 12/31				
	1982	1982* (9 mos.)	1983	1984	1985	1986	1987
Net Investment Income ($)	.09	.02	.07	.03	.02	.04	.01
Dividends from Net Investment Income ($)	.22	.11	.06	.04	.04	.02	.05
Net Gains (Losses) on Investments ($)	(1.75)	1.91	(.36)	(.98)	.37	1.07	2.07
Distributions from Net Realized Capital Gains ($)	.62	.04	.05	.10	—	—	.32
Net Asset Value End of Year ($)	2.76	4.54	4.14	3.05	3.40	4.49	6.20
Ratio of Expenses to Net Assets (%)	2.12	1.50	1.50	1.50	1.50	1.50	1.28
Portfolio Turnover Rate (%)	5	43	16	17	30	15	14
Total Assets: End of Year (Millions $)	0.9	3.8	7.0	7.5	12.4	24.6	104.9

Annual Rate of Return (%) Years Ending 12/31	38.1	*	(6.4)	(23.7)	13.0	32.7	46.3

Five-Year Total Return(%)	56.5[D]	Degree of Diversification	E	Beta	.38	Bull (%)	133.6[A]	Bear (%)	(15.5)[C]

Changed fiscal year-end from 3/31 to 12/31 and changed management company. All annual return figures are for full years ending 12/31.

Objective: Seeks capital appreciation and a hedge against inflation through investment in gold bullion and debt and equity securities of domestic and foreign firms engaged in mining or processing gold. May buy repos and CDs.

Portfolio: (12/31/87) Common stocks 67%, gold bullion 24%, short-term securities 9%. Largest stock holdings: North American gold mining 34%, Australian gold mining 14%.

Distributions: Income: Feb, Aug   **Capital Gains:** Feb

12b-1: Yes   **Amount:** 0.25%

Minimum: Initial: $1,000   Subsequent: $50

Min IRA: Initial: $250   Subsequent: $50

Services: IRA, Keogh, Corp, SEP, 403(b), Withdraw, Deduct

Tel Exchange: Yes   **With MMF:** Yes

Registered: All states except NH, WI

LEXINGTON GROWTH

Aggressive Growth

Lexington Management Corp.
P.O. Box 1515
Park 80 W. Plaza 2
Saddle Brook, NJ 07662
(800) 526-0056

	Years Ending 12/31					
	1982	1983	1984	1985	1986	1987
Net Investment Income ($)	.11	.20	.25	.18	.16	.14
Dividends from Net Investment Income ($)	.22	.11	.30	.12	.20	.38
Net Gains (Losses) on Investments ($)	.34	.74	(1.48)	1.92	1.88	.12
Distributions from Net Realized Capital Gains ($)	.94	.06	.73	—	—	3.67
Net Asset Value End of Year ($)	9.47	10.24	7.98	9.96	11.80	8.01
Ratio of Expenses to Net Assets (%)	1.56	1.21	1.50	1.43	1.32	1.34
Portfolio Turnover Rate (%)	24	57	141	151	54	83
Total Assets: End of Year (Millions $)	27.6	35.0	22.7	28.0	29.9	25.6

Annual Rate of Return (%) Years Ending 12/31	6.7	9.9	(12.0)	26.7	20.6	0.0

Five-Year Total Return(%)	47.7ᴱ	Degree of Diversification	A	Beta	.99	Bull (%)	135.1ᴬ	Bear (%)	(25.9)ᴱ

Objective: Seeks capital growth. May invest in securities of newer, less seasoned companies, companies whose earnings are cyclically depressed but that have good potential for recovery, or established companies experiencing important changes such as product innovation. May also buy repos.

Portfolio: (12/31/87) Common stocks 91%, short-term securities 6%, bonds 3%. Largest stock holdings: drugs & health care 15%, consumer products 12%.

Distributions: Income: Feb **Capital Gains:** Feb
12b-1: Yes **Amount:** 0.25%
Minimum: Initial: $1,000 Subsequent: $50
Min IRA: Initial: $250 Subsequent: $50
Services: IRA, Keogh, Corp, SEP, 403(b), Withdraw, Deduct
Tel Exchange: Yes **With MMF:** Yes
Registered: All states except NH

LEXINGTON
RESEARCH
Growth

Lexington Management Corp.
P.O. Box 1515
Park 80 W. Plaza 2
Saddle Brook, NJ 07662
(800) 526-0056

	Years Ending 12/31					
	1982	1983	1984	1985	1986	1987
Net Investment Income ($)	.75	.80	.63	.60	.47	.43
Dividends from Net Investment Income ($)	.65	.72	.80	.60	.66	.51
Net Gains (Losses) on Investments ($)	.99	3.87	(1.75)	3.36	3.06	.02
Distributions from Net Realized Capital Gains ($)	.68	1.11	2.73	.11	2.33	5.52
Net Asset Value End of Year ($)	17.18	20.02	15.37	18.62	19.16	13.58
Ratio of Expenses to Net Assets (%)	1.07	.95	1.00	1.00	.95	.96
Portfolio Turnover Rate (%)	27	64	59	86	82	95
Total Assets: End of Year (Millions $)	93.4	111.7	100.0	114.3	124.7	112.8
Annual Rate of Return (%) Years Ending 12/31	12.0	28.7	(4.3)	26.3	20.2	0.0

Five-Year Total Return(%)	86.9[B]	Degree of Diversification	A	Beta	.90	Bull (%)	120.7[B]	Bear (%)	(22.9)[D]

Objective: Seeks capital growth over the long-term through investments in stocks of large, ably-managed and well-financed companies. Income is a secondary objective. May buy repos.

Portfolio: (12/31/87) Common stocks 84%, short-term securities 7%, CDs 6%, bonds 3%. Largest stock holdings: drugs & health care 16%, electronics & electrical equipment 12%.

Distributions: Income: Feb, May, Aug, Nov **Capital Gains:** Feb

12b-1: Yes **Amount:** 0.25%

Minimum: Initial: $1,000 **Subsequent:** $50

Min IRA: Initial: $250 **Subsequent:** $50

Services: IRA, Keogh, Corp, SEP, 403(b), Withdraw, Deduct

Tel Exchange: Yes **With MMF:** Yes

Registered: All states except NH

LIBERTY
Bond

Neuberger and Berman
Management Inc.
342 Madison Avenue
New York, NY 10173
(800) 367-0770/(212) 850-8300

	Years Ending 3/31					
	1982	1983	1984	1985	1986	1987
Net Investment Income ($)	.44	.34	.36	.37	.32	.43
Dividends from Net Investment Income ($)	.47	.36	.30	.40	.32	.38
Net Gains (Losses) on Investments ($)	(.44)	.58	.02	(.01)	.68	.20
Distributions from Net Realized Capital Gains ($)	–	–	–	–	–	–
Net Asset Value End of Year ($)	3.33	3.89	3.97	3.93	4.61	4.86
Ratio of Expenses to Net Assets (%)	1.50	1.50	1.50	2.00	2.00	1.98
Portfolio Turnover Rate (%)	58	171	225	110	256	186
Total Assets: End of Year (Millions $)	7.5	8.6	8.1	8.0	9.9	12.3

Annual Rate of Return (%) Years Ending 12/31	21.1	16.7	6.1	20.9	18.2	(4.6)

Five-Year Total Return(%)	68.8ᶜ	Degree of Diversification	NA	Beta	.26	Bull (%)	60.7ᴰ	Bear (%)	(8.0)ᶜ

Objective: Seeks a high level of current income by investing in a diversified portfolio of higher-yielding, lower-rated (BBB or lower) fixed-income securities. May invest in foreign securities.

Portfolio: (9/30/87) Corporate bonds 79%, corporate short-term notes 18%, preferred stocks 10%. Largest bond holdings: consumer goods & products 18%, retailing 10%.

Distributions: Income: Feb, April, July, Oct **Capital Gains:** May

12b-1: No

Minimum: Initial: $500 Subsequent: $50

Min IRA: Initial: $250 Subsequent: $50

Services: IRA, Keogh, Withdraw, Deduct

Tel Exchange: Yes **With MMF:** Yes

Registered: All states except AZ, IA, IL, LA, ME, MS, NC, NH, TN

LINDNER
DIVIDEND FUND
Balanced

Lindner Management Corp.
200 South Bemiston
P.O. Box 11208
St. Louis, MO 63105
(314) 727-5305

	9/30		Years Ending 2/28			
	1982	1983	1984* (5 mos.)	1985	1986	1987
Net Investment Income ($)	1.52	1.41	.62	1.76	1.90	1.85
Dividends from Net Investment Income ($)	1.45	1.47	.31	1.38	1.79	2.17
Net Gains (Losses) on Investments ($)	2.02	8.64	.44	1.83	1.92	3.17
Distributions from Net Realized Capital Gains ($)	–	–	5.24	.86	.01	3.26
Net Asset Value End of Year ($)	17.44	26.02	21.53	22.88	24.90	24.49
Ratio of Expenses to Net Assets (%)	1.00	.94	.42	1.14	.95	1.00
Portfolio Turnover Rate (%)	1	14	1	11	26	56
Total Assets: End of Year (Millions $)	.9	1.3	1.2	51.6	67.1	67.0

Annual Rate of Return (%) Years Ending 12/31	30.8	43.8	14.9	16.8	20.8	(4.1)

Five-Year Total Return(%)	123.7ᴬ	Degree of Diversification	NA	Beta	.30	Bull (%)	65.8ᴰ	Bear (%)	(9.2)ᶜ

Fiscal year changed from 9/30 to 2/28.

Objective: Seeks current income; capital appreciation is a secondary objective. Invests in high-yielding common stocks, preferred stocks, convertible securities and bonds. Under normal circumstances, the fund will invest at least 65% of its assets in common and preferred stocks.

Portfolio: (10/31/87) Preferred stocks 35%, common stocks 27%, convertible bonds 19%, non-convertible bonds 14%. Largest holdings: electric and gas utilities 35%, oil 13%.

Distributions: Income: Quarterly   **Capital Gains:** Annually

12b-1: No

Minimum: Initial: $2,000   Subsequent: $100

Min IRA: Initial: $250   Subsequent: $100

Services: IRA, Withdraw

Tel Exchange: No

Registered: CA, HI, IL, MO, NV, NJ, NY

LMH
Growth & Income

Heine Management Group, Inc.
253 Post Rd. West
P.O. Box 830
Westport, CT 06881
(800) 225-8558/(203) 222-1624

	Years Ending 6/30					
	1982	1983	1984	1985	1986	1987
Net Investment Income ($)	–	–	.20	.46	1.10	1.13
Dividends from Net Investment Income ($)	–	–	–	.11	.52	1.10
Net Gains (Losses) on Investments ($)	–	–	.35	4.51	4.12	.68
Distributions from Net Realized Capital Gains ($)	–	–	–	.11	.80	4.42
Net Asset Value End of Year ($)	–	–	20.55	25.30	29.20	25.49
Ratio of Expenses to Net Assets (%)	–	–	2.60	1.42	1.25	1.29
Portfolio Turnover Rate (%)	–	–	13	25	50	19
Total Assets: End of Year (Millions $)	–	–	30.5	77.1	83.9	76.7
Annual Rate of Return (%) Years Ending 12/31	–	–	9.4	22.8	14.1	(6.4)

Five-Year Total Return(%)	NA	Degree of Diversification	D	Beta	.50	Bull (%)	71.2[c]	Bear (%)	(14.5)[c]

Objective: Seeks capital appreciation through investment in common stocks of well-established, dividend-paying companies that are currently undervalued considering the strength of their financial position. May also invest in preferred stocks and convertible securities as well as up to 10% of total assets in U.S.-traded foreign securities.

Portfolio: (9/30/87) Commercial paper 55%, common stocks 44%, other assets 1%. Largest stock holdings: conglomerates 6%, life insurance 6%.

Distributions: Income: Annually   **Capital Gains:** Annually

12b-1: No

Minimum: Initial: $2,500   Subsequent: $1,000

Min IRA: Initial: $500   Subsequent: $500

Services: IRA, Keogh

Tel Exchange: No

Registered: All states except AL, TX

LOOMIS-SAYLES MUTUAL
Balanced

Loomis Sayles & Co., Inc.
P.O. Box 449
Back Bay Annex
Boston, MA 02117
(800) 345-4048/(617) 578-4200

	Years Ending 12/31					
	1982	1983	1984	1985	1986	1987
Net Investment Income ($)	1.09	.94	1.08	.94	.82	.87
Dividends from Net Investment Income ($)	1.09	1.09	.95	1.08	.94	1.06
Net Gains (Losses) on Investments ($)	4.26	.80	(.07)	4.66	4.20	2.25
Distributions from Net Realized Capital Gains ($)	–	–	1.86	–	2.75	4.52
Net Asset Value End of Year ($)	18.16	18.81	17.01	21.53	22.86	20.40
Ratio of Expenses to Net Assets (%)	.84	.87	.85	.86	.84	.94
Portfolio Turnover Rate (%)	102	194	135	186	127	197
Total Assets: End of Year (Millions $)	86.9	95.5	90.6	121.1	203.4	303.0

Annual Rate of Return (%) Years Ending 12/31	40.9	10.0	6.4	34.4	24.8	13.6

Five-Year Total Return(%) 123.2[A]	Degree of Diversification NA	Beta .92	Bull (%) 154.3[A]	Bear (%) (12.9)[C]

Objective: Seeks high total return from income and capital growth by investing in a diversified portfolio of stocks and bonds of seasoned, well-established, dividend-paying companies.

Portfolio: (12/31/87) Common stocks 65%, bonds and notes 27%, preferred stocks 6%, short-term securities 2%. Largest stock holdings: aluminum 15%, mining 10%.

Distributions: Income: Quarterly   **Capital Gains:** Annually

12b-1: No

Minimum: Initial: $250   Subsequent: $50

Min IRA: Initial: $25   Subsequent: $25

Services: IRA, Keogh, SEP, Withdraw, Deduct

Tel Exchange: Yes   **With MMF:** Yes

Registered: All states

MANHATTAN
Growth

Neuberger and Berman
Management Inc.
342 Madison Ave.
New York, NY 10173
(800) 367-0770/(212) 850-8300

	Years Ending 12/31					
	1982	1983	1984	1985	1986	1987
Net Investment Income ($)	.18	.19	.11	.07	.10	.14
Dividends from Net Investment Income ($)	.13	.17	.18	.11	.08	.26
Net Gains (Losses) on Investments ($)	.96	1.16	.31	2.34	1.31	(.07)
Distributions from Net Realized Capital Gains ($)	–	–	–	–	1.24	.95
Net Asset Value End of Year ($)	5.14	6.32	6.56	8.86	8.95	7.81
Ratio of Expenses to Net Assets (%)	1.50	1.30	1.50	1.40	1.10	1.0
Portfolio Turnover Rate (%)	177	173	186	155	96	111
Total Assets: End of Year (Millions $)	65.8	75.5	79.4	158.9	293.6	329.2

Annual Rate of Return (%) Years Ending 12/31	28.7	26.8	7.1	37.1	17.0	0.4

Five-Year Total Return(%)	118.7ᴬ	Degree of Diversification	A	Beta	1.11	Bull (%)	153.8ᴬ	Bear (%)	(27.5)ᴱ

Objective:	Seeks capital growth; any income received is incidental to growth objective. May invest in preferred stocks and debt securities without limitation as defensive tactic. Common stock investment is in well-established, leading companies with maximum growth potential.
Portfolio:	(12/31/87) Common stocks 102%, short-term corporate notes 10%. Largest stock holdings: oil & gas 9%, health care 9%.
Distributions:	Income: Feb **Capital Gains:** Feb
12b-1:	No
Minimum:	Initial: $1,000 Subsequent: $100
Min IRA:	Initial: $250 Subsequent: $50
Services:	IRA, Keogh, Withdraw, Deduct
Tel Exchange:	Yes **With MMF:** Yes
Registered:	All states except NH

MATHERS
Growth

Mathers & Company, Inc.
100 Corporate North, Suite 201
Bannockburn, IL 60015
(800) 926-3863/(312) 295-7400

	Years Ending 12/31					
	1982	1983	1984	1985	1986	1987
Net Investment Income ($)	.68	.86	.61	.75	.34	.43
Dividends from Net Investment Income ($)	.65	.63	.86	.55	.81	.88
Net Gains (Losses) on Investments ($)	2.11	2.49	(1.17)	4.30	2.16	3.92
Distributions from Net Realized Capital Gains ($)	1.00	1.49	2.68	1.82	7.38	5.97
Net Asset Value End of Year ($)	22.84	24.07	19.97	22.65	16.96	14.46
Ratio of Expenses to Net Assets (%)	.63	.60	.69	.74	.77	.82
Portfolio Turnover Rate (%)	35	85	71	278	174	202
Total Assets: End of Year (Millions $)	214.7	217.2	182.1	187.3	134.8	151.5
Annual Rate of Return (%) Years Ending 12/31	16.2	16.1	(1.5)	27.5	12.9	26.2

Five-Year Total Return(%)	107.9[A]	Degree of Diversification	D	Beta	.73	Bull (%)	117.3[B]	Bear (%)	(3.7)[C]

Objective: Long-term capital appreciation principally through investment in common stocks of growth companies and a small percentage of companies in special situations (mergers, etc.) or that are unseasoned. Current income is a secondary consideration.

Portfolio: (12/31/87) Common stocks 101%. Largest stock holdings: technology/electronics 15%, chemicals 10%.

Distributions: Income: Annually   **Capital Gains:** Annually

12b-1: No

Minimum: Initial: $1,000   Subsequent: $200

Min IRA: Initial: None   Subsequent: None

Services: IRA, Keogh

Tel Exchange: No

Registered: All states except AK, ID, ME, MT, ND, NH, SD, UT, VT, WY

MEDICAL
TECHNOLOGY
Aggressive Growth

AMA Advisers, Inc.
5 Sentry Pkwy. West
Suite 120, P.O. Box 1111
Blue Bell, PA 19422
(800) 262-3863/(215) 825-0400

	Years Ending 6/30					
	1982	**1983**	**1984**	**1985**	**1986**	**1987**
Net Investment Income ($)	.03	.03	(.04)	.02	(.02)	(.18)
Dividends from Net Investment Income ($)	.03	.02	.02	–	.02	–
Net Gains (Losses) on Investments ($)	(1.23)	6.04	(4.45)	2.00	5.56	1.12
Distributions from Net Realized Capital Gains ($)	.31	.02	.04	.07	.06	.19
Net Asset Value End of Year ($)	6.97	13.00	8.46	10.41	15.87	16.62
Ratio of Expenses to Net Assets (%)	1.56	1.40	1.56	1.49	1.44	1.90
Portfolio Turnover Rate (%)	18	8	23	21	15	6
Total Assets: End of Year (Millions $)	17.9	72.7	49.8	66.7	97.6	59.0

Annual Rate of Return (%) Years Ending 12/31	37.9	(0.7)	(12.5)	39.0	15.3	(1.9)

Five-Year Total Return(%)	36.7ᴱ	Degree of Diversification	D	Beta	1.19	Bull (%)	126.1ᴬ	Bear (%)	(25.2)ᴱ

Objective: Seeks capital appreciation through concentration of investments in companies engaged in the design, manufacture or sale of products or services which are derived from technology for use in medicine or health care. May move up to 75% of assets into defensive positions. May invest in foreign securities.

Portfolio: (9/30/87) Common stocks 94%, commercial paper 6%. Largest stock holdings: therapeutic technology 34%, supplies & equipment 19%.

Distributions: Income: July   **Capital Gains:** July

12b-1: Yes   **Amount:** 0.50%

Minimum: Initial: $1,000   **Subsequent:** None

Min IRA: Initial: $500   **Subsequent:** $50

Services: IRA, Keogh, Corp, 403(b), SEP, Withdraw, Deduct

Tel Exchange: Yes   **With MMF:** Yes

Registered: All states

MERIT
U.S. GOVERNMENT
Bond

Sav/Vest Securities Corp.
121 South Broad Street, 8th Floor
Philadelphia, PA 19107
(800) 992-2206

	Years Ending 12/31					
	1982	1983	1984	1985	1986 (3 mos.)	1987
Net Investment Income ($)	–	–	–	–	.22	.91
Dividends from Net Investment Income ($)	–	–	–	–	.22	.91
Net Gains (Losses) on Investments ($)	–	–	–	–	.20	(.60)
Distributions from Net Realized Capital Gains ($)	–	–	–	–	–	.10
Net Asset Value End of Year ($)	–	–	–	–	12.70	12.00
Ratio of Expenses to Net Assets (%)	–	–	–	–	–	.71
Portfolio Turnover Rate (%)	–	–	–	–	11	500
Total Assets: End of Year (Millions $)	–	–	–	–	12.1	11.7

Annual Rate of Return (%) Years Ending 12/31	–	–	–	–	–	2.9

Five-Year Total Return(%)	NA	Degree of Diversification	NA	Beta	NA	Bull (%)	NA	Bear (%)	4.4^A

Objective: Seeks high current income, preservation of capital and the maintenance of liquidity by investing primarily in debt securities issued or guaranteed by the U.S. government and its agencies. Will invest at least 65% of assets in U.S. government securities. May also invest in put and call options and futures contracts.

Portfolio: (12/31/87) U.S. Treasury notes 42%, FNMA obligations 26%, GNMA obligations 25%, repos 4%, other assets 3%.

Distributions: Income: Monthly   **Capital Gains:** Annually

12b-1: Yes   **Amount:** 0.25%

Minimum: Initial: $1,000   Subsequent: $100

Min IRA: Initial: $500   Subsequent: $100

Services: IRA, Keogh, Corp, SEP, 403(b), Withdraw, Deduct

Tel Exchange: Yes   **With MMF:** Yes

Registered: CA, CT, DC, DE, FL, GA, IL, IN, KY, LA, MA, MD, MI, MN, NC, NJ, NY, OH, PA, VA, WV.

MUTUAL OF OMAHA AMERICA

Bond

Mutual of Omaha Fund
Management Co.
10235 Regency Circle
Omaha, NE 68114
(800) 228-9596/(402) 397-8555

	Years Ending 12/31					
	1982	1983	1984	1985	1986	1987
Net Investment Income ($)	1.09	.97	1.01	.90	.92	.82
Dividends from Net Investment Income ($)	1.14	.94	1.03	.91	.92	.83
Net Gains (Losses) on Investments ($)	.37	(.39)	.05	.68	.21	(.76)
Distributions from Net Realized Capital Gains ($)	—	—	—	—	—	.03
Net Asset Value End of Year ($)	10.10	9.74	9.77	10.44	10.65	9.85
Ratio of Expenses to Net Assets (%)	1.38	1.21	1.11	1.05	.98	.98
Portfolio Turnover Rate (%)	NA	NA	NA	168	76	35
Total Assets: End of Year (Millions $)	11.0	20.4	19.1	28.3	49.1	53.1
Annual Rate of Return (%) Years Ending 12/31	15.4	6.6	11.7	16.9	11.1	0.7

Five-Year Total Return(%)	55.7[D]	Degree of Diversification	NA	Beta	.02	Bull (%)	37.4[E]	Bear (%)	3.6[A]

Objective:	Seeks current income through investing at least 80% of its total assets in the securities of the U.S. government or its instrumentalities.
Portfolio:	(12/31/87) U.S. government and agency securities 50%, U.S. government sponsored securities 41%, short-term securities 9%.
Distributions:	Income: Mar, June, Sept, Dec **Capital Gains:** Dec
12b-1:	No
Minimum:	Initial: $250 Subsequent: $50
Min IRA:	Initial: $250 Subsequent: $50
Services:	IRA, Keogh, Corp, 403(b), Withdraw, Deduct
Tel Exchange:	Yes **With MMF:** Yes
Registered:	All states

MUTUAL QUALIFIED INCOME
Balanced

Heine Securities Corporation
26 Broadway
New York, NY 10004
(800) 553-3014/(212) 908-4047

	Years Ending 12/31					
	1982	1983	1984	1985	1986	1987
Net Investment Income ($)	.31	.36	.42	.61	.90	.77
Dividends from Net Investment Income ($)	.30	.39	.35	.61	.85	.88
Net Gains (Losses) on Investments ($)	1.52	4.19	1.90	3.57	2.42	.86
Distributions from Net Realized Capital Gains ($)	.25	1.33	1.13	1.17	1.56	1.44
Net Asset Value End of Year ($)	13.08	15.91	16.75	19.15	20.06	19.37
Ratio of Expenses to Net Assets (%)	1.48	1.11	.81	.70	.68	.71
Portfolio Turnover Rate (%)	125	79	107	96	124	74
Total Assets: End of Year (Millions $)	28.9	56.3	178.1	432.5	561.4	686.3

Annual Rate of Return (%) Years Ending 12/31	15.4	34.9	14.7	25.5	16.9	7.6

Five-Year Total Return(%)	144.1[A]	Degree of Diversification	NA	Beta	.61	Bull (%)	105.6[B]	Bear (%)	(15.6)[C]

Objective: Primary objective is capital appreciation from either short- or long-term investment in companies involved in prospective mergers, consolidations, liquidations and reorganizations. Current income is a secondary objective.

Portfolio: (12/31/87) Common stocks 45%, short-term investments 17%, corporate bonds 12%, foreign investments 10%, bonds and notes in reorganization 7%, preferred stocks 6%, companies in liquidation 2%. Largest stock holdings: banking and financial institutions 7%, industrials 5%.

Distributions: Income: Annually   **Capital Gains:** Annually

12b-1: No

Minimum: Initial: $1,000   Subsequent: $50

Min IRA: Initial: $1,000   Subsequent: $50

Services: IRA, Keogh, 403(b), Withdraw, Deduct

Tel Exchange: No

Registered: All states except NE

MUTUAL SHARES
Balanced

Heine Securities Corporation
26 Broadway
New York, NY 10004
(800) 553-3014/(212) 908-4047

	Years Ending 12/31					
	1982	1983	1984	1985	1986	1987
Net Investment Income ($)	2.00	1.40	1.45	1.93	2.43	2.23
Dividends from Net Investment Income ($)	2.12	1.37	1.42	1.88	2.34	2.52
Net Gains (Losses) on Investments ($)	3.15	13.51	5.61	11.34	7.29	1.78
Distributions from Net Realized Capital Gains ($)	2.68	4.63	4.83	4.12	4.52	4.09
Net Asset Value End of Year ($)	40.58	49.49	50.30	57.57	60.43	57.83
Ratio of Expenses to Net Assets (%)	.78	.83	.73	.67	.70	.69
Portfolio Turnover Rate (%)	78	70	102	91	122	78
Total Assets: End of Year (Millions $)	154.1	241.1	496.0	1,076.2	1,402.6	1,684.6

Annual Rate of Return (%) Years Ending 12/31	13.4	37.0	14.4	26.6	16.9	6.2

Five-Year Total Return(%)	146.3[A]	Degree of Diversification	NA	Beta	.60	Bull (%)	104.7[B]	Bear (%)	(15.7)[C]

Objective: Primary objective is capital appreciation from either short- or long-term investment in the debt or equity securities of companies involved in prospective mergers, consolidations, liquidations and reorganizations. Income is secondary objective.

Portfolio: (12/31/87) Common stocks 47%, temporary investments 20%, corporate bonds 8%, foreign investments 8%, bonds and notes in reorganization 7%, preferred stocks 6%, companies in liquidation 2%. Largest stock holdings: banking and financial institutions 7%, transportation 6%.

Distributions: **Income:** Annually **Capital Gains:** Annually
12b-1: No
Minimum: **Initial:** $5,000 **Subsequent:** $100
Min IRA: **Initial:** $2,000 **Subsequent:** $100
Services: IRA, Keogh, 403(b), Withdraw, Deduct
Tel Exchange: No
Registered: All states except NE

NAESS & THOMAS SPECIAL

Aggressive Growth

Vanguard Group
Vanguard Financial Center
Valley Forge, PA 19482
(800) 662-7447/(215) 648-6000

	Years Ending 9/30					
	1982	1983	1984	1985	1986	1987
Net Investment Income ($)	.97	(.25)	.43	(.11)	(.03)	(.11)
Dividends from Net Investment Income ($)	.10	.91	—	.45	—	—
Net Gains (Losses) on Investments ($)	6.70	25.72	(12.76)	(1.54)	4.70	13.27
Distributions from Net Realized Capital Gains ($)	6.32	2.76	7.53	2.31	—	5.67
Net Asset Value End of Year ($)	37.51	59.31	39.45	35.04	39.71	47.20
Ratio of Expenses to Net Assets (%)	2.19	1.41	1.05	1.00	.92	.92
Portfolio Turnover Rate (%)	114	83	100	103	88	92
Total Assets: End of Year (Millions $)	16.0	41.2	37.1	31.6	30.8	35.1

Annual Rate of Return (%) Years Ending 12/31	47.2	17.9	(25.1)	21.7	0.0	(7.2)

Five-Year Total Return(%)	(0.2)[E]	Degree of Diversification	C	Beta 1.23	Bull (%) 60.5[D]	Bear (%) (31.6)[E]

Objective: Fund is intended for that portion of an investor's funds that can appropriately be invested in special risks of various kinds with the basic aim growth of principal. Invests in securities of small companies from different sectors of the economy. May invest up to 25% of assets in foreign securities.

Portfolio: (9/30/87) Common stocks 96%, cash 7%. Largest stock holdings: technology 19%, health care 13%.

Distributions: Income: Nov   **Capital Gains:** Nov

12b-1: No

Minimum: Initial: $3,000   Subsequent: $100

Min IRA: Initial: $500   Subsequent: $100

Services: IRA, Keogh, 403(b), Corp, SEP, Withdraw, Deduct

Tel Exchange: No

Registered: All states

NATIONAL INDUSTRIES FUND

Growth

Stonebridge Capital Mgmt., Inc.
5990 Greenwood Plaza Blvd.
Englewood, CO 80111
(303) 220-8500

	Years Ending 11/30					
	1982	1983	1984	1985	1986	1987
Net Investment Income ($)	.61	.38	.33	.25	.13	.09
Dividends from Net Investment Income ($)	.48	.61	.39	.34	.25	.13
Net Gains (Losses) on Investments ($)	(.78)	1.50	(1.14)	.99	1.39	(.68)
Distributions from Net Realized Capital Gains ($)	1.36	.43	1.17	.18	.50	1.32
Net Asset Value End of Year ($)	13.12	13.96	11.59	12.31	13.08	11.04
Ratio of Expenses to Net Assets (%)	1.70	1.67	1.70	1.70	1.68	1.65
Portfolio Turnover Rate (%)	76	50	57	70	74	68
Total Assets: End of Year (Millions $)	29.1	31.2	27.8	27.9	28.0	24.3

Annual Rate of Return (%) Years Ending 12/31	4.7	11.3	(2.3)	10.5	9.8	2.6

Five-Year Total Return(%)	35.4E	Degree of Diversification	B	Beta	.92	Bull (%)	70.9C	Bear (%)	(22.0)D

Objective: Seeks long-term capital appreciation and growth in income. Current income is a secondary consideration. Invests in companies that appear to have good prospects for increased earnings and dividends.

Portfolio: (11/30/87) Common stocks 82%, short-term securities 10%, U.S. government obligations 4%, cash 3%. Largest stock holdings: pharmaceuticals 14%, miscellaneous 11%.

Distributions: Income: Annually   **Capital Gains:** Annually

12b-1: No

Minimum: Initial: $250   Subsequent: $25

Min IRA: Initial: NA   Subsequent: NA

Services: Withdraw

Tel Exchange: No

Registered: All states

NEUBERGER & BERMAN MONEY MARKET PLUS
Bond

Neuberger & Berman
Management Inc.
342 Madison Ave.
New York, NY 10173
(800) 367-0770/(212) 850-8300

	Years Ending 2/28					
	1982	1983	1984	1985	1986	1987 (4 mos.)
Net Investment Income ($)	–	–	–	–	–	.18
Dividends from Net Investment Income ($)	–	–	–	–	–	.18
Net Gains (Losses) on Investments ($)	–	–	–	–	–	(.01)
Distributions from Net Realized Capital Gains ($)	–	–	–	–	–	–
Net Asset Value End of Year ($)	–	–	–	–	–	9.98
Ratio of Expenses to Net Assets (%)	–	–	–	–	–	.50
Portfolio Turnover Rate (%)	–	–	–	–	–	39
Total Assets: End of Year (Millions $)	–	–	–	–	–	66.8

Annual Rate of Return (%) Years Ending 12/31	–	–	–	–	–	5.5

Five-Year Total Return(%)	NA	Degree of Diversification	NA	Beta	NA	Bull (%)	NA	Bear (%)	2.2ᴬ

Objective: Seeks a higher total return than a conventional money market fund, while providing liquidity and a minimal risk to principal. The fund's average maturity can be expected to vary from as short as 30 days to as long as one year. Invests in short-term U.S. government securities and commerical paper.

Portfolio: (1/15/88) Corporate commerical paper 54%, U.S. government agency securities 10%, certificates of deposit 10%, corporate debt securities 9%, U.S. Treasury obligations 8%, mortgage-backed securities 8%, cash 1%.

Distributions: **Income:** Monthly   **Capital Gains:** Annually

12b-1: Yes   **Amount:** 0.15%

Minimum: **Initial:** $5,000   **Subsequent:** $200

Min IRA: **Initial:** $250   **Subsequent:** $200

Services: IRA, Keogh, Withdraw, Deduct

Tel Exchange: Yes   **With MMF:** Yes

Registered: All states except NH

NEUWIRTH
Aggressive Growth

Wood, Struthers & Winthrop
Management Corp.
140 Broadway
New York, NY 10005
(800) 225-8011/(816) 283-1700

	Years Ending 12/31					
	1982	1983	1984	1985	1986	1987
Net Investment Income ($)	.18	(.03)	.06	.05	(.07)	(.07)
Dividends from Net Investment Income ($)	.06	.16	—	.08	.04	—
Net Gains (Losses) on Investments ($)	2.20	1.62	(1.28)	4.27	1.47	(1.23)
Distributions from Net Realized Capital Gains ($)	—	—	.37	—	3.21	.54
Net Asset Value End of Year ($)	11.13	12.56	10.98	15.21	13.35	11.52
Ratio of Expenses to Net Assets (%)	1.79	1.58	1.64	1.55	1.78	1.69
Portfolio Turnover Rate (%)	120	81	83	86	74	117
Total Assets: End of Year (Millions $)	20.1	23.0	18.2	23.9	23.3	21.1
Annual Rate of Return (%) Years Ending 12/31	28.1	15	(8.0)	39.1	8.7	(10.7)

Five-Year Total Return(%)	42.8ᴱ	Degree of Diversification	D	Beta	1.14	Bull (%)	110.8ᴮ	Bear (%)	(29.4)ᴱ

Objective: Seeks capital growth through investment in securities of established companies in growth industries. May invest in lesser-known emerging growth companies and up to 20% of total assets may be invested in foreign securities. May write put and call options.

Portfolio: (12/30/87) Common stocks 94%, U.S. government obligations 5%, convertible preferred stocks 1%, equity funds 1%. Largest stock holdings: consumer cyclicals 28%, technology 19%.

Distributions: Income: Dec   Capital Gains: Dec

12b-1: Yes   Amount: 0.85%

Minimum: Initial: $1,000   Subsequent: $100

Min IRA: Initial: $250   Subsequent: $100

Services: IRA, Keogh, Withdraw

Tel Exchange: No

Registered: All states except AR, AZ, CA, TN, TX, WI

NEW BEGINNING GROWTH
Aggressive Growth

Sit Investment Associates, Inc.
1714 First Bank Place West
Minneapolis, MN 55402
(612) 332-3223

		Years Ending 6/30				
	1982	1983	1984	1985	1986	1987
Net Investment Income ($)	–	.07	.20	.21	.04	.02
Dividends from Net Investment Income ($)	–	.08	.17	.23	–	.05
Net Gains (Losses) on Investments ($)	–	13.36	(3.77)	4.87	9.75	4.61
Distributions from Net Realized Capital Gains ($)	–	1.01	.39	.76	–	3.82
Net Asset Value End of Year ($)	–	23.01	18.88	22.97	32.76	33.52
Ratio of Expenses to Net Assets (%)	–	1.50	1.50	1.50	1.32	1.20
Portfolio Turnover Rate (%)	–	67	80	130	99	81
Total Assets: End of Year (Millions $)	–	9.4	13.3	19.6	40.8	56.1

Annual Rate of Return (%) Years Ending 12/31	–	27.0	(3.1)	43.6	10.4	5.5

Five-Year Total Return(%)	106.0[A]	Degree of Diversification	C	Beta	1.13	Bull (%)	132.9[A]	Bear (%)	(24.6)[D]

Objective: Seeks to maximize long-term capital appreciation. Invests primarily in the common stock of small emerging-growth companies. For defensive purposes, can invest 100% of assets in corporate or government fixed-income securities.

Portfolio: (9/30/87) Common stocks 90%, other assets 9%, convertible bonds 1%. Largest stock holdings: technology 24%, capital goods/construction 16%.

Distributions: Income: Annually   **Capital Gains:** Annually

12b-1: No

Minimum: Initial: $10,000   Subsequent: $100

Min IRA: Initial: None   Subsequent: None

Services: IRA, Keogh, Corp, SEP, Deduct

Tel Exchange: Yes   **With MMF:** No

Registered: CA, CO, CT, DC, DE, FL, IA, IL, IN, KS, MA, MD, MI, MN, MO, MS, NJ, NY, OH, PA, TX, VA, WA, WI, WY

NEWTON GROWTH
Growth

M&I Investment Management Corp.
330 E. Kilbourn Ave.
Two Plaza East, #1150
Milwaukee, WI 53202
(800) 247-7039/(414) 347-1141

	Years Ending 12/31					
	1982	**1983**	**1984**	**1985**	**1986**	**1987**
Net Investment Income ($)	.56	.20	.55	.69	.41	.26
Dividends from Net Investment Income ($)	.55	.19	.52	–	1.06	.27
Net Gains (Losses) on Investments ($)	6.09	5.30	(2.74)	6.25	1.83	(1.01)
Distributions from Net Realized Capital Gains ($)	.77	1.89	–	–	11.73	1.30
Net Asset Value End of Year ($)	23.64	27.06	24.35	31.29	20.74	18.42
Ratio of Expenses to Net Assets (%)	1.21	1.16	1.17	1.18	1.23	1.20
Portfolio Turnover Rate (%)	72	55	44	143	136	96
Total Assets: End of Year (Millions $)	21.6	31.5	30.0	33.9	33.9	31.9

Annual Rate of Return (%) Years Ending 12/31	36.1	23.5	(8.2)	28.7	9.1	(3.6)

Five-Year Total Return(%)	53.3[D]	Degree of Diversification	C	Beta	1.07	Bull (%)	105.7[B]	Bear (%)	(31.2)[E]

Objective: Long-term growth of capital through investment primarily in common stocks of large, established companies that are dividend-paying. Current income of lesser importance.

Portfolio: (12/31/87) Common stocks 86%, short-term securities 11%, convertible corporate bonds 2%, other assets 1%. Largest stock holdings: capital goods 46%, consumer goods & services 12%.

Distributions: Income: Annually   **Capital Gains:** Annually

12b-1: Yes   **Amount:** 0.25%

Minimum: Initial: $1,000   Subsequent: $50

Min IRA: Initial: $500   Subsequent: $50

Services: IRA, Keogh, Corp, SEP, 403(b), Withdraw, Deduct

Tel Exchange: Yes   **With MMF:** Yes

Registered: All states except DE, ID, KY, MS, MT, NE, OK, SC, SD, VT

NEWTON INCOME
Bond

M&I Investment Mgmt. Corp.
330 E. Kilbourn
Two Plaza East, #1150
Milwaukee, WI 53202
(800) 247-7039/(414) 347-1141

	Years Ending 7/31					
	1982	1983	1984	1985	1986	1987
Net Investment Income ($)	.87	.87	.82	.76	.78	.61
Dividends from Net Investment Income ($)	.87	.87	.82	.77	.60	.66
Net Gains (Losses) on Investments ($)	(.11)	1.05	.03	.31	.14	(.30)
Distributions from Net Realized Capital Gains ($)	—	—	—	—	—	—
Net Asset Value End of Year ($)	6.84	7.89	7.92	8.22	8.54	8.19
Ratio of Expenses to Net Assets (%)	1.72	1.49	1.66	1.60	1.51	1.46
Portfolio Turnover Rate (%)	43	41	0	480	56	15
Total Assets: End of Year (Millions $)	5.1	6.3	7.1	11.7	11.5	13.9
Annual Rate of Return (%) Years Ending 12/31	30.2	11.6	12.2	12.8	9.0	2.5

Five-Year Total Return(%)	58.0ᴰ	Degree of Diversification	NA	Beta	.02	Bull (%)	31.4ᴱ	Bear (%)	2.1ᴬ

Objective: Seeks above-average income through investment in investment-grade bonds (rated Baa or BBB or better) varying in maturity as fits in relationship with current economic conditions. May invest in income-producing common stocks.

Portfolio: (7/31/87) Corporate bonds 34%, federal agency securities 33%, U.S. government securities 22%, short-term securities 13%.

Distributions: Income: Feb, May, Aug, Nov   **Capital Gains:** Aug

12b-1: Yes   **Amount:** 0.25%

Minimum: Initial: $1,000   Subsequent: $50

Min IRA: Initial: $500   Subsequent: $50

Services: IRA, Keogh, Corp, SEP, 403(b), Withdraw, Deduct

Tel Exchange: Yes   **With MMF:** Yes

Registered: Call for availability

NICHOLAS
Growth

Nicholas Company, Inc.
700 N. Water St., #1010
Milwaukee, WI 53202
(800) 227-5987/(414) 272-6133

	Years Ending 3/31					
	1982	1983	1984	1985	1986	1987
Net Investment Income ($)	.63	.68	.66	.62	.89	1.03
Dividends from Net Investment Income ($)	.52	.62	.64	.64	.57	.88
Net Gains (Losses) on Investments ($)	(1.74)	8.99	.44	6.37	6.31	4.72
Distributions from Net Realized Capital Gains ($)	.84	1.01	1.07	1.58	.61	.19
Net Asset Value End of Year ($)	17.04	25.08	24.47	29.24	35.26	39.94
Ratio of Expenses to Net Assets (%)	1.03	.95	.87	.82	.86	.86
Portfolio Turnover Rate (%)	45	31	22	14	14	27
Total Assets: End of Year (Millions $)	56.6	126.1	153.4	309.0	955.5	1,298.9
Annual Rate of Return (%) Years Ending 12/31	35.5	23.9	9.9	29.7	11.7	(1.3)

Five-Year Total Return(%)	94.7[B]	Degree of Diversification	C	Beta	.68	Bull (%)	101.5[B]	Bear (%)	(19.1)[C]

Objective: Capital appreciation through investment primarily in common stocks showing favorable long-term prospects. Investment in unseasoned companies is limited to 5%.

Portfolio: (9/30/87) Common stocks 69%, short-term securities 27%, convertible bonds 3%, convertible preferred stocks 1%. Largest stock holdings: insurance 11%, banks and savings & loan 11%.

Distributions: Income: Annually   **Capital Gains:** Annually
12b-1: No
Minimum: Initial: $500   Subsequent: $100
Min IRA: Initial: $500   Subsequent: $100
Services: IRA, Keogh, SEP, Withdraw, Deduct
Tel Exchange: No
Registered: All states

NICHOLAS II
Growth

Nicholas Company, Inc.
700 N. Water St., #1010
Milwaukee, WI 53202
(800) 227-5987/(414) 272-6133

	\multicolumn{6}{c}{Years Ending 9/30}
	1982	1983	1984	1985	1986	1987
Net Investment Income ($)	–	–	.09	.18	.40	.24
Dividends from Net Investment Income ($)	–	–	–	.09	.16	.42
Net Gains (Losses) on Investments ($)	–	–	1.57	2.83	2.33	4.80
Distributions from Net Realized Capital Gains ($)	–	–	–	.19	.06	.51
Net Asset Value End of Year ($)	–	–	11.66	14.39	16.90	21.01
Ratio of Expenses to Net Assets (%)	–	–	1.85	1.11	.79	.74
Portfolio Turnover Rate (%)	–	–	29	10	15	26
Total Assets: End of Year (Millions $)	–	–	11.4	140.1	299.2	432.3
Annual Rate of Return (%) Years Ending 12/31	–	–	16.9	33.8	10.3	7.2

Five-Year Total Return(%)	NA	Degree of Diversification	C	Beta	.81	Bull (%)	124.2ᴬ	Bear (%)	(19.1)ᶜ

Objective: Primary objective is long-term growth; current income is a secondary consideration. Invests primarily in common stocks which are believed to have favorable long-term growth prospects. May invest 5% of the fund's assets in unseasoned companies which have an operating history of less than three years.

Portfolio: (9/30/87) Common stocks 80%, short-term securities 18%, convertible preferred stocks 1%, convertible bonds 1%. Largest stock holdings: insurance 9%, retail trade 6%.

Distributions: **Income:** Annually **Capital Gains:** Annually
12b-1: No
Minimum: **Initial:** $1,000 **Subsequent:** $100
Min IRA: **Initial:** $1,000 **Subsequent:** $100
Services: IRA, Keogh, SEP, Withdraw, Deduct
Tel Exchange: No
Registered: All states

NICHOLAS INCOME
Bond

Nicholas Company, Inc.
700 N. Water St., #1010
Milwaukee, WI 53202
(800) 227-5987/(414) 272-6133

	Years Ending 12/31					
	1982	1983	1984	1985	1986	1987
Net Investment Income ($)	.46	.44	.45	.43	.40	.38
Dividends from Net Investment Income ($)	.46	.44	.44	.42	.38	.47
Net Gains (Losses) on Investments ($)	.54	(.01)	(.03)	.30	.03	(.28)
Distributions from Net Realized Capital Gains ($)	—	—	—	—	—	—
Net Asset Value End of Year ($)	3.68	3.67	3.65	3.96	4.01	3.64
Ratio of Expenses to Net Assets (%)	1.00	1.00	1.00	1.00	.96	.86
Portfolio Turnover Rate (%)	31	19	14	12	20	48
Total Assets: End of Year (Millions $)	13.2	14.6	16.9	34.8	65.0	69.7
Annual Rate of Return (%) Years Ending 12/31	34.9	12.4	12.6	21.2	11.4	2.6

Five-Year Total Return(%)	75.3[C]	Degree of Diversification	NA	Beta	.11	Bull (%)	53.7[D]	Bear (%)	0.2[B]

Objective: High current income and consistent conservation of capital. Must invest at least 25% of total assets in geographically diversified and state-regulated electric utilities and systems. Balance is invested in investment-grade debt securities and may include repos and other cash investments.

Portfolio: (12/31/87) Non-convertible bonds 84%, short-term securities 7%, convertible bonds 3%, preferred stocks 3%, cash 3%.

Distributions: Income: Jan, April, July, Oct   **Capital Gains:** Jan
12b-1: No
Minimum: Initial: $500   Subsequent: $50
Min IRA: Initial: $500   Subsequent: $50
Services: IRA, Keogh, SEP, Withdraw, Deduct
Tel Exchange: No
Registered: All states

NODDINGS CONVERTIBLE STRATEGIES
Growth & Income

Noddings Investment Group, Inc.
Two Mid America Plaza
Suite 920
Oakbrook Terrace, IL 60181
(800) 544-7785/(312) 954-1322

	Years Ending 4/30						10/31
	1982	1983	1984	1985	1986 (10 mos.)	1987	1987* (6 mos.)
Net Investment Income ($)	–	–	–	–	.35	.45	.34
Dividends from Net Investment Income ($)	–	–	–	–	.15	.42	.20
Net Gains (Losses) on Investments ($)	–	–	–	–	1.57	.33	(.86)
Distributions from Net Realized Capital Gains ($)	–	–	–	–	–	.60	.21
Net Asset Value End of Year ($)	–	–	–	–	11.77	11.53	10.60
Ratio of Expenses to Net Assets (%)	–	–	–	–	2.0	1.7	1.70
Portfolio Turnover Rate (%)	–	–	–	–	37	62	40
Total Assets: End of Year (Millions $)	–	–	–	–	5.4	12.7	8.7

Annual Rate of Return (%) Years Ending 12/31	–	–	–	–	15.6	(2.9)	*

Five-Year Total Return(%)	NA	Degree of Diversification	NA	Beta	NA	Bull (%)	NA	Bear (%)	(9.4)c

*Fiscal year end changed from 4/30 to 10/31. All annual return figures are for full years ending 12/31.

Objective: Seeks long-term capital appreciation through investment in a diversified portfolio of convertible securities. During normal conditions at least 65% of the fund's assets will be invested in convertibles, some of which are rated BB or lower by Standard & Poor's. May also sell stocks short against their convertible positions.

Portfolio: (10/31/87) Convertible bonds 74%, index put options 10%, demand notes 10%, other assets 5%, warrants 3%. Largest holdings: capital goods-technology 23%, consumer growth staples 21%.

Distributions: Income: Quarterly   **Capital Gains:** Annually
12b-1: No
Minimum: Initial: $5,000   Subsequent: None
Min IRA: Initial: $2,000   Subsequent: None
Services: IRA, Keogh, SEP, Withdraw, Deduct
Tel Exchange: No
Registered: Call for availability

NOMURA PACIFIC BASIN
International

Nomura Capital Management
180 Maiden Lane
New York, NY 10038
(800) 833-0018/(212) 208-9366

	Years Ending 3/31					
	1982	1983	1984	1985	1986 (9 mos.)	1987
Net Investment Income ($)	–	–	–	–	.06	.03
Dividends from Net Investment Income ($)	–	–	–	–	–	–
Net Gains (Losses) on Investments ($)	–	–	–	–	5.62	8.85
Distributions from Net Realized Capital Gains ($)	–	–	–	–	–	.36
Net Asset Value End of Year ($)	–	–	–	–	15.68	24.20
Ratio of Expenses to Net Assets (%)	–	–	–	–	1.50	1.45
Portfolio Turnover Rate (%)	–	–	–	–	3	46
Total Assets: End of Year (Millions $)	–	–	–	–	32.4	81.8

Annual Rate of Return (%) Years Ending 12/31	–	–	–	–	74.4	33.8

Five-Year Total Return(%)	NA	Degree of Diversification	NA	Beta	NA	Bull (%)	NA	Bear (%)	(9.6)^c

Objective: Seeks long-term capital appreciation primarily through investment of 70% of the fund's assets in equity securities of corporations located in the Pacific Basin, including Japan, Australia and the Philippines. Portfolio companies will range from large and well-established to small and unseasoned.

Portfolio: (9/30/87) Common stocks 84%, short-term securities 13%. Largest country holdings: Japan 71%, Australia 5%.

Distributions: Income: Semiannually   **Capital Gains:** Annually

12b-1: Yes   **Amount:** Pd. by Advisor

Minimum: Initial: $10,000   **Subsequent:** $5,000

Min IRA: Initial: $10,000   **Subsequent:** $5,000

Services: IRA

Tel Exchange: No

Registered: AK, AZ, CA, CO, CT, DE, FL, GA, HI, ID, IL, IN, MA, MD, MI, MN, MO, MS, NJ, NV, NY, OH, OR, PA, TN, TX, UT, VA, WA, WI, WV, WY

NORTHEAST INVESTORS GROWTH

Growth

Northeast Management &
Research Co., Inc.
50 Congress Street
Boston, MA 02109
(800) 225-6704/(617) 523-3588

	Years Ending 12/31					
	1982	1983	1984	1985	1986	1987
Net Investment Income ($)	.30	.13	.13	.11	.08	.14
Dividends from Net Investment Income ($)	.22	.21	.12	.05	.13	.12
Net Gains (Losses) on Investments ($)	.91	1.05	.29	3.91	3.56	(.79)
Distributions from Net Realized Capital Gains ($)	.12	.15	.30	.09	.52	.62
Net Asset Value End of Year ($)	10.54	11.36	11.36	15.24	18.23	16.84
Ratio of Expenses to Net Assets (%)	2.47	2.01	2.02	2.00	1.87	1.60
Portfolio Turnover Rate (%)	66	63	34	37	13	36
Total Assets: End of Year (Millions $)	2.8	4.0	4.1	6.4	20.5	20.8
Annual Rate of Return (%) Years Ending 12/31	15.2	9.6	3.9	36.7	24.3	(4.3)

Five-Year Total Return(%)	85.2[B]	Degree of Diversification	B	Beta	.99	Bull (%)	149.7[A]	Bear (%)	(27.2)[E]

Objective: Seeks long-term growth of both capital and future income. Invests in stocks, bonds and short-term money market instruments. Ordinarily no more than 25% of the fund's assets will be invested in fixed-income securities.

Portfolio: (12/31/87) Common stocks 95%, repurchase agreements 5%. Largest stock holdings: drug companies and health 20%, food and beverages 20%.

Distributions: Income: Annually   **Capital Gains:** Annually

12b-1: No

Minimum: Initial: $1,000   Subsequent: None

Min IRA: Initial: $500   Subsequent: None

Services: IRA, Keogh, 403(b)

Tel Exchange: Yes   **With MMF:** No

Registered: All states except AL

NORTHEAST INVESTORS TRUST
Bond

Trustees, Northeast
Investor's Trust
50 Congress St.
Boston, MA 02109
(800) 225-6704/(617) 523-3588

	Years Ending 9/30					
	1982	1983	1984	1985	1986	1987
Net Investment Income ($)	1.43	1.47	1.45	1.48	1.47	1.55
Dividends from Net Investment Income ($)	1.41	1.44	1.46	1.46	1.46	1.46
Net Gains (Losses) on Investments ($)	1.48	.92	(.84)	1.19	1.40	(.80)
Distributions from Net Realized Capital Gains ($)	—	—	—	—	—	—
Net Asset Value End of Year ($)	10.88	11.83	10.98	12.19	13.60	12.89
Ratio of Expenses to Net Assets (%)	.69	.67	.67	.72	.72	.76
Portfolio Turnover Rate (%)	7	30	14	22	43	52
Total Assets: End of Year (Millions $)	145.4	169.4	168.2	218.1	313.3	347.9
Annual Rate of Return (%) Years Ending 12/31	36.9	11.2	13.9	25.6	20.4	0.1

Five-Year Total Return(%)	91.7[B]	Degree of Diversification	NA	Beta	.16	Bull (%)	80.7[C]	Bear (%)	(5.1)[C]

Objective: Seeks production of income with capital growth as a secondary objective. Between 25% and 50% of the trust's assets will be invested in the electric utility industry. Common stock investments will be in established, dividend-paying companies. May use leverage.

Portfolio: (9/30/87) Corporate bonds 111%. Largest bond holdings: banks and finance 19%, retail 18%.

Distributions: Income: Feb, May, Aug, Nov   **Capital Gains:** Sept

12b-1: No

Minimum: Initial: $1,000   **Subsequent:** None

Min IRA: Initial: $500   **Subsequent:** None

Services: IRA, Keogh, 403(b)

Tel Exchange: Yes   **With MMF:** No

Registered: All states

100 FUND
Aggressive Growth

Berger Associates, Inc.
899 Logan St., Suite 211
Denver, CO 80203
(800) 333-1001/(303) 837-1020

	Years Ending 9/30					
	1982	**1983**	**1984**	**1985**	**1986**	**1987**
Net Investment Income ($)	.14	(.09)	.32	(.10)	(.12)	(.10)
Dividends from Net Investment Income ($)	.27	.13	—	.34	—	—
Net Gains (Losses) on Investments ($)	.25	7.51	(6.34)	.99	5.25	5.75
Distributions from Net Realized Capital Gains ($)	—	—	—	—	—	1.16
Net Asset Value End of Year ($)	13.20	20.49	14.47	15.02	20.15	24.64
Ratio of Expenses to Net Assets (%)	1.75	1.70	1.90	2.00	1.71	1.61
Portfolio Turnover Rate (%)	137	155	272	130	122	106
Total Assets: End of Year (Millions $)	10.3	14.4	9.6	8.9	10.6	11.7

Annual Rate of Return (%) Years Ending 12/31	13.0	17.0	(20.1)	25.7	20.0	15.7

Five-Year Total Return(%) 63.1ᴰ	Degree of Diversification E	Beta .89	Bull (%) 88.1ᶜ	Bear (%) (10.7)ᶜ

Objective: Long-term capital appreciation through investment in common stocks of established companies on the basis of fundamental analysis, industry trends and earnings trends in relation to the current market environment.

Portfolio: (9/30/87) Common stocks 89%, U.S. government obligations 9%, other assets 2%. Largest stock holdings: information services 12%, pollution control 9%.

Distributions: Income: Oct   **Capital Gains:** Annually

12b-1: Yes   **Amount:** 0.30%

Minimum: Initial: $250   Subsequent: $50

Min IRA: Initial: $250   Subsequent: $50

Services: IRA, Keogh, Withdraw

Tel Exchange: Yes   **With MMF:** No

Registered: CA, CO, FL, HI, MA, MD, MI, MS, NJ, NY, TX, WA

101 FUND
Growth

Berger Associates, Inc.
899 Logan St., Suite 211
Denver, CO 80203
(800) 333-1001/(303) 837-1020

	Years Ending 9/30					
	1982	**1983**	**1984**	**1985**	**1986**	**1987**
Net Investment Income ($)	.50	.49	.52	.33	.57	.66
Dividends from Net Investment Income ($)	.53	.48	.45	.43	.57	.60
Net Gains (Losses) on Investments ($)	(.47)	5.41	(.69)	1.11	3.86	2.30
Distributions from Net Realized Capital Gains ($)	—	—	1.00	—	.29	3.00
Net Asset Value End of Year ($)	9.48	14.90	13.28	14.29	17.86	17.22
Ratio of Expenses to Net Assets (%)	2.00	2.00	2.00	2.00	1.96	1.79
Portfolio Turnover Rate (%)	120	168	267	166	187	241
Total Assets: End of Year (Millions $)	0.9	1.3	1.4	1.6	2.7	2.8

Annual Rate of Return (%) Years Ending 12/31	13.8	35.2	(0.3)	29.1	15.0	(2.6)

Five-Year Total Return(%)	95.0[B]	Degree of Diversification	C	Beta	.80	Bull (%)	84.8[C]	Bear (%)	(19.2)[D]

Objective: Seeks capital appreciation and a moderate level of current income through investment in dividend-paying common stocks of large, established companies and senior debt securities.

Portfolio: (9/30/87) Convertible debentures 54%, common stocks 25%, corporate debentures 14%, convertible preferred stocks 5%, other assets 3%. Largest stock holdings: electric utilities 6%, insurance 5%.

Distributions: Income: Quarterly   **Capital Gains:** Annually
12b-1: Yes   **Amount:** 0.30%
Minimum: Initial: $250   **Subsequent:** $50
Min IRA: Initial: $250   **Subsequent:** $50
Services: IRA, Keogh, Withdraw
Tel Exchange: Yes   **With MMF:** No
Registered: CA, CO, FL, HI, MA, MD, MI, MS, NJ, NY, TX, WA

PARTNERS
Growth & Income

Neuberger and Berman
Management Inc.
342 Madison Ave.
New York, NY 10173
(800) 367-0770/(212) 850-8300

	Years Ending 6/30					
	1982	1983	1984	1985	1986	1987
Net Investment Income ($)	1.20	.83	.74	.65	.42	.44
Dividends from Net Investment Income ($)	.95	1.11	.84	.72	.65	.44
Net Gains (Losses) on Investments ($)	(.74)	4.47	(1.02)	3.63	4.71	2.45
Distributions from Net Realized Capital Gains ($)	3.30	–	1.96	.27	1.27	2.25
Net Asset Value End of Year ($)	13.02	17.21	14.13	17.42	20.63	20.83
Ratio of Expenses to Net Assets (%)	1.08	.97	.91	.93	.89	.86
Portfolio Turnover Rate (%)	244	232	227	146	181	169
Total Assets: End of Year (Millions $)	74.4	139.3	146.3	221.9	433.3	757.8

Annual Rate of Return (%) Years Ending 12/31	26.6	19.1	8.2	29.8	17.3	4.2

Five-Year Total Return(%)	104.4[A]	Degree of Diversification	A	Beta	.79	Bull (%)	122.3[B]	Bear (%)	(19.5)[D]

Objective: Seeks capital growth by investing primarily in securities of large, established, dividend-paying companies which are believed to offer appreciation potential. Seeks short-term gains. May invest in investment-grade debt securities, repurchase agreements and foreign securities, and may write covered call options.

Portfolio: (6/30/87) Common stocks 77%, U.S. government obligations 19%, repos 3%, corporate notes 1%. Largest stock holdings: retailing 8%, banking & financial services 8%.

Distributions: Income: Aug   **Capital Gains:** Aug

12b-1: No

Minimum: Initial: $500   Subsequent: $50

Min IRA: Initial: $250   Subsequent: $50

Services: IRA, Keogh, Withdraw, Deduct

Tel Exchange: Yes   **With MMF:** Yes

Registered: All states except NH

PAX WORLD
International

Pax World Management Corp.
224 State St.
Portsmouth, NH 03801
(603) 431-8022

	Years Ending 12/31					
	1982	1983	1984	1985	1986	1987
Net Investment Income ($)	.46	.49	.56	.53	.46	.58
Dividends from Net Investment Income ($)	.41	.49	.51	.52	.50	.75
Net Gains (Losses) on Investments ($)	1.13	1.88	.22	2.23	.60	(.20)
Distributions from Net Realized Capital Gains ($)	.21	.28	.77	.37	.71	1.24
Net Asset Value End of Year ($)	10.37	11.97	11.47	13.34	13.19	11.58
Ratio of Expenses to Net Assets (%)	1.50	1.40	1.50	1.40	1.20	1.10
Portfolio Turnover Rate (%)	38	29	34	48	57	124
Total Assets: End of Year (Millions $)	7.1	12.2	16.9	32.7	53.8	65.8

Annual Rate of Return (%) Years Ending 12/31	18.4	24.1	7.5	25.5	8.4	2.2

Five-Year Total Return(%)	85.5[B]	Degree of Diversification	B	Beta	.62	Bull (%)	86.9[C]	Bear (%)	(14.9)[C]

Objective: Primarily seeks income and, secondarily, long-term capital growth. Endeavors to contribute to world peace through investment in companies producing life-supportive goods and services. Will not invest in companies engaging in or contributing to military activities or those in the liquor, gambling or tobacco industries.

Portfolio: (12/31/87) Common stocks 68%, government bonds 29%, cash 2%, CDs 1%. Largest stock holdings: natural gas 15%, drugs 13%.

Distributions: Income: July, Dec   **Capital Gains:** Dec

12b-1: Yes   **Amount:** 0.25%

Minimum: Initial: $250   Subsequent: $50

Min IRA: Initial: $250   Subsequent: $50

Services: IRA, Keogh, SEP, 403(b), Withdraw

Tel Exchange: No

Registered: All states except NE

PENN SQUARE MUTUAL
Growth & Income

Penn Square Management Corp.
P.O. Box 1419
Reading, PA 19603
(800) 523-8440/(215) 670-1031

	Years Ending 12/31					
	1982	1983	1984	1985	1986	1987
Net Investment Income ($)	.46	.41	.41	.38	.39	.34
Dividends from Net Investment Income ($)	.49	.43	.42	.37	.39	.35
Net Gains (Losses) on Investments ($)	.97	1.85	(.39)	1.72	.76	.15
Distributions from Net Realized Capital Gains ($)	.56	.61	.70	.53	1.25	.78
Net Asset Value End of Year ($)	8.38	9.60	8.50	9.70	9.21	8.57
Ratio of Expenses to Net Assets (%)	.66	.63	.65	.74	.80	.81
Portfolio Turnover Rate (%)	21	34	16	24	22	15
Total Assets: End of Year (Millions $)	155.3	182.2	171.3	198.8	198.9	188.8

Annual Rate of Return (%) Years Ending 12/31	20.7	29.3	0.5	26.6	12.9	4.9

Five-Year Total Return(%)	95.0[B]	Degree of Diversification	A	Beta	.85	Bull (%)	112.2[B]	Bear (%)	(21.3)[D]

Objective: Seeks long-term capital growth through the common stocks of only 30 to 50 large, well-established companies from a cross-section of industries.

Portfolio: (12/31/87) Common stocks 80%, short-term securities 19%. Largest stock holdings: health care 10%, electronics and telecommunications 9%.

Distributions: Income: Jan, April, July, Oct   **Capital Gains:** Dec

12b-1: No

Minimum: Initial: $500   Subsequent: $100

Min IRA: Initial: $250   Subsequent: None

Services: IRA, Keogh, Corp, SEP, Withdraw

Tel Exchange: Yes   **With MMF:** Yes

Registered: All states

PERMANENT PORTFOLIO†
Growth

World Money Managers
7 Fourth Street, Suite 14
Petaluma, CA 94952
(800) 531-5142/(512) 453-7558

	12/31		Years Ending 1/31			
	1982	1983	1984* (1 mo.)	1985	1986	1987
Net Investment Income ($)	1.26	.38	.02	.39	.33	.33
Dividends from Net Investment Income ($)	–	–	Nil	–	–	–
Net Gains (Losses) on Investments ($)	–	.24	(.15)	(1.32)	.73	1.45
Distributions from Net Realized Capital Gains ($)	–	–	Nil	–	–	–
Net Asset Value End of Year ($)	11.26	11.88	11.75	10.82	11.88	13.66
Ratio of Expenses to Net Assets (%)	.82	.92	.92	.90	.90	1.17
Portfolio Turnover Rate (%)	0	2	0	11	17	31
Total Assets: End of Year (Millions $)	5.5	69.9	68.9	71.1	73.0	72.5

Annual Rate of Return (%) Years Ending 12/31	–	5.5	(12.9)	12.2	13.6	13.1

Five-Year Total Return(%)	32.5ᴱ	Degree of Diversification	E	Beta	.24	Bull (%)	48.1ᴱ	Bear (%)	(3.5)ᴮ

Changed fiscal year-end from 12/31 to 1/31.

Objective: Invests a fixed "target percentage" of its net assets in gold, silver, Swiss francs, real estate and natural resource company stocks, and other stocks with the aim of preserving and increasing "purchasing power." Strives for long-term asset appreciation.

Portfolio: (7/31/87) U.S. government securities 35%, common stocks 30%, silver & gold 26%, Swiss franc assets 10%. Largest stock holdings: natural resources 9%, real estate 6%.

Distributions: **Income:** Annually   **Capital Gains:** Annually
12b-1: Yes   **Amount:** 0.25%
Minimum: **Initial:** $1,000   **Subsequent:** $100
Min IRA: **Initial:** $1,000   **Subsequent:** $100
Services: IRA, Withdraw
Tel Exchange: Yes   **With MMF:** Yes
Registered: All states

†The fund has a one-time $35 start-up fee.

PINE STREET
Growth & Income

Wood, Struthers & Winthrop
Management Corp.
140 Broadway
New York, NY 10005
(800) 225-8011/(816) 283-1700

| | Years Ending 6/30 | | | | | |
	1982	1983	1984	1985	1986	1987
Net Investment Income ($)	.62	.56	.46	.56	.56	.46
Dividends from Net Investment Income ($)	.62	.56	.47	.56	.55	.37
Net Gains (Losses) on Investments ($)	(2.05)	5.25	(1.74)	3.39	3.23	1.21
Distributions from Net Realized Capital Gains ($)	.28	1.33	1.45	1.26	1.96	1.10
Net Asset Value End of Year ($)	10.25	14.17	10.97	13.10	14.38	14.58
Ratio of Expenses to Net Assets (%)	1.22	1.15	1.15	1.09	1.17	1.14
Portfolio Turnover Rate (%)	59	103	104	65	90	48
Total Assets: End of Year (Millions $)	34.5	45.0	39.3	52.1	65.9	70.8

Annual Rate of Return (%) Years Ending 12/31	20.4	19.1	5.1	30.7	14.3	(5.8)

Five-Year Total Return(%) 76.2[C]	Degree of Diversification A	Beta .94	Bull (%) 112.5[B]	Bear (%) (24.8)[E]

Objective: Seeks to combine continuity of income with opportunity for growth through investment in common stocks of well-established companies. May invest in debt or equity securities of foreign countries.

Portfolio: (9/30/87) Common stocks 84%, convertible bonds 13%, convertible preferred stocks 2%, other assets 1%. Largest stock holdings: business equipment 11%, oil & gas 10%.

Distributions: Income: Mar, June, Sept, Dec   **Capital Gains:** June

12b-1: Yes   **Amount:** 0.30%

Minimum: Initial: $1,000   Subsequent: $100

Min IRA: Initial: $1,000   Subsequent: $100

Services: IRA, Keogh, Withdraw

Tel Exchange: No

Registered: All states except ME

T. ROWE PRICE CAPITAL APPRECIATION
Aggressive Growth

T. Rowe Price Associates
100 East Pratt Street
Baltimore, MD 21202
(800) 638-5660/(301) 547-2308

	Years Ending 12/31					
	1982	1983	1984	1985	1986 (6 mos.)	1987
Net Investment Income ($)	–	–	–	–	.14	.35
Dividends from Net Investment Income ($)	–	–	–	–	–	.48
Net Gains (Losses) on Investments ($)	–	–	–	–	.71	.28
Distributions from Net Realized Capital Gains ($)	–	–	–	–	–	1.85
Net Asset Value End of Year ($)	–	–	–	–	10.85	9.15
Ratio of Expenses to Net Assets (%)	–	–	–	–	1.20	1.20
Portfolio Turnover Rate (%)	–	–	–	–	375	291
Total Assets: End of Year (Millions $)	–	–	–	–	69.0	63.9

Annual Rate of Return (%) Years Ending 12/31	–	–	–	–	–	5.9

Five-Year Total Return(%)	NA	Degree of Diversification	NA	Beta	NA	Bull (%)	NA	Bear (%)	(10.8)c

Objective: Seeks capital appreciation through investment primarily in common stocks. Portfolio consists of two categories: long-term "core" holdings of undervalued growth stocks; and short-term holdings, where the stock price is expected to rise over the short term. Can invest up to 35% of the fund's assets in corporate debt.

Portfolio: (12/31/87) Common stocks 93%, short-term securities 8%, U.S. government obligations 6%, preferred stocks 3%. Largest stock holdings: financial 22%, technology 14%.

Distributions: Income: Annually   **Capital Gains:** Annually

12b-1: No

Minimum: Initial: $1,000   Subsequent: $100

Min IRA: Initial: $500   Subsequent: $50

Services: IRA, Keogh, Corp, SEP, 403(b), Withdraw, Deduct

Tel Exchange: Yes   **With MMF:** Yes

Registered: All states

T. ROWE PRICE EQUITY INCOME
Growth & Income

T. Rowe Price Associates
100 East Pratt Street
Baltimore, MD 21202
(800) 638-5660/(301) 547-2308

	1982	1983	1984	1985 (2 mos.)	1986	1987
Net Investment Income ($)	–	–	–	.14	.66	.64
Dividends from Net Investment Income ($)	–	–	–	–	.65	.82
Net Gains (Losses) on Investments ($)	–	–	–	.86	2.21	(.14)
Distributions from Net Realized Capital Gains ($)	–	–	–	–	.26	1.35
Net Asset Value End of Year ($)	–	–	–	11.00	12.96	11.29
Ratio of Expenses to Net Assets (%)	–	–	–	1.00	1.00	1.10
Portfolio Turnover Rate (%)	–	–	–	37	73	80
Total Assets: End of Year (Millions $)	–	–	–	16.6	94.0	185.0
Annual Rate of Return (%) Years Ending 12/31	–	–	–	–	26.6	3.5

Five-Year Total Return(%)	NA	Degree of Diversification	NA	Beta	NA	Bull (%)	NA	Bear (%)	(15.8)c

Objective: Seeks high income through investment in dividend-paying common stocks of established companies that also have capital appreciation potential. May invest in investment grade (BBB or higher) debt securities without limit. Will invest at least 65% of fund's assets in income-producing common stocks.

Portfolio: (12/31/87) Common stocks 70%, corporate bonds 8%, convertible bonds 7%, short-term securities 7%, preferred stocks 3%, convertible preferred stocks 2%, U.S. government and agency obligations 1%. Largest stock holdings: financial 14%, consumer nondurables 10%.

Distributions: Income: Quarterly   **Capital Gains:** Annually

12b-1: No

Minimum: Initial: $1,000   Subsequent: $100

Min IRA: Initial: $500   Subsequent: $50

Services: IRA, Keogh, Corp, SEP, 403(b), Withdraw, Deduct

Tel Exchange: Yes   **With MMF:** Yes

Registered: All states

T. ROWE PRICE GNMA
Bond

T. Rowe Price Associates, Inc.
100 E. Pratt St.
Baltimore, MD 21202
(800) 638-5660/(301) 547-2308

	Years Ending 2/28					
	1982	1983	1984	1985	1986 (3 mos.)	1987
Net Investment Income ($)	–	–	–	–	.26	.90
Dividends from Net Investment Income ($)	–	–	–	–	.26	.90
Net Gains (Losses) on Investments ($)	–	–	–	–	.12	.15
Distributions from Net Realized Capital Gains ($)	–	–	–	–	–	–
Net Asset Value End of Year ($)	–	–	–	–	10.12	10.27
Ratio of Expenses to Net Assets (%)	–	–	–	–	1.00	1.00
Portfolio Turnover Rate (%)	–	–	–	–	51	226
Total Assets: End of Year (Millions $)	–	–	–	–	123.6	377.5

Annual Rate of Return (%) Years Ending 12/31		–	–	–	–	11.0		.8
Five-Year Total Return(%)	NA	Degree of Diversification	NA	Beta	NA	Bull (%)	NA	Bear (%)	1.5^

Objective: Seeks high level of current income consistent with preservation of capital. Invests in securities backed by the U.S. government, principally GNMAs.

Portfolio: (8/31/87) GNMA securities 97%, U.S. Treasury notes 2%.

Distributions: Income: Monthly   **Capital Gains:** Annually
12b-1: No
Minimum: Initial: $1,000   Subsequent: $100
Min IRA: Initial: $500   Subsequent: $50
Services: IRA, Keogh, Corp, SEP, 403(b), Withdraw, Deduct
Tel Exchange: Yes   **With MMF:** Yes
Registered: All states

T. ROWE PRICE GROWTH & INCOME

Growth & Income

T. Rowe Price Associates
100 E. Pratt St.
Baltimore, MD 21202
(800) 638-5660/(301) 547-2308

	\ 1982	Years Ending 12/31 \ 1983	\ 1984	\ 1985	\ 1986	\ 1987
Net Investment Income ($)	–	.77	.81	.59	.75	.66
Dividends from Net Investment Income ($)	–	.60	.79	.61	.71	.88
Net Gains (Losses) on Investments ($)	–	2.88	(.57)	1.76	.33	(1.09)
Distributions from Net Realized Capital Gains ($)	–	–	.06	–	1.57	1.04
Net Asset Value End of Year ($)	–	13.05	12.44	14.18	12.98	10.63
Ratio of Expenses to Net Assets (%)	–	.90	.94	.94	.96	1.03
Portfolio Turnover Rate (%)	–	48	52	121	100	114
Total Assets: End of Year (Millions $)	–	234.5	309.1	356.8	388.6	365.6
Annual Rate of Return (%) Years Ending 12/31	–	32.6	1.9	19.7	7.9	(4.3)

Five-Year Total Return(%)	67.1c	Degree of Diversification	B	Beta	.88	Bull (%)	86.3c	Bear (%)	(23.2)D

Objective:	Seeks long-term growth of capital, a reasonable level of current income, and an increase in future income through investment primarily in income-producing equity securities that have prospects for both capital growth and dividend income.
Portfolio:	(12/31/87) Common stocks 88%, convertible bonds 6%, short-term securities 5%, corporate bonds 1%. Largest stock holdings: financial 23%, energy 10%.
Distributions:	Income: Jan, April, July, Oct **Capital Gains:** Jan
12b-1:	No
Minimum:	Initial: $1,000 Subsequent: $100
Min IRA:	Initial: $500 Subsequent: $50
Services:	IRA, Keogh, Corp, SEP, 403(b), Withdraw, Deduct
Tel Exchange:	Yes **With MMF:** Yes
Registered:	All states

T. ROWE PRICE GROWTH STOCK

Growth

T. Rowe Price Associates
100 E. Pratt St.
Baltimore, MD 21202
(800) 638-5660/(301) 547-2308

	Years Ending 12/31					
	1982	1983	1984	1985	1986	1987
Net Investment Income ($)	.49	.34	.34	.38	.31	.32
Dividends from Net Investment Income ($)	.53	.50	.36	.34	.38	.63
Net Gains (Losses) on Investments ($)	1.48	1.30	(.54)	4.35	3.26	.28
Distributions from Net Realized Capital Gains ($)	.09	—	.45	.64	4.18	2.66
Net Asset Value End of Year ($)	14.07	15.21	14.20	17.95	16.96	14.27
Ratio of Expenses to Net Assets (%)	.51	.50	.52	.52	.57	.67
Portfolio Turnover Rate (%)	54	63	60	69	60	51
Total Assets: End of Year (Millions $)	1,007.4	1,013.0	965.5	1,158.4	1,273.2	1,267.9

Annual Rate of Return (%) Years Ending 12/31		16.3	12.3	(0.7)	35.1	21.7	3.3
Five-Year Total Return(%)	89.2[B]	Degree of Diversification	B	Beta .94	Bull (%) 142.5[A]	Bear (%) (22.1)[D]	

Objective: Seeks long-term capital appreciation primarily through investment in common stocks of well-established growth companies. May invest up to 25% of assets in foreign securities and write covered call options.

Portfolio: (12/31/87) Common & preferred stocks 95%, short-term securities 6%, convertible bonds 1%. Largest stock holdings: technology 20%, foreign 19%.

Distributions: Income: Jan   **Capital Gains:** Jan

12b-1: No

Minimum: Initial: $1,000   Subsequent: $100

Min IRA: Initial: $500   Subsequent: $50

Services: IRA, Keogh, Corp, SEP, 403(b), Withdraw, Deduct

Tel Exchange: Yes   **With MMF:** Yes

Registered: All states

T. ROWE PRICE HIGH YIELD
Bond

T. Rowe Price Associates, Inc.
100 E. Pratt St.
Baltimore, MD 21202
(800) 638-5660/(301) 547-2308

	Years Ending 2/28					
	1982	1983	1984	1985 (2 mos.)	1986	1987
Net Investment Income ($)	–	–	–	.22	1.37	1.29
Dividends from Net Investment Income ($)	–	–	–	.22	1.37	1.28
Net Gains (Losses) on Investments ($)	–	–	–	(.01)	1.00	.39
Distributions from Net Realized Capital Gains ($)	–	–	–	–	–	.13
Net Asset Value End of Year ($)	–	–	–	9.99	10.99	11.26
Ratio of Expenses to Net Assets (%)	–	–	–	1.00	1.00	.99
Portfolio Turnover Rate (%)	–	–	–	6	164	166
Total Assets: End of Year (Millions $)	–	–	–	22.5	456.7	939.5

Annual Rate of Return (%) Years Ending 12/31			–	–	–	22.5	15.1	2.9
Five-Year Total Return(%)	NA	Degree of Diversification	NA	Beta	.21	Bull (%)	NA	Bear (%)	4.01c

Objective: Seeks high level of current income by investing in long-term, high-yielding, lower and medium quality fixed-income securities. May lend its securities, write options, and purchase foreign debt securities.

Portfolio: (8/31/87) Corporate bonds & notes 88%, U.S. government obligations 8%, convertible bonds 2%, preferred stocks 2%, convertible preferred stocks 1%, common stocks 1%.

Distributions: Income: Monthly   **Capital Gains:** February
12b-1: No
Minimum: Initial: $1,000   Subsequent: $100
Min IRA: Initial: $500   Subsequent: $50
Services: IRA, Keogh, Corp, SEP, 403(b), Withdraw, Deduct
Tel Exchange: Yes   **With MMF:** Yes
Registered: All states

T. ROWE PRICE INTERNATIONAL BOND

International

T. Rowe Price Associates
100 East Pratt Street
Baltimore, MD 21202
(800) 638-5660/(301) 547-2308

	Years Ending 12/31					
	1982	1983	1984	1985	1986 (4 mos.)	1987
Net Investment Income ($)	–	–	–	–	.28	1.01
Dividends from Net Investment Income ($)	–	–	–	–	.28	1.01
Net Gains (Losses) on Investments ($)	–	–	–	–	.01	1.64
Distributions from Net Realized Capital Gains ($)	–	–	–	–	–	.05
Net Asset Value End of Year ($)	–	–	–	–	10.01	11.60
Ratio of Expenses to Net Assets (%)	–	–	–	–	1.25	1.25
Portfolio Turnover Rate (%)	–	–	–	–	218	284
Total Assets: End of Year (Millions $)	–	–	–	–	70.0	400.0

Annual Rate of Return (%) Years Ending 12/31	–	–	–	–	–	28.1

Five-Year Total Return(%)	NA	Degree of Diversification	NA	Beta NA	Bull (%) NA	Bear (%) 18.6ᴬ

Objective: To achieve a high level of current income through investment in foreign bonds. Also seeks capital appreciation and protection of its principal through actively managing its maturity structure and currency exposure.

Portfolio: (12/31/87) Netherlands 19%, United Kingdom 18%, New Zealand 14%.

Distributions: Income: Monthly   **Capital Gains:** Annually

12b-1: No

Minimum: Initial: $1,000   Subsequent: $100

Min IRA: Initial: $500   Subsequent: $50

Services: IRA, Keogh, Corp, SEP, 403(b), Withdraw, Deduct

Tel Exchange: Yes   **With MMF:** Yes

Registered: All states

T. ROWE PRICE INTERNATIONAL STOCK
(formerly T. ROWE PRICE INTERNATIONAL)

International

T. Rowe Price Associates
100 E. Pratt St.
Baltimore, MD 21202
(800) 638-5660/(301) 547-2308

	Years Ending 12/31					
	1982	1983	1984	1985	1986	1987
Net Investment Income ($)	.16	.08	.15	.11	.11	.12
Dividends from Net Investment Income ($)	.15	.11	.08	.15	.11	.23
Net Gains (Losses) on Investments ($)	.16	1.52	(.56)	2.72	5.23	.74
Distributions from Net Realized Capital Gains ($)	—	—	.08	.23	1.38	4.98
Net Asset Value End of Year ($)	5.67	7.16	6.59	9.04	12.89	8.54
Ratio of Expenses to Net Assets (%)	1.16	1.14	1.11	1.11	1.10	1.14
Portfolio Turnover Rate (%)	79	69	38	62	56	77
Total Assets: End of Year (Millions $)	101.0	130.0	180.6	376.9	790.0	642.5
Annual Rate of Return (%) Years Ending 12/31	6.2	28.4	(5.6)	45.2	60.5	8.0

Five-Year Total Return(%)	204.9[A]	Degree of Diversification	E	Beta	.62	Bull (%)	233.1[A]	Bear (%)	(17.5)[C]

Objective:	Seeks long-term capital growth and income by investing in a diversified portfolio of marketable securities of established non-U.S. issuers.
Portfolio:	(12/31/87) United Kingdom 30%, Japan 26%, Hong Kong 8%.
Distributions:	Income: Jan **Capital Gains:** Jan
12b-1:	No
Minimum:	Initial: $1,000 Subsequent: $100
Min IRA:	Initial: $500 Subsequent: $50
Services:	IRA, Keogh, Corp, SEP, 403(b), Withdraw, Deduct
Tel Exchange:	Yes **With MMF:** Yes
Registered:	All states

T. ROWE PRICE NEW AMERICA GROWTH

Growth

T. Rowe Price Associates
100 East Pratt Street
Baltimore, MD 21202
(800) 638-5660/(301) 547-2308

	Years Ending 12/31					
	1982	1983	1984	1985 (3 mos.)	1986	1987
Net Investment Income ($)	–	–	–	.10	.06	(.01)
Dividends from Net Investment Income ($)	–	–	–	–	.10	.06
Net Gains (Losses) on Investments ($)	–	–	–	1.75	1.63	(1.23)
Distributions from Net Realized Capital Gains ($)	–	–	–	–	.30	1.39
Net Asset Value End of Year ($)	–	–	–	11.85	13.14	10.45
Ratio of Expenses to Net Assets (%)	–	–	–	1.00	1.00	1.23
Portfolio Turnover Rate (%)	–	–	–	49	81	72
Total Assets: End of Year (Millions $)	–	–	–	30.5	83.4	62.4
Annual Rate of Return (%) Years Ending 12/31	–	–	–	–	14.3	(9.9)

Five-Year Total Return(%)	NA	Degree of Diversification	NA	Beta	NA	Bull (%)	NA	Bear (%)	(26.4)E

Objective: Seeks long-term growth of capital through investment primarily in common stocks of companies that operate in the service sector of the economy. Will invest at least 75% of net assets in service sector stocks. May also write covered call options and buy puts.

Portfolio: (12/31/87) Common stocks 94%, short-term securities 6%. Largest stock holdings: consumer services 34%, financial services 31%.

Distributions: Income: Jan   **Capital Gains:** Jan

12b-1: No

Minimum: Initial: $1,000   Subsequent: $100

Min IRA: Initial: $500   Subsequent: $50

Services: IRA, Keogh, Corp, SEP, 403(b), Withdraw, Deduct

Tel Exchange: Yes   **With MMF:** Yes

Registered: All states

T. ROWE PRICE NEW ERA
Growth

T. Rowe Price Associates
100 E. Pratt St.
Baltimore, MD 21202
(800) 638-5660/(301) 547-2308

	Years Ending 12/31					
	1982	1983	1984	1985	1986	1987
Net Investment Income ($)	.84	.58	.67	.49	.38	.61
Dividends from Net Investment Income ($)	.86	.81	.61	.68	.50	.98
Net Gains (Losses) on Investments ($)	(.74)	3.21	(.08)	3.14	2.46	2.46
Distributions from Net Realized Capital Gains ($)	3.05	.07	1.29	1.41	3.25	1.77
Net Asset Value End of Year ($)	15.53	18.44	17.13	18.67	17.76	18.08
Ratio of Expenses to Net Assets (%)	.71	.68	.68	.69	.73	.82
Portfolio Turnover Rate (%)	62	37	39	37	32	30
Total Assets: End of Year (Millions $)	411.5	485.1	472.1	529.4	496.2	756.7

Annual Rate of Return (%) Years Ending 12/31	1.7	26.4	3.5	22.9	16.2	17.5

Five-Year Total Return(%) 119.6[A]	Degree of Diversification C	Beta .95	Bull (%) 131.3[A]	Bear (%) (19.1)[C]

Objective: Seeks long-term growth of capital through investment primarily in common stocks of companies that own or develop natural resources, and selected growth companies with capable management, sound financial and accounting policies, effective R&D, and efficient service. May invest in foreign securities, loan its portfolio securities (up to 30% of assets), and write covered call options.

Portfolio: (12/31/87) Common stocks 85%, short-term securities 15%. Largest stock holdings: natural resource-related companies 67%, science & technology 10%.

Distributions: Income: Jan   **Capital Gains:** Jan

12b-1: No

Minimum: Initial: $1,000   Subsequent: $100

Min IRA: Initial: $500   Subsequent: $50

Services: IRA, Keogh, Corp, SEP, 403(b), Withdraw, Deduct

Tel Exchange: Yes   **With MMF:** Yes

Registered: All states

T. ROWE PRICE NEW HORIZONS
Aggressive Growth

T. Rowe Price Associates
100 E. Pratt St.
Baltimore, MD 21202
(800) 638-5660/(301) 547-2308

	Years Ending 12/31					
	1982	1983	1984	1985	1986	1987
Net Investment Income ($)	.19	.16	.14	.09	.02	.04
Dividends from Net Investment Income ($)	.35	.20	.16	.14	.09	.06
Net Gains (Losses) on Investments ($)	2.62	2.80	(1.38)	2.92	(.04)	(.92)
Distributions from Net Realized Capital Gains ($)	2.62	.76	3.72	.52	2.64	1.93
Net Asset Value End of Year ($)	15.90	17.90	12.78	15.13	12.38	9.51
Ratio of Expenses to Net Assets (%)	.56	.61	0.71	.70	.73	.78
Portfolio Turnover Rate (%)	36	45	32	31	35	50
Total Assets: End of Year (Millions $)	1,198.7	1,355.1	1,273.2	1,474.9	1,033.9	855.8

Annual Rate of Return (%) Years Ending 12/31	22.5	19.7	(11.8)	24.0	(0.2)	(7.6)

Five-Year Total Return(%)	20.8[E]	Degree of Diversification	C	Beta 1.20	Bull (%) 65.5[D]	Bear (%) (28.4)[E]

Objective: Seeks long-term growth of capital through investment primarily in common stocks of small growth companies that have the potential to become major companies in the future.

Portfolio: (12/31/87) Common stocks 88%, short-term investments 11%. Largest stock holdings: technology 21%, consumer services 20%.

Distributions: Income: Annually   **Capital Gains:** Annually

12b-1: No

Minimum: Initial: $1,000   Subsequent: $100

Min IRA: Initial: $500   Subsequent: $50

Services: IRA, Keogh, Corp, SEP, 403(b), Withdraw, Deduct

Tel Exchange: Yes   **With MMF:** Yes

Registered: All states

T. ROWE PRICE NEW INCOME
Bond

T. Rowe Price Associates, Inc.
100 E. Pratt St.
Baltimore, MD 21202
(800) 638-5660/(301) 547-2308

	12/31	Years Ending 2/28				
	1982	1983* (2 mos.)	1984	1985	1986	1987
Net Investment Income ($)	1.07	.17	.94	.94	.88	.75
Dividends from Net Investment Income ($)	1.07	.17	.95	.94	.88	.75
Net Gains (Losses) on Investments ($)	.67	.10	(.31)	(.06)	.77	.22
Distributions from Net Realized Capital Gains ($)	—	—	—	—	—	—
Net Asset Value End of Year ($)	8.46	8.56	8.24	8.18	8.95	9.17
Ratio of Expenses to Net Assets (%)	.59	.57	.62	.64	.66	.65
Portfolio Turnover Rate (%)	96	67	84	155	185	125
Total Assets: End of Year (Millions $)	611.3	640.3	695.5	707.8	936.0	938.9
Annual Rate of Return (%) Years Ending 12/31	24.1	9.7	11.9	17.6	14.0	2.1

Five-Year Total Return(%) 68.0ᶜ	Degree of Diversification NA	Beta .05	Bull (%) 40.6ᴱ	Bear (%) 4.3ᴬ

Fiscal year end changed from 12/31 to 2/28.

Objective: Seeks high current income with reasonable stability through investment in high grade fixed-income securities.

Portfolio: (8/31/87) U.S. government securities 51%, corporate bonds and notes 30%, other foreign securities 10%, Canadian securities 5%, commercial paper 1%, CDs 1%. Largest bond holdings: finance & credit 10%, petroleum 7%.

Distributions: Income: Monthly   **Capital Gains:** March

12b-1: No

Minimum: Initial: $1,000   Subsequent: $100

Min IRA: Initial: $500   Subsequent: $50

Services: IRA, Keogh, Corp, SEP, 403(b), Withdraw, Deduct

Tel Exchange: Yes   **With MMF:** Yes

Registered: All states

T. ROWE PRICE SHORT-TERM BOND
Bond

T. Rowe Price Associates, Inc.
100 E. Pratt St.
Baltimore, MD 21202
(800) 638-5660/(301) 547-2308

	Years Ending 2/28					
	1982	1983	1984	1985 (10 mos.)	1986	1987
Net Investment Income ($)	–	–	–	.53	.47	.40
Dividends from Net Investment Income ($)	–	–	–	.53	.47	.40
Net Gains (Losses) on Investments ($)	–	–	–	(.03)	.20	.04
Distributions from Net Realized Capital Gains ($)	–	–	–	–	–	–
Net Asset Value End of Year ($)	–	–	–	4.97	5.17	5.21
Ratio of Expenses to Net Assets (%)	–	–	–	.90	1.31	.94
Portfolio Turnover Rate (%)	–	–	–	73	21	7
Total Assets: End of Year (Millions $)	–	–	–	42.0	96.1	218.2
Annual Rate of Return (%) Years Ending 12/31	–	–	–	12.8	9.0	5.2

Five-Year Total Return(%)	NA	Degree of Diversification	NA	Beta	.01	Bull (%)	NA	Bear (%)	3.3ᴬ

Objective: Seeks high level of income with minimum fluctuation of principal value and liquidity. Portfolio will consist of short- and intermediate-term securities.

Portfolio: (8/31/87) Corporate bonds & notes 35%, U.S. government securities 32%, CDs 22%, foreign securities 5%, commercial paper 4%. Largest bond holdings: finance & credit 13%, banking 6%.

Distributions: Income: Monthly   **Capital Gains:** Mar
12b-1: No
Minimum: Initial: $1,000   Subsequent: $100
Min IRA: Initial: $500   Subsequent: $50
Services: IRA, Keogh, Corp, SEP, 403(b), Withdraw, Deduct
Tel Exchange: Yes   **With MMF:** Yes
Registered: All states

PRIMARY TREND FUND
Growth & Income

Arnold Investment Counsel, Inc.
First Financial Centre
700 North Water Street
Milwaukee, WI 53202
(800) 443-6544/(414) 271-7870

	Years Ending 6/30					
	1982	1983	1984	1985	1986	1987 (9 mos.)
Net Investment Income ($)	–	–	–	–	–	.19
Dividends from Net Investment Income ($)	–	–	–	–	–	–
Net Gains (Losses) on Investments ($)	–	–	–	–	–	1.43
Distributions from Net Realized Capital Gains ($)	–	–	–	–	–	–
Net Asset Value End of Year ($)	–	–	–	–	–	11.62
Ratio of Expenses to Net Assets (%)	–	–	–	–	–	1.05
Portfolio Turnover Rate (%)	–	–	–	–	–	20
Total Assets: End of Year (Millions $)	–	–	–	–	–	31.3

Annual Rate of Return (%) Years Ending 12/31	–	–	–	–	–	3.7

Five-Year Total Return(%)	NA	Degree of Diversification	NA	Beta	NA	Bull (%)	NA	Bear (%)	(13.2)c

Objective: Seeks to maximize total return without exposing capital to undue risk. Invests in common stock and convertible and fixed-income securities. Attempts to align the portfolio with primary market trends which can last from several quarters up to several years.

Portfolio: (12/31/87) Common stocks 96%, short-term securities 3%, other assets 1%. Largest stock holdings: Navistar International Corp. 21%, Northern Indiana Public Service Company 10%.

Distributions: Income: Annually   **Capital Gains:** Annually
12b-1: No
Minimum: Initial: $5,000   Subsequent: $100
Min IRA: Initial: $2,000   Subsequent: $100
Services: IRA, Keogh, Corp, SEP, 403(b), Withdraw
Tel Exchange: No
Registered: All states except AR, IA, ID, ND, NH, NM, VT

QUEST FOR VALUE
Aggressive Growth

Oppenheimer Capital Corp.
Oppenheimer Tower
World Financial Center
New York, NY 10281
(212) 667-7587

	Years Ending 4/30					10/31
	1983	**1984**	**1985**	**1986**	**1987**	**1987*** (6 mos.)
Net Investment Income ($)	.54	.30	.29	.19	.27	.10
Dividends from Net Investment Income ($)	.30	.52	.34	.27	.20	.27
Net Gains (Losses) on Investments ($)	10.63	1.45	2.99	6.99	2.42	(3.40)
Distributions from Net Realized Capital Gains ($)	.60	4.84	3.82	.70	2.59	.91
Net Asset Value End of Year ($)	26.69	23.08	22.20	28.41	28.31	23.83
Ratio of Expenses to Net Assets (%)	2.48	2.29	2.34	2.18	2.17	2.24
Portfolio Turnover Rate (%)	93	74	42	68	34	21
Total Assets: End of Year (Millions $)	8.9	13.4	28.1	64.3	104.5	91.2
Annual Rate of Return (%) Years Ending 12/31	38.2	4.8	27.4	14.3	(2.1)	*

Five-Year Total Return(%)	106.5ᴬ	Degree of Diversification	C	Beta	.78	Bull (%)	95.6ᶜ	Bear (%)	(21.1)ᴰ

*Fiscal year changed from 4/30 to 10/31. All annual return figures are for full years ending 12/31.

Objective: Seeks capital appreciation through investment in common stocks of small, unseasoned companies as well as established companies believed to be undervalued. Defensively, may convert to long- and short-term debt securities.

Portfolio: (10/31/87) Common stocks 86%, short-term corporate notes 13%, short-term government securities 2%, short-term foreign government securities 2%. Largest stock holdings: consumer cyclicals 24%, financial 19%.

Distributions: Income: May   **Capital Gains:** May
12b-1: No
Minimum: Initial: $2,000   Subsequent: $25
Min IRA: Initial: $250   Subsequent: $25
Services: IRA, Keogh, Corp, 403(b), Withdraw, Deduct
Tel Exchange: No
Registered: All states except AL, AR, IA, KS, MO, MS, MT, NE, NH, OH, OK, SD, WV

RAINBOW
Growth

Furman, Anderson & Co.
19 Rector St.
New York, NY 10006
(212) 509-8532

	Years Ending 5/31					
	1982	**1983**	**1984**	**1985**	**1986**	**1987**
Net Investment Income ($)	.03	(.01)	.02	.11	.01	(.05)
Dividends from Net Investment Income ($)	–	–	–	–	–	–
Net Gains (Losses) on Investments ($)	(.89)	1.04	(.32)	.44	1.18	.78
Distributions from Net Realized Capital Gains ($)	–	–	–	–	–	–
Net Asset Value End of Year ($)	2.98	4.01	3.71	4.26	5.45	6.18
Ratio of Expenses to Net Assets (%)	3.42	4.65	4.32	3.02	3.46	3.27
Portfolio Turnover Rate (%)	127	291	247	164	190	113
Total Assets: End of Year (Millions $)	1.6	1.8	1.5	1.7	2.0	2.2
Annual Rate of Return (%) Years Ending 12/31	(3.2)	22.2	(4.9)	20.7	15.8	(4.0)

Five-Year Total Return(%) 55.9ᴰ	Degree of Diversification	C	Beta	.90	Bull (%)	88.4ᶜ	Bear (%)	(24.7)ᴰ

Objective: Seeks capital appreciation through investment in common stocks of established companies. Employs speculative market techniques such as listed put and call options. May write covered and uncovered put and call options, buy and write options on stock indexes. May sell securities short, invest up to 20% of its assets in warrants and up to 25% in foreign securities.

Portfolio: (11/30/87) Common stocks 37%, U.S. government obligations 28%, short-term securities 27%, other assets 8%. Largest stock holdings: drugs 14%, insurance 5%.

Distributions: Income: Annually   **Capital Gains:** Annually

12b-1: No

Minimum: Initial: $300   Subsequent: $50

Min IRA: Initial: $300   Subsequent: $50

Services: IRA, Keogh, Withdraw

Tel Exchange: No

Registered: NJ, NY

REICH & TANG EQUITY

Aggressive Growth

Reich & Tang, Inc.
100 Park Avenue
New York, NY 10017
(212) 370-1252

	Years Ending 12/31					
	1982	**1983**	**1984**	**1985** (11 mos.)	**1986**	**1987**
Net Investment Income ($)	–	–	–	.31	.35	.34
Dividends from Net Investment Income ($)	–	–	–	.30	.28	.40
Net Gains (Losses) on Investments ($)	–	–	–	3.43	1.62	.45
Distributions from Net Realized Capital Gains ($)	–	–	–	–	.63	1.78
Net Asset Value End of Year ($)	–	–	–	13.44	14.50	13.11
Ratio of Expenses to Net Assets (%)	–	–	–	.99	1.21	1.11
Portfolio Turnover Rate (%)	–	–	–	20	35	43
Total Assets: End of Year (Millions $)	–	–	–	54.2	110.5	101.6

Annual Rate of Return (%) Years Ending 12/31			–	–	–	–	14.7	5.1

Five-Year Total Return(%)	NA	Degree of Diversification	NA	Beta	NA	Bull (%)	NA	Bear (%)	(19.6)[D]

Objective: Seeks long-term capital appreciation; current income is a secondary consideration. Invests in common stocks of undervalued companies showing good growth potential. May convert entirely to debt securities and money market instruments for defensive purposes. May enter into repos, buy warrants, invest in foreign securities and restricted securities.

Portfolio: (12/31/87) Common stocks 83%, short-term securities 17%. Largest stock holdings: food & beverages 11%, consumer products 10%.

Distributions: Income: Semiannually   **Capital Gains:** Annually

12b-1: Yes   Amount: 0.05%

Minimum: Initial: $5,000   Subsequent: None

Min IRA: Initial: $250   Subsequent: None

Services: IRA, Corp, Withdraw

Tel Exchange: Yes   With MMF: Yes

Registered: AL, AR, CA, CO, CT, DC, DE, FL, GA, HI, IL, IN, KY, MA, MD, ME, MI, MN, MO, MT, NC, NE, NH, NJ, NM, NV, NY, OH, OK, OR, PA, SC, TN, TX, UT, VA, VT, WA, WI, WY

RESERVE EQUITY TRUST—DREMAN CONTRARIAN PORTFOLIO
Growth & Income

R.D. Partners, L.P.
810 Seventh Avenue
New York, NY 10019
(800) 421-0261/(212) 977-9675

			Years Ending 5/31			
	1982	1983	1984 (4 mos.)	1985	1986	1987
Net Investment Income ($)	–	–	.10	.45	.44	.36
Dividends from Net Investment Income ($)	–	–	–	.30	.49	.27
Net Gains (Losses) on Investments ($)	–	–	(.82)	3.20	4.32	1.53
Distributions from Net Realized Capital Gains ($)	–	–	–	–	.01	.46
Net Asset Value End of Year ($)	–	–	9.28	12.63	16.89	18.05
Ratio of Expenses to Net Assets (%)	–	–	1.00	1.00	1.00	1.50
Portfolio Turnover Rate (%)	–	–	5	6	26	25
Total Assets: End of Year (Millions $)	–	–	.2	5.3	20.9	27.3

Annual Rate of Return (%) Years Ending 12/31	–	–	–	40.5	10.8	(6.8)

Five-Year Total Return(%)	NA	Degree of Diversification	B	Beta	.97	Bull (%)	140.2ᴬ	Bear (%)	(30.6)ᴱ

Objective: Seeks dividend income and capital appreciation through investment in securities believed by the advisor to be undervalued in relation to securities of other companies in the same industry and those overlooked due to pessimistic appraisals by the investing public.

Portfolio: (11/30/87) Common stocks 84%, repos 15%. Largest stock holdings: automotive 15%, office equipment 12%.

Distributions: Income: Quarterly   **Capital Gains:** Annually

12b-1: Yes   **Amount:** 0.75%

Minimum: Initial: $10,000   **Subsequent:** $1,000

Min IRA: Initial: $500   **Subsequent:** $250

Services: IRA

Tel Exchange: Yes   **With MMF:** Yes

Registered: All states

RIGHTIME

Growth

Rightime Econometrics
The Benson East Office Plaza
Jenkintown, PA 19046
(800) 242-1421/(215) 927-7880

	1982	1983	1984	1985 (2 mos.)	1986	1987
Years Ending 10/31						
Net Investment Income ($)	—	—	—	(.01)	(.53)	.51
Dividends from Net Investment Income ($)	—	—	—	—	.05	—
Net Gains (Losses) on Investments ($)	—	—	—	.88	6.96	3.73
Distributions from Net Realized Capital Gains ($)	—	—	—	—	.20	1.94
Net Asset Value End of Year ($)	—	—	—	25.87	32.05	34.35
Ratio of Expenses to Net Assets (%)	—	—	—	1.99	1.57	1.35
Portfolio Turnover Rate (%)	—	—	—	—	231	166
Total Assets: End of Year (Millions $)	—	—	—	14.7	145.2	211.3
Annual Rate of Return (%) Years Ending 12/31	—	—	—	—	11.0	19.5

Five-Year Total Return(%)	NA	Degree of Diversification	NA	Beta	NA	Bull (%)	NA	Bear (%)	2.5ᴬ

Objective: Seeks high total return through investment in other investment companies. Looks at past performance and investment structure. Investment companies may be open- or closed-end, load or no-load.

Portfolio: (10/31/87) Short-term securities 57%, money market funds 25%, equity funds 15%, other assets 3%. Largest fund holdings: IDS Cash Management 20%, Delaware Cash Reserve 12%.

Distributions: Income: Annually   **Capital Gains:** Annually
12b-1: Yes   **Amount:** 1.20%
Minimum: Initial: $2,000   Subsequent: $100
Min IRA: Initial: $1,000   Subsequent: $100
Services: IRA, Keogh, 403(b), Withdraw
Tel Exchange: Yes   **With MMF:** No
Registered: All states except AL, CA, IA, NC, NH, TX, WI

RIGHTIME GOVERNMENT SECURITIES
Bond

Rightime Econometrics
The Benson East Office Plaza
Jenkintown, PA 19046
(800) 242-1421/(215) 927-7880

	Years Ending 10/31					
	1982	1983	1984	1985	1986	1987 (10 mos.)
Net Investment Income ($)	—	—	—	—	—	.96
Dividends from Net Investment Income ($)	—	—	—	—	—	.85
Net Gains (Losses) on Investments ($)	—	—	—	—	—	(1.62)
Distributions from Net Realized Capital Gains ($)	—	—	—	—	—	—
Net Asset Value End of Year ($)	—	—	—	—	—	13.49
Ratio of Expenses to Net Assets (%)	—	—	—	—	—	.12
Portfolio Turnover Rate (%)	—	—	—	—	—	111
Total Assets: End of Year (Millions $)	—	—	—	—	—	8.4
Annual Rate of Return (%) Years Ending 12/31	—	—	—	—	—	(3.1)

Five-Year Total Return(%)	NA	Degree of Diversification	NA	Beta	NA	Bull (%)	NA	Bear (%)	2.6ᴬ

Objective: Seeks high level of current income consistent with safety and liquidity of principal through investment in the debt obligations of the U.S. government and its agencies. Under normal circumstances 65% of fund assets will be invested in U.S. government securities. Can invest in put and call options and futures contracts.

Portfolio: (10/31/87) U.S. Treasury bonds 93%, other assets 7%.

Distributions: **Income:** Monthly   **Capital Gains:** Annually

12b-1: Yes   **Amount:** 0.50%

Minimum: **Initial:** $2,000   **Subsequent:** $100

Min IRA: **Initial:** $1,000   **Subsequent:** $100

Services: IRA, Keogh, 403(b), Withdraw

Tel Exchange: Yes   **With MMF:** Yes

Registered: Call for availability

RODNEY SQUARE BENCHMARK U.S. TREASURY
Bond

Scudder Fund Distributors, Inc.
175 Federal Street
Boston, MA 02110
(800) 225-5084

	Years Ending 10/31					
	1982	1983	1984	1985	1986	1987
Net Investment Income ($)	–	–	–	–	–	.64
Dividends from Net Investment Income ($)	–	–	–	–	–	.64
Net Gains (Losses) on Investments ($)	–	–	–	–	–	(.59)
Distributions from Net Realized Capital Gains ($)	–	–	–	–	–	–
Net Asset Value End of Year ($)	–	–	–	–	–	9.41
Ratio of Expenses to Net Assets (%)	–	–	–	–	–	1.04
Portfolio Turnover Rate (%)	–	–	–	–	–	257
Total Assets: End of Year (Millions $)	–	–	–	–	–	62.7

Annual Rate of Return (%) Years Ending 12/31		–	–	–	–	–	4.7
Five-Year Total Return(%)	NA	Degree of Diversification	NA	Beta NA	Bull (%) NA	Bear (%) 6.5ᴬ	

Objective: Seeks a high total return consistent with the preservation of capital and liquidity by investing in U.S. Treasury securities. The average maturity of the portfolio can range from one to 30 years. Can also sell or buy futures contracts.

Portfolio: (10/31/87) U.S. Treasury bonds 89%, repos 8%.

Distributions: **Income:** Monthly   **Capital Gains:** Annually

12b-1: Yes   **Amount:** 0.35%

Minimum: **Initial:** $1,000   **Subsequent:** None

Min IRA: **Initial:** $1,000   **Subsequent:** None

Services: IRA, Keogh, Corp, 403(b), Withdraw

Tel Exchange: Yes   **With MMF:** Yes

Registered: All states

RUSHMORE STOCK MARKET INDEX PLUS
Growth & Income

Money Management Associates
4922 Fairmont Avenue
Bethesda, MD 20814
(800) 343-3355/(301) 657-1500

	Years Ending 8/31					
	1982	1983	1984	1985	1986 (8 mos.)	1987
Net Investment Income ($)	–	–	–	–	.25	.44
Dividends from Net Investment Income ($)	–	–	–	–	.18	.29
Net Gains (Losses) on Investments ($)	–	–	–	–	1.71	3.81
Distributions from Net Realized Capital Gains ($)	–	–	–	–	–	–
Net Asset Value End of Year ($)	–	–	–	–	11.78	15.75
Ratio of Expenses to Net Assets (%)	–	–	–	–	1.00	.75
Portfolio Turnover Rate (%)	–	–	–	–	7	188
Total Assets: End of Year (Millions $)	–	–	–	–	1.2	29.0
Annual Rate of Return (%) Years Ending 12/31	–	–	–	–	17.6	8.9

Five-Year Total Return(%)	NA	Degree of Diversification	NA	Beta	NA	Bull (%)	NA	Bear (%)	(21.5)ᴰ

Objective: The fund's objective is to provide investment results that closely correlate to the performance of the common stocks comprising the Standard & Poor's 100 index. Index options are also used in an attempt to enhance the performance of the fund.

Portfolio: (8/31/87) Common stocks 70%, repos 29%, options 1%.

Distributions: Income: Monthly   **Capital Gains:** Annually

12b-1: No

Minimum: Initial: $2,500   **Subsequent:** None

Min IRA: Initial: $500   **Subsequent:** None

Services: IRA, Keogh, Deduct

Tel Exchange: Yes   **With MMF:** Yes

Registered: All states

SAFECO EQUITY
Growth & Income

Safeco Asset Management Co.
Safeco Plaza
Seattle, WA 98185
(800) 426-6730/(206) 545-5530

	Years Ending 9/30					
	1982	**1983**	**1984**	**1985**	**1986**	**1987**
Net Investment Income ($)	.66	.48	.45	.40	.29	.21
Dividends from Net Investment Income ($)	.68	.52	.45	.41	.34	.22
Net Gains (Losses) on Investments ($)	(.59)	2.63	(.26)	1.19	2.46	2.83
Distributions from Net Realized Capital Gains ($)	.81	.83	.58	.72	1.22	2.03
Net Asset Value End of Year ($)	8.86	10.62	9.79	10.25	11.44	12.23
Ratio of Expenses to Net Assets (%)	.65	.65	.64	.68	.88	.97
Portfolio Turnover Rate (%)	22	16	20	56	86	85
Total Assets: End of Year (Millions $)	28.3	34.5	31.4	34.9	46.7	64.7

Annual Rate of Return (%) Years Ending 12/31	11.4	21.1	2.8	32.6	12.6	(4.8)

Five-Year Total Return(%) 77.1ᴮ	Degree of Diversification	A	Beta 1.04	Bull (%) 130.2ᴬ	Bear (%) (29.2)ᴱ

Objective: Seeks reasonable balance of long-term growth of capital and reasonable current income for shareholders. Fund invests primarily in common stocks or convertibles of well-established, dividend-paying companies.

Portfolio: (9/30/87) Common stocks 97%, bonds 3%, short-term securities 1%, preferred stocks 1%. Largest stock holdings: health care 13%, electrical equipment & electronics 13%.

Distributions: Income: March, June, Sept, Dec   **Capital Gains:** Dec

12b-1: No

Minimum: Initial: $1,000   Subsequent: $100

Min IRA: Initial: $250   Subsequent: $100

Services: IRA, SEP, Withdraw, Deduct

Tel Exchange: Yes   **With MMF:** Yes

Registered: All states except ME, NH, VT

SAFECO GROWTH
Growth

Safeco Asset Management Co.
Safeco Plaza
Seattle, WA 98185
(800) 426-6730/(206) 545-5530

	Years Ending 9/30					
	1982	**1983**	**1984**	**1985**	**1986**	**1987**
Net Investment Income ($)	.52	.42	.51	.51	.31	.24
Dividends from Net Investment Income ($)	.59	.44	.46	.56	.42	.23
Net Gains (Losses) on Investments ($)	.43	7.56	(2.37)	1.19	1.62	4.31
Distributions from Net Realized Capital Gains ($)	1.22	.67	1.20	1.16	2.98	1.59
Net Asset Value End of Year ($)	13.50	20.38	16.87	16.86	15.40	18.13
Ratio of Expenses to Net Assets (%)	.64	.61	.61	.63	.85	.92
Portfolio Turnover Rate (%)	13	19	23	29	46	24
Total Assets: End of Year (Millions $)	40.6	64.5	63.5	66.3	68.4	82.7
Annual Rate of Return (%) Years Ending 12/31	19.0	31.8	(7.0)	19.6	1.8	7.0

Five-Year Total Return(%)	59.7[D]	Degree of Diversification	B	Beta	.95	Bull (%)	80.4[C]	Bear (%)	(19.8)[D]

Objective: Seeks capital growth and increased shareholder income through investment in large, well-established, dividend-paying companies. Short-term investments are only made when deemed beneficial. The aim is to keep portfolio turnover rates low.

Portfolio: (9/30/87) Common stocks 80%, short-term securities 17%, bonds 2%. Largest stock holdings: office equipment 11%, drugs 7%.

Distributions: **Income:** Semiannually   **Capital Gains:** Annually

12b-1: No

Minimum: **Initial:** $1,000   **Subsequent:** $100

Min IRA: **Initial:** $250   **Subsequent:** $100

Services: IRA, SEP, Withdraw, Deduct

Tel Exchange: Yes   **With MMF:** Yes

Registered: All states except ME, NH, VT

SAFECO INCOME
Balanced

Safeco Asset Management Co.
Safeco Plaza
Seattle, WA 98185
(800) 426-6730/(206) 545-5530

	Years Ending 9/30					
	1982	1983	1984	1985	1986	1987
Net Investment Income ($)	.86	.83	.87	.77	.78	.78
Dividends from Net Investment Income ($)	.86	.83	.85	.80	.79	.78
Net Gains (Losses) on Investments ($)	.41	3.62	.04	1.53	3.12	2.36
Distributions from Net Realized Capital Gains ($)	.44	.44	.87	1.17	.56	.73
Net Asset Value End of Year ($)	10.26	13.44	12.63	12.96	15.52	17.16
Ratio of Expenses to Net Assets (%)	.63	.63	.63	.73	.95	.94
Portfolio Turnover Rate (%)	28	32	34	29	29	33
Total Assets: End of Year (Millions $)	15.4	21.5	19.8	31.5	102.3	313.2
Annual Rate of Return (%) Years Ending 12/31	22.0	28.3	10.7	31.4	19.9	(5.9)

Five-Year Total Return(%) 110.6[A]	Degree of Diversification NA	Beta .77	Bull (%) 118.9[B]	Bear (%) (21.6)[D]

Objective: Seeks high current income and capital growth through investments in common stocks and convertible securities of medium- to large-sized companies that pay dividends.

Portfolio: (9/30/87) Common stocks 62%, corporate bonds 24%, preferred stocks 11%, short-term securities 2%. Largest stock holdings: banking & finance 9%, utilities/telephone 9%.

Distributions: Income: March, June, Sept, Dec   **Capital Gains:** Dec

12b-1: No

Minimum: Initial: $1,000   Subsequent: $100

Min IRA: Initial: $250   Subsequent: $100

Services: IRA, SEP, Withdraw, Deduct

Tel Exchange: Yes   **With MMF:** Yes

Registered: All states except ME, NH, VT

SAFECO
U.S. GOVERNMENT
SECURITIES
Bond

Safeco Asset Management Co.
Safeco Plaza
Seattle, WA 98185
(800) 426-6730/(206) 545-5530

			Years Ending 9/30			
	1982	1983	1984	1985	1986 (5 mos.)	1987
Net Investment Income ($)	–	–	–	–	.33	.82
Dividends from Net Investment Income ($)	–	–	–	–	.33	.82
Net Gains (Losses) on Investments ($)	–	–	–	–	–	(.87)
Distributions from Net Realized Capital Gains ($)	–	–	–	–	–	–
Net Asset Value End of Year ($)	–	–	–	–	10.00	9.13
Ratio of Expenses to Net Assets (%)	–	–	–	–	1.25	1.05
Portfolio Turnover Rate (%)	–	–	–	–	33	101
Total Assets: End of Year (Millions $)	–	–	–	–	8.1	20.3

Annual Rate of Return (%) Years Ending 12/31	–	–	–	–	–	0.9

Five-Year Total Return(%)	NA	Degree of Diversification	NA	Beta	NA	Bull (%)	NA	Bear (%)	1.2^A

Objective: Seeks high current income consistent with the preservation of capital through investment in U.S. government and its agencies' debt obligations. During normal market conditions the fund will invest at least 65% of its assets in U.S. government securities, principally GNMAs. May invest in other no-load government bond funds.

Portfolio: (9/30/87) U.S. government and agency obligations 92%, short-term securities 8%.

Distributions: **Income:** Monthly   **Capital Gains:** Annually

12b-1: No

Minimum: **Initial:** $1,000   **Subsequent:** $100

Min IRA: **Initial:** $250   **Subsequent:** $100

Services: IRA, SEP, Withdraw, Deduct

Tel Exchange: Yes   **With MMF:** Yes

Registered: All states except ME, NH, VT

SALEM GROWTH
Growth

Salem Funds
99 High Street
Boston, MA 02110
(800) 343-3424/(704) 331-0710

	Years Ending 3/31					
	1982	1983	1984	1985 (7 mos.)	1986	1987
Net Investment Income ($)	–	–	–	.04	.19	.15
Dividends from Net Investment Income ($)	–	–	–	–	.20	.13
Net Gains (Losses) on Investments ($)	–	–	–	0	2.32	2.38
Distributions from Net Realized Capital Gains ($)	–	–	–	–	–	.09
Net Asset Value End of Year ($)	–	–	–	10.04	12.35	14.66
Ratio of Expenses to Net Assets (%)	–	–	–	2.00	2.00	1.97
Portfolio Turnover Rate (%)	–	–	–	0	20	20
Total Assets: End of Year (Millions $)	–	–	–	.1	5.6	23.2

Annual Rate of Return (%) Years Ending 12/31	–	–	–	–	16.6	1.6

Five-Year Total Return(%)	NA	Degree of Diversification	NA	Beta	NA	Bull (%)	NA	Bear (%)	(21.6)^D

Objective: Primary objective is long-term capital growth; income is a secondary objective. Invests in companies with at least $100 million in equity. Will also invest in convertible securities rated at least BBB by Standard & Poor's.

Portfolio: (9/30/87) Common stocks 89%, short-term securities 11%. Largest stock holdings: consumer staples 17%, technology 13%.

Distributions: **Income:** Quarterly   **Capital Gains:** Annually

12b-1: Yes   **Amount:** 0.35%

Minimum: **Initial:** $1,000   **Subsequent:** None

Min IRA: **Initial:** $1,000   **Subsequent:** None

Services: IRA, Keogh, Withdraw, Deduct

Tel Exchange: No

Registered: DC, FL, GA, IL, KY, MS, NC, NJ, NY, SC, VA

SBSF FUND
Growth

Spears, Benzak, Salomon &
Farrell, Inc.
45 Rockefeller Plaza
New York, NY 10111
(212) 903-1200

	Years Ending 11/30					
	1982	1983	1984	1985	1986	1987
Net Investment Income ($)	–	–	.44	.31	.37	.39
Dividends from Net Investment Income ($)	–	–	.18	.40	.32	.37
Net Gains (Losses) on Investments ($)	–	–	.55	2.81	1.13	(1.33)
Distributions from Net Realized Capital Gains ($)	–	–	–	–	.55	1.05
Net Asset Value End of Year ($)	–	–	10.81	13.53	14.16	11.80
Ratio of Expenses to Net Assets (%)	–	–	1.37	1.40	1.17	1.10
Portfolio Turnover Rate (%)	–	–	87	80	65	66
Total Assets: End of Year (Millions $)	–	–	23.5	60.7	90.1	83.3
Annual Rate of Return (%) Years Ending 12/31	–	–	11.8	28.3	8.1	(3.1)

Five-Year Total Return(%)	NA	Degree of Diversification	B	Beta	.70	Bull (%)	92.0ᶜ	Bear (%)	(20.6)ᴰ

Objective: Seeks high total return over the long term consistent with reasonable risk. Using common stocks, bonds and convertible securities, the fund looks for above-average capital appreciation during up markets and capital preservation during down markets.

Portfolio: (11/30/87) Common stocks 59%, government bonds 18%, short-term securities 11%, cash 8%, preferred stocks 2%, convertible bonds 2%. Largest stock holdings: insurance 15%, oil and gas production and services 14%.

Distributions: Income: Semiannually   **Capital Gains:** Annually

12b-1: Yes   **Amount:** 0.25%

Minimum: Initial: None   Subsequent: None

Min IRA: Initial: $500   Subsequent: None

Services: IRA, Keogh, Withdraw

Tel Exchange: Yes   **With MMF:** Yes

Registered: All states

SCUDDER CAPITAL GROWTH
Growth

Scudder, Stevens & Clark
175 Federal St.
Boston, MA 02110
(800) 453-3305/(617) 439-4640

	Years Ending 9/30					
	1982	1983	1984	1985	1986	1987
Net Investment Income ($)	.34	.28	.29	.26	.26	.16
Dividends from Net Investment Income ($)	.67	–	.26	.29	.23	.23
Net Gains (Losses) on Investments ($)	.82	4.93	(.83)	2.19	3.67	5.77
Distributions from Net Realized Capital Gains ($)	–	–	.72	.51	1.88	2.46
Net Asset Value End of Year ($)	10.01	15.22	13.70	15.35	17.17	20.41
Ratio of Expenses to Net Assets (%)	1.00	.82	.90	.86	.84	.88
Portfolio Turnover Rate (%)	57	48	36	58	56	58
Total Assets: End of Year (Millions $)	110.5	237.5	236.3	302.4	413.9	583.0
Annual Rate of Return (%) Years Ending 12/31	28.6	22.1	0.5	36.2	16.5	(0.8)

Five-Year Total Return(%)	93.1[B]	Degree of Diversification	B	Beta	1.09	Bull (%)	133.0[A]	Bear (%)	(25.4)[E]

Objective: Seeks to maximize long-term growth of capital by investing in common stocks with growth potential, in special situations and in foreign companies. The fund may also invest in debt securities for defensive purposes and foreign securities.

Portfolio: (9/30/87) Common stocks 93%, short-term securities 6%, preferred stocks 2%. Largest stock holdings: media & service 33%, technology 15%.

Distributions: Income: Annually   **Capital Gains:** Annually

12b-1: No

Minimum: Initial: $1,000   Subsequent: None

Min IRA: Initial: $240   Subsequent: None

Services: IRA, Keogh, 403(b), Corp, Withdraw, Deduct

Tel Exchange: Yes   **With MMF:** Yes

Registered: All states

SCUDDER
DEVELOPMENT
Aggressive Growth

Scudder, Stevens & Clark
175 Federal St.
Boston, MA 02110-2267
(800) 453-3305/(617) 439-4640

	Years Ending 6/30					
	1982	1983	1984	1985	1986	1987
Net Investment Income ($)	.52	.32	.31	.14	(.01)	(.07)
Dividends from Net Investment Income ($)	.26	.45	.34	.28	.17	—
Net Gains (Losses) on Investments ($)	(3.45)	9.33	(4.47)	2.33	5.81	1.67
Distributions from Net Realized Capital Gains ($)	1.45	—	.44	.35	.92	1.33
Net Asset Value End of Year ($)	14.31	23.51	18.57	20.41	25.12	25.39
Ratio of Expenses to Net Assets (%)	1.22	1.26	1.31	1.29	1.25	1.38
Portfolio Turnover Rate (%)	19	22	20	26	29	24
Total Assets: End of Year (Millions $)	89.0	253.0	206.4	254.0	358.7	386.5

Annual Rate of Return (%) Years Ending 12/31	15.6	18.2	(10.3)	19.8	7.6	(1.6)

Five-Year Total Return(%)	34.5ᴱ	Degree of Diversification	C	Beta 1.18	Bull (%)	80.1ᶜ	Bear (%)	(26.5)ᴱ

Objective: Seeks long-term capital growth by investing in marketable equity securities of small or little-known companies with promise of expanding in size and profitability and/or of gaining increased market recognition for their securities. May invest in restricted securities and foreign securities. May convert to debt instruments as defensive measure.

Portfolio: (9/30/87) Common stocks 94%, short-term securities 3%, other assets 3%. Largest stock holdings: technology 25%, media & service 24%.

Distributions: Income: Aug, Dec   **Capital Gains:** Aug, Dec

12b-1: No

Minimum: Initial: $1,000   Subsequent: None

Min IRA: Initial: $240   Subsequent: None

Services: IRA, Keogh, 403(b), Corp, Withdraw, Deduct

Tel Exchange: Yes   **With MMF:** Yes

Registered: All states

SCUDDER GLOBAL
International

Scudder, Stevens & Clark
175 Federal Street
Boston, MA 02110-2267
(800) 225-2470/(617) 439-4640

	Years Ending 6/30					
	1982	**1983**	**1984**	**1985**	**1986**	**1987** (11 mos.)
Net Investment Income ($)	–	–	–	–	–	.05
Dividends from Net Investment Income ($)	–	–	–	–	–	–
Net Gains (Losses) on Investments ($)	–	–	–	–	–	3.37
Distributions from Net Realized Capital Gains ($)	–	–	–	–	–	–
Net Asset Value End of Year ($)	–	–	–	–	–	15.42
Ratio of Expenses to Net Assets (%)	–	–	–	–	–	1.84
Portfolio Turnover Rate (%)	–	–	–	–	–	32
Total Assets: End of Year (Millions $)	–	–	–	–	–	101.9
Annual Rate of Return (%) Years Ending 12/31	–	–	–	–	–	2.9

Five-Year Total Return(%)	NA	Degree of Diversification	NA	Beta	NA	Bull (%)	NA	Bear (%)	(22.9)ᴰ

Objective: Seeks long-term growth of capital through worldwide investment in equity securities. Will be invested in at least three different countries, one of which will be the U.S. Income is an incidental consideration. Can buy and sell index and foreign currency futures as a hedge.

Portfolio: (9/30/87) Common stocks 84%, repos 6%, bonds 6%, other assets 3%, preferred stocks 1%. Largest country holdings: United States 39%, United Kingdom 13%.

Distributions: **Income:** Annually   **Capital Gains:** Annually

12b-1: No

Minimum: **Initial:** $1,000   **Subsequent:** None

Min IRA: **Initial:** $240   **Subsequent:** None

Services: IRA, Keogh, Corp, 403(b), Withdraw

Tel Exchange: Yes   **With MMF:** Yes

Registered: All states

SCUDDER GNMA
(formerly SCUDDER GOVERNMENT MORTGAGE SECURITIES)
Bond

Scudder, Stevens & Clark
175 Federal St.
Boston, MA 02110
(800) 453-3305/(617) 439-4640

	Years Ending 3/31					
	1982	1983	1984	1985	1986 (8 mos.)	1987
Net Investment Income ($)	–	–	–	–	1.12	1.34
Dividends from Net Investment Income ($)	–	–	–	–	1.12	1.34
Net Gains (Losses) on Investments ($)	–	–	–	–	.41	.11
Distributions from Net Realized Capital Gains ($)	–	–	–	–	–	.08
Net Asset Value End of Year ($)	–	–	–	–	15.41	15.44
Ratio of Expenses to Net Assets (%)	–	–	–	–	1.02	1.05
Portfolio Turnover Rate (%)	–	–	–	–	124	59
Total Assets: End of Year (Millions $)	–	–	–	–	153.8	293.8
Annual Rate of Return (%) Years Ending 12/31	–	–	–	–	11.3	1.5

Five-Year Total Return(%)	NA	Degree of Diversification	NA	Beta	NA	Bull (%)	NA	Bear (%)	2.2ᴬ

Objective: Seeks high current income and safety of principal through investment of at least 65% of its net assets in GNMA securities. Invests in other U.S. government-backed securities. May also buy and sell options and futures contracts.

Portfolio: (9/30/87) GNMAs 70%, U.S. Treasury obligations 29%, repos 1%.

Distributions: Income: Monthly   Capital Gains: Apr
12b-1: No
Minimum: Initial: $1,000   Subsequent: None
Min IRA: Initial: $240   Subsequent: None
Services: IRA, Keogh, Corp. 403(b), Withdraw, Deduct
Tel Exchange: Yes   With MMF: Yes
Registered: All states

SCUDDER
GROWTH & INCOME
Growth & Income

Scudder, Stevens & Clark
175 Federal St.
Boston, MA 02110-2267
(800) 453-3305/(617) 439-4640

	Years Ending 12/31					
	1982	1983	1984*	1985	1986	1987
Net Investment Income ($)	.50	.44	.41	.59	.67	.68
Dividends from Net Investment Income ($)	.49	.43	.40	.58	.68	.68
Net Gains (Losses) on Investments ($)	1.99	1.38	(1.12)	3.44	1.96	(.07)
Distributions from Net Realized Capital Gains ($)	1.36	.49	1.78	–	2.28	2.64
Net Asset Value End of Year ($)	13.89	14.79	11.90	15.35	15.02	12.31
Ratio of Expenses to Net Assets (%)	.86	.92	.89	.84	.83	.89
Portfolio Turnover Rate (%)	52	84	79	73	45	60
Total Assets: End of Year (Millions $)	188.6	260.1	223.6	302.1	384.5	391.8

Annual Rate of Return (%) Years Ending 12/31	22.6	13.3	(3.7)	34.5	17.8	3.4

Five-Year Total Return(%)	78.8B	Degree of Diversification	A	Beta	.86	Bull (%) 128.6A	Bear (%) (18.0)C

Changed name and objectives.

Objective: Seeks long-term capital growth and current income by purchasing seasoned and readily marketable dividend-paying securities of leading companies. May invest in foreign securities and sell covered call options and futures contracts. May also lend portfolio securities and enter into repos.

Portfolio: (12/31/87) Common stocks 62%, convertible securities 34%, short-term securities 7%. Largest stock holdings: utilities 15%, electric 11%.

Distributions: Income: April, July, Oct, Dec   **Capital Gains:** Dec

12b-1: No

Minimum: Initial: $1,000   Subsequent: None

Min IRA: Initial: $240   Subsequent: None

Services: IRA, Keogh, Corp, 403(b), Withdraw, Deduct

Tel Exchange: Yes   **With MMF:** Yes

Registered: All states

SCUDDER INCOME
Bond

Scudder, Stevens & Clark
175 Federal St.
Boston, MA 02110-2267
(800) 453-3305/(617) 439-4640

	Years Ending 12/31					
	1982	1983	1984	1985	1986	1987
Net Investment Income ($)	1.27	1.26	1.25	1.29	1.22	1.08
Dividends from Net Investment Income ($)	1.27	1.25	1.25	1.29	1.22	1.10
Net Gains (Losses) on Investments ($)	1.55	(.04)	.06	1.12	.59	(.99)
Distributions from Net Realized Capital Gains ($)	—	—	—	—	—	—
Net Asset Value End of Year ($)	11.67	11.64	11.70	12.82	13.41	12.40
Ratio of Expenses to Net Assets (%)	.93	.97	1.02	.91	.88	.94
Portfolio Turnover Rate (%)	41	40	40	30	24	34
Total Assets: End of Year (Millions $)	91.2	110.5	122.9	171.7	248.5	241.8

Annual Rate of Return (%) Years Ending 12/31	30.0	10.8	12.3	21.7	14.6	0.8

Five-Year Total Return(%)	74.9ᶜ	Degree of Diversification	NA	Beta	.08	Bull (%)	53.8ᴰ	Bear (%)	2.7ᴬ

Objective: Seeks current income through investment in fixed-income securities, dividend-paying common stocks and government obligations. May invest in foreign securities and CDs of both foreign and domestic banks, and may sell covered call options and enter into repos.

Portfolio: (12/31/87) Long-term bonds 57%, intermediate-term bonds 19%, short-term securities 14%, common stocks 5%, preferred stocks 2%, other assets 2%, convertible bonds 1%. Largest bond holdings: utilities 23%, financial 9%.

Distributions: Income: April, July, Oct, Dec   **Capital Gains:** Dec

12b-1: No

Minimum: Initial: $1,000   **Subsequent:** None

Min IRA: Initial: $240   **Subsequent:** None

Services: IRA, Keogh, Corp, 403(b), Withdraw, Deduct

Tel Exchange: Yes   **With MMF:** Yes

Registered: All states

SCUDDER INTERNATIONAL
International

Scudder, Stevens & Clark
175 Federal St.
Boston, MA 02110
(800) 453-3305/(617) 439-4640

	7/31		Years Ending 3/31			
	1982	1983	1984* (8 mos.)	1985	1986	1987
Net Investment Income ($)	.54	.40	.15	.51	.74	.47
Dividends from Net Investment Income ($)	.40	.54	.31	.10	.41	.49
Net Gains (Losses) on Investments ($)	(2.69)	6.37	3.24	(1.09)	13.70	13.07
Distributions from Net Realized Capital Gains ($)	.03	—	—	.58	.13	5.93
Net Asset Value End of Year ($)	14.98	21.21	24.29	23.03	36.93	44.05
Ratio of Expenses to Net Assets (%)	1.16	1.13	1.05	1.04	.99	1.09
Portfolio Turnover Rate (%)	42	39	17	20	36	67
Total Assets: End of Year (Millions $)	56.7	110.8	188.9	222.9	597	791.3

Annual Rate of Return (%) Years Ending 12/31	1.2	29.2	(0.7)	48.9	50.5	1.0

Five-Year Total Return(%)	190.3ᴬ	Degree of Diversification	E	Beta .70	Bull (%) 212.3ᴬ	Bear (%) (21.8)ᴰ

Fiscal year changed from 7/31 to 3/31.

Objective: Seeks long-term capital growth through investment in marketable equity securities selected primarily to permit participation in established non-U.S. companies and economies with prospects for growth. Also invests in fixed-income securities of foreign governments and companies with a view toward total investment return.

Portfolio: (9/30/87) Common stocks 91%, convertible bonds 3%, short-term securities 2%, preferred stocks 2%, bonds 1%. Largest country holdings: Japan 18%, United Kingdom 15%.

Distributions: Income: May   **Capital Gains:** May

12b-1: No

Minimum: Initial: $1,000   **Subsequent:** None

Min IRA: Initial: $240   **Subsequent:** None

Services: IRA, Keogh, 403(b), Corp, Withdraw, Deduct

Tel Exchange: Yes   **With MMF:** Yes

Registered: All states

SCUDDER TARGET GENERAL 1990
Bond

Scudder, Stevens & Clark
175 Federal St.
Boston, MA 02110-2267
(800) 453-3305/(617) 439-4640

	10/31			Years Ending 12/31			
	1982	1983	1984	1984* (2 mos.)	1985	1986	1986
Net Investment Income ($)	—	.59	.82	.14	.83	.66	.56
Dividends from Net Investment Income ($)	—	.59	.82	.14	.83	.66	.56
Net Gains (Losses) on Investments ($)	—	(.67)	.05	.15	.85	.54	(.25)
Distributions from Net Realized Capital Gains ($)	—	—	—	—	—	.39	.12
Net Asset Value End of Year ($)	—	9.33	9.38	9.53	10.38	10.53	10.16
Ratio of Expenses to Net Assets (%)	—	1.00	1.06	1.00	1.00	1.25	1.41
Portfolio Turnover Rate (%)	—	4	13	0	49	35	41
Total Assets: End of Year (Millions $)	—	6.0	8.8	9.3	12.5	16.2	15.4
Annual Rate of Return (%) Years Ending 12/31	—	(0.4)	12.9	*	18.3	12.0	2.9

Five-Year Total Return(%)	53.3ᴰ	Degree of Diversification	NA	Beta	.03	Bull (%)	48.8ᴰ	Bear (%)	2.2ᴬ

Fiscal year end changed from 10/31 to 12/31. All annual return figures are for full years ending 12/31.

Objective: Seeks current income plus preservation of capital. Invests in high grade corporate bonds and notes plus U.S. Treasury securities. The portfolio is designed to be liquidated in 1990.

Portfolio: (12/31/87) Corporate bonds 64%, U.S. Treasury obligations 26%, U.S. government-backed obligations 10%. Largest bond holdings: utilities 28%, transportation 15%.

Distributions: **Income:** Monthly   **Capital Gains:** Annually

12b-1: No

Minimum: **Initial:** $1,000   **Subsequent:** None

Min IRA: **Initial:** $240   **Subsequent:** None

Services: IRA, Keogh, Corp, 403(b), Withdraw, Deduct

Tel Exchange: Yes   **With MMF:** Yes

Registered: All states

SELECTED AMERICAN SHARES

Growth & Income

Prescott Asset Mgmt., Inc.
230 W. Monroe St., 28th Flr.
Chicago, IL 60606
(800) 621-7321/(312) 641-7862

	Years Ending 12/31					
	1982	1983	1984	1985	1986	1987
Net Investment Income ($)	.58	.56	.46	.48	.42	.34
Dividends from Net Investment Income ($)	.56	.56	.48	.40	.48	.42
Net Gains (Losses) on Investments ($)	1.08	1.19	.93	2.90	1.65	(.22)
Distributions from Net Realized Capital Gains ($)	—	—	.05	.17	2.29	.92
Net Asset Value End of Year ($)	8.49	9.68	10.54	13.35	12.65	11.43
Ratio of Expenses to Net Assets (%)	1.02	.94	.99	.87	.85	1.11
Portfolio Turnover Rate (%)	15	66	49	33	40	45
Total Assets: End of Year (Millions $)	76.6	81.3	84.3	122.6	160.5	263.2

Annual Rate of Return (%) Years Ending 12/31	24.3	22.6	13.9	33.2	17.0	0.2

Five-Year Total Return(%)	118.0ᴬ	Degree of Diversification	B	Beta .78	Bull (%) 126.3ᴬ	Bear (%) (21.4)ᴰ

Objective: To provide growth of capital and income. The fund invests in common stocks and fixed-income securities in varying proportions of companies with large capitalizations and long records of earnings growth and dividends. May lend portfolio securities and write covered call options.

Portfolio: (12/31/87) Common stocks 100%. Largest stock holdings: insurance 17%, food 9%.

Distributions: Income: Jan, Mar, June, Sept   **Capital Gains:** Jan

12b-1: Yes   **Amount:** 1.00%

Minimum: Initial: $1,000   **Subsequent:** $100

Min IRA: Initial: $1,000   **Subsequent:** $100

Services: IRA, Keogh, Corp, SEP, Withdraw, Deduct

Tel Exchange: Yes   **With MMF:** Yes

Registered: All states

SELECTED
SPECIAL SHARES
Growth

Prescott Asset Mgmt., Inc.
230 W. Monroe St., 28th Flr.
Chicago, IL 60606
(800) 621-7321/(312) 641-7862

	Years Ending 12/31					
	1982	1983	1984	1985	1986	1987
Net Investment Income ($)	.43	.65	.40	.67	.49	.18
Dividends from Net Investment Income ($)	.42	.38	.56	.49	.64	.64
Net Gains (Losses) on Investments ($)	2.22	4.45	(1.14)	3.32	.88	(.06)
Distributions from Net Realized Capital Gains ($)	—	—	4.28	.65	3.45	1.40
Net Asset Value End of Year ($)	18.56	23.28	17.70	20.55	17.83	15.91
Ratio of Expenses to Net Assets (%)	1.32	1.21	1.38	1.23	1.08	1.10
Portfolio Turnover Rate (%)	62	101	68	73	133	89
Total Assets: End of Year (Millions $)	31.0	36.6	32.7	35.9	32.8	36.1
Annual Rate of Return (%) Years Ending 12/31	16.8	28.0	(4.2)	23.5	7.2	0.6

Five-Year Total Return(%)	63.3[C]	Degree of Diversification	B	Beta	1.02	Bull (%)	102.4[B]	Bear (%)	(26.7)[E]

Objective: Seeks growth of capital through investment in common stocks and convertible securities of growing companies that are undervalued. Looks for strong management and growth record. Current income is incidental to this objective.

Portfolio: (12/31/87) Common stocks 92%, short-term securities 14%. Largest stock holdings: consumer goods & services 21%, distribution 15%.

Distributions: Income: Jan   **Capital Gains:** Jan

12b-1: Yes   **Amount:** 1.00%

Minimum: Initial: $1,000   Subsequent: $100

Min IRA: Initial: $1,000   Subsequent: $100

Services: IRA, Keogh, Corp, SEP, Withdraw, Deduct

Tel Exchange: Yes   **With MMF:** Yes

Registered: All states

SHERMAN, DEAN
Aggressive Growth

Sherman, Dean
Management and Research Corp.
6061 N.W. Expressway
Suite 465
San Antonio, TX 78201
(512) 735-7700

	Years Ending 5/31					
	1982	1983	1984	1985	1986	1987
Net Investment Income ($)	.06	.05	.02	.00	(.11)	(.20)
Dividends from Net Investment Income ($)	–	.12	.03	.01	.04	–
Net Gains (Losses) on Investments ($)	(3.49)	2.88	(2.25)	(.74)	(.75)	3.13
Distributions from Net Realized Capital Gains ($)	–	–	–	–	–	–
Net Asset Value End of Year ($)	6.31	9.12	6.86	6.11	5.21	8.14
Ratio of Expenses to Net Assets (%)	1.91	1.91	2.01	2.04	2.36	3.38
Portfolio Turnover Rate (%)	10	4	12	21	13	0
Total Assets: End of Year (Millions $)	4.9	5.1	4.3	3.8	2.3	2.9

Annual Rate of Return (%) Years Ending 12/31	(3.9)	(3.8)	(32.0)	13.1	(4.7)	.2

Five-Year Total Return(%) (29.2)ᴱ	Degree of Diversification	E	Beta .58	Bull (%) 47.3ᴱ	Bear (%) (37.9)ᴱ

Objective: Seeks long-term capital appreciation through investment in common stocks of companies with apparently unusually favorable prospects including small, unseasoned and special situation companies. May concentrate 50% of assets in two companies—25% each.

Portfolio: (11/30/87) Common stocks 96%, cash and other assets 4%, bonds 1%. Largest stock holdings: mining 58%, technology 19%.

Distributions: Income: June   **Capital Gains:** June
12b-1: Yes   **Amount:** 0.25%
Minimum: Initial: $1,000   Subsequent: $100
Min IRA: Initial: NA   Subsequent: NA
Services: NA
Tel Exchange: No
Registered: CA, CO, CT, DC, FL, GA, HI, IL, IN, MA, MD, MI, MN, MO, NJ, NV, NY, OR, PA, TX, VA, WA, WI, WY

SOUND SHORE
Growth

McConnell & Miller, Inc.
8 Sound Shore Drive
Greenwich, CT 06836
(203) 629-1980

| | Years Ending 3/31 | | | | | |
	1982	1983	1984	1985	1986 (11 mos.)	1987
Net Investment Income ($)	–	–	–	–	.15	.14
Dividends from Net Investment Income ($)	–	–	–	–	.14	.08
Net Gains (Losses) on Investments ($)	–	–	–	–	3.66	2.63
Distributions from Net Realized Capital Gains ($)	–	–	–	–	–	.39
Net Asset Value End of Year ($)	–	–	–	–	13.67	15.97
Ratio of Expenses to Net Assets (%)	–	–	–	–	1.48	1.45
Portfolio Turnover Rate (%)	–	–	–	–	82	91
Total Assets: End of Year (Millions $)	–	–	–	–	13.9	31.5

Annual Rate of Return (%) Years Ending 12/31	–	–	–	–	20.5	(3.7)

Five-Year Total Return(%)	NA	Degree of Diversification	NA	Beta	NA	Bull (%)	NA	Bear (%)	(21.6)ᴰ

Objective: Seeks capital growth with current income as a secondary objective. Invests in a diversified group of growth stocks selected on the basis of price, earnings expectations, balance sheet characteristics, and perceived management skills. May not invest more than 25% of net assets in any particular industry.

Portfolio: (9/30/87) Common stocks 91%, cash 5%, short-term securities 4%. Largest stock holdings: insurance 18%, savings and loan 12%.

Distributions: Income: Semiannually   **Capital Gains:** Annually

12b-1: Yes   **Amount:** 1.00%

Minimum: Initial: $20,000   **Subsequent:** None

Min IRA: Initial: $250   **Subsequent:** None

Services: IRA, Withdraw

Tel Exchange: Yes   **With MMF:** Yes

Registered: All states

STEADMAN AMERICAN INDUSTRY

Growth

Steadman Security Corp.
1730 K St., N.W.
Washington, DC 20006
(800) 424-8570/(202) 223-1000

	Years Ending 1/31					
	1982	1983	1984	1985	1986	1987
Net Investment Income ($)	.14	.05	(.02)	(.04)	(.04)	(.14)
Dividends from Net Investment Income ($)	–	.15	.03	–	–	–
Net Gains (Losses) on Investments ($)	(.46)	.26	.04	(.36)	–	(.07)
Distributions from Net Realized Capital Gains ($)	–	–	.02	–	–	–
Net Asset Value End of Year ($)	3.20	3.36	3.33	2.93	2.89	2.68
Ratio of Expenses to Net Assets (%)	3.61	4.33	3.75	4.83	5.03	6.26
Portfolio Turnover Rate (%)	81	143	78	227	249	420
Total Assets: End of Year (Millions $)	13.1	12.8	11.2	9.3	9.3	6.5

Annual Rate of Return (%) Years Ending 12/31	4.7	6.7	(23.2)	7.8	(19.7)	.9

Five-Year Total Return(%)	(28.5)ᴱ	Degree of Diversification	D	Beta .98	Bull (%) 14.4ᴱ	Bear (%) (28.0)ᴱ

Objective: Seeks to provide long-term capital growth through investment in common stocks of large, established companies, debt securities, precious metals, oil and gas leases and limited partnerships, and real estate. Realization of current income is secondary. May employ leverage, effect short sales, write options and enter into repos.

Portfolio: (7/31/87) Common stocks 97%, short-term securities 2%. Largest stock holdings: consumer goods 27%, utilities 19%.

Distributions: Income: Annually   **Capital Gains:** Annually

12b-1: Yes   **Amount:** 0.25%

Minimum: Initial: $500   Subsequent: $25

Min IRA: Initial: $500   Subsequent: $25

Services: IRA, Keogh, 403(b), Withdraw

Tel Exchange: Yes   **With MMF:** No

Registered: All states

STEADMAN ASSOCIATED

Growth & Income

Steadman Security Corp.
1730 K St., N.W.
Washington, DC 20006
(800) 424-8570/(202) 223-1000

	Years Ending 9/30					
	1982	1983*	1984	1985	1986	1987
Net Investment Income ($)	.07	.06	.05	Nil	(.01)	.02
Dividends from Net Investment Income ($)	.07	.06	.05	.01	—	.02
Net Gains (Losses) on Investments ($)	.08	.15	(.14)	.01	.11	.12
Distributions from Net Realized Capital Gains ($)	—	.02	—	.04	.08	.06
Net Asset Value End of Year ($)	.87	1.00	.86	.82	.85	.91
Ratio of Expenses to Net Assets (%)	2.18	1.99	2.6	2.85	2.88	3.06
Portfolio Turnover Rate (%)	41	78	304	211	375	302
Total Assets: End of Year (Millions $)	30.9	32.7	25.2	20.5	19.8	20.6

Annual Rate of Return (%) Years Ending 12/31	27.3	6.0	(8.6)	21.5	2.8	(23.9)

Five-Year Total Return(%) (8.0)ᴱ	Degree of Diversification D	Beta 1.04	Bull (%) 38.9ᴱ	Bear (%) (31.0)ᴱ

*Was an income (bond) fund. Changed 10/83 to growth fund.

Objective: Seeks capital growth through use of a broad range of investments and techniques including purchase and sale of put and call options. Income is secondary goal. Emphasis is on large, well-established, dividend-paying companies.

Portfolio: (9/30/87) Common stocks 86%, restricted securities 5%, convertible preferred stocks 5%, short-term securities 4%. Largest stock holdings: consumer goods 18%, metals 16%.

Distributions: Income: Mar, June, Sept, Dec   **Capital Gains:** Sept

12b-1: Yes   **Amount:** 0.25%

Minimum: Initial: $500   **Subsequent:** $25

Min IRA: Initial: $500   **Subsequent:** $25

Services: IRA, Keogh, 403(b), Withdraw

Tel Exchange: Yes   **With MMF:** No

Registered: All states

STEADMAN INVESTMENT
Growth

Steadman Security Corp.
1730 K St., NW
Washington, DC 20006
(800) 424-8570/(202) 223-1000

	Years Ending 12/31					
	1982	1983	1984	1985	1986	1987
Net Investment Income ($)	.07	.01	.03	.13	.06	.01
Dividends from Net Investment Income ($)	.09	.04	.02	.02	–	–
Net Gains (Losses) on Investments ($)	.03	.11	(.20)	(.05)	.09	(.29)
Distributions from Net Realized Capital Gains ($)	–	–	–	–	–	–
Net Asset Value End of Year ($)	1.49	1.58	1.39	1.46	1.61	1.32
Ratio of Expenses to Net Assets (%)	2.71	2.61	3.52	5.15	3.97	4.32
Portfolio Turnover Rate (%)	162	186	262	406	129	96
Total Assets: End of Year (Millions $)	14.1	13.6	9.7	9.0	8.1	5.7

Annual Rate of Return (%) Years Ending 12/31	7.4	8.0	(10.9)	5.3	10.3	(17.5)

Five-Year Total Return(%) (7.8)ᴱ	Degree of Diversification	D	Beta .92	Bull (%) 50.7ᴰ	Bear (%) (30.9)ᴱ

Objective: Long-term capital appreciation through investing in common stocks and other equity-related securities. May invest up to 10% of assets in foreign securities and use option techniques.

Portfolio: (12/31/87) Common stocks 44%, convertible bonds 21%, short-term securities 19%, convertible preferred stocks 16%, put options purchased 1%. Largest stock holdings: Sudbury Holdings, Inc. 38%, Toll Brothers, Inc. 29%.

Distributions:	Income: Annually	**Capital Gains:**	Annually
12b-1:	Yes	Amount: 0.25%	
Minimum:	Initial: $500	Subsequent: $25	
Min IRA:	Initial: $500	Subsequent: $25	
Services:	IRA, Keogh, 403(b), Withdraw		
Tel Exchange:	Yes	With MMF: No	
Registered:	All states		

STEADMAN OCEANOGRAPHIC, TECHNOLOGY & GROWTH

Aggressive Growth

Steadman Security Corp.
1730 K St., NW
Washington, DC 20006
(800) 424-8570/(202) 223-1000

	Years Ending 12/31					
	1982	1983	1984	1985	1986	1987
Net Investment Income ($)	.13	(.06)	(.09)	(.22)	(.33)	(.27)
Dividends from Net Investment Income ($)	.15	.07	—	—	—	—
Net Gains (Losses) on Investments ($)	(.24)	.68	(.64)	(.61)	(.25)	(.09)
Distributions from Net Realized Capital Gains ($)	—	.06	—	—	—	—
Net Asset Value End of Year ($)	6.13	6.62	5.89	5.06	4.48	4.12
Ratio of Expenses to Net Assets (%)	4.13	3.67	4.43	5.30	5.81	6.34
Portfolio Turnover Rate (%)	214	225	270	260	197	196
Total Assets: End of Year (Millions $)	8.0	8.0	6.5	4.9	3.8	3.1

Annual Rate of Return (%) Years Ending 12/31	(1.7)	10.2	(10.9)	(14.3)	(11.3)	(8.5)

Five-Year Total Return(%) (31.6)[E]	Degree of Diversification D	Beta 1.46	Bull (%) 15.1[E]	Bear (%) (37.5)[E]

Objective: Seeks capital growth through investment in common stocks of companies primarily engaged in basic industries. May employ leverage, short-selling; may invest in foreign securities; may buy and sell option contracts.

Portfolio: (12/31/87) Common stocks 75%, short-term securities 17%, convertible bonds 7%, put options purchased 1%. Largest stock holdings: Sudbury Holdings, Inc. 29%, Automatic Language Processing Systems, Inc. 17%.

Distributions: Income: Annually   **Capital Gains:** Annually

12b-1: Yes   **Amount:** 0.25%

Minimum: Initial: $500   Subsequent: $25

Min IRA: Initial: $500   Subsequent: $25

Services: IRA, Keogh, 403(b), Withdraw

Tel Exchange: Yes   **With MMF:** No

Registered: All states

STEINROE CAPITAL OPPORTUNITIES

Aggressive Growth

Stein Roe & Farnham
P.O. Box 1143
Chicago, IL 60690
(800) 338-2550/(312) 368-7826

	Years Ending 12/31					
	1982	1983	1984	1985	1986	1987
Net Investment Income ($)	.24	.11	.30	.20	.06	.06
Dividends from Net Investment Income ($)	.33	.19	.12	.29	.20	.09
Net Gains (Losses) on Investments ($)	4.57	2.80	(4.69)	4.53	3.93	1.24
Distributions from Net Realized Capital Gains ($)	.64	.65	2.55	–	.85	6.73
Net Asset Value End of Year ($)	24.36	26.43	19.37	23.81	26.75	21.23
Ratio of Expenses to Net Assets (%)	.95	.89	.92	.95	.95	.95
Portfolio Turnover Rate (%)	95	72	85	90	116	133
Total Assets: End of Year (Millions $)	197.9	292.5	176.1	176.1	191.4	171.9
Annual Rate of Return (%) Years Ending 12/31	24.9	11.9	(16.8)	24.6	16.8	8.7

Five-Year Total Return(%)	47.2ᴱ	Degree of Diversification	D	Beta	1.21	Bull (%)	119.7ᴮ	Bear (%)	(27.0)ᴱ

Objective: To provide long-term capital appreciation by investing in selected common stocks of both seasoned and smaller companies that have potential for success with new products or services, technological developments, or management shifts. May invest in foreign securities.

Portfolio: (12/31/87) Common stocks 95%, other assets 5%. Largest stock holdings: technology 35%, business services 17%.

Distributions: Income: Annually   **Capital Gains:** Annually
12b-1: No
Minimum: Initial: $1,000   Subsequent: $100
Min IRA: Initial: $500   Subsequent: $50
Services: IRA, Keogh, SEP, Withdraw
Tel Exchange: Yes   **With MMF:** Yes
Registered: All states

STEINROE DISCOVERY

Aggressive Growth

Stein Roe & Farnham
P.O. Box 1143
Chicago, IL 60690
(800) 621-0320/(312) 368-7826

	1982	1983	1984 (11 mos.)	1985	1986	1987
			Years Ending 6/30			
Net Investment Income ($)	–	–	.02	.04	.03	.03
Dividends from Net Investment Income ($)	–	–	–	.03	.04	.04
Net Gains (Losses) on Investments ($)	–	–	(2.53)	2.72	3.55	(.48)
Distributions from Net Realized Capital Gains ($)	–	–	–	–	–	.03
Net Asset Value End of Year ($)	–	–	7.49	10.22	13.76	13.24
Ratio of Expenses to Net Assets (%)	–	–	1.49	1.42	1.29	1.36
Portfolio Turnover Rate (%)	–	–	64	101	157	207
Total Assets: End of Year (Millions $)	–	–	33.2	97.2	133.4	65.7

| Annual Rate of Return (%) Years Ending 12/31 | – | – | (12.2) | 45.3 | (5.3) | (3.2) |

| Five-Year Total Return(%) | NA | Degree of Diversification | D | Beta 1.36 | Bull (%) 100.9C | Bear (%) (28.1)E |

Objective: Seeks long-term capital appreciation by investing in the common stock of smaller companies with less than $250 million in market capitalization and in larger companies with new products, technological developments or other favorable business developments. May include new issues. May write covered call options and enter into repurchase agreements.

Portfolio: (9/30/87) Common stocks 95%, short-term obligations 6%. Largest stock holdings: technology 32%, health care 17%.

Distributions: Income: Aug   **Capital Gains:** Aug

12b-1: No

Minimum: Initial: $1,000   Subsequent: $100

Min IRA: Initial: $500   Subsequent: $50

Services: IRA, Keogh, SEP, Withdraw

Tel Exchange: Yes   **With MMF:** Yes

Registered: All states except CA

STEINROE
HIGH-YIELD BONDS

Bond

Stein Roe & Farnham
P.O. Box 1143
Chicago, IL 60690
(800) 621-0320/(312) 368-7826

	Years Ending 6/30					
	1982	1983	1984	1985	1986 (4 mos.)	1987
Net Investment Income ($)	–	–	–	–	.30	.98
Dividends from Net Investment Income ($)	–	–	–	–	.30	.98
Net Gains (Losses) on Investments ($)	–	–	–	–	(.06)	(.23)
Distributions from Net Realized Capital Gains ($)	–	–	–	–	–	–
Net Asset Value End of Year ($)	–	–	–	–	9.94	9.71
Ratio of Expenses to Net Assets (%)	–	–	–	–	2.01	.96
Portfolio Turnover Rate (%)	–	–	–	–	84	153
Total Assets: End of Year (Millions $)	–	–	–	–	32.0	91.9

Annual Rate of Return (%) Years Ending 12/31	–	–	–	–	–	4.0

Five-Year Total Return(%)	NA	Degree of Diversification	NA	Beta	NA	Bull (%)	NA	Bear (%)	3.0ᴬ

Objective: Seeks high level of current income; capital appreciation is of secondary importance. Invests in below invest-ment-grade (BBB) bonds and convertible securities. May invest up to 35% of its assets in preferred and common stocks.

Portfolio: (9/30/87) Long-term obligations 93%, short-term obliga-tions 9%. Largest holdings: electric utilities 24%, tele-phone 8%.

Distributions: Income: Monthly   **Capital Gains:** Annually

12b-1: No

Minimum: Initial: $1,000   Subsequent: $100

Min IRA: Initial: $500   Subsequent: $50

Services: IRA, Keogh, SEP, Withdraw

Tel Exchange: Yes   **With MMF:** Yes

Registered: All states

STEINROE MANAGED BONDS
Bond

Stein Roe & Farnham
P.O. Box 1143
Chicago, IL 60690
(800) 621-0320/(312) 368-7826

	Years Ending 6/30					
	1982	1983	1984	1985	1986	1987
Net Investment Income ($)	1.10	.97	.94	.89	.84	.74
Dividends from Net Investment Income ($)	1.10	.97	.94	.89	.84	.74
Net Gains (Losses) on Investments ($)	(.20)	1.08	(1.04)	1.14	1.03	(.41)
Distributions from Net Realized Capital Gains ($)	–	–	.21	–	–	.74
Net Asset Value End of Year ($)	7.92	9.00	7.75	8.89	9.92	8.77
Ratio of Expenses to Net Assets (%)	1.07	.81	.78	.70	.69	.65
Portfolio Turnover Rate (%)	241	185	152	286	334	230
Total Assets: End of Year (Millions $)	28.3	84.1	86.5	134.6	183.4	188.7

Annual Rate of Return (%) Years Ending 12/31	27.4	6.9	11.8	22.9	16.3	1.1

Five-Year Total Return(%)	72.6ᶜ	Degree of Diversification	NA	Beta	.06	Bull (%)	51.6ᴰ	Bear (%)	3.3ᴬ

Objective: Seeks high current income through investment in marketable, investment-grade debt securities. May enter into interest rate futures contracts and covered call options as a hedge. May invest in foreign debt securities. Any common stock investment would be in dividend-paying companies.

Portfolio: (9/30/87) U.S. government obligations 50%, corporate bonds 28%, short-term obligations 22%. Largest holdings: financial 8%, telephone 7%.

Distributions: Income: Monthly   **Capital Gains:** July
12b-1: No
Minimum: Initial: $1,000   Subsequent: $100
Min IRA: Initial: $500   Subsequent: $50
Services: IRA, Keogh, SEP, Withdraw
Tel Exchange: Yes   **With MMF:** Yes
Registered: All states

STEINROE SPECIAL
Aggressive Growth

Stein Roe & Farnham
P.O. Box 1143
Chicago, IL 60690
(800) 338-2550/(312) 368-7826

	Years Ending 12/31					
	1982	1983	1984	1985	1986	1987
Net Investment Income ($)	.23	.23	.28	.25	.35	.23
Dividends from Net Investment Income ($)	.29	.23	.23	.19	.34	.57
Net Gains (Losses) on Investments ($)	3.50	4.21	(.61)	4.01	2.33	.12
Distributions from Net Realized Capital Gains ($)	1.26	.57	2.29	.54	3.80	3.90
Net Asset Value End of Year ($)	14.09	17.73	14.88	18.41	16.95	12.83
Ratio of Expenses to Net Assets (%)	.96	.93	.96	.92	.92	.96
Portfolio Turnover Rate (%)	61	81	89	96	116	103
Total Assets: End of Year (Millions $)	78.2	145.2	152.0	278.0	253.7	187.9
Annual Rate of Return (%) Years Ending 12/31	36.7	32.9	0.0	29.4	14.8	3.5

Five-Year Total Return(%)	104.2[A]	Degree of Diversification	B	Beta	1.00	Bull (%)	122.8[B]	Bear (%)	(21.6)[D]

Objective: Seeks capital appreciation through investment in the common stocks of companies expected to benefit from special factors or trends or having unusual capital appreciation potential, including new issues.

Portfolio: (12/31/87) Common stocks 90%, short-term obligations 5%, convertible subordinated debentures 3%, bonds and notes 3%, convertible preferred stocks 1%. Largest stock holdings: media 20%, technology 16%.

Distributions: Income: Annually   **Capital Gains:** Annually

12b-1: No

Minimum: Initial: $1,000   Subsequent: $100

Min IRA: Initial: $500   Subsequent: $50

Services: IRA, Keogh, SEP, Withdraw

Tel Exchange: Yes   **With MMF:** Yes

Registered: All states

STEINROE STOCK

Aggressive Growth

Stein Roe & Farnham
P.O. Box 1143
Chicago, IL 60690
(800) 338-2550/(312) 368-7826

	Years Ending 12/31					
	1982	**1983**	**1984**	**1985**	**1986**	**1987**
Net Investment Income ($)	.48	.25	.36	.31	.26	.24
Dividends from Net Investment Income ($)	.45	.28	.38	.30	.25	.29
Net Gains (Losses) on Investments ($)	4.62	2.41	(2.60)	3.38	2.75	.46
Distributions from Net Realized Capital Gains ($)	1.48	1.43	4.70	—	3.22	2.71
Net Asset Value End of Year ($)	20.41	21.36	14.04	17.43	16.97	14.67
Ratio of Expenses to Net Assets (%)	.66	.63	.67	.67	.67	.65
Portfolio Turnover Rate (%)	116	173	195	114	137	143
Total Assets: End of Year (Millions $)	234.9	269.3	216.5	224.4	226.6	232.7

Annual Rate of Return (%) Years Ending 12/31	33.4	14.0	(9.8)	26.5	17.3	5.1

Five-Year Total Return(%)	60.5[D]	Degree of Diversification	A	Beta 1.12	Bull (%) 127.3[A]	Bear (%) (26.1)[E]

Objective: Seeks long-term capital appreciation through investment primarily in common stocks and convertible securities of established companies. May write covered call options on up to 25% of assets.

Portfolio: (12/31/87) Common stocks 94%, short-term obligations 8%. Largest stock holdings: food, beverages & tobacco 8%, utilities—telephone 8%.

Distributions: Income: Feb, May, Aug, Nov   **Capital Gains:** Feb

12b-1: No

Minimum: Initial: $1,000   Subsequent: $100

Min IRA: Initial: $500   Subsequent: $50

Services: IRA, Keogh, SEP, Withdraw

Tel Exchange: Yes   **With MMF:** Yes

Registered: All states

STEINROE
TOTAL RETURN
Balanced

Stein Roe & Farnham
P.O. Box 1143
Chicago, IL 60690
(800) 338-2550/(312) 368-7826

	Years Ending 12/31					
	1982	1983	1984	1985	1986	1987
Net Investment Income ($)	1.23	1.30	1.41	1.41	1.33	1.32
Dividends from Net Investment Income ($)	1.15	1.26	1.41	1.42	1.35	1.63
Net Gains (Losses) on Investments ($)	3.03	1.61	(.48)	3.87	2.75	(1.06)
Distributions from Net Realized Capital Gains ($)	.43	–	1.55	.19	2.70	1.45
Net Asset Value End of Year ($)	21.75	23.40	21.37	25.04	25.07	22.25
Ratio of Expenses to Net Assets (%)	.73	.73	.73	.77	.79	.80
Portfolio Turnover Rate (%)	84	79	50	100	108	86
Total Assets: End of Year (Millions $)	84.7	93.0	95.7	128.7	149.8	140.2

Annual Rate of Return (%) Years Ending 12/31	24.3	13.5	5.2	25.6	16.9	0.4

Five-Year Total Return(%)	76.1ᶜ	Degree of Diversification	NA	Beta	.60	Bull (%)	89.3ᶜ	Bear (%)	(13.2)ᶜ

Objective: To maintain and increase the purchasing power of invested capital while providing income by investing in high-quality bonds, preferred stocks and common stocks of established companies. Stocks will comprise no more than 75% of assets. May write (sell) covered call options.

Portfolio: (12/31/87) Common stocks 31%, bonds and notes 27%, convertible subordinated debentures 25%, convertible preferred stocks 9%, short-term obligations 8%. Largest stock holdings: consumer products 4%; food, beverages and tobacco 4%.

Distributions: Income: Feb, May, Aug, Nov   **Capital Gains:** Feb
12b-1: No
Minimum: Initial: $1,000   Subsequent: $100
Min IRA: Initial: $500   Subsequent: $50
Services: IRA, Keogh, SEP, Withdraw
Tel Exchange: Yes   **With MMF:** Yes
Registered: All states

STEINROE UNIVERSE
Growth

Stein Roe & Farnham
P.O. Box 1143
Chicago, IL 60690
(800) 621-0320/(312) 368-7826

	Years Ending 6/30					
	1982	1983	1984	1985	1986	1987
Net Investment Income ($)	.36	.16	.28	.29	.21	.26
Dividends from Net Investment Income ($)	.14	.36	.17	.28	.27	.21
Net Gains (Losses) on Investments ($)	(2.12)	10.86	(6.94)	3.06	6.35	.87
Distributions from Net Realized Capital Gains ($)	–	–	.64	–	–	3.62
Net Asset Value End of Year ($)	11.79	22.45	14.98	18.05	24.34	21.64
Ratio of Expenses to Net Assets (%)	1.16	1.10	1.09	1.19	1.20	1.19
Portfolio Turnover Rate (%)	81	75	130	179	147	242
Total Assets: End of Year (Millions $)	115.0	336.4	182.5	116.8	114.7	94.4

Annual Rate of Return (%) Years Ending 12/31	31.6	20.6	(18.8)	28.3	13.2	(1.6)

Five-Year Total Return(%)	39.9ᴱ	Degree of Diversification	B	Beta 1.11	Bull (%) 100.3ᶜ	Bear (%) (26.7)ᴱ

Objective: Seeks capital appreciation primarily through investment in common stocks of growth companies including small and unseasoned companies or securities convertible into common stocks selected by its computerized database, which includes financial forecasts and estimates of indicated market value. May write covered call options, invest in foreign securities and enter into repos.

Portfolio: (9/30/87) Common stocks 97%, short-term obligations 10%. Largest stock holdings: computers & office equipment 11%, services 10%.

Distributions: Income: Aug   **Capital Gains:** Aug

12b-1: No

Minimum: Initial: $1,000   Subsequent: $100

Min IRA: Initial: $500   Subsequent: $50

Services: IRA, Keogh, SEP, Withdraw

Tel Exchange: Yes   **With MMF:** Yes

Registered: All states except CA

STRATTON GROWTH
Growth

Stratton Management Co.
Plymouth Meeting Executive
Campus
610 W. Germantown Pike
Suite 361
Plymouth Meeting, PA 19462
(800) 634-5726/(215) 941-0255

	Years Ending 5/31					
	1982	1983	1984	1985	1986	1987
Net Investment Income ($)	.25	.18	.15	.20	.28	.37
Dividends from Net Investment Income ($)	.28	.29	.13	.14	.20	.28
Net Gains (Losses) on Investments ($)	(1.36)	7.09	(2.27)	3.82	5.93	(.03)
Distributions from Net Realized Capital Gains ($)	–	–	–	.70	.61	2.07
Net Asset Value End of Year ($)	10.94	17.92	15.67	18.85	24.25	22.24
Ratio of Expenses to Net Assets (%)	1.90	1.80	1.61	1.61	1.49	1.50
Portfolio Turnover Rate (%)	47	70	36	35	29	23
Total Assets: End of Year (Millions $)	6.7	11.8	11.4	14.3	19.3	19.3
Annual Rate of Return (%) Years Ending 12/31	32.6	26.3	(4.6)	27.2	10.7	(4.3)

Five-Year Total Return(%)	62.4ᴰ	Degree of Diversification	C	Beta	.95	Bull (%)	89.9ᶜ	Bear (%)	(22.7)ᴰ

Objective: Seeks growth of capital with current income as a secondary consideration. The fund will normally invest in common stocks and convertible securities of medium to large, well-established, dividend-paying companies.

Portfolio: (11/30/87) Common stocks 78%, cash 16%, convertible debentures 5%. Largest stock holdings: banking 15%, business services 12%.

Distributions: Income: June   **Capital Gains:** June

12b-1: No

Minimum: Initial: $1,000   Subsequent: $100

Min IRA: Initial: None   Subsequent: None

Services: IRA, Keogh, 403(b), Withdraw

Tel Exchange: Yes   **With MMF:** No

Registered: CA, CO, CT, DC, DE, FL, GA, HI, IL, IN, MA, MD, MI, MN, NE, NJ, NY, OH, OR, PA, RI, TX, VA, WA, WY

STRATTON MONTHLY DIVIDEND SHARES

Balanced

Stratton Management Co.
Plymouth Meeting Executive Campus
610 W. Germantown Pike
Plymouth Meeting, PA 19462
(800) 634-5726/(215) 941-0255

	Years Ending 1/31					
	1982	**1983**	**1984**	**1985**	**1986**	**1987**
Net Investment Income ($)	2.01	2.08	1.85	1.96	1.83	2.09
Dividends from Net Investment Income ($)	1.76	1.83	1.93	2.05	2.17	2.28
Net Gains (Losses) on Investments ($)	.21	2.52	(.19)	2.24	5.69	3.96
Distributions from Net Realized Capital Gains ($)	—	—	—	—	—	.10
Net Asset Value End of Year ($)	17.82	20.59	20.32	22.47	27.82	31.09
Ratio of Expenses to Net Assets (%)	1.99	1.98	1.74	1.72	1.49	1.24
Portfolio Turnover Rate (%)	30	33	30	28	14	15
Total Assets: End of Year (Millions $)	7.5	8.5	9.0	10.4	21.3	53.6

Annual Rate of Return (%) Years Ending 12/31	20.4	11.8	21.0	29.7	20.4	(11.3)

Five-Year Total Return(%)	87.3[B]	Degree of Diversification	NA	Beta	.46	Bull (%)	92.4[c]	Bear (%)	(11.3)[c]

Objective: Seeks high dividend and interest income from common stocks and convertible securities. Of these investments, 25% must be in public utility companies in electric energy, gas, water or telephone service. May convert to cash equivalents for defensive purposes.

Portfolio: (10/31/87) Common stocks 52%, convertible debentures 25%, cash 12%, convertible preferred stocks 11%. Largest stock holdings: electric utilities 27%, electric and gas utilities 17%.

Distributions: Income: Monthly   **Capital Gains:** Annually

12b-1: No

Minimum: Initial: $1,000   Subsequent: $100

Min IRA: Initial: None   Subsequent: None

Services: IRA, Keogh, 403(b), Withdraw

Tel Exchange: Yes   **With MMF:** No

Registered: AL, AZ, CA, CO, CT, DC, DE, FL, GA, HI, IL, IN, KS, KY, MA, MD, MI, MN, MO, NJ, NY, OH, OR, PA, RI, TN, TX, VA, WA, WI, WY

STRONG GOVERNMENT SECURITIES

Bond

Strong/Corneliuson Capital Mgmt.
815 E. Mason St.
Milwaukee, WI 53202
(800) 368-3863/(414) 765-0934

	Years Ending 12/31					
	1982	1983	1984	1985	1986 (2 mos.)	1987
Net Investment Income ($)	–	–	–	–	.13	.65
Dividends from Net Investment Income ($)	–	–	–	–	.13	.65
Net Gains (Losses) on Investments ($)	–	–	–	–	.09	(.34)
Distributions from Net Realized Capital Gains ($)	–	–	–	–	–	–
Net Asset Value End of Year ($)	–	–	–	–	10.09	9.75
Ratio of Expenses to Net Assets (%)	–	–	–	–	.6	1.0
Portfolio Turnover Rate (%)	–	–	–	–	0	715
Total Assets: End of Year (Millions $)	–	–	–	–	.9	11.4

Annual Rate of Return (%) Years Ending 12/31	–	–	–	–	–	3.4

Five-Year Total Return(%)	NA	Degree of Diversification	NA	Beta	NA	Bull (%)	NA	Bear (%)	9.4^

Objective:	Seeks high level of current income from investments in the debt obligations of the U.S. government and its agencies. Can use futures contracts and options to hedge the portfolio. May invest in short-term cash instruments and repurchase agreements.
Portfolio:	(12/31/87) U.S. government issues 97%, short-term securities and other assets 3%.
Distributions:	Income: Monthly **Capital Gains:** Annually
12b-1:	No
Minimum:	Initial: $1,000 Subsequent: $200
Min IRA:	Initial: $250 Subsequent: None
Services:	IRA, Keogh, Corp, SEP, 403(b), Withdraw, Deduct
Tel Exchange:	Yes With MMF: Yes
Registered:	All states

STRONG INCOME
Balanced

Strong/Corneliuson Capital Mgmt.
815 E. Mason St.
Milwaukee, WI 53202
(800) 368-3863/(414) 765-0934

	Years Ending 12/31					
	1982	1983	1984	1985 (1 mo.)	1986	1987
Net Investment Income ($)	–	–	–	.03	.98	1.23
Dividends from Net Investment Income ($)	–	–	–	–	.71	1.53
Net Gains (Losses) on Investments ($)	–	–	–	.27	2.08	(.67)
Distributions from Net Realized Capital Gains ($)	–	–	–	–	–	.04
Net Asset Value End of Year ($)	–	–	–	10.30	12.65	11.64
Ratio of Expenses to Net Assets (%)	–	–	–	1.1	1.0	1.1
Portfolio Turnover Rate (%)	–	–	–	7	205	245
Total Assets: End of Year (Millions $)	–	–	–	2.5	118.7	137.8
Annual Rate of Return (%) Years Ending 12/31	–	–	–	–	29.9	4.3

Five-Year Total Return(%)	NA	Degree of Diversification	NA	Beta	NA	Bull (%)	NA	Bear (%)	(1.6)[B]

Objective: Seeks high level of current income from investments in a diversified portfolio of fixed-income securities and dividend-paying common stocks. The fixed-income securities may be unrated or as low as CC. May also enter into repos and invest in foreign securities, convertibles and preferred stocks.

Portfolio: (12/31/87) Short-term securities and other assets 46%, corporate bonds 44%, U.S. government issues 7%, preferred stocks 3%.

Distributions: Income: Monthly   **Capital Gains:** Annually

12b-1: No

Minimum: Initial: $1,000   Subsequent: $200

Min IRA: Initial: $250   Subsequent: None

Services: IRA, Keogh, Corp, SEP, 403(b), Withdraw, Deduct

Tel Exchange: Yes   **With MMF:** Yes

Registered: All states

TRANSATLANTIC GROWTH
(formerly TRANSATLANTIC FUND)
International

Kleinwort Benson International
200 Park Ave. Suite 5610
New York, NY 10166
(800) 237-4218/(212) 687-2515

	Years Ending 12/31					
	1982	1983	1984	1985	1986	1987
Net Investment Income ($)	.32	.18	.07	.09	.06	.08
Dividends from Net Investment Income ($)	.30	.17	.03	.06	–	–
Net Gains (Losses) on Investments ($)	(2.66)	3.53	(2.03)	6.21	9.09	2.03
Distributions from Net Realized Capital Gains ($)	1.54	.06	1.00	.16	4.18	11.82
Net Asset Value End of Year ($)	11.38	14.86	11.87	17.95	22.92	13.21
Ratio of Expenses to Net Assets (%)	1.44	1.28	1.53	1.94	1.49	1.72
Portfolio Turnover Rate (%)	45	96	60	73	76	59
Total Assets: End of Year (Millions $)	27.8	35.4	28.0	41.3	92.6	53.8
Annual Rate of Return (%) Years Ending 12/31	(15.3)	32.9	(14.4)	54.2	51.7	9.2

Five-Year Total Return(%)	190.6ᴬ	Degree of Diversification	E	Beta	.60	Bull (%)	223.6ᴬ	Bear (%)	(16.9)ᶜ

Objective: Seeks long-term capital growth through investment in equity securities of companies domiciled in countries other than the United States. For defensive purposes, can invest all or a portion of assets in U.S. government securities or other domestic issues.

Portfolio: (12/31/87) Common stocks and convertible securities 88%, bank deposits 18%. Largest country holdings: Japan 28%, United Kingdom 23%.

Distributions: Income: Semiannually   **Capital Gains:** Annually

12b-1: Yes   **Amount:** 0.20%

Minimum: Initial: $1,000   Subsequent: $500

Min IRA: Initial: $500   Subsequent: $500

Services: IRA

Tel Exchange: Yes   With MMF: No

Registered: All states except: AL, AR, AZ, IA, ID, ME, MS, MT, ND, NE, NJ, NM, OK, SD, TN, UT, VT, WV, WY

TREASURY FIRST
Bond

Vintage Advisors, Inc.
29 W. Susquehanna Ave.
Suite 112
Towson, MD 21204
(301) 494-8488

	Years Ending 10/31					
	1982	1983	1984	1985	1986	1987 (11 mos.)
Net Investment Income ($)	–	–	–	–	–	.72
Dividends from Net Investment Income ($)	–	–	–	–	–	.72
Net Gains (Losses) on Investments ($)	–	–	–	–	–	.12
Distributions from Net Realized Capital Gains ($)	–	–	–	–	–	.05
Net Asset Value End of Year ($)	–	–	–	–	–	10.07
Ratio of Expenses to Net Assets (%)	–	–	–	–	–	.54
Portfolio Turnover Rate (%)	–	–	–	–	–	307
Total Assets: End of Year (Millions $)	–	–	–	–	–	24.4
Annual Rate of Return (%) Years Ending 12/31	–	–	–	–	–	8.9

Five-Year Total Return(%)	NA	Degree of Diversification	NA	Beta	NA	Bull (%)	NA	Bear (%)	5.0ᴬ

Objective: Seeks to achieve a high level of current income, consistent with the preservation of capital and the maintenance of liquidity. Invests in debt obligations issued or guaranteed by the U.S. government, its agencies or instrumentalities. Intends to invest in puts, calls, interest rate futures contracts and options.

Portfolio: (10/31/87) U.S. Treasury notes 77%, GNMAs 19%, options 3%.

Distributions: Income: Monthly   **Capital Gains:** Annually

12b-1: Yes   **Amount:** 0.25%

Minimum: Initial: $10,000   **Subsequent:** None

Min IRA: Initial: $1,000   **Subsequent:** None

Services: IRA, Keogh, SEP

Tel Exchange: No

Registered: CA, CT, DC, DE, FL, GA, HI, IL, MA, MD, MI, NJ, NY, OH, PA, SC, TN, VA, WV, WY

TUDOR
Aggressive Growth

Tudor Management Co.
One New York Plaza
New York, NY 10004
(800) 223-3332/(212) 908-9582

	3/31		Years Ending 12/31				
	1982	**1983**	**1983*** (9 mos.)	**1984**	**1985**	**1986**	**1987**
Net Investment Income ($)	.29	.30	.13	.40	.08	(.04)	(.04)
Dividends from Net Investment Income ($)	.10	.22	.28	.11	.37	.07	–
Net Gains (Losses) on Investments ($)	(.66)	8.72	1.67	(1.98)	5.37	2.92	.47
Distributions from Net Realized Capital Gains ($)	–	–	.54	1.56	–	5.48	1.69
Net Asset Value End of Year ($)	11.14	19.94	20.92	17.67	22.75	20.08	18.82
Ratio of Expenses to Net Assets (%)	1.58	1.35	1.01	1.01	.95	1.01	1.03
Portfolio Turnover Rate (%)	134	99	55	83	123	128	113
Total Assets: End of Year (Millions $)	18.4	53.3	91.5	94.0	155.9	163.8	142.5
Annual Rate of Return (%) Years Ending 12/31	45.3	28.4	*	(7.2)	31.2	12.3	1.1

Five-Year Total Return(%)	77.5[B]	Degree of Diversification	B	Beta	1.24	Bull (%)	126.8[A]	Bear (%)	(27.7)[E]

*Fiscal year-end changed from 3/31 to 12/31. All annual return figures are for full years ending 12/31.

Objective: Seeks capital appreciation through investment in common stocks. The fund invests approximately 50% of its assets in "special situations" and may write covered call options. May enter into repos.

Portfolio: (12/31/87) Common stocks 93%, repos 9%. Largest stock holdings: basic industries 13%, semi-conductors and related 11%.

Distributions: Income: March, Aug   **Capital Gains:** March

12b-1: No

Minimum: Initial: $1,000   Subsequent: $50

Min IRA: Initial: $250   Subsequent: $50

Services: IRA, Keogh, Withdraw

Tel Exchange: Yes   **With MMF:** Yes

Registered: All states except ID, ND

20th CENTURY GROWTH

Aggressive Growth

Investors Research Corp.
P.O. Box 200
Kansas City, MO 64141
(800) 345-2021/(816) 531-5575

	Years Ending 10/31					
	1982	**1983**	**1984**	**1985**	**1986**	**1987**
Net Investment Income ($)	.06	.06	.16	.17	.12	.01
Dividends from Net Investment Income ($)	–	.05	.05	.15	.18	.09
Net Gains (Losses) on Investments ($)	(.45)	4.03	(1.77)	1.85	5.37	1.30
Distributions from Net Realized Capital Gains ($)	.60	–	1.82	–	–	5.08
Net Asset Value End of Year ($)	11.73	15.77	12.29	14.16	19.47	15.62
Ratio of Expenses to Net Assets (%)	1.08	1.02	1.01	1.01	1.01	1.00
Portfolio Turnover Rate (%)	132	98	132	116	105	114
Total Assets: End of Year (Millions $)	388.5	659.1	678.2	759.9	964.5	1,187.6

Annual Rate of Return (%) Years Ending 12/31	9.3	24.5	(10.2)	33.9	19.4	13.0

Five-Year Total Return(%)	101.9[A]	Degree of Diversification	A	Beta	1.27	Bull (%)	168.3[A]	Bear (%)	(26.8)[E]

Objective: Capital growth through investment in common stocks of smaller companies that management considers to possess better than average growth prospects based on fundamental and technical analysis and three-year history.

Portfolio: (10/31/87) Common stocks 99%, temporary cash investments 4%. Largest stock holdings: electronic components 11%, computer systems 10%.

Distributions: Income: Jan   **Capital Gains:** Jan

12b-1: No

Minimum: Initial: None   Subsequent: None

Min IRA: Initial: None   Subsequent: None

Services: IRA, Keogh Corp, 403(b), Withdraw, Deduct

Tel Exchange: Yes   **With MMF:** Yes

Registered: All states

20th CENTURY SELECT
Aggressive Growth

Investors Research Corp.
P.O. Box 200
Kansas City, MO 64141
(800) 345-2021/(816) 531-5575

	Years Ending 10/31					
	1982	**1983**	**1984**	**1985**	**1986**	**1987**
Net Investment Income ($)	.08	.11	.45	.56	.43	.33
Dividends from Net Investment Income ($)	.12	.14	.14	.47	.52	.38
Net Gains (Losses) on Investments ($)	3.68	7.98	(2.74)	4.04	9.01	.80
Distributions from Net Realized Capital Gains ($)	.31	—	.69	—	—	3.46
Net Asset Value End of Year ($)	17.51	25.46	22.35	26.48	35.40	32.69
Ratio of Expenses to Net Assets (%)	1.08	1.02	1.01	1.01	1.01	1.00
Portfolio Turnover Rate (%)	145	57	112	119	85	123
Total Assets: End of Year (Millions $)	93.4	648.9	840.5	1,143.1	1,978.4	2,416.9

Annual Rate of Return (%) Years Ending 12/31	42.4	30.0	(7.6)	33.8	20.7	5.7

Five-Year Total Return(%)	105.1^	Degree of Diversification	A	Beta	1.10	Bull (%)	147.3^	Bear (%)	(23.9)^D

Objective: Primarily capital growth but designed for investors also interested in income. Invests in securities of companies with above-average growth prospects that also pay dividends or interest.

Portfolio: (10/31/87) Common stocks 98%, temporary cash investments 4%. Largest stock holdings: pharmaceuticals 16%, diversified companies 9%.

Distributions: Income: Jan   **Capital Gains:** Jan

12b-1: No

Minimum: Initial: None   **Subsequent:** None

Min IRA: Initial: None   **Subsequent:** None

Services: IRA, Keogh, Corp, 403(b), Withdraw, Deduct

Tel Exchange: Yes   **With MMF:** Yes

Registered: All states

20TH CENTURY
U.S. GOVERNMENTS
Bond

Investors Research Corp.
P.O. Box 200
Kansas City, MO 64141
(800) 345-2021/(816) 531-5575

		Years Ending 10/31				
	1982	1983 (10 mos.)	1984	1985	1986	1987
Net Investment Income ($)	–	8.02	10.25	9.97	8.71	7.92
Dividends from Net Investment Income ($)	–	8.02	10.25	9.97	8.71	7.92
Net Gains (Losses) on Investments ($)	–	(2.42)	(.80)	2.72	2.63	(4.88)
Distributions from Net Realized Capital Gains ($)	–	–	–	–	.56	1.22
Net Asset Value End of Year ($)	–	97.58	96.79	99.51	101.58	95.48
Ratio of Expenses to Net Assets (%)	–	1.02	1.01	1.01	1.01	1.00
Portfolio Turnover Rate (%)	–	403	352	573	464	468
Total Assets: End of Year (Millions $)	–	34.7	58.8	98.8	254.7	335.6
Annual Rate of Return (%) Years Ending 12/31	–	7.0	12.3	12.9	9.9	3.8

Five-Year Total Return(%)	54.8[D]	Degree of Diversification	NA	Beta	.00	Bull (%)	35.4[E]	Bear (%)	3.2[A]

Objective: Seeks income through investment in U.S. government securities, with its portfolio averaging four years or less maturity.

Portfolio: (10/31/87) U.S. government securities 90%, other 8%, cash 2%.

Distributions: **Income:** Monthly   **Capital Gains:** Annually

12b-1: No

Minimum: **Initial:** None   **Subsequent:** None

Min IRA: **Initial:** None   **Subsequent:** None

Services: IRA, Keogh, Corp, 403(b), Withdraw, Deduct

Tel Exchange: Yes   **With MMF:** Yes

Registered: All states

UMB BOND
Bond

Jones & Babson, Inc.
Three Crown Center
2440 Pershing Road
Kansas City, MO 64108
(800) 821-5591/(816) 471-5200

	Years Ending 6/30					
	1982	1983 (7 mos.)	1984	1985	1986	1987
Net Investment Income ($)	–	.35	1.02	.93	.88	.82
Dividends from Net Investment Income ($)	–	.36	1.06	.46	1.29	.40
Net Gains (Losses) on Investments ($)	–	(.01)	(.87)	1.25	.56	(.30)
Distributions from Net Realized Capital Gains ($)	–	–	–	–	.08	–
Net Asset Value End of Year ($)	–	9.98	9.07	10.79	10.86	10.98
Ratio of Expenses to Net Assets (%)	–	.85	.87	.88	.88	.87
Portfolio Turnover Rate (%)	–	–	–	51	23	12
Total Assets: End of Year (Millions $)	–	4.6	6.0	9.8	19.0	31.1
Annual Rate of Return (%) Years Ending 12/31	–	4.8	13.5	16.2	12.3	2.9

Five-Year Total Return(%)	59.8ᴰ	Degree of Diversification	NA	Beta	.02	Bull (%)	43.5ᴱ	Bear (%)	3.3ᴬ

Objective: To provide maximum current income while preserving capital. Invests in the guaranteed obligations of the U.S. government and its agencies, including Treasury securities and GNMAs. Will also invest in corporate debt rated A or better by Standard & Poor's.

Portfolio: (9/30/87) Corporate bonds 43%, U.S. government agency 40%, U.S. government securities 11%, repos 2%, short-term corporate notes 2%, other assets 2%.

Distributions: Income: Semiannually   **Capital Gains:** Annually

12b-1: No

Minimum: Initial: $1,000   Subsequent: $100

Min IRA: Initial: $50   Subsequent: None

Services: IRA, Keogh, Corp, SEP, 403(b), Withdraw

Tel Exchange: Yes   **With MMF:** Yes

Registered: AR, CA, DC, FL, IA, IL, IN, KS, MA, MN, MO, MT, NE, OH, OK, PA, SD

UMB STOCK
Growth & Income

Jones & Babson, Inc.
Three Crown Center
2440 Pershing Road
Kansas City, MO 64108
(800) 821-5591/(816) 471-5200

		Years Ending 6/30				
	1982	1983 (7 mos.)	1984	1985	1986	1987
Net Investment Income ($)	—	.15	.48	.49	.48	.43
Dividends from Net Investment Income ($)	—	.19	.60	.25	.71	.20
Net Gains (Losses) on Investments ($)	—	1.96	(.75)	1.96	2.57	1.91
Distributions from Net Realized Capital Gains ($)	—	.42	.54	—	1.11	.40
Net Asset Value End of Year ($)	—	11.50	10.09	12.29	13.52	15.26
Ratio of Expenses to Net Assets (%)	—	.85	.87	.88	.87	.87
Portfolio Turnover Rate (%)	—	76	80	65	38	50
Total Assets: End of Year (Millions $)	—	6.8	11.2	18.3	31.7	42.3
Annual Rate of Return (%) Years Ending 12/31	—	23.7	5.9	23.1	12.3	5.1

Five-Year Total Return(%)	90.3[B]	Degree of Diversification	A	Beta	.87	Bull (%)	102.8[B]	Bear (%)	(19.4)[D]

Objective: Seeks long-term growth of both capital and dividend income. Normally will invest 80% of its assets in common stocks that have demonstrated a consistent and above-average ability to increase earnings and dividends.

Portfolio: (9/30/87) Common stocks 80%, short-term corporate notes 14%, convertible corporate bonds 4%, repos 2%, convertible preferred stocks 1%. Largest stock holdings: basic materials 16%, consumer staples 15%.

Distributions: Income: Semiannually   **Capital Gains:** Annually

12b-1: No

Minimum: Initial: $1,000   Subsequent: $100

Min IRA: Initial: $250   Subsequent: None

Services: IRA, Keogh, Corp, SEP, 403(b), Withdraw

Tel Exchange: Yes   **With MMF:** Yes

Registered: AR, CA, DC, FL, IA, IL, IN, KS, MA, MN, MO, MT, NE, OH, OK, PA, SD

UNIFIED GROWTH

Growth

Unified Management Corp.
429 N. Pennsylvania St.
Indianapolis, IN 46204-1897
(800) 862-7283/(317) 634-3300

	Years Ending 4/30					
	1982	1983	1984	1985	1986	1987
Net Investment Income ($)	.46	.33	.54	.40	.36	.32
Dividends from Net Investment Income ($)	.46	.33	.55	.40	.35	.33
Net Gains (Losses) on Investments ($)	(2.29)	5.45	(1.39)	3.25	5.64	1.94
Distributions from Net Realized Capital Gains ($)	—	1.08	—	—	—	2.45
Net Asset Value End of Year ($)	12.34	16.71	15.31	18.56	24.21	23.69
Ratio of Expenses to Net Assets (%)	1.34	1.28	1.16	1.10	1.00	1.01
Portfolio Turnover Rate (%)	33	99	16	37	27	61
Total Assets: End of Year (Millions $)	3.8	8.5	10.9	15.0	25.5	28.1

Annual Rate of Return (%) Years Ending 12/31	28.2	11.3	7.5	26.0	13.5	(11.6)

Five-Year Total Return(%)	51.2[D]	Degree of Diversification	B	Beta 1.01	Bull (%) 99.1[C]	Bear (%) (26.7)[E]

Objective: Seeks long-term appreciation by investing primarily in common stocks and convertible securities of medium and smaller companies with attractive profit margins and high return on equity. Current income is a secondary consideration. May take defensive posture with debt instruments.

Portfolio: (10/31/87) Common stocks 90%, commercial paper 6%, short-term notes 4%. Largest stock holdings: chemical/specialty 13%, drug manufacturing/ethical and consumer 11%.

Distributions: Income: April   **Capital Gains:** April

12b-1: No

Minimum: Initial: $200   Subsequent: $25

Min IRA: Initial: $25   Subsequent: $25

Services: IRA, Keogh, Corp, 403(b), Withdraw, Deduct

Tel Exchange: Yes   **With MMF:** Yes

Registered: All states

UNIFIED INCOME

Balanced

Unified Management Corp.
429 N. Pennsylvania St.
Indianapolis, IN 46204-1897
(800) 862-7283/(317) 634-3300

	Years Ending 10/31					
	1982	1983	1984	1985	1986	1987
Net Investment Income ($)	.88	.89	1.17	1.10	.89	.91
Dividends from Net Investment Income ($)	.89	.90	1.16	1.10	.89	.90
Net Gains (Losses) on Investments ($)	2.06	1.41	(1.00)	.58	1.00	(2.29)
Distributions from Net Realized Capital Gains ($)	—	.44	—	—	—	—
Net Asset Value End of Year ($)	11.20	12.16	11.17	11.75	12.75	10.47
Ratio of Expenses to Net Assets (%)	1.86	1.33	1.30	1.22	1.12	1.10
Portfolio Turnover Rate (%)	15	19	25	18	49	75
Total Assets: End of Year (Millions $)	2.5	7.5	7.1	8.7	13.6	11.2

Annual Rate of Return (%) Years Ending 12/31	32.2	17.9	(0.5)	20.5	9.8	(11.6)

Five-Year Total Return(%)	37.4[E]	Degree of Diversification	NA	Beta	.55	Bull (%)	56.6[D]	Bear (%)	(18.2)[C]

Objective: Seeks current income and preservation of capital by investing in fixed and convertible corporate debt, common and preferred stock, and short-term instruments.

Portfolio: (10/31/87) Corporate and convertible bonds 50%, common stocks 35%, convertible preferred stocks 11%, short-term notes 5%. Largest stock holdings: electric utility 6%, drug manufacturing 5%.

Distributions: Income: April, Oct   **Capital Gains:** Oct
12b-1: No
Minimum: Initial: $500   Subsequent: $25
Min IRA: Initial: $25   Subsequent: $25
Services: IRA, Keogh, Corp, 403(b), Withdraw, Deduct
Tel Exchange: Yes   **With MMF:** Yes
Registered: All states

UNIFIED MUTUAL SHARES

Growth & Income

Unified Management Corp.
429 N. Pennsylvania St.
Indianapolis, IN 46204-1897
(800) 862-7283/(317) 634-3300

	Years Ending 7/31					
	1982	1983	1984	1985	1986	1987
Net Investment Income ($)	.63	.50	.59	.55	.62	.56
Dividends from Net Investment Income ($)	.64	.50	.59	.55	.59	.59
Net Gains (Losses) on Investments ($)	(1.88)	3.74	(1.12)	3.51	2.55	2.68
Distributions from Net Realized Capital Gains ($)	—	—	—	—	.17	2.25
Net Asset Value End of Year ($)	8.26	12.00	10.88	14.39	16.80	17.20
Ratio of Expenses to Net Assets (%)	1.32	1.23	1.21	1.11	1.02	1.03
Portfolio Turnover Rate (%)	7	51	12	5	41	49
Total Assets: End of Year (Millions $)	6.1	9.8	8.8	12.6	18.9	23.5
Annual Rate of Return (%) Years Ending 12/31	17.6	21.7	8.5	30.8	11.6	(2.3)

Five-Year Total Return(%)	88.3[B]	Degree of Diversification	B	Beta	.78	Bull (%)	106.9[B]	Bear (%)	(19.3)[D]

Objective: The fund seeks capital growth and current income principally through the purchase of high-quality, income-producing common stocks and convertible securities whose markets, profit margins and rates of return indicate future growth potentials. May write covered options.

Portfolio: (7/31/87) Common stocks 77%, short-term securities 12%, bonds 11%. Largest stock holdings: pharmaceuticals 13%, banking 8%.

Distributions: Income: Jan, July   **Capital Gains:** July

12b-1: No

Minimum: Initial: $200   Subsequent: $25

Min IRA: Initial: $25   Subsequent: $25

Services: IRA, Keogh, Corp, 403(b), Withdraw, Deduct

Tel Exchange: Yes   **With MMF:** Yes

Registered: All states

USAA CORNERSTONE
Balanced

USAA Investment Mgmt. Co.
9800 Fredericksburg Rd.
San Antonio, TX 78288
(800) 531-8000/(512) 498-8000

	Years Ending 9/30					
	1982	**1983**	**1984** (1 mo.)	**1985**	**1986**	**1987**
Net Investment Income ($)	—	—	.09	.51	.45	.60
Dividends from Net Investment Income ($)	—	—	—	.04	.32	.30
Net Gains (Losses) on Investments ($)	—	—	(.11)	.16	3.83	5.18
Distributions from Net Realized Capital Gains ($)	—	—	—	.02	.06	.21
Net Asset Value End of Year ($)	—	—	9.98	10.58	14.49	19.76
Ratio of Expenses to Net Assets (%)	—	—	1.90	1.50	1.50	1.07
Portfolio Turnover Rate (%)	—	—	9	15	70	15
Total Assets: End of Year (Millions $)	—	—	3.3	13.6	29.0	822.6

Annual Rate of Return (%) Years Ending 12/31	—	—	—	14.7	40.7	9.0

Five-Year Total Return(%)	NA	Degree of Diversification	NA	Beta	.61	Bull (%)	NA	Bear (%)	(18.5)c

Objective: Seeks to preserve purchasing power of capital and achieve reasonably stable value of fund shares and positive, inflation-adjusted rate of return despite shifting inflation and volatility in markets. Will invest 20% in each of five asset categories: gold stocks, foreign stocks, real estate stocks, basic value stocks and U.S. government securities.

Portfolio: (9/30/87) Common stocks 79%, U.S. government and agency issues 32%. Largest stock holdings: foreign stocks 20%, basic value stocks 20%.

Distributions: Income: Nov   **Capital Gains:** Nov

12b-1: No

Minimum: Initial: $1,000   Subsequent: $100

Min IRA: Initial: $1,000   Subsequent: $100

Services: IRA, Keogh, SEP, 403(b), Withdraw, Deduct

Tel Exchange: Yes   **With MMF:** Yes

Registered: All states

USAA GOLD
Precious Metals

USAA Investment Mgmt. Co.
9800 Fredericksburg Rd.
San Antonio, TX 78288
(800) 531-8000/(512) 498-8000

			Years Ending 9/30			
	1982	1983	1984 (1 mo.)	1985	1986	1987
Net Investment Income ($)	–	–	.06	.28	.10	.10
Dividends from Net Investment Income ($)	–	–	–	.02	.12	.10
Net Gains (Losses) on Investments ($)	–	–	(.86)	(2.63)	1.46	8.81
Distributions from Net Realized Capital Gains ($)	–	–	–	–	–	–
Net Asset Value End of Year ($)	–	–	9.20	6.83	8.27	17.07
Ratio of Expenses to Net Assets (%)	–	–	1.93	1.50	1.50	1.14
Portfolio Turnover Rate (%)	–	–	–	–	62	54
Total Assets: End of Year (Millions $)	–	–	3.3	15.1	29.5	309.9

Annual Rate of Return (%) Years Ending 12/31	–	–	–	(20.7)	55.6	15.8

Five-Year Total Return(%)	NA	Degree of Diversification	E	Beta	.62	Bull (%)	NA	Bear (%)	(34.7)E

Objective: Seeks long-term capital appreciation and protection of capital against inflation through investment in common stock of companies engaged in gold exploration, mining or processing. Up to 20% of assets may be in other precious metals, diamonds or minerals.

Portfolio: (9/30/87) Common stocks 91%, U.S. government & agency issues 13%, Australian notes 1%. Largest stock holdings: Australian gold mines 48%, North American gold mines 43%.

Distributions: Income: Nov   **Capital Gains:** Nov
12b-1: No
Minimum: Initial: $1,000   Subsequent: $100
Min IRA: Initial: $1,000   Subsequent: $100
Services: IRA, Keogh, SEP, 403(b), Withdraw, Deduct
Tel Exchange: Yes   **With MMF:** Yes
Registered: All states

USAA GROWTH
Growth

USAA Investment Mgmt. Co.
9800 Fredericksburg Rd.
San Antonio, TX 78288
(800) 531-8000/(512) 498-8000

	Years Ending 9/30					
	1982	1983	1984	1985	1986	1987
Net Investment Income ($)	.34	.19	.29	.26	.22	.30
Dividends from Net Investment Income ($)	.29	.32	.14	.23	.28	.19
Net Gains (Losses) on Investments ($)	.25	5.43	(2.51)	.65	2.54	5.17
Distributions from Net Realized Capital Gains ($)	.29	—	.47	—	.31	1.59
Net Asset Value End of Year ($)	10.62	15.91	13.08	13.76	15.94	19.63
Ratio of Expenses to Net Assets (%)	1.23	1.03	1.00	1.06	1.09	1.09
Portfolio Turnover Rate (%)	91	94	69	128	110	124
Total Assets: End of Year (Millions $)	60.7	107.2	128.6	145.2	173.8	272.3

Annual Rate of Return (%) Years Ending 12/31	20.9	15.8	(7.5)	19.9	10.1	5.5

Five-Year Total Return(%)	49.3[D]	Degree of Diversification	A	Beta 1.01	Bull (%) 97.2[C]	Bear (%) (21.9)[D]

Objective: Long-term growth of capital. Invests in common stocks of companies that are established and have substantial capitalizations with exceptional prospects for growth in earnings. May invest up to 10% of its assets in foreign securities listed on U.S. exchanges.

Portfolio: (9/30/87) Common stocks 92%, short-term notes 5%, bonds 2%. Largest stock holdings: health care 7%, chemicals 7%.

Distributions: Income: Nov   **Capital Gains:** Nov

12b-1: No

Minimum: Initial: $1,000   Subsequent: $25

Min IRA: Initial: $1,000   Subsequent: $25

Services: IRA, Keogh, 403(b), SEP, Withdraw, Deduct

Tel Exchange: Yes   **With MMF:** Yes

Registered: All states

USAA INCOME
Bond

USAA Investment Mgmt. Co.
9800 Fredericksburg Rd.
San Antonio, TX 78288
(800) 531-8000/(512) 498-8000

	Years Ending 9/30					
	1982	**1983**	**1984**	**1985**	**1986**	**1987**
Net Investment Income ($)	1.08	1.14	1.16	1.23	1.15	.91
Dividends from Net Investment Income ($)	1.00	1.05	1.06	1.21	1.12	1.24
Net Gains (Losses) on Investments ($)	1.51	.51	(.22)	.76	.61	(.81)
Distributions from Net Realized Capital Gains ($)	.01	–	.12	–	.02	.06
Net Asset Value End of Year ($)	10.34	10.93	10.68	11.46	12.08	10.89
Ratio of Expenses to Net Assets (%)	1.13	1.09	.75	.68	.65	.61
Portfolio Turnover Rate (%)	116	166	116	79	38	36
Total Assets: End of Year (Millions $)	19.7	39.0	92.1	138.8	213.6	249.9
Annual Rate of Return (%) Years Ending 12/31	28.9	10.7	13.9	19.0	12.6	3.5

Five-Year Total Return(%)	75.0ᶜ	Degree of Diversification	NA	Beta	.06	Bull (%)	50.1ᴰ	Bear (%)	2.9ᴬ

Objective: Seeks high yields from marketable income-producing securities with a mix of maturities and qualities. May invest in restricted securities.

Portfolio: (9/30/87) U.S. government & agency issues 61%, corporate bonds 37%, short-term notes 1%.

Distributions: Income: Monthly   **Capital Gains:** Nov

12b-1: No

Minimum: Initial: $1,000   Subsequent: $25

Min IRA: Initial: $1,000   Subsequent: $25

Services: IRA, Keogh, SEP, 403(b), Withdraw, Deduct

Tel Exchange: Yes   **With MMF:** Yes

Registered: All states

USAA SUNBELT ERA
Aggressive Growth

USAA Investment Mgmt. Co.
9800 Fredericksburg Rd.
San Antonio, TX 78288
(800) 531-8000/(512) 498-8000

	Years Ending 9/30					
	1982	1983	1984	1985	1986	1987
Net Investment Income ($)	.10	.10	.07	.10	.07	.11
Dividends from Net Investment Income ($)	.09	.04	.06	.08	.11	.07
Net Gains (Losses) on Investments ($)	1.04	7.46	(3.83)	.56	2.55	4.81
Distributions from Net Realized Capital Gains ($)	–	–	.25	–	–	.35
Net Asset Value End of Year ($)	10.74	18.27	14.20	14.78	17.29	21.79
Ratio of Expenses to Net Assets (%)	1.45	1.06	1.06	1.11	1.05	.97
Portfolio Turnover Rate (%)	76	49	52	74	57	35
Total Assets: End of Year (Millions $)	9.8	79.9	98.2	108.9	119.0	149.8

Annual Rate of Return (%) Years Ending 12/31	24.6	23.9	(18.1)	23.0	5.5	(0.8)

Five-Year Total Return(%)	30.6[E]	Degree of Diversification	C	Beta 1.16	Bull (%) 85.4[C]	Bear (%) (26.1)[E]

Objective: Seeks appreciation of capital through investment primarily in common stocks of smaller, emerging companies located in or doing business in the sunbelt region of the United States.

Portfolio: (9/30/87) Common stocks 86%, short-term notes 9%, bonds 3%, preferred stocks 1%. Largest stock holdings: electronics 11%, health care 9%.

Distributions: Income: Nov   **Capital Gains:** Nov

12b-1: No

Minimum: Initial: $1,000   Subsequent: $25

Min IRA: Initial: $1,000   Subsequent: $25

Services: IRA, Keogh, SEP, 403(b), Withdraw, Deduct

Tel Exchange: Yes   **With MMF:** Yes

Registered: All states

US GNMA
Bond

United Services Advisors
P.O. Box 29467
San Antonio, TX 78229
(800) 873-8637/(512) 696-1234

	Years Ending 6/30					
	1982	**1983**	**1984**	**1985**	**1986** (3 mos.)	**1987**
Net Investment Income ($)	—	—	—	—	.12	.76
Dividends from Net Investment Income ($)	—	—	—	—	.11	.78
Net Gains (Losses) on Investments ($)	—	—	—	—	(.11)	(.41)
Distributions from Net Realized Capital Gains ($)	—	—	—	—	—	—
Net Asset Value End of Year ($)	—	—	—	—	9.90	9.47
Ratio of Expenses to Net Assets (%)	—	—	—	—	—	.08
Portfolio Turnover Rate (%)	—	—	—	—	—	107
Total Assets: End of Year (Millions $)	—	—	—	—	.8	6.7

Annual Rate of Return (%) Years Ending 12/31	—	—	—	—	—	(1.3)

Five-Year Total Return(%)	NA	Degree of Diversification	NA	Beta	NA	Bull (%)	NA	Bear (%)	3.3^

Objective: Seeks to provide a high level of current income, consistent with safety of principal and maintenance of liquidity. At least 65% of the fund's assets will be invested in GNMAs. Also uses put and call options to hedge the portfolio.

Portfolio: (9/30/87) Long-term U.S. government or government guaranteed securities 87%, short-term government securities 11%, other assets 2%.

Distributions: Income: Monthly   **Capital Gains:** Annually

12b-1: No

Minimum: Initial: $100   Subsequent: $50

Min IRA: Initial: None   Subsequent: None

Services: IRA, 403(b), Corp, Withdraw, Deduct

Tel Exchange: Yes   With MMF: No

Registered: All states

US GOLD SHARES
Precious Metals

United Services Advisors, Inc.
P.O. Box 29467
San Antonio, TX 78229-0467
(800) 873-8637/(512) 696-1234

	Years Ending 6/30.					
	1982	**1983**	**1984**	**1985**	**1986**	**1987**
Net Investment Income ($)	.43	.37	.33	.24	.30	.33
Dividends from Net Investment Income ($)	.64	.34	.41	.29	.26	.35
Net Gains (Losses) on Investments ($)	(1.46)	5.63	(.97)	(2.48)	(2.05)	3.02
Distributions from Net Realized Capital Gains ($)	—	—	—	.06	—	—
Net Asset Value End of Year ($)	3.31	8.97	7.92	5.33	3.32	6.32
Ratio of Expenses to Net Assets (%)	1.15	1.11	1.06	1.15	1.27	1.32
Portfolio Turnover Rate (%)	7	4	11	10	14	24
Total Assets: End of Year (Millions $)	61.4	314.9	443.1	389.6	214.8	407.7

Annual Rate of Return (%) Years Ending 12/31	71.5	1.2	(29.7)	(26.9)	37.5	31.6

Five-Year Total Return(%)	(5.8)^E	Degree of Diversification	E	Beta .32	Bull (%) 45.7^E	Bear (%) (18.3)^C

Objective: Seeks long-term capital growth as well as protection against inflation and monetary instability. Fund concentrates its investments in common stocks of companies involved in exploration for, mining of, processing of, or dealing in gold, with emphasis on stocks of foreign companies.

Portfolio: (9/30/87) Common stocks 96%, U.S. government obligations 2%, other assets 1%. Largest holdings: long-life gold mines 28%, gold-uranium mines 22%.

Distributions: Income: Feb, Aug   **Capital Gains:** Aug
12b-1: No
Minimum: **Initial:** $100   **Subsequent:** $50
Min IRA: **Initial:** None   **Subsequent:** None
Services: IRA, Keogh, Corp, 403(b), SEP, Withdraw, Deduct
Tel Exchange: Yes   **With MMF:** No
Registered: All states

US GOOD AND BAD TIMES

Growth

United Services Advisors
P.O. Box 29467
San Antonio, TX 78229-0467
(800) 873-8637/(512) 696-1234

	Years Ending 6/30					
	1982* (6 mos.)	**1983**	**1984**	**1985**	**1986**	**1987**
Net Investment Income ($)	.16	.10	.34	.24	.35	.32
Dividends from Net Investment Income ($)	.18	.15	.11	.49	.17	.38
Net Gains (Losses) on Investments ($)	(.16)	3.52	(1.20)	2.84	3.65	1.92
Distributions from Net Realized Capital Gains ($)	—	—	—	—	—	—
Net Asset Value End of Year ($)	9.46	12.93	11.96	14.55	18.38	20.24
Ratio of Expenses to Net Assets (%)	2.18	2.20	1.45	1.50	1.40	1.35
Portfolio Turnover Rate (%)	47	156	92	99	91	58
Total Assets: End of Year (Millions $)	1.8	15.3	12.8	36.1	32.7	36.4

Annual Rate of Return (%) Years Ending 12/31	23.4	11.1	2.7	23.9	11.3	0.6

Five-Year Total Return(%)	58.2ᴰ	Degree of Diversification	A	Beta	.95	Bull (%)	100.3ᶜ	Bear (%)	(23.6)ᴰ

Fiscal year changed from 12/31 to 6/30.

Objective: Invests in common stock of industrial corporations with little or no debt that are believed to be able to have capital appreciation in good economic times and preservation of capital in bad economic times. May invest up to 50% of assets in debt instruments as a defensive tactic.

Portfolio: (9/30/87) Common stocks 83%, government obligations 14%, other assets 3%. Largest stock holdings: miscellaneous 18%, consumer products 16%.

Distributions: Income: Aug   **Capital Gains:** Aug
12b-1: No
Minimum: Initial: $100   Subsequent: $50
Min IRA: Initial: None   Subsequent: None
Services: IRA, Keogh, Corp, 403(b), SEP, Withdraw, Deduct
Tel Exchange: Yes   **With MMF:** No
Registered: All states

US GROWTH
Aggressive Growth

United Services Advisors
P.O. Box 29467
San Antonio, TX 78229-0467
(800) 873-8637/(512) 696-1234

	Years Ending 6/30					
	1982	**1983**	**1984**	**1985**	**1986**	**1987**
Net Investment Income ($)	–	–	.09	.03	.06	.06
Dividends from Net Investment Income ($)	–	–	–	.07	.06	.07
Net Gains (Losses) on Investments ($)	–	–	(2.47)	.02	2.27	.27
Distributions from Net Realized Capital Gains ($)	–	–	–	–	–	–
Net Asset Value End of Year ($)	–	–	7.62	7.60	9.87	10.13
Ratio of Expenses to Net Assets (%)	–	–	1.45	1.67	1.52	1.71
Portfolio Turnover Rate (%)	–	–	161	163	60	64
Total Assets: End of Year (Millions $)	–	–	6.3	12.7	11.9	9.2

Annual Rate of Return (%) Years Ending 12/31	–	–	(25.6)	21.0	11.5	(11.2)

Five-Year Total Return(%)	NA	Degree of Diversification	C	Beta 1.05	Bull (%) 57.6[D]	Bear (%) (27.2)[E]

Objective: Seeks capital appreciation through investment in common stocks of established, well-known and newer, less-seasoned companies. Fundamental analysis is employed to identify underpriced stocks, cyclical companies and companies changing for what looks like the better. May invest up to 25% of assets in foreign securities traded on U.S. exchanges.

Portfolio: (9/30/87) Common stocks 85%, U.S. government obligations 19%. Largest stock holdings: miscellaneous 40%, communications equipment 7%.

Distributions: Income: Aug   **Capital Gains:** Aug
12b-1: No
Minimum: Initial: $100   Subsequent: $50
Min IRA: Initial: None   Subsequent: None
Services: IRA, Keogh, Corp, 403(b), SEP, Withdraw, Deduct
Tel Exchange: Yes   **With MMF:** No
Registered: All states

US INCOME

Balanced

United Services Advisors
P.O. Box 29467
San Antonio, TX 78229-0467
(800) 873-8637/(512) 696-1234

	Years Ending 6/30					
	1982	1983	1984 (8 mos.)	1985	1986	1987
Net Investment Income ($)	–	–	.14	.55	.34	.63
Dividends from Net Investment Income ($)	–	–	.11	.61	.38	.50
Net Gains (Losses) on Investments ($)	–	–	(.84)	1.29	.89	(.27)
Distributions from Net Realized Capital Gains ($)	–	–	–	–	.07	.56
Net Asset Value End of Year ($)	–	–	9.19	10.42	11.20	10.50
Ratio of Expenses to Net Assets (%)	–	–	1.80	1.66	1.63	1.60
Portfolio Turnover Rate (%)	–	–	279	271	179	174
Total Assets: End of Year (Millions $)	–	–	1.2	2.5	2.9	3.6
Annual Rate of Return (%) Years Ending 12/31	–	–	3.9	15.3	5.5	(4.3)

Five-Year Total Return(%)	NA	Degree of Diversification	NA	Beta	.39	Bull (%)	36.3ᴱ	Bear (%)	(8.4)ᶜ

Objective: Seeks preservation of capital and current income. Secondarily, seeks capital appreciation through investment in common stocks of companies with a long record of paying cash dividends and U.S. Treasury debt securities and convertibles. May write covered call options.

Portfolio: (9/30/87) Common stocks 43%, corporate bonds 30%, convertible bonds 11%, government obligations 8%, other assets 7%, convertible preferred stocks 4%. Largest stock holdings: real estate investment trusts 17%, electric, water & gas utilities 17%.

Distributions: Income: Mar, June, Sep, Dec   **Capital Gains:** Annually
12b-1: No
Minimum: Initial: $100   Subsequent: $50
Min IRA: Initial: None   Subsequent: None
Services: IRA, Keogh, Corp, 403(b), SEP, Withdraw, Deduct
Tel Exchange: Yes   **With MMF:** No
Registered: All states

US LOCAP
Aggressive Growth

United Services Advisors
P.O. Box 29467
San Antonio, TX 78229-0467
(800) 873-8637/(512) 696-1234

	Years Ending 6/30					
	1982	1983	1984	1985 (5 mos.)	1986	1987
Net Investment Income ($)	–	–	–	.02	.02	(.05)
Dividends from Net Investment Income ($)	–	–	–	–	.02	.02
Net Gains (Losses) on Investments ($)	–	–	–	(2.38)	.79	.03
Distributions from Net Realized Capital Gains ($)	–	–	–	–	–	–
Net Asset Value End of Year ($)	–	–	–	7.64	8.43	8.39
Ratio of Expenses to Net Assets (%)	–	–	–	1.67	1.84	2.27
Portfolio Turnover Rate (%)	–	–	–	6	70	52
Total Assets: End of Year (Millions $)	–	–	–	2.1	3.2	4.3

Annual Rate of Return (%) Years Ending 12/31	–	–	–	–	(6.6)	(13.2)

Five-Year Total Return(%) NA	Degree of Diversification NA	Beta NA	Bull (%) NA	Bear (%) (33.6)E

Objective: To provide above-average capital appreciation. Current income is not a consideration. Invests in companies with a market capitalization in the bottom 10% of the combined group of common stocks listed on the New York and American stock exchanges.

Portfolio: (9/30/87) Common stocks 99%, government obligations 2%. Largest stock holdings: miscellaneous 22%, electronics & electrical 13%.

Distributions: Income: Aug   **Capital Gains:** Aug

12b-1: No

Minimum: **Initial:** $100   **Subsequent:** $50

Min IRA: **Initial:** None   **Subsequent:** None

Services: IRA, Keogh, Corp, 403(b), SEP, Withdraw, Deduct

Tel Exchange: Yes   **With MMF:** No

Registered: All states

US NEW PROSPECTOR

Precious Metals

United Services Advisors
P.O. Box 29467
San Antonio, TX 78229-0467
(800) 873-8637/(512) 696-1234

	Years Ending 6/30					
	1982	1983	1984	1985	1986 (7 mos.)	1987
Net Investment Income ($)	—	—	—	—	.00	.00
Dividends from Net Investment Income ($)	—	—	—	—	—	—
Net Gains (Losses) on Investments ($)	—	—	—	—	(.04)	1.11
Distributions from Net Realized Capital Gains ($)	—	—	—	—	—	.02
Net Asset Value End of Year ($)	—	—	—	—	.96	2.05
Ratio of Expenses to Net Assets (%)	—	—	—	—	1.51	1.47
Portfolio Turnover Rate (%)	—	—	—	—	31	44
Total Assets: End of Year (Millions $)	—	—	—	—	27.3	127.0
Annual Rate of Return (%) Years Ending 12/31	—	—	—	—	38.5	31.1

Five-Year Total Return(%)	NA	Degree of Diversification	NA	Beta	NA	Bull (%)	NA	Bear (%)	(28.2)E

Objective: Seeks long-term growth of capital as well as protection against inflation and monetary instability. Current income is not a consideration. Invests in companies involved in the natural resource industry, including gold, silver, timber and oil.

Portfolio: (9/30/87) Common stocks and warrants 91%, government obligations 9%, convertible bonds 1%. Largest stock holdings: major gold-producing companies 43%, other gold-producing companies 20%.

Distributions: Income: Aug   **Capital Gains:** Aug
12b-1: No
Minimum: **Initial:** $100   **Subsequent:** $50
Min IRA: **Initial:** None   **Subsequent:** None
Services: IRA, Keogh, Corp, 403(b), SEP, Withdraw, Deduct
Tel Exchange: Yes   **With MMF:** No
Registered: All states

VALLEY FORGE
Growth & Income

Valley Forge Mgmt. Corp.
P.O. Box 262
Valley Forge, PA 19481
(215) 688-6839

	Years Ending 12/31					
	1982	**1983**	**1984**	**1985**	**1986**	**1987**
Net Investment Income ($)	.63	.72	.67	.58	.66	.56
Dividends from Net Investment Income ($)	.73	.42	.54	.47	.69	1.31
Net Gains (Losses) on Investments ($)	1.47	1.05	.01	.40	(.05)	(.10)
Distributions from Net Realized Capital Gains ($)	.06	.78	.96	.06	.41	.19
Net Asset Value End of Year ($)	10.96	11.53	10.71	11.16	10.67	9.63
Ratio of Expenses to Net Assets (%)	2.00	1.60	1.70	1.40	1.40	1.30
Portfolio Turnover Rate (%)	38	39	70	87	40	56
Total Assets: End of Year (Millions $)	2.2	3.2	7.8	10.1	9.2	9.4

Annual Rate of Return (%) Years Ending 12/31	28.7	17.9	6.7	10.5	5.5	4.6

Five-Year Total Return(%)	53.3ᴰ	Degree of Diversification	E	Beta	.15	Bull (%)	31.9ᴱ	Bear (%)	(3.6)ᶜ

Objective: Seeks capital appreciation and, secondarily, current income through investment in common stocks of established companies chosen on the basis of fundamental analysis and technical market considerations. May convert to short-term debt securities during adverse stock market conditions.

Portfolio: (12/31/87) Short-term money market securities 84%, common stocks 10%, bonds 3%, preferred stocks 3%. Largest stock holdings: energy & related 4%, miscellaneous 4%.

Distributions: Income: Dec   **Capital Gains:** Dec

12b-1: No

Minimum: Initial: $2,500   Subsequent: $100

Min IRA: Initial: $1,000   Subsequent: $100

Services: IRA

Tel Exchange: No

Registered: All states

VALUE LINE AGGRESSIVE INCOME
Bond

Value Line, Inc.
711 Third Avenue
New York, NY 10017
(800) 223-0818/(212) 687-3965

	Years Ending 1/31					
	1982	1983	1984	1985	1986	1987
Net Investment Income ($)	–	–	–	–	–	1.16
Dividends from Net Investment Income ($)	–	–	–	–	–	1.16
Net Gains (Losses) on Investments ($)	–	–	–	–	–	(.21)
Distributions from Net Realized Capital Gains ($)	–	–	–	–	–	–
Net Asset Value End of Year ($)	–	–	–	–	–	9.90
Ratio of Expenses to Net Assets (%)	–	–	–	–	–	1.33
Portfolio Turnover Rate (%)	–	–	–	–	–	110
Total Assets: End of Year (Millions $)	–	–	–	–	–	57.5
Annual Rate of Return (%) Years Ending 12/31	–	–	–	–	–	(2.0)

Five-Year Total Return(%) NA	Degree of Diversification NA	Beta NA	Bull (%) NA	Bear (%)	(8.0)c

Objective: Seeks to maximize current income; capital appreciation is of secondary importance. Invests primarily in high-yielding fixed-income corporate securities issued by companies rated B++ or lower for relative strength in the Value Line Investment Survey.

Portfolio: (7/31/87) Corporate bonds 92%, U.S. Treasury obligations 5%, repos 3%. Largest corporate holdings: broadcasting/cable TV 15%, building 6%.

Distributions: Income: Monthly   **Capital Gains:** Annually

12b-1: No

Minimum: Initial: $1,000   Subsequent: $250

Min IRA: Initial: $1,000   Subsequent: $250

Services: IRA, Keogh, Corp, SEP, 403(b), Withdraw, Deduct

Tel Exchange: Yes   **With MMF:** Yes

Registered: All states

VALUE LINE
CONVERTIBLE
Balanced

Value Line Inc.
711 Third Ave.
New York, NY 10017
(800) 223-0818/(212) 687-3965

	1982	1983	1984	1985	1986 (10 mos.)	1987
Years Ending 4/30						
Net Investment Income ($)	–	–	–	–	.38	.57
Dividends from Net Investment Income ($)	–	–	–	–	.24	.54
Net Gains (Losses) on Investments ($)	–	–	–	–	2.28	.59
Distributions from Net Realized Capital Gains ($)	–	–	–	–	–	.71
Net Asset Value End of Year ($)	–	–	–	–	12.45	12.36
Ratio of Expenses to Net Assets (%)	–	–	–	–	1.31	1.04
Portfolio Turnover Rate (%)	–	–	–	–	164	234
Total Assets: End of Year (Millions $)	–	–	–	–	49.8	89.2

Annual Rate of Return (%) Years Ending 12/31	–	–	–	–	16.1	(6.1)

Five-Year Total Return(%)	NA	Degree of Diversification	NA	Beta	NA	Bull (%)	NA	Bear (%)	(17.1)ᶜ

Objective: Seeks high current income and capital appreciation through investment primarily in convertible securities. May also invest in non-convertible debt and equity securities.

Portfolio: (10/31/87) Convertible bonds & notes 71%, convertible preferred stocks 22%, other assets 4%, common stocks 3%. Largest holdings: publishing 9%, computer & peripherals 9%.

Distributions: Income: Quarterly   **Capital Gains:** Annually
12b-1: No
Minimum: Initial: $1,000   Subsequent: $250
Min IRA: Initial: $1,000   Subsequent: $250
Services: IRA, Keogh, 403(b), SEP, Withdraw, Deduct
Tel Exchange: Yes   **With MMF:** Yes
Registered: All states

VALUE LINE FUND
Growth

Value Line, Inc.
711 Third Ave.
New York, NY 10017
(800) 223-0818/(212) 687-3965

	Years Ending 12/31					
	1982	1983	1984	1985	1986	1987
Net Investment Income ($)	1.00	.32	.18	.20	.22	.24
Dividends from Net Investment Income ($)	.80	.55	.20	.20	.23	.27
Net Gains (Losses) on Investments ($)	2.21	(.43)	(2.08)	3.50	2.17	.50
Distributions from Net Realized Capital Gains ($)	3.20	.75	—	—	1.75	2.64
Net Asset Value End of Year ($)	14.28	12.87	10.77	14.27	14.68	12.51
Ratio of Expenses to Net Assets (%)	.67	.77	.83	.81	.73	.69
Portfolio Turnover Rate (%)	87	97	110	129	145	118
Total Assets: End of Year (Millions $)	109.0	203.2	166.5	206.0	212.6	204.7

Annual Rate of Return (%) Years Ending 12/31	28.5	(1.3)	(14.7)	34.6	16.7	4.7

Five-Year Total Return(%)	38.3E	Degree of Diversification	B	Beta 1.10	Bull (%) 126.7A	Bear (%) (20.2)D

Objective: Primary objective is long-term growth of capital through investment in common stocks chosen on the basis of the Value Line Ranking System for Timeliness. May write covered call options, invest in restricted securities, and enter into repurchase agreements. May take defensive posture in debt investments.

Portfolio: (12/31/87) Common stocks 91%, repos 8%, U.S. Treasury obligations 5%. Largest stock holdings: computer software & services 9%, drugs 8%.

Distributions: Income: Quarterly   **Capital Gains:** Annually
12b-1: No
Minimum: Initial: $1,000   Subsequent: $100
Min IRA: Initial: $1,000   Subsequent: $100
Services: IRA, Keogh, 403(b), SEP, Corp, Withdraw, Deduct
Tel Exchange: Yes   **With MMF:** Yes
Registered: All states

VALUE LINE INCOME
Balanced

Value Line, Inc.
711 Third Ave.
New York, NY 10017
(800) 223-0818/(212) 687-3965

	Years Ending 12/31					
	1982	1983	1984	1985	1986	1987
Net Investment Income ($)	.60	.39	.43	.50	.47	.50
Dividends from Net Investment Income ($)	.56	.56	.48	.48	.48	.43
Net Gains (Losses) on Investments ($)	1.05	.07	(.30)	.91	.64	(.62)
Distributions from Net Realized Capital Gains ($)	1.45	.14	.26	—	.91	.69
Net Asset Value End of Year ($)	7.01	6.77	6.16	7.09	6.81	5.57
Ratio of Expenses to Net Assets (%)	.78	.78	.89	.83	.77	.76
Portfolio Turnover Rate (%)	82	72	114	148	167	96
Total Assets: End of Year (Millions $)	94.7	125.9	117.9	134.4	162.8	140.2

Annual Rate of Return (%) Years Ending 12/31	29.8	6.7	2.9	23.7	16.3	(2.4)

Five-Year Total Return(%)	54.1ᴰ	Degree of Diversification	NA	Beta	.68	Bull (%)	94.4ᶜ	Bear (%)	(17.5)ᶜ

Objective: Seeks current income but considers capital appreciation to be an important secondary objective. Substantially all its investments are in common stocks or convertibles chosen on the basis of the Value Line Ranking System for Timeliness. May shift portfolio to debt investments as defensive posture. May invest in repurchase agreements and restricted securities and write covered call options.

Portfolio: (12/31/87) Common stocks 70%, corporate bonds 21%, U.S. government agency obligations 5%, U.S. Treasury obligations 2%, repos 2%. Largest stock holdings: drugs 6%, insurance—diversified 5%.

Distributions: Income: Quarterly   **Capital Gains:** Annually
12b-1: No
Minimum: Initial: $1,000   Subsequent: $100
Min IRA: Initial: $1,000   Subsequent: $100
Services: IRA, Keogh, Corp, SEP, 403(b), Withdraw, Deduct
Tel Exchange: Yes   **With MMF:** Yes
Registered: All states

VALUE LINE LEVERAGED GROWTH

Growth

Value Line, Inc.
711 Third Ave.
New York, NY 10017
(800) 223-0818/(212) 687-3965

	Years Ending 12/31					
	1982	1983	1984	1985	1986	1987
Net Investment Income ($)	.71	.36	.16	.29	.20	.29
Dividends from Net Investment Income ($)	.65	.65	.31	.13	.34	.46
Net Gains (Losses) on Investments ($)	3.48	1.15	(1.96)	4.18	4.64	.45
Distributions from Net Realized Capital Gains ($)	3.25	.02	.99	–	2.60	4.93
Net Asset Value End of Year ($)	18.82	19.66	16.56	20.90	22.80	18.15
Ratio of Expenses to Net Assets (%)	.84	.80	.86	.80	.96	.95
Portfolio Turnover Rate (%)	95	105	89	121	115	148
Total Assets: End of Year (Millions $)	115.1	216.1	181.5	228.6	290.0	282.9

Annual Rate of Return (%) Years Ending 12/31	28.6	7.9	(8.8)	27.1	23.3	3.0

Five-Year Total Return(%)	59.0[D]	Degree of Diversification	A	Beta	1.13	Bull (%)	136.2[A]	Bear (%)	(23.4)[D]

Objective: Capital growth through investment in common stocks chosen on the basis of Value Line Ranking System for Timeliness. No consideration is given to current income in the choice of investments. May employ leverage from banks and may write covered call options. May enter into repurchase agreements.

Portfolio: (12/31/87) Common stocks 101%. Largest stock holdings: computer & peripherals 9%, beverage 7%.

Distributions: Income: Annually   **Capital Gains:** Annually

12b-1: No

Minimum: Initial: $1,000   Subsequent: $100

Min IRA: Initial: $1,000   Subsequent: $100

Services: IRA, Keogh, Corp, 403(b), SEP, Withdraw, Deduct

Tel Exchange: Yes   **With MMF:** Yes

Registered: All states

VALUE LINE SPECIAL SITUATIONS
Aggressive Growth

Value Line, Inc.
711 Third Ave.
New York, NY 10017
(800) 223-0818/(212) 687-3965

	Years Ending 12/31					
	1982	1983	1984	1985	1986	1987
Net Investment Income ($)	.46	.12	.09	.04	.06	.06
Dividends from Net Investment Income ($)	.30	.45	.02	.05	.04	.12
Net Gains (Losses) on Investments ($)	2.13	2.61	(4.19)	2.47	.68	(1.46)
Distributions from Net Realized Capital Gains ($)	–	–	.08	–	–	2.56
Net Asset Value End of Year ($)	13.83	16.11	11.91	14.37	15.07	10.99
Ratio of Expenses to Net Assets (%)	1.02	1.00	1.06	1.07	1.02	1.01
Portfolio Turnover Rate (%)	50	63	75	88	73	41
Total Assets: End of Year (Millions $)	199.5	337.9	240.1	242.7	193.6	123.8

Annual Rate of Return (%) Years Ending 12/31	23.1	19.4	(25.5)	21.1	5.1	(9.8)

Five-Year Total Return(%) 2.1ᴱ	Degree of Diversification	C	Beta 1.29	Bull (%) 65.3ᴰ	Bear (%) (29.1)ᴱ

Objective: Seeks long-term capital growth. Experiences wider than average price fluctuations and a period of years without substantial current investment income; 80% of its assets are invested in securities of companies in special situations (unusual developments in the operations of the company such as a new product or a merger). Uses Value Line Ranking System for Timeliness for determining possible undervaluation.

Portfolio: (12/31/87) Common stocks 90%, repos 9%, units 1%. Largest stock holdings: computer & peripherals 14%, computer software & services 9%.

Distributions: **Income:** Annually   **Capital Gains:** Annually
12b-1: No
Minimum: **Initial:** $1,000   **Subsequent:** $100
Min IRA: **Initial:** $1,000   **Subsequent:** $100
Services: IRA, Keogh, Corp, 403(b), SEP, Withdraw, Deduct
Tel Exchange: Yes   **With MMF:** Yes
Registered: All states

VALUE LINE
U.S. GOVERNMENT
SECURITIES
Bond

Value Line, Inc.
711 Third Ave.
New York, NY 10017
(800) 223-0818/(212) 687-3965

	Years Ending 8/31					
	1982	1983	1984	1985	1986	1987
Net Investment Income ($)	1.33	1.35	1.33	1.32	1.30	1.19
Dividends from Net Investment Income ($)	.96	1.36	1.28	1.30	1.32	1.23
Net Gains (Losses) on Investments ($)	1.44	.22	(.36)	1.41	.51	(.77)
Distributions from Net Realized Capital Gains ($)	—	—	.28	—	.15	.23
Net Asset Value End of Year ($)	11.56	11.77	11.18	12.61	12.95	11.91
Ratio of Expenses to Net Assets (%)	.98	.82	.92	.86	.76	.72
Portfolio Turnover Rate (%)	0.0	7	31	64	73	48
Total Assets: End of Year (Millions $)	35.9	48.6	51.4	68.3	112.4	217.7
Annual Rate of Return (%) Years Ending 12/31	32.9	6.0	13.7	21.2	10.7	3.4

Five-Year Total Return(%)	67.2[C]	Degree of Diversification	NA	Beta	.01	Bull (%)	52.5[D]	Bear (%)	3.1[A]

Objective: Seeks income as high and dependable as is consistent with reasonable risk through investment of 80% of its net assets in investment grade bonds rated B++ or better by Value Line. Capital preservation and possible capital appreciation are secondary objectives. May invest up to 10% of its assets in unregistered securities. May lend its portfolio's securities and engage in repos.

Portfolio: (8/31/87) U.S. government agency obligations 85%, U.S. Treasury obligations 14%.

Distributions: Income: Quarterly   **Capital Gains:** Annually

12b-1: No

Minimum: Initial: $1,000   Subsequent: $250

Min IRA: Initial: $1,000   Subsequent: $250

Services: IRA, Keogh, Corp, 403(b), SEP, Withdraw, Deduct

Tel Exchange: Yes   **With MMF:** Yes

Registered: All states

VANGUARD
BOND MARKET
Bond

Vanguard Group
Vanguard Financial Center
Valley Forge, PA 19482
(800) 662-7447/(215) 648-6000

	Years Ending 12/31					
	1982	**1983**	**1984**	**1986**	**1986** (1 mo.)	**1987**
Net Investment Income ($)	–	–	–	–	.03	.83
Dividends from Net Investment Income ($)	–	–	–	–	.03	.83
Net Gains (Losses) on Investments ($)	–	–	–	–	(.06)	(.74)
Distributions from Net Realized Capital Gains ($)	–	–	–	–	–	–
Net Asset Value End of Year ($)	–	–	–	–	9.94	9.20
Ratio of Expenses to Net Assets (%)	–	–	–	–	0	.14
Portfolio Turnover Rate (%)	–	–	–	–	0	77
Total Assets: End of Year (Millions $)	–	–	–	–	2.7	43.3

Annual Rate of Return (%) Years Ending 12/31	–	–	–	–	–	1.2

Five-Year Total Return(%)	NA	Degree of Diversification	NA	Beta	NA	Bull (%)	NA	Bear (%)	3.1ᴬ

Objective: This is an index fund. Its objective is to duplicate the total return of the Salomon Brothers broad investment-grade bond index. Bonds in the index have maturities greater than one year, have a minimum rating of BBB, and have general availability in the marketplace. Included are Treasury bonds, GNMAs and corporate bonds.

Portfolio: (12/31/87) U.S. government & agency obligations 79%, corporate bonds 18%, repos 2%, other assets 1%. Largest bond holdings: industrial 8%, finance 5%.

Distributions: Income: Quarterly   **Capital Gains:** Annually

12b-1: No

Minimum: Initial: $3,000   Subsequent: $100

Min IRA: Initial: $500   Subsequent: $100

Services: IRA, Keogh, SEP, 403(b), Corp, Withdraw, Deduct

Tel Exchange: Yes   **With MMF:** Yes

Registered: All states

VANGUARD CONVERTIBLE SECURITIES

Growth & Income

Vanguard Group
Vanguard Financial Center
Valley Forge, PA 19482
(800) 662-7447/(215) 648-6000

	Years Ending 11/30					
	1982	1983	1984	1985	1986 (5 mos.)	1987
Net Investment Income ($)	–	–	–	–	.26	.60
Dividends from Net Investment Income ($)	–	–	–	–	.17	.51
Net Gains (Losses) on Investments ($)	–	–	–	–	(.29)	(1.95)
Distributions from Net Realized Capital Gains ($)	–	–	–	–	–	–
Net Asset Value End of Year ($)	–	–	–	–	9.80	7.94
Ratio of Expenses to Net Assets (%)	–	–	–	–	.80	.85
Portfolio Turnover Rate (%)	–	–	–	–	13	13
Total Assets: End of Year (Millions $)	–	–	–	–	72.8	72.8

Annual Rate of Return (%) Years Ending 12/31		–	–	–	–	–	(10.7)
Five-Year Total Return(%)	NA	Degree of Diversification	NA	Beta NA	Bull (%) NA	Bear (%)	(19.2)ᴰ

Objective: Seeks high level of current income together with long-term capital appreciation. At least 80% of the fund's assets will be invested in convertible bonds, debentures, corporate notes, and preferred stocks. Can invest up to 20% of assets in non-convertible corporate or government debt securities.

Portfolio: (11/30/87) Convertible bonds 87%, repos 8%, convertible preferred stocks 4%, common stocks 3%. Largest bond holdings: building 10%, technology 9%.

Distributions: Income: Quarterly   **Capital Gains:** April

12b-1: No

Minimum: Initial: $3,000   Subsequent: $100

Min IRA: Initial: $500   Subsequent: $100

Services: IRA, Keogh, Corp, SEP, 403(b), Withdraw

Tel Exchange: Yes   **With MMF:** Yes

Registered: All states

VANGUARD EXPLORER II

Aggressive Growth

Vanguard Group
Vanguard Financial Center
Valley Forge, PA 19482
(800) 662-7447/(215) 648-6000

	Years Ending 10/31					
	1982	1983	1984	1985 (4 mos.)	1986	1987
Net Investment Income ($)	−	−	−	.08	.04	.06
Dividends from Net Investment Income ($)	−	−	−	−	.08	.04
Net Gains (Losses) on Investments ($)	−	−	−	(.83)	.87	(2.72)
Distributions from Net Realized Capital Gains ($)	−	−	−	−	−	.47
Net Asset Value End of Year ($)	−	−	−	19.25	20.08	16.91
Ratio of Expenses to Net Assets (%)	−	−	−	1.06	1.17	.62
Portfolio Turnover Rate (%)	−	−	−	3	27	4
Total Assets: End of Year (Millions $)	−	−	−	13.8	36.5	45.1

Annual Rate of Return (%) Years Ending 12/31	−	−	−	−	(7.3)	(4.5)

Five-Year Total Return(%)	NA	Degree of Diversification	NA	Beta	NA	Bull (%)	NA	Bear (%)	(27.5)[E]

Objective: Seeks long-term growth of capital by investing in common stocks of small unseasoned companies with less than $100 million in annual revenues and more than three years of operating history.

Portfolio: (10/31/87) Common stocks 99%, repos 5%. Largest stock holdings: medical and biotechnology 21%, automation and controls 20%.

Distributions: **Income:** Annually   **Capital Gains:** Annually

12b-1: No

Minimum: **Initial:** $3,000   **Subsequent:** $100

Min IRA: **Initial:** $500   **Subsequent:** $100

Services: IRA, Keogh, Corp, 403(b), SEP, Withdraw, Deduct

Tel Exchange: No

Registered: All states

VANGUARD GNMA
Bond

Vanguard Group
Vanguard Financial Center
Valley Forge, PA 19482
(800) 662-7447/(215) 648-6000

	Years Ending 1/31					
	1982	1983	1984	1985	1986	1987
Net Investment Income ($)	1.12	1.11	1.07	1.08	1.04	.97
Dividends from Net Investment Income ($)	1.12	1.11	1.07	1.08	1.04	.97
Net Gains (Losses) on Investments ($)	(.83)	1.29	(.01)	.05	.67	.19
Distributions from Net Realized Capital Gains ($)	—	—	—	—	—	.01
Net Asset Value End of Year ($)	7.92	9.21	9.20	9.25	9.92	10.10
Ratio of Expenses to Net Assets (%)	.89	.57	.58	.58	.50	.38
Portfolio Turnover Rate (%)	17	41	21	23	32	28
Total Assets: End of Year (Millions $)	25.0	84.7	172.4	298.9	1,262.1	2,380.3

Annual Rate of Return (%) Years Ending 12/31	31.5	9.7	14.0	20.6	11.5	2.3

Five-Year Total Return(%)	72.1^C	Degree of Diversification	NA	Beta −.01	Bull (%) 50.3^D	Bear (%) 3.3^A

Objective: Seeks current income through investing at least 80% of assets in GNMA mortgage-backed securities whose interest and principal payment is guaranteed by the U.S. government. Balance invested in other U.S. government guaranteed securities.

Portfolio: (7/31/87) GNMA obligations 97%, repos 4%.

Distributions: **Income:** Monthly **Capital Gains:** Annually

12b-1: No

Minimum: **Initial:** $3,000 **Subsequent:** $100

Min IRA: **Initial:** $500 **Subsequent:** $100

Services: IRA, Keogh, SEP, Corp, 403(b), Withdraw, Deduct

Tel Exchange: Yes **With MMF:** Yes

Registered: All states

VANGUARD HIGH YIELD BOND

Bond

Vanguard Group
Vanguard Financial Center
Valley Forge, PA 19482
(800) 662-7447/(215) 648-6000

	Years Ending 1/31					
	1982	1983	1984	1985	1986	1987
Net Investment Income ($)	1.24	1.28	1.20	1.18	1.13	1.09
Dividends from Net Investment Income ($)	1.24	1.28	1.20	1.18	1.14	1.08
Net Gains (Losses) on Investments ($)	(.62)	1.08	.01	(.45)	.33	.60
Distributions from Net Realized Capital Gains ($)	–	–	–	–	–	.12
Net Asset Value End of Year ($)	7.88	8.96	8.97	8.52	8.84	9.33
Ratio of Expenses to Net Assets (%)	.93	.71	.68	.65	.60	.45
Portfolio Turnover Rate (%)	87	52	82	71	61	67
Total Assets: End of Year (Millions $)	13.0	51.2	116.8	252.5	634.6	1,370.0

Annual Rate of Return (%) Years Ending 12/31	27.2	15.7	7.5	21.9	16.9	2.7

Five-Year Total Return(%)	82.0[B]	Degree of Diversification	NA	Beta	.19	Bull (%)	64.1[D]	Bear (%)	(2.1)[B]

Objective: Seeks current income primarily from investment in high-yielding, medium- and lower-quality bonds. Normally only 20% can be in debt securities rated below B, convertibles, preferred stocks or short-term investments. May invest in foreign securities and restricted securities. Fund performs own credit analysis.

Portfolio: (7/31/87) Corporate bonds 89%, government obligations 6%, other assets 4%. Largest corporate holdings: industrial 59%, communications & entertainment 9%.

Distributions: Income: Monthly   **Capital Gains:** Annually

12b-1: No

Minimum: Initial: $3,000   **Subsequent:** $100

Min IRA: Initial: $500   **Subsequent:** $100

Services: IRA, Keogh, SEP, Corp, 403(b), Withdraw, Deduct

Tel Exchange: Yes   **With MMF:** Yes

Registered: All states

VANGUARD INDEX 500
(formerly VANGUARD INDEX TRUST)

Growth & Income

Vanguard Group
Vanguard Financial Center
Valley Forge, PA 19482
(800) 662-7447/(215) 648-6000

	Years Ending 12/31					
	1982	1983	1984	1985	1986	1987
Net Investment Income ($)	.83	.87	.88	.91	.89	.88
Dividends from Net Investment Income ($)	.83	.87	.88	.91	.89	.69
Net Gains (Losses) on Investments ($)	2.29	2.85	.30	5.08	3.30	.36
Distributions from Net Realized Capital Gains ($)	.25	.71	.48	1.61	2.02	.17
Net Asset Value End of Year ($)	17.56	19.70	19.52	22.99	24.27	24.65
Ratio of Expenses to Net Assets (%)	.39	.28	.27	.28	.28	.26
Portfolio Turnover Rate (%)	11	35	14	36	29	15
Total Assets: End of Year (Millions $)	110.0	233.7	289.7	394.2	485.0	826.5
Annual Rate of Return (%) Years Ending 12/31	19.3	21.3	6.2	31.1	18.3	4.7

Five-Year Total Return(%)	109.2^A	Degree of Diversification	A	Beta 1.00	Bull (%) 143.5^A	Bear (%) (24.5)^D

Objective: Seeks to duplicate stock market price and yield perform-ance by owning all stocks in the Standard & Poor's 500 stock index. Established fund shareholders may ex-change their shares of S&P 500 stocks for fund shares.

Portfolio: (12/31/87) Common stocks 100%, repos 1%. Owns all S&P 500 companies.

Distributions: Income: Mar, June, Sept, Dec   **Capital Gains:** Dec

12b-1: No

Minimum: Initial: $1,500   Subsequent: $100

Min IRA: Initial: $500   Subsequent: $100

Services: IRA, Keogh, Corp, SEP, 403(b), Withdraw, Deduct

Tel Exchange: No

Registered: All states

VANGUARD INVESTMENT GRADE BOND
Bond

Vanguard Group
Vanguard Financial Center
Valley Forge, PA 19482
(800) 662-7447/(215) 648-6000

	Years Ending 1/31					
	1982	1983	1984	1985	1986	1987
Net Investment Income ($)	.93	.96	.95	.96	.92	.85
Dividends from Net Investment Income ($)	.93	.96	.95	.96	.92	.85
Net Gains (Losses) on Investments ($)	(.35)	.94	(.16)	—	.58	.47
Distributions from Net Realized Capital Gains ($)	—	—	—	—	—	.12
Net Asset Value End of Year ($)	7.06	8.00	7.84	7.84	8.42	8.77
Ratio of Expenses to Net Assets (%)	.93	.75	.67	.62	.55	.41
Portfolio Turnover Rate (%)	156	122	62	55	56	47
Total Assets: End of Year (Millions $)	36.4	62.5	68.6	106.5	318.3	753.2

Annual Rate of Return (%) Years Ending 12/31	28.5	6.7	14.2	21.9	14.3	.3

Five-Year Total Return(%)	70.3[c]	Degree of Diversification	NA	Beta	.05	Bull (%)	51.9[D]	Bear (%)	3.8[A]

Objective: Seeks current income through investment primarily in long-term corporate bonds with high coupons of Baa or higher grade. Fund performs own credit analysis. May invest in foreign securities and restricted securities and engage in repos of similar quality.

Portfolio: (7/31/87) Corporate bonds 91%, government obligations 7%, repos 1%. Largest corporate holdings: industrial 43%, utilities 25%.

Distributions: Income: Monthly   **Capital Gains:** Annually

12b-1: No

Minimum: Initial: $3,000   Subsequent: $100

Min IRA: Initial: $500   Subsequent: $100

Services: IRA, Keogh, SEP, Corp, 403(b), Withdraw, Deduct

Tel Exchange: Yes   **With MMF:** Yes

Registered: All states

VANGUARD PRIMECAP

Growth

Vanguard Group
Vanguard Financial Center
Valley Forge, PA 19482
(800) 662-7447/(215) 648-6000

	Years Ending 12/31					
	1982	1983	1984 (2 mos.)	1985	1986	1987
Net Investment Income ($)	–	–	.06	.24	.32	.45
Dividends from Net Investment Income ($)	–	–	–	.03	.56	.40
Net Gains (Losses) on Investments ($)	–	–	1.16	9.13	7.98	(1.45)
Distributions from Net Realized Capital Gains ($)	–	–	–	–	.73	.94
Net Asset Value End of Year ($)	–	–	26.22	35.56	42.57	40.23
Ratio of Expenses to Net Assets (%)	–	–	–	.98	.82	.83
Portfolio Turnover Rate (%)	–	–	51	14	15	21
Total Assets: End of Year (Millions $)	–	–	1.8	54.1	132.6	164.9

Annual Rate of Return (%) Years Ending 12/31	–	–	–	35.8	23.5	(2.3)

Five-Year Total Return(%)	NA	Degree of Diversification	C	Beta	1.06	Bull (%)	NA	Bear (%)	(24.3)ᴰ

Objective: Seeks long-term growth of capital, income is not an objective. Under normal conditions the fund will invest 80% of its assets in equity securities, including common stocks and convertibles. Looks for companies with superior earnings growth and consistency. May also invest in out of favor cyclical stocks.

Portfolio: (12/31/87) Common stocks 99%, other assets 1%. Largest stock holdings: computer and related 21%, medical technonolgy 15%.

Distributions: Income: Annually   **Capital Gains:** Annually

12b-1: No

Minimum: Initial: $25,000   Subsequent: $1,000

Min IRA: Initial: $500   Subsequent: $100

Services: IRA, Keogh, SEP, 403(b), Corp, Withdraw, Deduct

Tel Exchange: Yes   **With MMF:** Yes

Registered: All states

VANGUARD QUANTITATIVE PORTFOLIOS

Growth & Income

Vanguard Group
Vanguard Financial Center
Valley Forge, PA 19482
(800) 662-7447/(215) 648-6000

	Years Ending 12/31					
	1982	1983	1984	1985	1986	1987
Net Investment Income ($)	–	–	–	–	.03	.33
Dividends from Net Investment Income ($)	–	–	–	–	–	.25
Net Gains (Losses) on Investments ($)	–	–	–	–	(.34)	.09
Distributions from Net Realized Capital Gains ($)	–	–	–	–	–	.06
Net Asset Value End of Year ($)	–	–	–	–	9.69	9.80
Ratio of Expenses to Net Assets (%)	–	–	–	–	0	.64
Portfolio Turnover Rate (%)	–	–	–	–	0	73
Total Assets: End of Year (Millions $)	–	–	–	–	7.4	149.1

Annual Rate of Return (%) Years Ending 12/31	–	–	–	–	–	3.3

Five-Year Total Return(%)	NA	Degree of Diversification	NA	Beta	NA	Bull (%)	NA	Bear (%)	(24.4)ᴰ

Objective: Seeks to provide a total return greater than the total return of the S&P 500 stock index. Over 65% of the fund's assets are invested in companies which are also included in the S&P 500. The advisor uses quantitative analysis to weight the portfolio toward the most attractive stocks in the universe of stocks monitored.

Portfolio: (12/31/87) Common stocks 97%, temporary cash investments 2%, other assets 1%. Largest stock holdings: Exxon Corp., American Telephone & Telegraph Co.

Distributions: **Income:** Semiannually   **Capital Gains:** Annually

12b-1: No

Minimum: **Initial:** $3,000   **Subsequent:** $100

Min IRA: **Initial:** $500   **Subsequent:** $100

Services: IRA, Keogh, SEP, 403(b), Corp, Withdraw, Deduct

Tel Exchange: Yes   **With MMF:** Yes

Registered: All states

VANGUARD
SHORT TERM BOND
Bond

Vanguard Group
Vanguard Financial Center
Valley Forge, PA 19482
(800) 662-7447/(215) 648-6000

	1982	1983 (3 mos.)	1984	1985	1986	1987
Net Investment Income ($)	–	.27	1.02	1.07	1.00	.88
Dividends from Net Investment Income ($)	–	.27	1.02	1.07	1.00	.88
Net Gains (Losses) on Investments ($)	–	.05	(.11)	.23	.38	.30
Distributions from Net Realized Capital Gains ($)	–	–	–	–	–	.18
Net Asset Value End of Year ($)	–	10.05	9.94	10.17	10.55	10.67
Ratio of Expenses to Net Assets (%)	–	.51	.56	.62	.49	.38
Portfolio Turnover Rate (%)	–	65	121	270	460	278
Total Assets: End of Year (Millions $)	–	64.1	135.8	119.1	198.5	400.7

Annual Rate of Return (%) Years Ending 12/31	–	9.1	14.2	14.9	11.3	4.4

Five-Year Total Return(%)	66.5ᶜ	Degree of Diversification	NA	Beta	.03	Bull (%)	42.9ᴱ	Bear (%)	2.8ᴬ

Objective: The fund invests primarily in short-term investment-grade bonds with maturities ranging from less than one year to four years. Has objective of obtaining the highest possible income consistent with minimum fluctuation in principal. May engage in repos and invest up to 20% of assets in foreign securities.

Portfolio: (7/31/87) Corporate bonds 37%, government obligations 34%, foreign securities 18%, repos 15%. Largest corporate holdings: finance–diversified 11%, finance–automobile 9%.

Distributions: Income: Monthly   **Capital Gains:** Annually
12b-1: No
Minimum: Initial: $3,000   Subsequent: $100
Min IRA: Initial: $500   Subsequent: $100
Services: IRA, Keogh, SEP, Corp, 403(b), Withdraw, Deduct
Tel Exchange: Yes   **With MMF:** Yes
Registered: All states

VANGUARD STAR
Growth

Vanguard Group
Vanguard Financial Center
Valley Forge, PA 19482
(800) 662-7447/(215) 648-6000

	1982	1983	1984	1985 (9 mos.)	1986	1987
Years Ending 12/31						
Net Investment Income ($)	–	–	–	.93	1.15	1.31
Dividends from Net Investment Income ($)	–	–	–	.05	.86	.85
Net Gains (Losses) on Investments ($)	–	–	–	.57	.31	(1.04)
Distributions from Net Realized Capital Gains ($)	–	–	–	–	.71	.75
Net Asset Value End of Year ($)	–	–	–	11.45	11.34	9.98
Ratio of Expenses to Net Assets (%)	–	–	–	0	0	0
Portfolio Turnover Rate (%)	–	–	–	–	–	–
Total Assets: End of Year (Millions $)	–	–	–	112.3	454.7	567.7

Annual Rate of Return (%) Years Ending 12/31	–	–	–	–	13.8	1.6

Five-Year Total Return(%)	NA	Degree of Diversification	NA	Beta	NA	Bull (%)	NA	Bear (%)	(13.4)c

Objective: Designed as a retirement portfolio. The fund invests in other Vanguard mutual funds, which in turn invest in common stocks and bonds. Seeks maximum total investment return. Will invest at least 60% in equity funds and not more than 40% in bond funds. May also invest in repurchase agreements.

Portfolio: (12/31/87) Growth and income 54%, fixed-income 25%, money market 13%, aggressive growth 8%.

Distributions: Income: Semiannually   **Capital Gains:** Annually

12b-1: No

Minimum: Initial: $500   Subsequent: $100

Min IRA: Initial: $500   Subsequent: $100

Services: IRA, Keogh, Corp, SEP, 403(b), Withdraw, Deduct

Tel Exchange: Yes   **With MMF:** Yes

Registered: All states

VANGUARD/ TRUSTEES' COMMINGLED— INTERNATIONAL PORTFOLIO
International

Vanguard Group
Vanguard Financial Center
Valley Forge, PA 19482
(800) 662-7447/(215) 648-6000

		Years Ending 12/31				
	1982	1983 (7 mos.)	1984	1985	1986	1987
Net Investment Income ($)	–	.51	1.02	.93	1.03	1.14
Dividends from Net Investment Income ($)	–	.44	1.09	.93	1.03	.75
Net Gains (Losses) on Investments ($)	–	.93	(1.21)	8.86	14.32	7.91
Distributions from Net Realized Capital Gains ($)	–	.02	.11	2.54	6.55	18.32
Net Asset Value End of Year ($)	–	25.98	24.59	30.91	38.68	28.66
Ratio of Expenses to Net Assets (%)	–	.90	.63	.56	.52	.50
Portfolio Turnover Rate (%)	–	-0-	8	29	24	48
Total Assets: End of Year (Millions $)	–	65.3	317.1	581.6	718.7	657.3

Annual Rate of Return (%) Years Ending 12/31	–	–	(0.7)	40.2	49.9	23.4

Five-Year Total Return(%)	NA	Degree of Diversification	E	Beta	.53	Bull (%) 216.4ᴬ	Bear (%) (12.8)ᶜ

Objective: Invests primarily in non-U.S. securities concentrating on areas apparently undervalued to achieve long-term total return. The contrarian approach is employed as well as computer modeling. May lend its portfolio securities.

Portfolio: (12/31/87) Common stocks 88%, temporary cash investments 14%. Largest stock holdings: Japan 24%, United Kingdom 16%.

Distributions: Income: Quarterly   **Capital Gains:** Annually
12b-1: No
Minimum: Initial: $10,000   Subsequent: $1,000
Min IRA: Initial: $500   Subsequent: $100
Services: IRA, Keogh, Corp, SEP, 403(b), Withdraw, Deduct
Tel Exchange: Yes   **With MMF:** Yes
Registered: All states

VANGUARD/ TRUSTEES' COMMINGLED— U.S. PORTFOLIO

Growth & Income

Vanguard Group
Vanguard Financial Center
Valley Forge, PA 19482
(800) 662-7447/(215) 648-6000

	Years Ending 12/31					
	1982	1983	1984	1985	1986	1987
Net Investment Income ($)	1.75	1.52	1.57	1.45	1.16	.92
Dividends from Net Investment Income ($)	1.75	1.52	1.57	1.45	1.16	.72
Net Gains (Losses) on Investments ($)	4.70	7.31	(2.65)	4.69	3.69	(.24)
Distributions from Net Realized Capital Gains ($)	1.19	2.15	2.51	4.10	6.15	5.88
Net Asset Value End of Year ($)	30.56	35.72	30.56	31.15	28.69	22.77
Ratio of Expenses to Net Assets (%)	.63	.50	.53	.48	.52	.52
Portfolio Turnover Rate (%)	43	30	33	25	19	44
Total Assets: End of Year (Millions $)	190.6	269.9	271.6	201.6	162.5	122.1

Annual Rate of Return (%) Years Ending 12/31	24.9	29.1	(2.9)	20.4	15.6	1.6

Five-Year Total Return(%)	77.3[B]	Degree of Diversification	B	Beta	1.03	Bull (%)	122.3[B]	Bear (%)	(27.3)[E]

Objective: Seeks long-term total return. Looks for securities of industries or companies unpopular in the marketplace, stocks not widely held by other institutions with low price-to-book value, and undervalued companies with under-utilized borrowing power.

Portfolio: (12/31/87) Common stocks 92%, temporary cash investments 8%. Largest stock holdings: Armco, Inc.; Middle South Utilities, Inc.

Distributions: Income: Quarterly   **Capital Gains:** Annually

12b-1: No

Minimum: Initial: $10,000   Subsequent: $1,000

Min IRA: Initial: $500   Subsequent: $100

Services: IRA, Keogh, Corp, SEP, 403(b), Withdraw, Deduct

Tel Exchange: Yes   **With MMF:** Yes

Registered: All states

VANGUARD U.S. TREASURY BOND
Bond

Vanguard Group
Vanguard Financial Center
Valley Forge, PA 19482
(800) 662-7447/(215) 648-6000

	Years Ending 1/31					
	1982	1983	1984	1985	1986	1987 (8 mos.)
Net Investment Income ($)	–	–	–	–	–	.53
Dividends from Net Investment Income ($)	–	–	–	–	–	.53
Net Gains (Losses) on Investments ($)	–	–	–	–	–	.31
Distributions from Net Realized Capital Gains ($)	–	–	–	–	–	.03
Net Asset Value End of Year ($)	–	–	–	–	–	10.28
Ratio of Expenses to Net Assets (%)	–	–	–	–	–	–
Portfolio Turnover Rate (%)	–	–	–	–	–	182
Total Assets: End of Year (Millions $)	–	–	–	–	–	34.7

Annual Rate of Return (%) Years Ending 12/31	–	–	–	–	–	(2.9)

Five-Year Total Return(%)	NA	Degree of Diversification	NA	Beta	NA	Bull (%)	NA	Bear (%)	4.0ᴬ

Objective: Seeks high level of current income consistent with safety of principal and liquidity. Invests at least 85% of its assets in long-term U.S. Treasury bonds and other "full faith and credit" obligations of the U.S. government. Can invest in zero coupon Treasury bonds and interest rate futures.

Portfolio: (7/31/87) U.S. Treasury securities 84%, repos 14%.

Distributions: Income: Monthly   **Capital Gains:** Annually

12b-1: No

Minimum: Initial: $3,000   Subsequent: $100

Min IRA: Initial: $500   Subsequent: $100

Services: IRA, Keogh, Corp, SEP, 403(b), Withdraw

Tel Exchange: Yes   **With MMF:** Yes

Registered: All states

VANGUARD/ WELLESLEY
Balanced

Vanguard Group
Vanguard Financial Center
Valley Forge, PA 19482
(800) 662-7447/(215) 648-6000

	Years Ending 12/31					
	1982	1983	1984	1985	1986	1987
Net Investment Income ($)	1.26	1.31	1.37	1.38	1.33	1.24
Dividends from Net Investment Income ($)	1.26	1.31	1.37	1.38	1.33	1.04
Net Gains (Losses) on Investments ($)	1.08	.84	.62	2.13	1.43	(1.52)
Distributions from Net Realized Capital Gains ($)	–	–	–	.10	.47	.38
Net Asset Value End of Year ($)	11.82	12.66	13.28	15.31	16.27	14.57
Ratio of Expenses to Net Assets (%)	.71	.70	.71	.60	.58	.49
Portfolio Turnover Rate (%)	60	38	36	21	31	40
Total Assets: End of Year (Millions $)	94.1	105.4	114.6	224.1	510.2	495.0

Annual Rate of Return (%) Years Ending 12/31	23.3	18.6	16.6	27.4	18.4	(1.9)

Five-Year Total Return(%) 104.5^A	Degree of Diversification NA	Beta .29	Bull (%) 78.5^C	Bear (%) (4.0)^C

Objective: Seeks to provide as much current income as management believes is consistent with reasonable risk. Invests approximately 70% of assets in investment grade fixed-income securities, with the balance invested in high yielding common stocks. May lend its portfolio securities and engage in repos.

Portfolio: (12/31/87) Corporate bonds 50%, common stocks 37%, U.S. government agency obligations 11%, repos 5%. Largest stock holdings: Union Electric Co., Pacific Gas & Electric Co.

Distributions: Income: Quarterly   **Capital Gains:** Annually
12b-1: No
Minimum: Initial: $1,500   Subsequent: $100
Min IRA: Initial: $500   Subsequent: $100
Services: IRA, Keogh, Corp, 403(b), SEP, Withdraw, Deduct
Tel Exchange: Yes   **With MMF:** Yes
Registered: All states

VANGUARD/ WELLINGTON
Balanced

Vanguard Group
Vanguard Financial Center
Valley Forge, PA 19482
(800) 662-7447/(215) 648-6000

	Years Ending 11/30					
	1982	1983	1984	1985	1986	1987
Net Investment Income ($)	.87	.91	.93	.91	.94	.95
Dividends from Net Investment Income ($)	.87	.91	.92	.92	.94	.54
Net Gains (Losses) on Investments ($)	1.01	1.88	.06	2.22	2.41	(1.55)
Distributions from Net Realized Capital Gains ($)	—	.44	.48	.30	.34	—
Net Asset Value End of Year ($)	11.05	12.49	12.08	13.99	16.06	14.92
Ratio of Expenses to Net Assets (%)	.69	.64	.59	.64	.53	.43
Portfolio Turnover Rate (%)	38	30	27	27	25	27
Total Assets: End of Year (Millions $)	555.0	617.3	604.2	783.8	1,102.1	1,273.6

Annual Rate of Return (%) Years Ending 12/31	23.0	24.6	10.7	28.4	18.2	2.3

Five-Year Total Return(%)	114.1^	Degree of Diversification	NA	Beta	.65	Bull (%)	112.7ᴮ	Bear (%)	(15.2)ᶜ

Objective: Seeks to provide conservation of principal, reasonable income return and profits without undue risk through balanced investments in common stocks, bonds and preferred stocks of well-established, dividend-paying companies. Common stocks generally amount from 60% to 70% of total portfolio.

Portfolio: (11/30/87) Common stocks 62%, bonds 22%, U.S. government and agency obligations 14%, repos 3%. Largest stock holdings: basic industries 26%, finance 10%.

Distributions: Income: Feb, May, Aug, Nov   Capital Gains: Nov
12b-1: No
Minimum: Initial: $1,500   Subsequent: $100
Min IRA: Initial: $500   Subsequent: $100
Services: IRA, Keogh, Corp, SEP, 403(b), Withdraw, Deduct
Tel Exchange: Yes   With MMF: Yes
Registered: All states

VANGUARD WINDSOR II
Growth & Income

Vanguard Group
Vanguard Financial Center
Valley Forge, PA 19482
(800) 662-7447/(215) 648-6000

| | | | Years Ending 10/31 | | | |
	1982	1983	1984	1985 (4 mos.)	1986	1987
Net Investment Income ($)	–	–	–	.11	.43	.52
Dividends from Net Investment Income ($)	–	–	–	.11	.43	.20
Net Gains (Losses) on Investments ($)	–	–	–	(.09)	3.09	(.39)
Distributions from Net Realized Capital Gains ($)	–	–	–	–	.52	–
Net Asset Value End of Year ($)	–	–	–	9.91	12.48	12.41
Ratio of Expenses to Net Assets (%)	–	–	–	.80	.65	.49
Portfolio Turnover Rate (%)	–	–	–	1	50	37
Total Assets: End of Year (Millions $)	–	–	–	133.0	814.0	1,322.8

Annual Rate of Return (%) Years Ending 12/31	–	–	–	–	21.4	(2.1)

Five-Year Total Return(%)	NA	Degree of Diversification	NA	Beta	NA	Bull (%)	NA	Bear (%)	(23.4)ᴰ

Objective:	Seeks long-term growth of capital and income through investment in common stocks characterized by above average income yields and below average price-earnings ratios. May hold cash or fixed-income securities for defensive purposes and engage in repos or lend its securities.
Portfolio:	(10/31/87) Common stocks 93%, repos 15%. Largest stock holdings: electric utilities 13%, insurance 13%.
Distributions:	Income: May, Dec **Capital Gains:** Dec
12b-1:	No
Minimum:	Initial: $1,500 Subsequent: $100
Min IRA:	Initial: $500 Subsequent: $100
Services:	IRA, Keogh, Corp, SEP, 403(b), Withdraw, Deduct
Tel Exchange:	Yes **With MMF:** Yes
Registered:	All states

VANGUARD/W.L. MORGAN GROWTH

Growth

Vanguard Group
Vanguard Financial Center
Valley Forge, PA 19482
(800) 662-7447/(215) 648-6000

	Years Ending 12/31					
	1982	1983	1984	1985	1986	1987
Net Investment Income ($)	.25	.31	.25	.23	.21	.23
Dividends from Net Investment Income ($)	.30	.25	.31	.25	.43	.20
Net Gains (Losses) on Investments ($)	2.32	2.81	(.94)	2.99	.78	.31
Distributions from Net Realized Capital Gains ($)	1.31	1.04	1.39	.60	2.88	2.45
Net Asset Value End of Year ($)	12.01	13.84	11.45	13.82	11.50	9.39
Ratio of Expenses to Net Assets (%)	1.04	.85	.68	.60	.54	.46
Portfolio Turnover Rate (%)	43	31	38	41	31	43
Total Assets: End of Year (Millions $)	288.5	401.7	467.8	665.0	594.3	538.0
Annual Rate of Return (%) Years Ending 12/31	27.2	28.0	(5.1)	29.5	7.8	4.7

Five-Year Total Return(%)	77.7ᴮ	Degree of Diversification	C	Beta	1.05	Bull (%)	117.0ᴮ	Bear (%)	(25.2)ᴱ

Objective: Primarily long-term capital growth. Fund follows a "three-tier" strategy of investing in established growth, emerging growth and cyclical growth companies chosen on the basis of greater than average earnings growth potential and quality of management.

Portfolio: (12/31/87) Common stocks 95%, temporary cash investments 7%. Largest stock holdings: established growth companies 47%, cyclical growth and other companies 24%.

Distributions: Income: Annually   **Capital Gains:** Annually

12b-1: No

Minimum: Initial: $1,500   Subsequent: $100

Min IRA: Initial: $500   Subsequent: $100

Services: IRA, Keogh, Corp, 403(b), SEP, Withdraw, Deduct

Tel Exchange: Yes   **With MMF:** Yes

Registered: All states

VANGUARD WORLD—INTERNATIONAL GROWTH

International

Vanguard Group
Vanguard Financial Center
Valley Forge, PA 19482
(800) 662-7447/(215) 648-6000

	1982	1983	1984	1985	1986 (11 mos.)	1987
Net Investment Income ($)	–	–	–	–	.07	.12
Dividends from Net Investment Income ($)	–	–	–	–	–	.07
Net Gains (Losses) on Investments ($)	–	–	–	–	5.41	3.29
Distributions from Net Realized Capital Gains ($)	–	–	–	–	–	.80
Net Asset Value End of Year ($)	–	–	–	–	11.67	14.21
Ratio of Expenses to Net Assets (%)	–	–	–	–	.78	.66
Portfolio Turnover Rate (%)	–	–	–	–	39	77
Total Assets: End of Year (Millions $)	–	–	–	–	451.3	606.7

Annual Rate of Return (%) Years Ending 12/31	–	–	–	–	56.6	12.4

Five-Year Total Return(%)	NA	Degree of Diversification	NA	Beta	NA	Bull (%)	NA	Bear (%)	(11.0)^c

Objective: Seeks long-term capital appreciation through investment in common stocks of seasoned foreign companies from a wide diversity of countries. May enter into foreign currency futures contracts and may lend its securities.

Portfolio: (8/31/87) Common stocks 96%, repos 3%, other assets 1%. Largest country holdings: Japan 34%, United Kingdom 26%.

Distributions: Income: Oct   **Capital Gains:** Oct

12b-1: No

Minimum: Initial: $1,500   Subsequent: $100

Min IRA: Initial: $500   Subsequent: $100

Services: IRA, Keogh, Corp, SEP, 403(b), Withdraw, Deduct

Tel Exchange: Yes   **With MMF:** Yes

Registered: All states

VANGUARD WORLD–U.S. GROWTH
Growth

Vanguard Group
Vanguard Financial Center
Valley Forge, PA 19482
(800) 662-7447/(215) 648-6000

	Years Ending 8/31					
	1982	1983	1984	1985	1986	1987
Net Investment Income ($)	–	–	–	–	.24	.30
Dividends from Net Investment Income ($)	–	–	–	–	–	.28
Net Gains (Losses) on Investments ($)	–	–	–	–	3.03	1.45
Distributions from Net Realized Capital Gains ($)	–	–	–	–	–	1.94
Net Asset Value End of Year ($)	–	–	–	–	13.21	12.74
Ratio of Expenses to Net Assets (%)	–	–	–	–	.80	.65
Portfolio Turnover Rate (%)	–	–	–	–	77	142
Total Assets: End of Year (Millions $)	–	–	–	–	188.0	184.1
Annual Rate of Return (%) Years Ending 12/31	–	–	–	–	7.6	(6.1)

Five-Year Total Return(%)	NA	Degree of Diversification	NA	Beta	NA	Bull (%)	NA	Bear (%)	(23.9)D

Objective: Seeks long-term capital appreciation through investment in common stock of primarily seasoned companies. May also invest in special situations and newer companies and, for defensive purposes, debt securities.

Portfolio: (8/31/87) Common stocks 86%, other assets 10%, repos 3%. Largest stock holdings: finance and insurance 17%, media 14%.

Distributions: Income: Oct   **Capital Gains:** Oct

12b-1: No

Minimum: Initial: $1,500   Subsequent: $100

Min IRA: Initial: $500   Subsequent: $100

Services: IRA, Keogh, Corp, SEP, (403)b, Withdraw, Deduct

Tel Exchange: Yes   **With MMF:** Yes

Registered: All states

VIKING
EQUITY INDEX—
GENERAL
Growth & Income

Viking Equity Index Fund, Inc.
232 Lakeside Drive
Horsham, PA 19044
(800) 441-3885

	Years Ending 1/31					
	1982	1983	1984	1985	1986	1987
Net Investment Income ($)	–	–	–	–	.38	.30
Dividends from Net Investment Income ($)	–	–	–	–	.37	.20
Net Gains (Losses) on Investments ($)	–	–	–	–	1.76	3.34
Distributions from Net Realized Capital Gains ($)	–	–	–	–	.13	–
Net Asset Value End of Year ($)	–	–	–	–	11.64	15.08
Ratio of Expenses to Net Assets (%)	–	–	–	–	.95	1.05
Portfolio Turnover Rate (%)	–	–	–	–	9	28
Total Assets: End of Year (Millions $)	–	–	–	–	2.2	7.2

Annual Rate of Return (%) Years Ending 12/31		–	–	–	–	16.7	3.3
Five-Year Total Return(%) NA	Degree of Diversification NA	Beta NA		Bull (%) NA		Bear (%) (24.6)[D]	

Objective: Designed to track the investment results of an equity index prepared by First Pennsylvania Bank. The index is substantially similar to the S&P 500 index.

Portfolio: (7/31/87) Common stocks 98%, short-term securities 1%. Largest stock holdings: oil 11%, drugs and medical 9%.

Distributions: Income: Quarterly **Capital Gains:** Annually

12b-1: No

Minimum: Initial: $250 Subsequent: None

Min IRA: Initial: $250 Subsequent: None

Services: IRA, Withdraw

Tel Exchange: Yes **With MMF:** Yes

Registered: DE, NJ, PA

WAYNE HUMMER GROWTH
Growth

Wayne Hummer Mgmt. Co.
175 W. Jackson Blvd.
Chicago, IL 60604
(800) 621-4477/(312) 431-1700

	1982	**1983**	**1984** (3 mos.)	**1985**	**1986**	**1987**
Net Investment Income ($)	–	–	.12	.44	.29	.27
Dividends from Net Investment Income ($)	–	–	–	.33	.30	.24
Net Gains (Losses) on Investments ($)	–	–	(.29)	.73	3.20	2.61
Distributions from Net Realized Capital Gains ($)	–	–	–	–	.01	.35
Net Asset Value End of Year ($)	–	–	9.83	10.67	13.85	16.14
Ratio of Expenses to Net Assets (%)	–	–	1.50	1.50	1.50	1.50
Portfolio Turnover Rate (%)	–	–	0	26	27	28
Total Assets: End of Year (Millions $)	–	–	1.7	4.3	10.1	18.8
Annual Rate of Return (%) Years Ending 12/31	–	–	4.0	24.4	13.8	9.3

Five-Year Total Return(%)	NA	Degree of Diversification	A	Beta	.97	Bull (%)	114.2B	Bear (%)	(19.4)D

Objective: Seeks long-term capital growth and secondarily current income through investment in established dividend-paying companies' common stock, preferred stock, bonds or convertibles. May temporarily invest in investment grade debt securities as defensive move.

Portfolio: (9/30/87) Common stocks 81%, commercial paper 19%. Largest stock holdings: chemical 10%, auto & machinery 10%.

Distributions: Income: Jan, April, July, Oct   **Capital Gains:** April
12b-1: Yes   Amount: 0.25%
Minimum: Initial: $1,000   Subsequent: $500
Min IRA: Initial: $500   Subsequent: $200
Services: IRA, Keogh, SEP, Corp
Tel Exchange: No
Registered: All states except DE, ID, NH, OK

WORLD OF TECHNOLOGY
International

Financial Programs
P.O. Box 2040
Denver, CO 80201
(800) 525-8085/(303) 779-1233

		Years Ending 2/28				
	1982	1983	1984 (11 mos.)	1985	1986	1987
Net Investment Income ($)	–	–	.09	(.04)	(.07)	(.04)
Dividends from Net Investment Income ($)	–	–	.09	–	–	–
Net Gains (Losses) on Investments ($)	–	–	(1.43)	.32	.72	3.0
Distributions from Net Realized Capital Gains ($)	–	–	–	–	–	–
Net Asset Value End of Year ($)	–	–	7.69	7.97	8.61	11.57
Ratio of Expenses to Net Assets (%)	–	–	1.44	1.50	1.50	1.50
Portfolio Turnover Rate (%)	–	–	56	99	121	147
Total Assets: End of Year (Millions $)	–	–	11.5	9.6	8.1	10.0

Annual Rate of Return (%) Years Ending 12/31	–	–	(17.5)	16.5	16.5	2.4

Five-Year Total Return(%)	NA	Degree of Diversification	E	Beta	.92	Bull (%)	79.1c	Bear (%)	(18.2)c

Objective: Seeks capital appreciation through investment in common stocks of smaller emerging companies involved in high technology. Invests worldwide but major portion of holdings are in U.S. companies.

Portfolio: (8/31/87) Common stocks 93%, fixed-income securities 7%. Largest stock holdings: electrical equipment 13%, pharmaceuticals 10%.

Distributions: Income: Feb   **Capital Gains:** Feb

12b-1: No

Minimum: Initial: $250   Subsequent: $50

Min IRA: Initial: $250   Subsequent: $50

Services: IRA, Keogh, Corp, 403(b), SEP, Withdraw, Deduct

Tel Exchange: Yes   **With MMF:** Yes

Registered: All states

WPG
Growth

Weiss, Peck & Greer
One New York Plaza, 30th Flr.
New York, NY 10004
(800) 223-3332/(212) 908-9582

	Years Ending 12/31					
	1982	**1983**	**1984**	**1985**	**1986**	**1987**
Net Investment Income ($)	.62	.31	.70	.49	.15	.24
Dividends from Net Investment Income ($)	.51	.47	.57	.65	.15	.15
Net Gains (Losses) on Investments ($)	3.63	3.01	(1.11)	5.26	2.77	1.36
Distributions from Net Realized Capital Gains ($)	—	.01	.54	—	6.55	3.36
Net Asset Value End of Year ($)	18.00	20.84	19.32	24.42	20.64	18.73
Ratio of Expenses to Net Assets (%)	1.78	1.32	1.17	1.21	1.23	1.19
Portfolio Turnover Rate (%)	212	63	104	108	71	84
Total Assets: End of Year (Millions $)	21.5	33.0	32.7	42.1	36.1	34.8

Annual Rate of Return (%) Years Ending 12/31	30.6	18.5	(1.6)	30.5	11.2	6.8

Five-Year Total Return(%)	80.7[B]	Degree of Diversification	A	Beta	1.07	Bull (%)	123.8[B]	Bear (%)	(22.9)[D]

Objective: Seeks both current income and capital growth. Portfolio generally consists of 75% equity securities and 25% debt securities of well-known, seasoned, established, dividend-paying companies. May write covered call options, buy options, lend its portfolio securities, and enter into repos.

Portfolio: (12/31/87) Common stocks 110%, repos 7%. Largest stock holdings: capital goods 16%, basic industries 15%.

Distributions: Income: Mar, June, Sept, Dec   **Capital Gains:** Dec

12b-1: No

Minimum: Initial: $1,000   Subsequent: $50

Min IRA: Initial: $250   Subsequent: $50

Services: IRA, Keogh, Withdraw

Tel Exchange: Yes   **With MMF:** Yes

Registered: All states

WPG GOVERNMENT SECURITIES
Bond

Weiss, Peck & Greer
One New York Plaza, 30th Flr.
New York, NY 10004
(800) 223-3332/(212) 908-9582

	Years Ending 12/31					
	1982	1983	1984	1985	1986 (10 mos.)	1987
Net Investment Income ($)	–	–	–	–	.30	.72
Dividends from Net Investment Income ($)	–	–	–	–	.30	.72
Net Gains (Losses) on Investments ($)	–	–	–	–	.50	(.49)
Distributions from Net Realized Capital Gains ($)	–	–	–	–	.17	.07
Net Asset Value End of Year ($)	–	–	–	–	10.33	9.77
Ratio of Expenses to Net Assets (%)	–	–	–	–	1.16	.87
Portfolio Turnover Rate (%)	–	–	–	–	203	108
Total Assets: End of Year (Millions $)	–	–	–	–	48.7	76.0

Annual Rate of Return (%) Years Ending 12/31	–	–	–	–	–	2.5

Five-Year Total Return(%)	NA	Degree of Diversification	NA	Beta	NA	Bull (%)	NA	Bear (%)	3.5A

Objective: Seeks high level of current income consistent with preservation of capital. Invests primarily in U.S. government securities having remaining maturities of one year or more. May also write (sell) and buy covered put and call options.

Portfolio: (12/31/87) Mortgage-backed securities 37%, U.S. Treasury notes 31%, U.S. Treasury bonds 14%, U.S. government instrumentalities 13%, repos 2%, other assets 2%.

Distributions: Income: Monthly   **Capital Gains:** Annually

12b-1: Yes   **Amount:** 0.05%

Minimum: Initial: $5,000   Subsequent: $1,000

Min IRA: Initial: $2,000   Subsequent: $50

Services: IRA, Corp, Withdraw

Tel Exchange: Yes   **With MMF:** Yes

Registered: All states

Tax-Exempt Bond Funds

On the following pages, we present 72 tax-exempt bond funds, listed alphabetically. All return figures are based on a calendar year-end, and assume monthly reinvestment of distributions. We did not calculate beta figures or degrees of diversification for tax-exempt bond funds, since they are measures relative to the stock market and are thus less meaningful for these funds.

AARP INSURED TAX FREE GENERAL BOND

Scudder Fund Distributors
175 Federal Street
Boston, MA 02110-2267
(800) 253-2277

	1982	1983	1984	1985 (10 mos.)	1986	1987
				Years Ending 9/30		
Dividends from Net Investment Income ($)	—	—	—	.64	1.01	1.07
Distributions from Net Realized Capital Gains ($)	—	—	—	—	.06	.20
Net Asset Value End of Year ($)	—	—	—	15.12	16.69	15.00
Ratio of Expenses to Net Assets (%)	—	—	—	1.29	1.13	1.00
Portfolio Turnover Rate (%)	—	—	—	91	36	135
Total Assets: End of Year (Millions $)	—	—	—	62.3	129.3	238.0
Annual Rate of Return (%) Years Ending 12/31	—	—	—	—	16.9	(1.4)

Distr: Income: Monthly
    Capital Gains: Annually
Minimum: Initial: $250
    Subsequent: None

Telephone Exchange: Yes
    With MMF: Yes
Registered In: All states
12b-1: No

AARP INSURED TAX FREE SHORT TERM

Scudder Fund Distributors
175 Federal Street
Boston, MA 02110-2267
(800) 253-2277

	1982	1983	1984	1985 (10 mos.)	1986	1987
				Years Ending 9/30		
Dividends from Net Investment Income ($)	—	—	—	.47	.73	.75
Distributions from Net Realized Capital Gains ($)	—	—	—	—	—	.05
Net Asset Value End of Year ($)	—	—	—	15.11	15.58	15.13
Ratio of Expenses to Net Assets (%)	—	—	—	1.50	1.48	1.31
Portfolio Turnover Rate (%)	—	—	—	—	23	22
Total Assets: End of Year (Millions $)	—	—	—	30.1	48.1	70.5
Annual Rate of Return (%) Years Ending 12/31	—	—	—	—	8.3	3.3

Distr: Income: Monthly
    Capital Gains: Annually
Minimum: Initial: $250
    Subsequent: None

Telephone Exchange: Yes
    With MMF: Yes
Registered In: All states
12b-1: No

BABSON TAX-FREE INCOME— PORTFOLIO L

Jones & Babson, Inc.
3 Crown Center
2440 Pershing Rd.
Kansas City, MO 64108
(800) 821-5591/(816) 471-5200

	Years Ending 6/30					
	1982	1983	1984	1985	1986	1987
Dividends from Net Investment Income ($)	.74	.74	.73	.72	.71	.63
Distributions from Net Realized Capital Gains ($)	—	—	—	—	—	.60
Net Asset Value End of Year ($)	6.94	8.30	7.66	8.76	9.45	8.64
Ratio of Expenses to Net Assets (%)	.75	.75	.92	1.00	1.00	.99
Portfolio Turnover Rate (%)	9	27	27	32	46	123
Total Assets: End of Year (Millions $)	3.5	10.6	11.9	16.0	20.9	22.0
Annual Rate of Return (%) Years Ending 12/31	39.6	9.0	9.1	20.4	18.2	(1.9)

Distr: Income: Monthly
    Capital Gains: Annually
Minimum: Initial: $1,000
    Subsequent: $100

Telephone Exchange: Yes
    With MMF: Yes
Registered In: All states
12b-1: No

BENHAM CALIFORNIA TAX-FREE INTERMEDIATE

Benham Management Corp.
755 Page Mill Road
Palo Alto, CA 94304
(800) 227-8380/(415) 858-3600

	Years Ending 8/31					
	1982	1983	1984	1985	1986	1987
Dividends from Net Investment Income ($)	—	—	.58	.69	.69	.62
Distributions from Net Realized Capital Gains ($)	—	—	—	—	—	—
Net Asset Value End of Year ($)	—	—	9.56	9.86	10.56	10.30
Ratio of Expenses to Net Assets (%)	—	—	.97	.96	.74	.67
Portfolio Turnover Rate (%)	—	—	93	48	23	52
Total Assets: End of Year (Millions $)	—	—	30.4	56.3	124.9	166.9
Annual Rate of Return (%) Years Ending 12/31	—	—	5.3	13.8	12.7	.8

Distr: Income: Monthly
    Capital Gains: Annually
Minimum: Initial: $1,000
    Subsequent: $100

Telephone Exchange: Yes
    With MMF: Yes
Registered In: AZ, CA, HI, NV, OR, WA
12b-1: No

BENHAM CALIFORNIA TAX-FREE LONG TERM

Benham Management Corp.
755 Page Mill Road
Palo Alto, CA 94304
(800) 227-8380/(415) 858-3600

	\multicolumn{6}{c}{Years Ending 8/31}
	1982	1983	1984	1985	1986	1987
Dividends from Net Investment Income ($)	–	–	.71	.84	.83	.85
Distributions from Net Realized Capital Gains ($)	–	–	–	–	–	–
Net Asset Value End of Year ($)	–	–	9.54	10.15	11.42	10.54
Ratio of Expenses to Net Assets (%)	–	–	.97	.95	.74	.65
Portfolio Turnover Rate (%)	–	–	107	91	48	82
Total Assets: End of Year (Millions $)	–	–	27.5	83.9	196.6	179.5
Annual Rate of Return (%) Years Ending 12/31	–	–	5.7	17.6	18.7	(4.6)

Distr: Income: Monthly
Capital Gains: Annually
Minimum: Initial: $1,000
Subsequent: $100

Telephone Exchange: Yes
With MMF: Yes
Registered In: AZ, CA, HI, NV, OR, WA
12b-1: No

BENHAM NATIONAL TAX-FREE TRUST INTERMEDIATE TERM

Benham Management Corp.
755 Page Mill Road
Palo Alto, CA 94304
(800) 227-8380/(415) 858-3600

	\multicolumn{6}{c}{Years Ending 5/31}
	1982	1983	1984	1985 (10 mos.)	1986	1987
Dividends from Net Investment Income ($)	–	–	–	.64	.72	.64
Distributions from Net Realized Capital Gains ($)	–	–	–	–	–	–
Net Asset Value End of Year ($)	–	–	–	9.55	9.91	9.87
Ratio of Expenses to Net Assets (%)	–	–	–	–	.27	.50
Portfolio Turnover Rate (%)	–	–	–	77	44	26
Total Assets: End of Year (Millions $)	–	–	–	3.1	12.2	19.5
Annual Rate of Return (%) Years Ending 12/31	–	–	–	12.5	14.2	2.2

Distr: Income: Monthly
Capital Gains: Annually
Minimum: Initial: $1,000
Subsequent: $100

Telephone Exchange: Yes
With MMF: Yes
Registered In: All states
12b-1: No

BENHAM NATIONAL TAX-FREE TRUST LONG TERM

Benham Management Corp.
755 Page Mill Road
Palo Alto, CA 94304
(800) 227-8380/(415) 858-3600

Years Ending 5/31

	1982	1983	1984	1985 (10 mos.)	1986	1987
Dividends from Net Investment Income ($)	–	–	–	.82	.94	.84
Distributions from Net Realized Capital Gains ($)	–	–	–	–	–	–
Net Asset Value End of Year ($)	–	–	–	10.56	11.37	10.79
Ratio of Expenses to Net Assets (%)	–	–	–	–	.26	.50
Portfolio Turnover Rate (%)	–	–	–	33	57	102
Total Assets: End of Year (Millions $)	–	–	–	7.1	22.8	24.0
Annual Rate of Return (%) Years Ending 12/31	–	–		19.2	18.7	(6.7)

Distr: Income: Monthly
    Capital Gains: Annually
Minimum: Initial: $1,000
    Subsequent: $100

Telephone Exchange: Yes
    With MMF: Yes
Registered In: All states
12b-1: No

BULL & BEAR TAX-FREE INCOME

Bull & Bear Advisors
11 Hanover Square
New York, NY 10005
(800) 847-4200/(212) 363-1100

Years Ending 12/31

	1982	1983	1984 (10 mos.)	1985	1986	1987
Dividends from Net Investment Income ($)	–	–	1.10	1.39	1.31	1.26
Distributions from Net Realized Capital Gains ($)	–	–	–	–	.58	–
Net Asset Value End of Year ($)	–	–	15.04	16.88	18.17	16.74
Ratio of Expenses to Net Assets (%)	–	–	.82	1.02	1.18	1.18
Portfolio Turnover Rate (%)	–	–	67	46	60	62
Total Assets: End of Year (Millions $)	–	–	4.2	11.0	21.8	16.1
Annual Rate of Return (%) Years Ending 12/31	–	–	–	22.4	19.6	(0.9)

Distr: Income: Monthly
    Capital Gains: Annually
Minimum: Initial: $1,000
    Subsequent: $100

Telephone Exchange: Yes
    With MMF: Yes
Registered In: All states
12b-1: Yes **Amount:** 0.50%

CALIFORNIA MUNI FUND

California Muni Fund
111 Broadway, Suite 1107
New York, NY 10006
(800) 225-6864/(212) 608-6864

		Years Ending 12/31				
	1982	1983	1984 (3 mos.)	1985	1986	1987
Dividends from Net Investment Income ($)	–	–	.28	.81	.76	.67
Distributions from Net Realized Capital Gains ($)	–	–	–	–	1.66	.17
Net Asset Value End of Year ($)	–	–	9.46	10.58	9.23	8.52
Ratio of Expenses to Net Assets (%)	–	–	NA	3.02	2.33	1.61
Portfolio Turnover Rate (%)	–	–	NA	228	34	32
Total Assets: End of Year (Millions $)	–	–	NA	10.7	6.3	7.8
Annual Rate of Return (%) Years Ending 12/31	–	–	–	21.2	10.5	1.4

Distr: Income: Monthly
    Capital Gains: Annually
Minimum: Initial: $1,000
    Subsequent: $100

Telephone Exchange: Yes
    With MMF: Yes
Registered In: CA
12b-1: Yes **Amount:** 0.50%

CALIFORNIA TAX-FREE INCOME

CCM Partners
44 Montgomery Street
Suite 2200
San Francisco, CA 94104
(800) 225-8778/(415) 398-2727

		Years Ending 8/31				
	1982	1983	1984	1985	1986 (9 mos.)	1987
Dividends from Net Investment Income ($)	–	–	–	–	.50	.85
Distributions from Net Realized Capital Gains ($)	–	–	–	–	–	–
Net Asset Value End of Year ($)	–	–	–	–	11.72	11.25
Ratio of Expenses to Net Assets (%)	–	–	–	–	.03	.39
Portfolio Turnover Rate (%)	–	–	–	–	50	87
Total Assets: End of Year (Millions $)	–	–	–	–	20.8	37.4
Annual Rate of Return (%) Years Ending 12/31	–	–	–	–	22.7	(1.2)

Distr: Income: Monthly
    Capital Gains: Annually
Minimum: Initial: $10,000
    Subsequent: $250

Telephone Exchange: Yes
    With MMF: Yes
Registered In: CA, HI, NV
12b-1: No

CALVERT TAX-FREE RESERVES— LIMITED TERM

Calvert Asset Management Co.
1700 Pennsylvania Ave., N.W.
Washington, DC 20006
(800) 368-2748/(301) 951-4820

	Years Ending 12/31					
	1982	1983	1984	1985	1986	1987
Dividends from Net Investment Income ($)	.84	.67	.71	.73	.64	.59
Distributions from Net Realized Capital Gains ($)	.03	.01	.01	.01	.04	—
Net Asset Value End of Year ($)	10.31	10.29	10.33	10.48	10.67	10.45
Ratio of Expenses to Net Assets (%)	1.00	1.00	.96	.88	.81	.76
Portfolio Turnover Rate (%)	86	79	155	90	67	52
Total Assets: End of Year (Millions $)	31.0	55.7	52.3	77.8	189.4	147.7
Annual Rate of Return (%) Years Ending 12/31	13.2	6.2	7.5	8.4	8.6	3.5

Distr: Income: Daily
    Capital Gains: Annually
Minimum: Initial: $2,000
    Subsequent: $250

Telephone Exchange: Yes
    With MMF: Yes
Registered In: All states
12b-1: No

DREYFUS CALIFORNIA TAX EXEMPT BOND

The Dreyfus Corp.
600 Madison Ave.
New York, NY 10022
(800) 645-6561/(718) 895-1206

	Years Ending 5/31					
	1982	1983	1984 (10 mos.)	1985	1986	1987
Dividends from Net Investment Income ($)	—	—	1.02	1.15	1.12	1.08
Distributions from Net Realized Capital Gains ($)	—	—	—	—	—	—
Net Asset Value End of Year ($)	—	—	12.54	13.87	14.70	14.45
Ratio of Expenses to Net Assets (%)	—	—	.55	.75	.72	.70
Portfolio Turnover Rate (%)	—	—	36	27	19	32
Total Assets: End of Year (Millions $)	—	—	216.1	529.3	973.2	1,175.2
Annual Rate of Return (%) Years Ending 12/31	—	—	—	18.0	17.7	(1.7)

Distr: Income: Monthly
    Capital Gains: June
Minimum: Initial: $2,500
    Subsequent: $100

Telephone Exchange: Yes
    With MMF: Yes
Registered In: Call for availability
12b-1: No

DREYFUS INSURED TAX EXEMPT BOND

The Dreyfus Corp.
600 Madison Ave.
New York, NY 10022
(800) 645-6561/(718) 895-1206

	Years Ending 4/30					
	1982	1983	1984	1985	1986 (10 mos.)	1987
Dividends from Net Investment Income ($)	–	–	–	–	1.14	1.24
Distributions from Net Realized Capital Gains ($)	–	–	–	–	–	–
Net Asset Value End of Year ($)	–	–	–	–	18.03	17.38
Ratio of Expenses to Net Assets (%)	–	–	–	–	.73	.84
Portfolio Turnover Rate (%)	–	–	–	–	51	75
Total Assets: End of Year (Millions $)	–	–	–	–	144.3	197.6
Annual Rate of Return (%) Years Ending 12/31	–	–	–	–	17.1	(1.9)

Distr: Income: Monthly
Capital Gains: Annually
Minimum: Initial: $2,500
Subsequent: $100

Telephone Exchange: Yes
With MMF: Yes
Registered In: All states
12b-1: Yes **Amount:** 0.20%

DREYFUS INTERMEDIATE TAX EXEMPT

Dreyfus Corp.
600 Madison Ave.
New York, NY 10022
(800) 645-6561/(718) 895-1206

	Years Ending 5/31					
	1982	1983	1984 (9 mos.)	1985	1986	1987
Dividends from Net Investment Income ($)	–	–	.82	1.02	1.03	.99
Distributions from Net Realized Capital Gains ($)	–	–	–	–	–	–
Net Asset Value End of Year ($)	–	–	11.84	12.93	13.47	13.46
Ratio of Expenses to Net Assets (%)	–	–	.69	.81	.75	.71
Portfolio Turnover Rate (%)	–	–	29	21	34	50
Total Assets: End of Year (Millions $)	–	–	228.5	548.7	920.2	1,089.9
Annual Rate of Return (%) Years Ending 12/31	–	–	–	16.1	15.4	1.1

Distr: Income: Monthly
Capital Gains: Annually
Minimum: Initial: $2,500
Subsequent: $100

Telephone Exchange: Yes
With MMF: Yes
Registered In: All states
12b-1: No

DREYFUS MASSACHUSETTS TAX EXEMPT BOND

The Dreyfus Corp.
600 Madison Ave.
New York, NY 10022
(800) 645-6561/(718) 895-1206

	1982	1983	1984	1985	1986	1987
Years Ending 5/31						
Dividends from Net Investment Income ($)	–	–	–	–	1.17	1.12
Distributions from Net Realized Capital Gains ($)	–	–	–	–	–	–
Net Asset Value End of Year ($)	–	–	–	–	15.89	15.48
Ratio of Expenses to Net Assets (%)	–	–	–	–	.26	.64
Portfolio Turnover Rate (%)	–	–	–	–	103	39
Total Assets: End of Year (Millions $)	–	–	–	–	54.7	81.7
Annual Rate of Return (%) Years Ending 12/31	–	–	–	–	17.9	(3.4)

Distr: Income: Monthly
Capital Gains: Annually
Minimum: Initial: $2,500
Subsequent: $100

Telephone Exchange: Yes
With MMF: Yes
Registered In: Call for availability
12b-1: No

DREYFUS NEW YORK TAX EXEMPT BOND

The Dreyfus Corp.
600 Madison Ave.
New York, NY 10022
(800) 645-6561/(718) 895-1206

	1982	1983	1984 (10 mos.)	1985	1986	1987
Years Ending 5/31						
Dividends from Net Investment Income ($)	–	–	.97	1.16	1.15	1.10
Distributions from Net Realized Capital Gains ($)	–	–	–	–	–	–
Net Asset Value End of Year ($)	–	–	12.41	14.10	15.05	14.73
Ratio of Expenses to Net Assets (%)	–	–	.77	.76	.71	.71
Portfolio Turnover Rate (%)	–	–	44	29	15	38
Total Assets: End of Year (Millions $)	–	–	252.1	652.9	1,246	1,538
Annual Rate of Return (%) Years Ending 12/31	–	–	–	20.6	17.1	(2.7)

Distr: Income: Monthly
Capital Gains: June
Minimum: Initial: $2,500
Subsequent: $100

Telephone Exchange: Yes
With MMF: Yes
Registered In: All states
12b-1: No

Tax-Exempt Bond Funds **347**

DREYFUS TAX EXEMPT

The Dreyfus Corporation
600 Madison Ave.
New York, NY 10022
(800) 645-6561/(718) 895-1206

	\multicolumn{6}{c}{Years Ending 8/31}
	1982	1983	1984	1985	1986	1987
Dividends from Net Investment Income ($)	.99	1.00	1.01	1.02	.99	.94
Distributions from Net Realized Capital Gains ($)	—	—	—	—	—	
Net Asset Value End of Year ($)	10.12	10.97	10.84	11.60	12.87	12.22
Ratio of Expenses to Net Assets (%)	.77	.73	.71	.69	.69	.68
Portfolio Turnover Rate (%)	40	37	22	28	53	67
Total Assets: End of Year (Millions $)	1,022.8	1,780.1	2,020.9	2,724.7	3,648.9	3,527.7
Annual Rate of Return (%) Years Ending 12/31	39.6	11.6	8.6	19.4	17.4	(1.7)

Distr: Income: Monthly
Capital Gains: Annually
Minimum: Initial: $2,500
Subsequent: $100

Telephone Exchange: Yes
With MMF: Yes
Registered In: All states
12b-1: No

FIDELITY AGGRESSIVE TAX-FREE PORTFOLIO

Fidelity Investments Co.
82 Devonshire St.
Boston, MA 02109
(800) 544-6666/(617) 523-1919

	\multicolumn{6}{c}{Years Ending 12/31}
	1982	1983	1984	1985 (3 mos.)	1986	1987
Dividends from Net Investment Income ($)	—	—	—	.31	.93	.90
Distributions from Net Realized Capital Gains ($)	—	—	—	—	—	—
Net Asset Value End of Year ($)	—	—	—	10.66	11.56	10.82
Ratio of Expenses to Net Assets (%)	—	—	—	.60	.65	.74
Portfolio Turnover Rate (%)	—	—	—	4	17	68
Total Assets: End of Year (Millions $)	—	—	—	101.4	394.1	352.8
Annual Rate of Return (%) Years Ending 12/31	—	—	—	—	17.6	1.4

Distr: Income: Monthly
Capital Gains: Annually
Minimum: Initial: $2,500
Subsequent: $250

Telephone Exchange: Yes
With MMF: Yes
Registered In: All states
12b-1: Yes **Amount:** Pd. by Advisor

FIDELITY CALIFORNIA TAX-FREE HIGH YIELD

Fidelity Investments Co.
82 Devonshire Street
Boston, MA 02109
(800) 544-6666/(617) 523-1919

			Years Ending 4/30		
	1982	1983	1984	1985 (10 mos.)	1986	1987
Dividends from Net Investment Income ($)	–	–	–	.77	.88	.78
Distributions from Net Realized Capital Gains ($)	–	–	–	–	–	.05
Net Asset Value End of Year ($)	–	–	–	10.43	11.51	10.95
Ratio of Expenses to Net Assets (%)	–	–	–	1.00	.72	.68
Portfolio Turnover Rate (%)	–	–	–	14	16	46
Total Assets: End of Year (Millions $)	–	–	–	30.2	323.5	460.8
Annual Rate of Return (%) Years Ending 12/31	–	–	–	16.6	17.7	(3.6)

Distr: Income: Monthly
    Capital Gains: Annually
Minimum: Initial: $2,500
    Subsequent: $250

Telephone Exchange: Yes
    With MMF: Yes
Registered In: CA
12b-1: Yes **Amount:** Pd. by Advisor

FIDELITY HIGH YIELD MUNICIPALS

Fidelity Investments Co.
82 Devonshire St.
Boston, MA 02109
(800) 544-6666/(617) 523-1919

			Years Ending 11/30		
	1982	1983	1984	1985	1986	1987
Dividends from Net Investment Income ($)	1.13	1.07	1.07	1.04	1.00	.94
Distributions from Net Realized Capital Gains ($)	–	–	–	–	.04	.52
Net Asset Value End of Year ($)	10.62	11.17	11.0	12.29	13.77	11.75
Ratio of Expenses to Net Assets (%)	.64	.65	.59	.56	.57	.71
Portfolio Turnover Rate (%)	109	81	73	57	49	80
Total Assets: End of Year (Millions $)	356.7	750.2	1,040.2	1,600.8	2,449.3	1,609.7
Annual Rate of Return (%) Years Ending 12/31	36.0	15.9	9.9	21.4	18.9	(2.9)

Distr: Income: Monthly
    Capital Gains: Annually
Minimum: Initial: $2,500
    Subsequent: $250

Telephone Exchange: Yes
    With MMF: Yes
Registered In: All states
12b-1: Yes **Amount:** Pd. by Advisor

FIDELITY INSURED TAX-FREE

Fidelity Investments Co.
82 Devonshire Street
Boston, MA 02109
(800) 544-6666/(617) 523-1919

	Years Ending 12/31					
	1982	1983	1984	1985 (2 mos.)	1986	1987
Dividends from Net Investment Income ($)	−	−	−	.07	.73	.72
Distributions from Net Realized Capital Gains ($)	−	−	−	−	−	.01
Net Asset Value End of Year ($)	−	−	−	10.23	11.33	10.36
Ratio of Expenses to Net Assets (%)	−	−	−	.60	.60	.62
Portfolio Turnover Rate (%)	−	−	−	−	23	57
Total Assets: End of Year (Millions $)	−	−	−	9.5	146.2	145.0
Annual Rate of Return (%) Years Ending 12/31	−	−	−	−	18.1	(2.2)

Distr: Income: Monthly
    Capital Gains: Annually
Minimum: Initial: $2,500
    Subsequent: $250

Telephone Exchange: Yes
    With MMF: Yes
Registered In: All states
12b-1: Yes **Amount:** Pd. by Advisor

FIDELITY LIMITED TERM MUNICIPALS

Fidelity Investments Co.
82 Devonshire St.
Boston, MA 02109
(800) 544-6666/(617) 523-1919

	Years Ending 12/31					
	1982	1983	1984	1985	1986	1987
Dividends from Net Investment Income ($)	.69	.62	.64	.63	.62	.58
Distributions from Net Realized Capital Gains ($)	−	−	−	−	−	−
Net Asset Value End of Year ($)	7.89	8.03	8.15	8.88	9.58	9.10
Ratio of Expenses to Net Assets (%)	.99	.83	.79	.71	.68	.74
Portfolio Turnover Rate (%)	210	146	152	73	30	59
Total Assets: End of Year (Millions $)	99.7	182.0	214.2	315.8	580.2	459.0
Annual Rate of Return (%) Years Ending 12/31	25.9	9.9	9.9	17.3	15.2	1.1

Distr: Income: Monthly
    Capital Gains: Annually
Minimum: Initial: $2,500
    Subsequent: $250

Telephone Exchange: Yes
    With MMF: Yes
Registered In: All states
12b-1: Yes **Amount:** Pd. by Advisor

FIDELITY MASSFREE HIGH YIELD
(formerly FIDELITY MASSFREE MUNI BOND)

Fidelity Investments Co.
82 Devonshire St.
Boston, MA 02109
(800) 544-6666/(617) 523-1919

	Years Ending 7/31					
	1982	1983	1984 (8 mos.)	1985	1986	1987
Dividends from Net Investment Income ($)	—	—	.72	.92	.87	.79
Distributions from Net Realized Capital Gains ($)	—	—	—	—	—	—
Net Asset Value End of Year ($)	—	—	9.64	10.54	11.18	11.12
Ratio of Expenses to Net Assets (%)	—	—	.89	.76	.64	.64
Portfolio Turnover Rate (%)	—	—	102	12	13	36
Total Assets: End of Year (Millions $)	—	—	56.2	203.1	500.2	641.9
Annual Rate of Return (%) Years Ending 12/31	—	—	—	19.6	16.9	(1.3)

Distr: Income: Monthly
Capital Gains: Aug
Minimum: Initial: $2,500
Subsequent: $250

Telephone Exchange: Yes
With MMF: Yes
Registered In: MA
12b-1: Yes **Amount:** Pd. by Advisor

FIDELITY MICHIGAN TAX-FREE

Fidelity Investments Co.
82 Devonshire St.
Boston, MA 02109
(800) 544-6666/(617) 523-1919

	Years Ending 12/31					
	1982	1983	1984	1985 (2 mos.)	1986	1987
Dividends from Net Investment Income ($)	—	—	—	.09	.79	.77
Distributions from Net Realized Capital Gains ($)	—	—	—	—	—	.04
Net Asset Value End of Year ($)	—	—	—	10.27	11.38	10.25
Ratio of Expenses to Net Assets (%)	—	—	—	.60	.60	.72
Portfolio Turnover Rate (%)	—	—	—	9	24	44
Total Assets: End of Year (Millions $)	—	—	—	6.6	127.6	128.3
Annual Rate of Return (%) Years Ending 12/31	—	—.	—	—	18.7	(3.2)

Distr: Income: Monthly
Capital Gains: Annually
Minimum: Initial: $2,500
Subsequent: $250

Telephone Exchange: Yes
With MMF: Yes
Registered In: MI
12b-1: Yes **Amount:** Pd. by Advisor

FIDELITY MINNESOTA TAX-FREE

Fidelity Investments Co.
82 Devonshire St.
Boston, MA 02109
(800) 544-6666/(617) 523-1919

	Years Ending 12/31					
	1982	1983	1984	1985 (1 mo.)	1986	1987
Dividends from Net Investment Income ($)	—	—	—	.07	.77	.72
Distributions from Net Realized Capital Gains ($)	—	—	—	—	—	.03
Net Asset Value End of Year ($)	—	—	—	10.09	10.99	9.82
Ratio of Expenses to Net Assets (%)	—	—	—	.60	.60	.79
Portfolio Turnover Rate (%)	—	—	—	—	23	63
Total Assets: End of Year (Millions $)	—	—	—	5.1	93.7	79.1
Annual Rate of Return (%) Years Ending 12/31	—	—	—	—	17.0	(4.1)

Distr: Income: Monthly
    Capital Gains: Annually
Minimum: Initial: $2,500
    Subsequent: $250

Telephone Exchange: Yes
    With MMF: Yes
Registered In: MN
12b-1: Yes **Amount:** Pd. by Advisor

FIDELITY MUNICIPAL BOND

Fidelity Investments Co.
82 Devonshire St.
Boston, MA 02109
(800) 544-6666/(617) 523-1919

	Years Ending 12/31					
	1982	1983	1984	1985	1986	1987
Dividends from Net Investment Income ($)	.62	.60	.59	.58	.55	.55
Distributions from Net Realized Capital Gains ($)	—	—	—	—	—	—
Net Asset Value End of Year ($)	6.71	6.72	6.70	7.42	8.28	7.60
Ratio of Expenses to Net Assets (%)	.62	.59	.53	.46	.51	.57
Portfolio Turnover Rate (%)	95	52	93	145	72	72
Total Assets: End of Year (Millions $)	634.6	703.5	741.2	905.8	1,141.3	903.2
Annual Rate of Return (%) Years Ending 12/31	39.7	9.3	9.0	20.1	19.5	(1.5)

Distr: Income: Monthly
    Capital Gains: Annually
Minimum: Initial: $2,500
    Subsequent: $250

Telephone Exchange: Yes
    With MMF: Yes
Registered In: All states
12b-1: Yes **Amount:** Pd. by Advisor

FIDELITY NEW YORK TAX-FREE HIGH YIELD

Fidelity Investments Co.
82 Devonshire St.
Boston, MA 02109
(800) 544-6666/(617) 523-1919

	Years Ending 4/30					
	1982	1983	1984	1985 (10 mos.)	1986	1987
Dividends from Net Investment Income ($)	–	–	–	.74	.89	.82
Distributions from Net Realized Capital Gains ($)	–	–	–	–	–	.17
Net Asset Value End of Year ($)	–	–	–	10.69	11.98	11.48
Ratio of Expenses to Net Assets (%)	–	–	–	1.00	.67	.60
Portfolio Turnover Rate (%)	–	–	–	8	62	51
Total Assets: End of Year (Millions $)	–	–	–	28.0	202.7	352.3
Annual Rate of Return (%) Years Ending 12/31	–	–	–	20.8	16.8	(2.4)

Distr: Income: Monthly
      Capital Gains: Annually
Minimum: Initial: $2,500
      Subsequent: $250

Telephone Exchange: Yes
      With MMF: Yes
Registered In: NY
12b-1: Yes **Amount:** Pd. by Advisor

FIDELITY NEW YORK TAX-FREE INSURED

Fidelity Investments Co.
82 Devonshire St.
Boston, MA 02109
(800) 544-6666/(617) 523-1919

	Years Ending 4/30					
	1982	1983	1984	1985	1986 (7 mos.)	1987
Dividends from Net Investment Income ($)	–	–	–	–	.41	.70
Distributions from Net Realized Capital Gains ($)	–	–	–	–	–	.01
Net Asset Value End of Year ($)	–	–	–	–	10.96	10.47
Ratio of Expenses to Net Assets (%)	–	–	–	–	.60	.60
Portfolio Turnover Rate (%)	–	–	–	–	8	30
Total Assets: End of Year (Millions $)	–	–	–	–	63.9	172.1
Annual Rate of Return (%) Years Ending 12/31	–	–	–	–	17.3	(3.2)

Distr: Income: Monthly
      Capital Gains: Annually
Minimum: Initial: $2,500
      Subsequent: $250

Telephone Exchange: Yes
      With MMF: Yes
Registered In: NY
12b-1: Yes **Amount:** Pd. by Advisor

FIDELITY OHIO TAX-FREE

Fidelity Investments Co.
82 Devonshire St.
Boston, MA 02109
(800) 544-6666/(617) 523-1919

		Years Ending 12/31				
	1982	1983	1984	1985 (2 mos.)	1986	1987
Dividends from Net Investment Income ($)	−	−	−	.09	.77	.74
Distributions from Net Realized Capital Gains ($)	−	−	−	−	−	−
Net Asset Value End of Year ($)	−	−	−	10.12	10.97	9.97
Ratio of Expenses to Net Assets (%)	−	−	−	.60	.60	.79
Portfolio Turnover Rate (%)	−	−	−	54	32	36
Total Assets: End of Year (Millions $)	−	−	−	4.4	107.1	116.7
Annual Rate of Return (%) Years Ending 12/31	−	−	−	−	16.4	(2.4)

Distr: Income: Monthly
Capital Gains: Annually
Minimum: Initial: $2,500
Subsequent: $250

Telephone Exchange: Yes
With MMF: Yes
Registered In: OH
12b-1: Yes **Amount:** Pd. by Advisor

FIDELITY PENNSYLVANIA TAX-FREE HIGH YIELD

Fidelity Investments Co.
82 Devonshire St.
Boston, MA 02109
(800) 544-6666/(617) 523-1919

		Years Ending 12/31				
	1982	1983	1984	1985	1986 (5 mos.)	1987
Dividends from Net Investment Income ($)	−	−	−	−	.27	.70
Distributions from Net Realized Capital Gains ($)	−	−	−	−	−	−
Net Asset Value End of Year ($)	−	−	−	−	10.35	9.07
Ratio of Expenses to Net Assets (%)	−	−	−	−	.30	.63
Portfolio Turnover Rate (%)	−	−	−	−	38	54
Total Assets: End of Year (Millions $)	−	−	−	−	24.3	41.7
Annual Rate of Return (%) Years Ending 12/31	−	−	−	−	−	(5.8)

Distr: Income: Monthly
Capital Gains: Annually
Minimum: Initial: $2,500
Subsequent: $250

Telephone Exchange: Yes
With MMF: Yes
Registered In: PA
12b-1: Yes **Amount:** Pd. by Advisor

FIDELITY SHORT-TERM TAX-FREE PORTFOLIO

Fidelity Investments Co.
82 Devonshire St.
Boston, MA 02109
(800) 544-6666/(617) 523-1919

Years Ending 12/31

	1982	1983	1984	1985	1986 (1 mo.)	1987
Dividends from Net Investment Income ($)	–	–	–	–	.01	.43
Distributions from Net Realized Capital Gains ($)	–	–	–	–	–	–
Net Asset Value End of Year ($)	–	–	–	–	9.92	9.51
Ratio of Expenses to Net Assets (%)	–	–	–	–	.60	.60
Portfolio Turnover Rate (%)	–	–	–	–	–	180
Total Assets: End of Year (Millions $)	–	–	–	–	2.5	59.2
Annual Rate of Return (%) Years Ending 12/31	–	–	–	–	–	0.2

Distr: Income: Monthly
    Capital Gains: Annually
Minimum: Initial: $2,500
    Subsequent: $250

Telephone Exchange: Yes
    With MMF: Yes
Registered In: All states
12b-1: Yes **Amount:** Pd. by Advisor

FIDELITY TEXAS TAX-FREE

Fidelity Investments Co.
82 Devonshire Street
Boston, MA 02109
(800) 544-6666/(617) 523-1919

Years Ending 12/31

	1982	1983	1984	1985	1986 (11 mos.)	1987
Dividends from Net Investment Income ($)	–	–	–	–	.70	.74
Distributions from Net Realized Capital Gains ($)	–	–	–	–	–	–
Net Asset Value End of Year ($)	–	–	–	–	10.38	9.58
Ratio of Expenses to Net Assets (%)	–	–	–	–	.65	1.04
Portfolio Turnover Rate (%)	–	–	–	–	13	64
Total Assets: End of Year (Millions $)	–	–	–	–	29.8	26.5
Annual Rate of Return (%) Years Ending 12/31	–	–	–	–	–	(0.7)

Distr: Income: Monthly
    Capital Gains: Annually
Minimum: Initial: $2,500
    Subsequent: $250

Telephone Exchange: Yes
    With MMF: Yes
Registered In: TX
12b-1: Yes **Amount:** Pd. by Advisor

FINANCIAL TAX-FREE INCOME SHARES

Financial Programs, Inc.
P.O. Box 2040
Denver, CO 80201
(800) 525-8085/(303) 779-1233

	1982	1983	1984	1985	1986	1987
	Years Ending 6/30					
Dividends from Net Investment Income ($)	1.21	1.31	1.24	1.27	1.21	1.09
Distributions from Net Realized Capital Gains ($)	.03	.15	.08	.70	.80	1.06
Net Asset Value End of Year ($)	12.46	14.47	13.07	14.32	15.20	13.86
Ratio of Expenses to Net Assets (%)	.40	.56	.59	.65	.68	.70
Portfolio Turnover Rate (%)	56	52	88	156	92	98
Total Assets: End of Year (Millions $)	21.2	61.7	60.3	85.5	108.5	117.9
Annual Rate of Return (%) Years Ending 12/31	34.6	8.0	9.1	22.9	22.1	(4.0)

Distr: Income: Monthly
    Capital Gains: July
Minimum: Initial: $250
    Subsequent: $50

Telephone Exchange: Yes
    With MMF: Yes
Registered In: All states
12b-1: No

GIT TAX-FREE HIGH YIELD

Bankers Finance Investment
    Management Corp.
1655 N. Fort Myer Dr.
Arlington, VA 22209
(800) 336-3063/(703) 528-6500

	1982	1983 (10 mos.)	1984	1985	1986	1987
	Years Ending 9/30					
Dividends from Net Investment Income ($)	–	.81	.89	.89	.86	.74
Distributions from Net Realized Capital Gains ($)	–	–	–	–	.81	.08
Net Asset Value End of Year ($)	–	10.32	9.87	10.49	11.20	10.38
Ratio of Expenses to Net Assets (%)	–	0.95	1.14	1.29	1.16	.99
Portfolio Turnover Rate (%)	–	222	252	173	117	66
Total Assets: End of Year (Millions $)	–	25.4	27.1	34.3	43.2	44.7
Annual Rate of Return (%) Years Ending 12/31	–	–	9.8	19.2	19.4	(0.6)

Distr: Income: Monthly
    Capital Gains: Annually
Minimum: Initial: $1,000
    Subsequent: None

Telephone Exchange: Yes
    With MMF: Yes
Registered In: All states except IN,
    LA, MT, OK
12b-1: Yes **Amount:** 1.00%

KENTUCKY TAX-FREE INCOME

Dupree & Co.
167 W. Main St.
Lexington, KY 40507
(800) 432-9518/(606) 254-7741

	1982	**1983**	**1984**	**1985**	**1986**	**1987**
Dividends from Net Investment Income ($)	.61	.58	.58	.57	.55	.50
Distributions from Net Realized Capital Gains ($)	—	—	—	—	—	—
Net Asset Value End of Year ($)	5.56	6.26	6.01	6.38	6.62	6.59
Ratio of Expenses to Net Assets (%)	.81	.79	.81	.76	.78	.79
Portfolio Turnover Rate (%)	152	59	57	30	28	54
Total Assets: End of Year (Millions $)	3.2	6.9	10.0	19.4	36.3	61.8
Annual Rate of Return (%) Years Ending 12/31	17.3	12.2	8.1	15.8	16.9	(1.0)

Years Ending 6/30

Distr: Income: Mar, June, Sep, Dec
    Capital Gains: Annually
Minimum: Initial: $2,500
    Subsequent: $100

Telephone Exchange: Yes
    With MMF: No
Registered In: KY
12b-1: No

LEXINGTON TAX EXEMPT BOND TRUST

Lexington Management Corp.
P.O. Box 1515
Park 80 W., Plaza 2
Saddle Brook, NJ 07662
(800) 526-0056

Years Ending 12/31

	1982	**1983**	**1984**	**1985**	**1986** (6 mos.)	**1987**
Dividends from Net Investment Income ($)	—	—	—	—	.32	.80
Distributions from Net Realized Capital Gains ($)	—	—	—	—	—	—
Net Asset Value End of Year ($)	—	—	—	—	10.55	9.67
Ratio of Expenses to Net Assets (%)	—	—	—	—	0	0
Portfolio Turnover Rate (%)	—	—	—	—	0	67
Total Assets: End of Year (Millions $)	—	—	—	—	8.4	3.3
Annual Rate of Return (%) Years Ending 12/31	—	—	—	—	—	0.0

Distr: Income: Monthly
    Capital Gains: Dec
Minimum: Initial: $1,000
    Subsequent: $50

Telephone Exchange: Yes
    With MMF: Yes
Registered In: All states
12b-1: Yes **Amount:** Pd. by Advisor

MERIT PENNSYLVANIA TAX-FREE TRUST

Sav/Vest Securities Corp.
121 South Broad St., 8th Flr.
Philadelphia, PA 19107
(800) 992-2206

	Years Ending 12/31					
	1982	1983	1984	1985	1986 (3 mos.)	1987
Dividends from Net Investment Income ($)	–	–	–	–	.19	.85
Distributions from Net Realized Capital Gains ($)	–	–	–	–	.03	–
Net Asset Value End of Year ($)	–	–	–	–	12.66	11.49
Ratio of Expenses to Net Assets (%)	–	–	–	–	–	.45
Portfolio Turnover Rate (%)	–	–	–	–	22	54
Total Assets: End of Year (Millions $)	–	–	–	–	14.7	26.6
Annual Rate of Return (%) Years Ending 12/31	–	–	–	–	–	(2.5)

Distr: Income: Monthly
Capital Gains: Annually
Minimum: Initial: $1,000
Subsequent: $100

Telephone Exchange: Yes
With MMF: Yes
Registered In: PA
12b-1: Yes **Amount:** 0.25%

NEW YORK MUNI

New York Muni Fund, Inc.
111 Broadway, Suite 1107
New York, NY 10006
(800) 225-6864/(212) 608-6864

	Years Ending 12/31					
	1982	1983	1984	1985	1986	1987
Dividends from Net Investment Income ($)	.08	.09	.08	.09	.09	.08
Distributions from Net Realized Capital Gains ($)	–	–	–	–	.06	.03
Net Asset Value End of Year ($)	1.04	1.07	1.07	1.19	1.25	1.05
Ratio of Expenses to Net Assets (%)	1.92	1.53	1.62	1.60	1.48	2.04
Portfolio Turnover Rate (%)	71	109	157	424	334	549
Total Assets: End of Year (Millions $)	14.4	79.4	129.2	174.4	261.2	220.3
Annual Rate of Return (%) Years Ending 12/31	NA	NA	8.1	20.3	17.7	(7.3)

Distr: Income: Monthly
Capital Gains: Dec
Minimum: Initial: $1,000
Subsequent: $100

Telephone Exchange: Yes
With MMF: Yes
Registered In: CT, FL, NJ, NY, PA
12b-1: Yes **Amount:** 0.50%

PARK AVENUE NEW YORK TAX EXEMPT— INTERMEDIATE

Park Ave. N.Y. Tax Exempt
Intermediate Bond Fund,
Inc.
600 Madison Ave.
New York, NY 10022
(800) 848-4350/(718) 895-1219

	1982	1983	1984	1985 (11 mos.)	1986	1987
Years Ending 10/31						
Dividends from Net Investment Income ($)	—	—	—	1.22	1.19	1.06
Distributions from Net Realized Capital Gains ($)	—	—	—	—	—	—
Net Asset Value End of Year ($)	—	—	—	17.39	18.97	17.87
Ratio of Expenses to Net Assets (%)	—	—	—	.21	.46	.89
Portfolio Turnover Rate (%)	—	—	—	32	38	67
Total Assets: End of Year (Millions $)	—	—	—	13.9	57.0	53.4
Annual Rate of Return (%) Years Ending 12/31	—	—	—	14.9	14.2	1.4

Distr: Income: Monthly
    Capital Gains: Annually
Minimum: Initial: $2,500
    Subsequent: $100

Telephone Exchange: Yes
    With MMF: Yes
Registered In: CT, FL, NJ, NY
12b-1: Yes **Amount:** 0.20%

T. ROWE PRICE CALIFORNIA TAX-FREE BOND

T. Rowe Price Associates, Inc.
100 East Pratt Street
Baltimore, MD 21202
(800) 638-5660/(301) 547-2308

	1982	1983	1984	1985	1986	1987 (5 mos.)
Years Ending 2/28						
Dividends from Net Investment Income ($)	—	—	—	—	—	.29
Distributions from Net Realized Capital Gains ($)	—	—	—	—	—	—
Net Asset Value End of Year ($)	—	—	—	—	—	10.48
Ratio of Expenses to Net Assets (%)	—	—	—	—	—	.85
Portfolio Turnover Rate (%)	—	—	—	—	—	88
Total Assets: End of Year (Millions $)	—	—	—	—	—	43.6
Annual Rate of Return (%) Years Ending 12/31	—	—	—	—	—	(6.8)

Distr: Income: Monthly
    Capital Gains: Annually
Minimum: Initial: $1,000
    Subsequent: $100

Telephone Exchange: Yes
    With MMF: Yes
Registered In: AZ, DC, HI, MD,
    NV, OR, WY
12b-1: No

T. ROWE PRICE NEW YORK TAX-FREE BOND

T. Rowe Price Associates, Inc.
100 E. Pratt St.
Baltimore, MD 21202
(800) 638-5660/(301) 547-2308

Years Ending 2/28

	1982	1983	1984	1985	1986	1987 (6 mos.)
Dividends from Net Investment Income ($)	–	–	–	–	–	.33
Distributions from Net Realized Capital Gains ($)	–	–	–	–	–	–
Net Asset Value End of Year ($)	–	–	–	–	–	10.34
Ratio of Expenses to Net Assets (%)	–	–	–	–	–	.85
Portfolio Turnover Rate (%)	–	–	–	–	–	126
Total Assets: End of Year (Millions $)	–	–	–	–	–	24.3
Annual Rate of Return (%) Years Ending 12/31	–	–	–	–	–	(2.5)

Distr: Income: Monthly
    Capital Gains: Annually
Minimum: Initial: $1,000
    Subsequent: $100

Telephone Exchange: Yes
    With MMF: Yes
Registered In: CT, DC, FL, HI, MA, MD, NJ, NV, NY, PA, RI, VT, WY
12b-1: No

T. ROWE PRICE TAX-FREE HIGH YIELD

T. Rowe Price Associates, Inc.
100 East Pratt St.
Baltimore, MD 21202
(800) 638-5660/(301) 547-2308

Years Ending 2/28

	1982	1983	1984	1985	1986	1987
Dividends from Net Investment Income ($)	–	–	–	–	.87	.87
Distributions from Net Realized Capital Gains ($)	–	–	–	–	–	–
Net Asset Value End of Year ($)	–	–	–	–	11.43	12.21
Ratio of Expenses to Net Assets (%)	–	–	–	–	1.00	.98
Portfolio Turnover Rate (%)	–	–	–	–	157	111
Total Assets: End of Year (Millions $)	–	–	–	–	168.2	324.2
Annual Rate of Return (%) Years Ending 12/31	–	–	–	–	20.4	.3

Distr: Income: Monthly
    Capital Gains: Annually
Minimum: Initial: $1,000
    Subsequent: $100

Telephone Exchange: Yes
    With MMF: Yes
Registered In: All states
12b-1: No

T. ROWE PRICE TAX-FREE INCOME

T. Rowe Price Associates, Inc.
100 E. Pratt St.
Baltimore, MD 21202
(800) 638-5660/(301) 547-2308

	12/31	Years Ending 2/28				
	1982	1983* (2 mos.)	1984	1985	1986	1987
Dividends from Net Investment Income ($)	.80	.13	.72	.65	.71	.68
Distributions from Net Realized Capital Gains ($)	—	—	—	—	—	—
Net Asset Value End of Year ($)	8.58	8.85	8.48	8.41	9.73	10.27
Ratio of Expenses to Net Assets (%)	.65	.62	.66	.63	.63	.61
Portfolio Turnover Rate (%)	224	170	221	277	188	237
Total Assets: End of Year (Millions $)	673.3	818.5	962.4	937.3	1,325.7	1,558.2
Annual Rate of Return (%) Years Ending 12/31	30.8	7.7	7.1	16.9	19.8	(4.2)

*Fiscal year changed from 12/31 to 2/28.

Distr: Income: Monthly
    Capital Gains: Mar
Minimum: Initial: $1,000
    Subsequent: $100

Telephone Exchange: Yes
    With MMF: Yes
Registered In: All states
12b-1: No

T. ROWE PRICE TAX-FREE SHORT-INTERMEDIATE

T. Rowe Price Associates, Inc.
100 E. Pratt Street
Baltimore, MD 21202
(800) 638-5660/(301) 547-2308

	Years Ending 2/28					
	1982	1983	1984 (2 mos.)	1985	1986	1987
Dividends from Net Investment Income ($)	—	—	.06	.32	.32	.29
Distributions from Net Realized Capital Gains ($)	—	—	—	—	—	—
Net Asset Value End of Year ($)	—	—	4.97	5.02	5.20	5.33
Ratio of Expenses to Net Assets (%)	—	—	.90	.90	.90	.73
Portfolio Turnover Rate (%)	—	—	111	301	129	120
Total Assets: End of Year (Millions $)	—	—	23.5	68.0	155.5	404.8
Annual Rate of Return (%) Years Ending 12/31	—	—	—	8.9	9.7	2.2

Distr: Income: Monthly
    Capital Gains: Annually
Minimum: Initial: $1,000
    Subsequent: $100

Telephone Exchange: Yes
    With MMF: Yes
Registered In: All states
12b-1: No

SAFECO CALIFORNIA TAX-FREE INCOME

Safeco Asset Management Co.
Safeco Plaza
Seattle, WA 98185
(800) 426-6730/(206) 545-5530

	Years Ending 3/31					
	1982	1983	1984 (8 mos.)	1985	1986	1987
Dividends from Net Investment Income ($)	–	–	.54	.78	.84	.80
Distributions from Net Realized Capital Gains ($)	–	–	–	–	–	.11
Net Asset Value End of Year ($)	–	–	9.90	9.99	11.68	12.14
Ratio of Expenses to Net Assets (%)	–	–	.90	.77	.76	.70
Portfolio Turnover Rate (%)	–	–	44	23	41	45
Total Assets: End of Year (Millions $)	–	–	8.1	11.5	21.1	34.8
Annual Rate of Return (%) Years Ending 12/31	–	–	7.6	21.0	19.7	(2.1)

Distr: Income: Monthly
Capital Gains: Annually
Minimum: Initial: $1,000
Subsequent: $100

Telephone Exchange: Yes
With MMF: Yes
Registered In: CA
12b-1: No

SAFECO MUNICIPAL

Safeco Asset Management Co.
Safeco Plaza
Seattle, WA 98185
(800) 426-6730/(206) 545-5530

	Years Ending 3/31					
	1982	1983	1984	1985	1986	1987
Dividends from Net Investment Income ($)	.53	1.05	1.05	1.07	1.06	.99
Distributions from Net Realized Capital Gains ($)	–	–	–	–	.02	.21
Net Asset Value End of Year ($)	9.36	11.87	11.38	11.69	13.74	14.16
Ratio of Expenses to Net Assets (%)	1.03	.72	.64	.63	.63	.59
Portfolio Turnover Rate (%)	99	40	92	47	21	23
Total Assets: End of Year (Millions $)	4.9	22.6	50.6	84.3	161.0	214.7
Annual Rate of Return (%) Years Ending 12/31	42.1	10.4	10.1	21.4	19.8	.2

Distr: Income: Monthly
Capital Gains: Annually
Minimum: Initial: $1,000
Subsequent: $100

Telephone Exchange: Yes
With MMF: Yes
Registered In: All states except ME, NH, VT
12b-1: No

SCUDDER CALIFORNIA TAX FREE

Scudder, Stevens & Clark
175 Federal St.
Boston, MA 02110
(800) 453-3305/(617) 439-4640

	Years Ending 3/31					
	1982	1983	1984 (8 mos.)	1985	1986	1987
Dividends from Net Investment Income ($)	—	—	.50	.80	.73	.71
Distributions from Net Realized Capital Gains ($)	—	—	—	—	—	.30
Net Asset Value End of Year ($)	—	—	9.61	9.54	10.95	11.18
Ratio of Expenses to Net Assets (%)	—	—	1.00	.99	.88	.84
Portfolio Turnover Rate (%)	—	—	92	168	93	68
Total Assets: End of Year (Millions $)	—	—	38.2	73.1	132.8	194.8
Annual Rate of Return (%) Years Ending 12/31	—	—	—	18.4	16.8	(1.7)

Distr: Income: Monthly
    Capital Gains: April
Minimum: Initial: $1,000
    Subsequent: None

Telephone Exchange: Yes
    With MMF: Yes
Registered In: All states
12b-1: No

SCUDDER MANAGED MUNICIPAL

Scudder, Stevens & Clark
175 Federal St.
Boston, MA 02110-2267
(800) 453-3305/(617) 439-4640

	Years Ending 12/31					
	1982	1983	1984	1985	1986	1987
Dividends from Net Investment Income ($)	.73	.70	.70	.59	.61	.61
Distributions from Net Realized Capital Gains ($)	—	—	—	—	.24	.11
Net Asset Value End of Year ($)	7.69	7.67	7.69	8.40	8.93	8.24
Ratio of Expenses to Net Assets (%)	.65	.65	.61	.58	.58	.63
Portfolio Turnover Rate (%)	146	83	120	98	78	73
Total Assets: End of Year (Millions $)	292.8	479.2	545.1	574.6	662.4	591.8
Annual Rate of Return (%) Years Ending 12/31	43.2	9.1	10.2	17.5	16.8	(0.3)

Distr: Income: Monthly
    Capital Gains: Annually
Minimum: Initial: $1,000
    Subsequent: None

Telephone Exchange: Yes
    With MMF: Yes
Registered In: All states
12b-1: No

SCUDDER NEW YORK TAX FREE

Scudder, Stevens & Clark
175 Federal St.
Boston, MA 02110
(800) 453-3305/(617) 439-4640

	1982	1983	1984 (8 mos.)	1985	1986	1987
Dividends from Net Investment Income ($)	—	—	.52	.83	.75	.75
Distributions from Net Realized Capital Gains ($)	—	—	—	—	—	.15
Net Asset Value End of Year ($)	—	—	9.97	10.11	11.19	11.43
Ratio of Expenses to Net Assets (%)	—	—	1.00	1.01	.88	.88
Portfolio Turnover Rate (%)	—	—	151	167	40	72
Total Assets: End of Year (Millions $)	—	—	27.7	61.6	102	153.7
Annual Rate of Return (%) Years Ending 12/31	—	—	—	16.0	14.1	(.7)

Years Ending 3/31

Distr: Income: Monthly
Capital Gains: April
Minimum: Initial: $1,000
Subsequent: None

Telephone Exchange: Yes
With MMF: Yes
Registered In: All states
12b-1: No

SCUDDER TAX FREE TARGET 1990

Scudder, Stevens & Clark
175 Federal Street
Boston, MA 02110-2267
(800) 225-2470/(617) 439-4640

	1982	1983 (9 mos.)	1984	1985	1986	1987
Dividends from Net Investment Income ($)	—	.45	.73	.68	.62	.54
Distributions from Net Realized Capital Gains ($)	—	—	—	—	.10	.05
Net Asset Value End of Year ($)	—	9.65	9.67	10.03	10.34	10.07
Ratio of Expenses to Net Assets (%)	—	1.00	.83	.85	.82	.80
Portfolio Turnover Rate (%)	—	97	96	132	44	33
Total Assets: End of Year (Millions $)	—	13.5	30.8	59.1	104.0	125.1
Annual Rate of Return (%) Years Ending 12/31	—	—	8.0	11.1	10.5	3.2

Years Ending 12/31

Distr: Income: Monthly
Capital Gains: Annually
Minimum: Initial: $1,000
Subsequent: None

Telephone Exchange: Yes
With MMF: Yes
Registered In: All states
12b-1: No

SCUDDER TAX FREE TARGET 1993

Scudder, Stevens & Clark
175 Federal Street
Boston, MA 02110-2267
(800) 225-2470/(617) 439-4640

			Years Ending 12/31			
	1982	1983 (9 mos.)	1984	1985	1986	1987
Dividends from Net Investment Income ($)	–	.49	.80	.75	.67	.61
Distributions from Net Realized Capital Gains ($)	–	–	–	–	.23	.14
Net Asset Value End of Year ($)	–	9.95	9.95	10.59	11.04	10.57
Ratio of Expenses to Net Assets (%)	–	1.00	.89	.86	.81	.80
Portfolio Turnover Rate (%)	–	190	78	265	80	64
Total Assets: End of Year (Millions $)	–	9.5	23.7	55.2	118.8	125.5
Annual Rate of Return (%) Years Ending 12/31	–	–	8.3	14.5	13.2	2.6

Distr: Income: Monthly
  Capital Gains: Annually
Minimum: Initial: $1,000
  Subsequent: None

Telephone Exchange: Yes
  With MMF: Yes
Registered In: All states
12b-1: No

SCUDDER TAX FREE TARGET 1996

Scudder Stevens & Clark
175 Federal Street
Boston, MA 02110
(800) 225-2470/(617) 482-3990

			Years Ending 12/31			
	1982	1983	1984	1985 (8 mos.)	1986	1987
Dividends from Net Investment Income ($)	–	–	–	.48	.67	.66
Distributions from Net Realized Capital Gains ($)	–	–	–	–	.02	.08
Net Asset Value End of Year ($)	–	–	–	10.35	11.17	10.59
Ratio of Expenses to Net Assets (%)	–	–	–	1.00	1.00	1.06
Portfolio Turnover Rate (%)	–	–	–	102	36	23
Total Assets: End of Year (Millions $)	–	–	–	7.2	21.6	28.1
Annual Rate of Return (%) Years Ending 12/31	–	–	–	–	14.7	1.5

Distr: Income: Monthly
  Capital Gains: Annually
Minimum: Initial: $1,000
  Subsequent: None

Telephone Exchange: Yes
  With MMF: Yes
Registered In: All states
12b-1: No

STEINROE HIGH-YIELD MUNICIPALS

Stein Roe & Farnham
P.O. Box 1143
Chicago, IL 60690
(800) 338-2550/(312) 368-7826

			Years Ending 12/31			
	1982	1983	1984 (10 mos.)	1985	1986	1987
Dividends from Net Investment Income ($)	–	–	.73	.94	.90	.87
Distributions from Net Realized Capital Gains ($)	–	–	–	–	.15	.11
Net Asset Value End of Year ($)	–	–	10.02	11.10	12.06	11.06
Ratio of Expenses to Net Assets (%)	–	–	1.43	.81	.76	.73
Portfolio Turnover Rate (%)	–	–	68	46	34	110
Total Assets: End of Year (Millions $)	–	–	32.8	99.8	225.9	181.7
Annual Rate of Return (%) Years Ending 12/31	–	–	–	20.9	19.0	(0.3)

Distr: Income: Monthly
   Capital Gains: Annually
Minimum: Initial: $1,000
   Subsequent: $100

Telephone Exchange: Yes
   With MMF: Yes
Registered In: All states
12b-1: No

STEINROE INTERMEDIATE MUNICIPALS

Stein Roe & Farnham
P.O. Box 1143
Chicago, IL 60690
(800) 338-2550/(312) 368-7826

				Years Ending 12/31		
	1982	1983	1984	1985 (3 mos.)	1986	1987
Dividends from Net Investment Income ($)	–	–	–	.12	.58	.57
Distributions from Net Realized Capital Gains ($)	–	–	–	–	–	.01
Net Asset Value End of Year ($)	–	–	–	10.14	10.76	10.37
Ratio of Expenses to Net Assets (%)	–	–	–	2.38	.94	.83
Portfolio Turnover Rate (%)	–	–	–	–	10	49
Total Assets: End of Year (Millions $)	–	–	–	23.0	104.7	96.1
Annual Rate of Return (%) Years Ending 12/31	–	–	–	–	12.1	1.7

Distr: Income: Monthly
   Capital Gains: Annually
Minimum: Initial: $1,000
   Subsequent: $100

Telephone Exchange: Yes
   With MMF: Yes
Registered In: All states
12b-1: No

STEINROE MANAGED MUNICIPALS

Stein Roe & Farnham
P.O. Box 1143
Chicago, IL 60690
(800) 338-2550/(312) 368-7826

	Years Ending 12/31					
	1982	1983	1984	1985	1986	1987
Dividends from Net Investment Income ($)	.68	.64	.67	.68	.67	.61
Distributions from Net Realized Capital Gains ($)	–	–	–	.03	.92	.13
Net Asset Value End of Year ($)	7.56	7.71	7.89	8.93	9.22	8.50
Ratio of Expenses to Net Assets (%)	.75	.65	.64	.65	.65	.65
Portfolio Turnover Rate (%)	166	114	190	113	92	113
Total Assets: End of Year (Millions $)	142.6	214.9	242.8	357.2	524.0	458.4
Annual Rate of Return (%) Years Ending 12/31	46.0	10.8	11.2	22.8	21.7	0.1

Distr: Income: Monthly
Capital Gains: Annually
Minimum: Initial: $1,000
Subsequent: $100

Telephone Exchange: Yes
With MMF: Yes
Registered In: All states
12b-1: No

STRONG TAX-FREE INCOME

Strong/Corneliuson Capital Mgmt.
815 E. Mason St.
Milwaukee, WI 53202
(800) 368-3863/(414) 765-0934

	Years Ending 12/31					
	1982	1983	1984	1985	1986 (2 mos.)	1987
Dividends from Net Investment Income ($)	–	–	–	–	.12	.67
Distributions from Net Realized Capital Gains ($)	–	–	–	–	–	–
Net Asset Value End of Year ($)	–	–	–	–	10.01	9.16
Ratio of Expenses to Net Assets (%)	–	–	–	–	.4	1.0
Portfolio Turnover Rate (%)	–	–	–	–	116	284
Total Assets: End of Year (Millions $)	–	–	–	–	2.2	19.1
Annual Rate of Return (%) Years Ending 12/31	–	–	–	–	–	(1.4)

Distr: Income: Monthly
Capital Gains: Annually
Minimum: Initial: $2,500
Subsequent: $200

Telephone Exchange: Yes
With MMF: Yes
Registered In: All states
12b-1: No

UNIFIED MUNICIPAL— GENERAL SERIES

Unified Management
Corporation
429 N. Pennsylvania St.
Indianapolis, IN 46204-1897
(800) 862-7283/(317) 634-3300

	Years Ending 4/30					
	1982	1983	1984	1985 (1 mo.)	1986	1987
Dividends from Net Investment Income ($)	—	—	—	—	.58	.65
Distributions from Net Realized Capital Gains ($)	—	—	—	—	.02	.08
Net Asset Value End of Year ($)	—	—	—	7.88	8.77	8.49
Ratio of Expenses to Net Assets (%)	—	—	—	—	1.24	1.06
Portfolio Turnover Rate (%)	—	—	—	—	19	45
Total Assets: End of Year (Millions $)	—	—	—	4.0	5.4	6.9
Annual Rate of Return (%) Years Ending 12/31	—	—	—	—	18.3	(1.0)

Distr: Income: April, Oct
Capital Gains: April
Minimum: Initial: $1,000
Subsequent: $25

Telephone Exchange: Yes
With MMF: Yes
Registered In: All states
12b-1: No

UNIFIED MUNICIPAL— INDIANA SERIES

Unified Management
Corporation
429 N. Pennsylvania St.
Indianapolis, IN 46204-1897
(800) 862-7283/(317) 634-3300

	Years Ending 4/30					
	1982	1983	1984	1985 (1 mo.)	1986	1987
Dividends from Net Investment Income ($)	—	—	—	—	.49	.60
Distributions from Net Realized Capital Gains ($)	—	—	—	—	—	.08
Net Asset Value End of Year ($)	—	—	—	7.91	8.77	8.62
Ratio of Expenses to Net Assets (%)	—	—	—	—	1.18	1.00
Portfolio Turnover Rate (%)	—	—	—	—	17	37
Total Assets: End of Year (Millions $)	—	—	—	3.8	8.0	11.5
Annual Rate of Return (%) Years Ending 12/31	—	—	—	—	19.0	.2

Distr: Income: April, Oct
Capital Gains: April
Minimum: Initial: $1,000
Subsequent: $25

Telephone Exchange: Yes
With MMF: Yes
Registered In: All states
12b-1: No

USAA TAX EXEMPT HIGH YIELD

USAA Investment Mgmt. Co.
9800 Fredericksburg Rd.
San Antonio, TX 78288
(800) 531-8000/(512) 498-8000

Years Ending 3/31

	1982 (4 mos.)	1983	1984	1985	1986	1987
Dividends from Net Investment Income ($)	—	1.40	1.08	1.13	1.13	1.04
Distributions from Net Realized Capital Gains ($)	—	—	—	—	—	.09
Net Asset Value End of Year ($)	10.38	12.02	11.76	11.88	13.52	13.96
Ratio of Expenses to Net Assets (%)	1.29	1.09	.68	.56	.50	.49
Portfolio Turnover Rate (%)	15	18	64	150	122	83
Total Assets: End of Year (Millions $)	3.2	50.3	148.2	272.8	648.0	1,039.0
Annual Rate of Return (%) Years Ending 12/31	—	11.3	10.2	19.7	17.2	(1.9)

Distr: Income: Mar, June, Sep, Dec
    Capital Gains: April
Minimum: Initial: $3,000
    Subsequent: $100

Telephone Exchange: Yes
    With MMF: Yes
Registered In: All states
12b-1: No

USAA TAX EXEMPT INTERMEDIATE-TERM

USAA Investment Mgmt. Co.
9800 Fredericksburg Rd.
San Antonio, TX 78288
(800) 531-8000/(512) 498-8000

Years Ending 3/31

	1982 (4 mos.)	1983	1984	1985	1986	1987
Dividends from Net Investment Income ($)	—	1.25	.98	1.00	.98	.88
Distributions from Net Realized Capital Gains ($)	—	—	—	—	—	—
Net Asset Value End of Year ($)	10.24	11.39	11.15	11.19	12.27	12.38
Ratio of Expenses to Net Assets (%)	1.24	1.18	.73	.64	.57	.60
Portfolio Turnover Rate (%)	—	38	49	127	80	91
Total Assets: End of Year (Millions $)	3.1	33.5	70.1	107.3	201.3	402.9
Annual Rate of Return (%) Years Ending 12/31	—	9.6	8.8	16.3	13.2	1.0

Distr: Income: Mar, June, Sep, Dec
    Capital Gains: April
Minimum: Initial: $3,000
    Subsequent: $100

Telephone Exchange: Yes
    With MMF: Yes
Registered In: All states
12b-1: No

USAA TAX EXEMPT SHORT-TERM

USAA Investment Mgmt. Co.
9800 Fredericksburg Rd.
San Antonio, TX 78288
(800) 531-8000/(512) 498-8000

	1982 (4 mos.)	1983	1984	1985	1986	1987
Years Ending 3/31						
Dividends from Net Investment Income ($)	–	1.01	.68	.74	.72	.62
Distributions from Net Realized Capital Gains ($)	–	–	–	–	–	–
Net Asset Value End of Year ($)	10.24	10.35	10.27	10.36	10.66	10.70
Ratio of Expenses to Net Assets (%)	1.26	1.15	.85	.70	.65	.57
Portfolio Turnover Rate (%)	–	57	56	159	101	142
Total Assets: End of Year (Millions $)	3.1	20.5	62.2	85.2	139.3	287.3
Annual Rate of Return (%) Years Ending 12/31	–	6.3	7.6	9.5	8.7	2.8

Distr: Income: Mar, June, Sep, Dec
    Capital Gains: April
Minimum: Initial: $3,000
    Subsequent: $100

Telephone Exchange: Yes
    With MMF: Yes
Registered In: All states
12b-1: No

US TAX FREE

United Services Advisors
P.O. Box 29467
San Antonio, TX 78229
(800) 873-8637/(512) 696-1234

	1982	1983	1984	1985 (8 mos.)	1986	1987
Years Ending 6/30						
Dividends from Net Investment Income ($)	–	–	–	–	.81	.66
Distributions from Net Realized Capital Gains ($)	–	–	–	–	–	.12
Net Asset Value End of Year ($)	–	–	–	10.48	11.15	10.98
Ratio of Expenses to Net Assets (%)	–	–	–	1.44	.38	.05
Portfolio Turnover Rate (%)	–	–	–	67	51	37
Total Assets: End of Year (Millions $)	–	–	–	1.0	2.3	7.5
Annual Rate of Return (%) Years Ending 12/31	–	–	–	11.2	17.0	(0.2)

Distr: Income: Quarterly
    Capital Gains: Annually
Minimum: Initial: $100
    Subsequent: $50

Telephone Exchange: Yes
    With MMF: No
Registered In: All states
12b-1: No

UST INTERMEDIATE TAX-EXEMPT BOND

U.S. Trust
One Boston Place
Boston, MA 02108
(800) 233-1136

			Years Ending 3/31			
	1982	1983	1984	1985	1986 (4 mos.)	1987
Dividends from Net Investment Income ($)	—	—	—	—	.12	.60
Distributions from Net Realized Capital Gains ($)	—	—	—	—	—	.15
Net Asset Value End of Year ($)	—	—	—	—	8.77	8.87
Ratio of Expenses to Net Assets (%)	—	—	—	—	.62	.81
Portfolio Turnover Rate (%)	—	—	—	—	85	126
Total Assets: End of Year (Millions $)	—	—	—	—	6.5	37.7
Annual Rate of Return (%) Years Ending 12/31	—	—	—	—	17.3	4.5

Distr: Income: Monthly
    Capital Gains: Annually
Minimum: Initial: $10,000
    Subsequent: $1,000

Telephone Exchange: Yes
    With MMF: Yes
Registered In: All states except WI
12b-1: No

VALUE LINE TAX EXEMPT HIGH YIELD

Value Line Securities
711 Third Ave.
New York, NY 10017
(800) 223-0818/(212) 687-3965

			Years Ending 2/28			
	1982	1983	1984	1985 (11 mos.)	1986	1987
Dividends from Net Investment Income ($)	—	—	—	.94	.98	.89
Distributions from Net Realized Capital Gains ($)	—	—	—	—	.02	.36
Net Asset Value End of Year ($)	—	—	—	9.97	11.12	11.01
Ratio of Expenses to Net Assets (%)	—	—	—	.17	.66	.68
Portfolio Turnover Rate (%)	—	—	—	187	254	79
Total Assets: End of Year (Millions $)	—	—	—	36.8	133.9	311.8
Annual Rate of Return (%) Years Ending 12/31	—	—	—	19.3	13.4	.5

Distr: Income: Monthly
    Capital Gains: Annually
Minimum: Initial: $1,000
    Subsequent: $250

Telephone Exchange: Yes
    With MMF: Yes
Registered In: All states
12b-1: No

VANGUARD CALIFORNIA TAX-FREE INSURED LONG-TERM

Vanguard Group
Vanguard Financial Center
Valley Forge, PA 19482
(800) 662-7447/(215) 648-6000

| | \multicolumn{6}{c}{Years Ending 11/30} |
	1982	1983	1984	1985	1986 (8 mos.)	1987
Dividends from Net Investment Income ($)	−	−	−	−	.41	.67
Distributions from Net Realized Capital Gains ($)	−	−	−	−	.01	−
Net Asset Value End of Year ($)	−	−	−	−	10.47	9.26
Ratio of Expenses to Net Assets (%)	−	−	−	−	.33	.31
Portfolio Turnover Rate (%)	−	−	−	−	12	37
Total Assets: End of Year (Millions $)	−	−	−	−	76.3	89.3
Annual Rate of Return (%) Years Ending 12/31	−	−	−	−	−	(3.9)

Distr: Income: Monthly
    Capital Gains: Annually
Minimum: Initial: $3,000
    Subsequent: $100

Telephone Exchange: Yes
    With MMF: Yes
Registered In: CA
12b-1: No

VANGUARD HIGH YIELD MUNICIPAL BOND

Vanguard Group
Vanguard Financial Center
Valley Forge, PA 19482
(800) 662-7447/(215) 648-6000

| | \multicolumn{6}{c}{Years Ending 8/31} |
	1982	1983	1984	1985	1986	1987
Dividends from Net Investment Income ($)	.91	.85	.87	.87	.85	.78
Distributions from Net Realized Capital Gains ($)	−	−	−	−	.39	−
Net Asset Value End of Year ($)	8.44	9.03	8.94	9.56	10.55	9.94
Ratio of Expenses to Net Assets (%)	.48	.46	.41	.39	.33	.26
Portfolio Turnover Rate (%)	207	206	90	41	38	83
Total Assets: End of Year (Millions $)	71.4	156.2	238.9	451.9	794.1	791.0
Annual Rate of Return (%) Years Ending 12/31	35.9	10.4	9.7	21.7	19.7	(1.6)

Distr: Income: Monthly
    Capital Gains: Annually
Minimum: Initial: $3,000
    Subsequent: $100

Telephone Exchange: Yes
    With MMF: Yes
Registered In: All states
12b-1: No

VANGUARD INSURED LONG-TERM MUNICIPAL BOND

Vanguard Group
Vanguard Financial Center
Valley Forge, PA 19482
(800) 662-7447/(215) 648-6000

	Years Ending 8/31					
	1982	1983	1984	1985 (10 mos.)	1986	1987
Dividends from Net Investment Income ($)	–	–	–	.83	.90	.85
Distributions from Net Realized Capital Gains ($)	–	–	–	–	.17	–
Net Asset Value End of Year ($)	–	–	–	10.50	11.73	11.24
Ratio of Expenses to Net Assets (%)	–	–	–	.36	.33	.26
Portfolio Turnover Rate (%)	–	–	–	16	20	50
Total Assets: End of Year (Millions $)	–	–	–	336.0	709.3	793.2
Annual Rate of Return (%) Years Ending 12/31	–	–	–	19.3	18.7	0.1

Distr: Income: Monthly
    Capital Gains: Annually
Minimum: Initial: $3,000
    Subsequent: $100

Telephone Exchange: Yes
    With MMF: Yes
Registered In: All states
12b-1: No

VANGUARD INTERMEDIATE-TERM MUNICIPAL BOND

Vanguard Group
Vanguard Financial Center
Valley Forge, PA 19482
(800) 662-7447/(215) 648-6000

	Years Ending 8/31					
	1982	1983	1984	1985	1986	1987
Dividends from Net Investment Income ($)	.91	.87	.90	.92	.89	.83
Distributions from Net Realized Capital Gains ($)	–	–	–	–	.02	–
Net Asset Value End of Year ($)	10.14	10.54	10.44	10.98	12.15	11.79
Ratio of Expenses to Net Assets (%)	.48	.46	.41	.39	.33	.26
Portfolio Turnover Rate (%)	107	117	55	26	13	57
Total Assets: End of Year (Millions $)	49.1	150.1	209.1	411.8	811.8	920.0
Annual Rate of Return (%) Years Ending 12/31	31.1	6.5	9.5	17.3	16.2	1.7

Distr: Income: Monthly
    Capital Gains: Annually
Minimum: Initial: $3,000
    Subsequent: $100

Telephone Exchange: Yes
    With MMF: Yes
Registered In: All states
12b-1: No

VANGUARD LONG-TERM MUNICIPAL BOND

Vanguard Group
Vanguard Financial Center
Valley Forge, PA 19482
(800) 662-7447/(215) 648-6000

	Years Ending 8/31					
	1982	1983	1984	1985	1986	1987
Dividends from Net Investment Income ($)	.88	.84	.86	.87	.85	.80
Distributions from Net Realized Capital Gains ($)	—	—	—	—	.19	—
Net Asset Value End of Year ($)	8.78	9.32	9.17	9.79	10.97	10.38
Ratio of Expenses to Net Assets (%)	.48	.46	.41	.39	.33	.26
Portfolio Turnover Rate (%)	191	211	99	72	32	67
Total Assets: End of Year (Millions $)	120.4	230.6	290.0	410.7	627.7	617.3
Annual Rate of Return (%) Years Ending 12/31	38.5	9.5	8.5	20.8	19.4	(1.1)

Distr: Income: Monthly
    Capital Gains: Annually
Minimum: Initial: $3,000
    Subsequent: $100

Telephone Exchange: Yes
    With MMF: Yes
Registered In: All states
12b-1: No

VANGUARD NEW YORK INSURED TAX-FREE

Vanguard Group
Vanguard Financial Center
Valley Forge, PA 19482
(800) 662-7447/(215) 648-6000

	Years Ending 11/30					
	1982	1983	1984	1985	1986 (8 mos.)	1987
Dividends from Net Investment Income ($)	—	—	—	—	.38	.63
Distributions from Net Realized Capital Gains ($)	—	—	—	—	—	—
Net Asset Value End of Year ($)	—	—	—	—	10.08	8.87
Ratio of Expenses to Net Assets (%)	—	—	—	—	.34	.35
Portfolio Turnover Rate (%)	—	—	—	—	8	31
Total Assets: End of Year (Millions $)	—	—	—	—	51.6	75.9
Annual Rate of Return (%) Years Ending 12/31	—	—	—	—	—	(3.5)

Distr: Income: Monthly
    Capital Gains: Annually
Minimum: Initial: $3,000
    Subsequent: $100

Telephone Exchange: Yes
    With MMF: Yes
Registered In: NY
12b-1: No

VANGUARD PENNSYLVANIA INSURED TAX-FREE

Vanguard Group
Vanguard Financial Center
Valley Forge, PA 19482
(800) 662-7447/(215) 648-6000

	Years Ending 11/30					
	1982	1983	1984	1985	1986 (8 mos.)	1987
Dividends from Net Investment Income ($)	—	—	—	—	.41	.68
Distributions from Net Realized Capital Gains ($)	—	—	—	—	—	—
Net Asset Value End of Year ($)	—	—	—	—	10.30	9.28
Ratio of Expenses to Net Assets (%)	—	—	—	—	.33	.31
Portfolio Turnover Rate (%)	—	—	—	—	0	15
Total Assets: End of Year (Millions $)	—	—	—	—	121.6	193.9
Annual Rate of Return (%) Years Ending 12/31	—	—	—	—	—	(1.3)

Distr: Income: Monthly
    Capital Gains: Annually
Minimum: Initial: $3,000
    Subsequent: $100

Telephone Exchange: Yes
    With MMF: Yes
Registered In: PA
12b-1: No

VANGUARD SHORT-TERM MUNICIPAL BOND

Vanguard Group
Vanguard Financial Center
Valley Forge, PA 19482
(800) 662-7447/(215) 648-6000

	Years Ending 8/31					
	1982	1983	1984	1985	1986	1987
Dividends from Net Investment Income ($)	1.16	.95	.92	.99	.90	.78
Distributions from Net Realized Capital Gains ($)	—	—	—	—	.01	—
Net Asset Value End of Year ($)	15.18	15.15	15.08	15.24	15.39	15.37
Ratio of Expenses to Net Assets (%)	.48	.46	.41	.39	.33	.26
Portfolio Turnover Rate (%)	224	136	102	55	57	12
Total Assets: End of Year (Millions $)	179.9	346.8	353.9	536.3	906.1	1,104.9
Annual Rate of Return (%) Years Ending 12/31	10.1	5.1	6.8	7.0	7.4	4.1

Distr: Income: Monthly
    Capital Gains: Annually
Minimum: Initial: $3,000
    Subsequent: $100

Telephone Exchange: Yes
    With MMF: Yes
Registered In: All states
12b-1: No

New Funds

AMA GLOBAL GROWTH

International

AMA Advisers, Inc.
5 Sentry Pkwy. W., Suite 120
P.O. Box 1111
Blue Bell, PA 19422
(800) 523-0864/(215) 825-0400

Investment Objectives/Policy: Seeks capital appreciation through investment in common stocks traded on exchanges worldwide. 30% of the portfolio may be invested in stocks not listed on American exchanges. May also invest in investment-grade debt securities.
Year First Offered: 1987
Distr: Income: Quarterly
    Capital Gains: Annually

12b-1: Yes   **Amount:** 0.50%
Minimum, Initial: $1,000
    Subsequent: None
Min IRA, Initial: $500
    Subsequent: $50
Investor Services: IRA, Keogh, Corp, SEP, 403(b), Withdraw, Deduct
Telephone Exchange: Yes
    With MMF: Yes
Registered In: All states

AVONDALE GOVERNMENT SECURITIES

Bond

Herbert R. Smith, Inc.
1105 Holliday
Wichita Falls, TX 76301
(817) 761-3777

Investment Objectives/Policy: Seeks current income consistent with preservation of capital. Invests in debt obligations issued or guaranteed by the U.S. government and its agencies. May write covered call options and may hedge using interest rate futures and options.
Year First Offered: 1987
Distr: Income: Monthly
    Capital Gains: Annually

12b-1: Yes   **Amount:** 0.25%
Minimum, Initial: $5,000
    Subsequent: $1,000
Min IRA, Initial: $1,000
    Subsequent: $250
Investor Services: IRA, Keogh, Corp, SEP, 403(b), Withdraw, Deduct
Telephone Exchange: No
Registered In: Call for availability

COUNSELLORS FIXED INCOME

Bond

Warburg, Pincus Counsellors, Inc.
466 Lexington Avenue
New York, NY 10017-3147
(800) 888-6878/(212) 878-0600

Investment Objectives/Policy: Primary objective is to generate high current income consistent with reasonable risk; capital appreciation is secondary. Invests in corporate bonds, debentures, notes, convertible securities, preferred stocks, government obligations and repurchase agreements. Normally will be 80% invested in fixed-income securities.
Year First Offered: 1987
Distr: Income: Monthly
    Capital Gains: Annually

12b-1: No
Minimum, Initial: $25,000
    Subsequent: $5,000
Min IRA, Initial: None
    Subsequent: None
Investor Services: Withdraw
Telephone Exchange: Yes
    With MMF: Yes
Registered In: All states

DREYFUS NEW JERSEY TAX EXEMPT BOND, L.P.

Tax-Exempt

The Dreyfus Corp.
600 Madison Ave.
New York, N.Y. 10022
(800) 645-6561/(718) 895-1206

Investment Objectives/Policy: Seeks to provide a high level of current income exempt from federal and New Jersey income taxes, consistent with the preservation of capital. A large proportion invested in New Jersey municipal obligations.
Year First Offered: 1987
Distr: Income: Monthly
    Capital Gains: Annually

12b-1: Yes   **Amount:** 0.25%
Minimum, Initial: $2,500
    Subsequent: $100
Investor Services: Withdraw
Telephone Exchange: Yes
    With MMF: Yes
Registered In: All states

DREYFUS NEW YORK INSURED TAX EXEMPT BOND

Tax-Exempt

The Dreyfus Corp.
600 Madison Ave.
New York, N.Y. 10022
(800) 645-6561/(718) 895-1206

Investment Objectives/Policy: Seeks to provide as high a level of current income exempt from federal, New York state, and New York City income taxes as is consistent with the preservation of capital. Invests in state of New York municipal securities which are insured as to the timely payment of interest and principal.
Year First Offered: 1987
Distr: Income: Monthly
    Capital Gains: Annually

12b-1: Yes   **Amount:** 0.25%
Minimum, Initial: $2,500
    Subsequent: $100
Investor Services: Withdraw, Deduct
Telephone Exchange: Yes
    With MMF: Yes
Registered In: CT, DC, HI, MA, NH, NJ, NY, PA, RI, VT, WY

DREYFUS SHORT-INTERMEDIATE TAX EXEMPT BOND

Tax-Exempt

The Dreyfus Corp.
600 Madison Ave.
New York, NY 10022
(800) 645-6561/(718) 895-1206

Investment Objectives/Policy: Seeks high level of current income exempt from federal income tax and consistent with preservation of capital. May invest in municipal bond index futures contracts and options.
Year First Offered: 1987
Distr: Income: Monthly
    Capital Gains: Annually

12b-1: Yes   **Amount:** 0.10%
Minimum, Initial: $2,500
    Subsequent: $100
Investor Services: Withdraw, Deduct
Telephone Exchange: Yes
    With MMF: Yes
Registered In: All states

DREYFUS U.S. GOVERNMENT INTERMEDIATE SECURITIES, L.P.

Bond

The Dreyfus Corp.
600 Madison Ave.
New York, NY 10022
(800) 645-6561/(718) 895-1206

Investment Objectives/Policy: Seeks high level of current income consistent with preservation of capital through investment in debt obligations of the U.S. government and its agencies. The fund is organized as a limited partnership in order to pass to investors state and local tax exemptions afforded to owners of such U.S. government securities.
Year First Offered: 1987
Distr: Income: Monthly
Capital Gains: Annually

12b-1: No
Minimum, Initial: $2,500
Subsequent: $100
Min IRA, Initial: $750
Subsequent: None
Investor Services: IRA, Keogh, Corp, 403(b), SEP, Withdraw
Telephone Exchange: Yes
With MMF: Yes
Registered In: All states except AZ

ECLIPSE EQUITY

Growth & Income

Towneley Capital Management
144 East 30th Street
New York, NY 10016
(800) 872-2710/(404) 631-0414

Investment Objectives/Policy: Seeks a high total return from equity investments. Buys stocks based on their intrinsic worth, expected future earnings growth, and current and expected dividend income. Generally invests in smaller companies whose market value is less than the average of the S&P 500.
Year First Offered: 1987
Distr: Income: Quarterly
Capital Gains: Annually

12b-1: Yes   **Amount:** 0.30%
Minimum, Initial: $10,000
Subsequent: None
Min IRA, Initial: $1,000
Subsequent: None
Investor Services: IRA, Corp, SEP
Telephone Exchange: Yes
With MMF: Yes
Registered In: All states

EVERGREEN VALUE TIMING

Growth & Income

Saxon Woods Asset Mgmt.
550 Mamaroneck Ave.
Harrison, NY 10528
(800) 235-0064/(914) 698-5711

Investment Objectives/Policy: Seeks capital appreciation and current income. Invests in the common stocks of companies that the advisor feels are undervalued relative to their assets, breakup value, earnings or potential earnings growth. May also invest in convertible and debt securities.
Year First Offered: 1987
Distr: Income: Annually
Capital Gains: Annually

12b-1: No
Minimum, Initial: $2,000
Subsequent: None
Min IRA, Initial: None
Subsequent: None
Investor Services: IRA, Keogh, SEP, Withdraw
Telephone Exchange: Yes
With MMF: Yes
Registered In: All states except MO

FIDELITY CONVERTIBLE SECURITIES

Growth & Income

Fidelity Investments Co.
82 Devonshire St.
Boston, MA 02109 .
(800) 544-6666/(617) 523-1919

Investment Objectives/Policy: Seeks a high level of total return from current income and capital appreciation, primarily through investment in convertible securities. Invests at least 65% of assets in convertibles including bonds, debentures, notes and preferred stocks.
Year First Offered: 1987
Distr: Income: Quarterly
Capital Gains: Annually

12b-1: Yes **Amount:** Pd. by Advisor
Minimum, Initial: $2,500
Subsequent: $250
Min IRA, Initial: $500
Subsequent: $250
Investor Services: IRA, Keogh, Corp, SEP, 403(b), Withdraw, Deduct
Telephone Exchange: Yes
With MMF: Yes
Registered In: All states

FIDELITY GLOBAL BOND

International

Fidelity Investments Co.
82 Devonshire St.
Boston, MA 02109
(800) 544-6666/(617) 523-1919

Investment Objectives/Policy: Seeks high total return through investment in debt securities issued worldwide. Will invest at least 65% of assets in debt securities rated not less than BB by Standard & Poor's. Considers factors such as currency relationships, interest rates and inflation. May invest in interest rate futures contracts.
Year First Offered: 1987
Distr: Income: Monthly
Capital Gains: Annually

12b-1: Yes **Amount:** Pd. by Advisor
Minimum, Initial: $2,500
Subsequent: $250
Min IRA, Initial: $500
Subsequent: $250
Investor Services: IRA, Keogh, Corp, SEP, 403(b), Withdraw, Deduct
Telephone Exchange: Yes
With MMF: Yes
Registered In: All states

FOUNDERS FRONTIER

Aggressive Growth

Founders Mutual Depositor Corp.
3033 East First Ave., #810
Denver, CO 80206
(800) 525-2440/(303) 394-4404

Investment Objectives/Policy: Seeks capital appreciation through investment in common stocks of small- and medium-sized companies, both foreign and domestic. Can invest up to 100% of the fund's assets in either foreign or domestic stocks, but it cannot have more than 25% invested in one foreign country. May also invest in put and call options.
Year First Offered: 1987
Distr: Income: Dec
Capital Gains: Dec

12b-1: Yes **Amount:** 0.25%
Minimum, Initial: $1,000
Subsequent: $100
Min IRA, Initial: $25
Subsequent: $25
Investor Services: IRA, Keogh, Corp, SEP, 403(b), Withdraw, Deduct
Telephone Exchange: Yes
With MMF: Yes
Registered In: All states except NH

IAI INTERNATIONAL
International

Investment Advisers, Inc.
1100 Dain Tower
P.O. Box 357
Minneapolis, MN 55440
(612) 371-2884

Investment Objectives/Policy: Seeks capital appreciation through investment in foreign equity securities. Income is a secondary objective. Under normal conditions the fund will invest 95% of its assets in foreign equities. Can also invest in put and call options, foreign currency futures and other financial futures.
Year First Offered: 1987
Distr: Income: Semiannually
    Capital Gains: Annually

12b-1: No
Minimum, Initial: $2,500
    Subsequent: $100
Min IRA, Initial: None
    Subsequent: None
Investor Services: IRA, Keogh, Corp, 403(b), Withdraw
Telephone Exchange: No
Registered In: AZ, CA, CO, IA, IL, MD, MI, MN, MO, MT, ND, NE, NY, PA, SD, TN, TX, WA, WI

NICHOLAS LIMITED EDITION
Growth

Nicholas Company, Inc.
700 N. Water St., #1010
Milwaukee, WI 53202
(800) 227-5987/(414) 272-6133

Investment Objectives/Policy: Seeks long-term capital appreciation through investment in common stocks. Income is a secondary consideration. Invests in small- to medium-sized companies that the advisor feels will have superior growth in sales and earnings. May also invest in debt securities and preferred stock.
Year First Offered: 1987
Distr: Income: Annually
    Capital Gains: Annually

12b-1: No
Minimum, Initial: $2,000
    Subsequent: $100
Min IRA, Initial: $2,000
    Subsequent: $100
Investor Services: IRA, Keogh, Corp, Withdraw
Telephone Exchange: No
Registered In: All states

T. ROWE PRICE MARYLAND TAX-FREE BOND
Tax-Exempt

T. Rowe Price Associates
100 E. Pratt St.
Baltimore, MD 21202
(800) 638-5660/(301) 547-2308

Investment Objectives/Policy: Seeks highest level of current income that is exempt from federal, Maryland state and local income taxes. Invests primarily in long-term Maryland municipal obligations rated BBB or higher.
Year First Offered: 1987
Distr: Income: Monthly
    Capital Gains: Annually

12b-1: No
Minimum, Initial: $1,000
    Subsequent: $100
Investor Services: Deduct, Withdraw
Telephone Exchange: Yes
    With MMF: Yes
Registered In: DC, DE, HI, MD, NJ, NV, PA, VA, WV, WY

T. ROWE PRICE SCIENCE & TECHNOLOGY

Aggressive Growth

T. Rowe Price Associates
100 E. Pratt St.
Baltimore, MD 21202
(800) 638-5660/(301) 547-2308

Investment Objectives/Policy: Seeks long-term growth of capital through investment in the common stocks of companies that are expected to benefit from the development, advancement, and use of science and technology. Looks for high-growth companies in the health care, information processing, waste management, synthetic materials, and communications industries.
Year First Offered: 1987
Distr: Income: Annually
　　Capital Gains: Annually

12b-1: No
Minimum, Initial: $1,000
　　Subsequent: $100
Min IRA, Initial: $500
　　Subsequent: $50
Investor Services: IRA, Keogh, Corp, 403(b), SEP, Withdraw
Telephone Exchange: Yes
　　With MMF: Yes
Registered In: All states

PRUDENT SPECULATOR LEVERAGED FUND

Aggressive Growth

Prudent Speculator Group
P.O. Box 75231
Los Angeles, CA 90075-0231
(800) 444-4778

Investment Objectives/Policy: Seeks long-term capital growth; current income is not an investment objective. Under normal conditions, at least 80% of the fund's assets will be invested in a diversified portfolio of common stocks. Looks for stocks that have lower than average price-earnings ratios, price-to-book-value ratios and price-to-sales ratios.
Year First Offered: 1987
Distr: Income: Annually
　　Capital Gains: Annually

12b-1: Yes　　**Amount:** 0.25%
Minimum, Initial: $5,000
　　Subsequent: $500
Min IRA, Initial: $2,000
　　Subsequent: $200
Investor Services: IRA, Keogh, Withdraw
Telephone Exchange: No
Registered In: All states except NE, NH

RODNEY SQUARE GROWTH PORTFOLIO

Growth

Scudder Fund Distributors, Inc.
175 Federal Street
Boston, MA 02110
(800) 225-5084

Investment Objectives/Policy: Seeks long-term capital appreciation through investment in growth stocks. Invests in stocks that have prospects for increased earnings due to new products, new management, technological developments and other factors. May invest up to 35% of the fund's assets in debt securities.
Year First Offered: 1987
Distr: Income: Quarterly
　　Capital Gains: Annually

12b-1: Yes　　**Amount:** 0.35%
Minimum, Initial: $1,000
　　Subsequent: None
Min IRA, Initial: $1,000
　　Subsequent: None
Investor Services: IRA, Keogh, Corp, 403(b), Withdraw
Telephone Exchange: Yes
　　With MMF: Yes
Registered In: All states

SCUDDER
EQUITY INCOME
Balanced

Scudder, Stevens & Clark
175 Federal Street
Boston, MA 02110-2267
(800) 453-3305/(617) 426-8300

Investment Objectives/Policy: Seeks high current income, primarily by investing in high-yielding common stocks and convertible securities. A secondary objective is growth of capital and income. Looks for stocks with price-earnings ratios lower than the S&P 500, with below average stock market risk. May also invest in debt securities.
Year First Offered: 1987
Distr: Income: Quarterly
    Capital Gains: Annually

12b-1: No
Minimum, Initial: $1,000
    Subsequent: None
Min IRA, Initial: $240
    Subsequent: None
Investor Services: IRA, Keogh, Corp, 403(b), Withdraw
Telephone Exchange: Yes
    With MMF: Yes
Registered In: All states

SCUDDER
HIGH YIELD
TAX FREE

Tax-Exempt

Scudder, Stevens & Clark
175 Federal Street
Boston, MA 02110-2267
(800) 453-3305/(617) 426-8300

Investment Objectives/Policy: Seeks high level of income exempt from federal income taxes through investment in investment-grade municipal securities. Invests primarily in bonds rated A or BBB by Standard & Poor's that have higher yields than higher-rated bonds. May also use futures contracts and options to hedge the portfolio.
Year First Offered: 1987
Distr: Income: Monthly
    Capital Gains: Annually

12b-1: No
Minimum, Initial: $1,000
    Subsequent: None
Investor Services: Withdraw, Deduct
Telephone Exchange: Yes
    With MMF: Yes
Registered In: All states

SCUDDER
JAPAN FUND

International

Scudder, Stevens & Clark
175 Federal Street
Boston, MA 02110-2267
(800) 453-3305/(617) 426-8300

Investment Objectives/Policy: Seeks capital appreciation by investing in the common stock of Japanese companies. The fund will invest at least 80% of its assets in Japan, but may keep up to 20% in short-term cash investments if conditions warrant. May also invest in Japanese debt securities and enter into foreign currency futures contracts.
Year First Offered: 1987*
Distr: Income: Annually
    Capital Gains: Annually

12b-1: No
Minimum, Initial: $1,000
    Subsequent: None
Min IRA, Initial: $240
    Subsequent: None
Investor Services: IRA, Keogh, Corp, 403(b), Withdraw, Deduct
Telephone Exchange: Yes
    With MMF: Yes
Registered In: All states

*Prior to August 1987, the fund was a closed-end investment company.

SHADOW STOCK FUND

Aggressive Growth

Investment Objectives/Policy: Seeks long-term growth of capital by investing in the stocks of small, neglected companies. These companies will have market capitalizations of between $20 million and $110 million and will have annual net profits of at least $1 million for the three most recent fiscal years. The fund will include more than 400 stocks.
Year First Offered: 1987
Distr: Income: Annually
    Capital Gains: Annually

Jones & Babson, Inc.
Three Crown Center
2440 Pershing Road
Kansas City, MO
(800) 821-5591/(816) 471-5200

12b-1: No
Minimum, Initial: $2,500
    Subsequent: $100
Min IRA, Initial: $250
    Subsequent: None
Investor Services: IRA, Keogh, Withdraw
Telephone Exchange: Yes
    With MMF: Yes
Registered In: All states

STEINROE PRIME EQUITIES

Growth & Income

Investment Objectives/Policy: Primary objective is growth of capital. Normally invests at least 65% of net assets in well-established companies with market capitalizations above $1 billion. May invest up to 10% of its assets in foreign securities. May also purchase fixed-income securities, options and futures contracts.
Year First Offered: 1987
Distr: Income: Quarterly
    Capital Gains: Annually

Stein Roe & Farnham
P.O. Box 1143
Chicago, IL 60690
(800) 621-0320/(312) 368-7826

12b-1: No
Minimum, Initial: $1,000
    Subsequent: $100
Min IRA, Initial: $500
    Subsequent: $50
Investor Services: IRA, Keogh, SEP, Withdraw
Telephone Exchange: Yes
    With MMF: Yes
Registered In: All states

STRONG SHORT-TERM BOND

Bond

Investment Objectives/Policy: Seeks to provide investors with the highest level of income consistent with minimum fluctuation in principal value and current liquidity. Invests in debt securities with maturities of up to 10 years. Under normal circumstances, 65% of the fund's assets will be invested in corporate bonds and securities issued or guaranteed by the U.S. government.
Year First Offered: 1987
Distr: Income: Monthly
    Capital Gains: Annually

Strong/Corneliuson Capital Mgmt.
815 E. Mason St.
Milwaukee, WI 53202
(800) 368-3863/(414) 765-0934

12b-1: No
Minimum, Initial: $1,000
    Subsequent: $200
Min IRA, Initial: $250
    Subsequent: None
Investor Services: IRA, Keogh, Corp, 403(b), SEP, Withdraw, Deduct
Telephone Exchange: Yes
    With MMF: Yes
Registered In: All states

TRANSATLANTIC INCOME

International

Kleinwort Benson International
200 Park Ave., Suite 5610
New York, NY 10166
(800) 237-4218/(212) 687-2515

Investment Objectives/Policy: Seeks high current income through investment in foreign and domestic fixed-income securities. Normally invests in three different currencies, but does not have more than 40% of assets in any one currency.
Year First Offered: 1987
Distr: Income: Semiannually
  Capital Gains: Annually

12b-1: Yes **Amount:** 0.20%
Minimum, Initial: $1,000
  Subsequent: $500
Min IRA, Initial: $500
  Subsequent: $500
Investor Services: IRA
Telephone Exchange: Yes
  With MMF: No
Registered In: Call for availability

TWENTIETH CENTURY LONG-TERM BOND

Bond

Investors Research Corp.
P.O. Box 200
Kansas City, MO 64141
(816) 531-5575

Investment Objectives/Policy: Seeks high level of income from investment in longer-term bonds, which generally have greater price volatility than short- or intermediate-term bonds. During normal conditions, the average weighted maturity of the portfolio will be 15 to 25 years. Invests in medium- to high-grade corporate bonds and U.S. government bonds.
Year First Offered: 1987
Distr: Income: Monthly
  Capital Gains: Annually

12b-1: No
Minimum, Initial: None
  Subsequent: None
Min IRA, Initial: None
  Subsequent: None
Investor Services: IRA, Corp, 403(b), Withdraw
Telephone Exchange: Yes
  With MMF: Yes
Registered In: All states

TWENTIETH CENTURY TAX-EXEMPT INTERMEDIATE TERM

Tax-Exempt

Investors Research Corp.
P.O. Box 200
Kansas City, MO 64141
(816) 531-5575

Investment Objectives/Policy: Seeks current income that is exempt from federal income tax. Invests in municipal securities with an average maturity of between five and seven years.
Year First Offered: 1987
Distr: Income: Monthly
  Capital Gains: Annually

12b-1: No
Minimum, Initial: None
  Subsequent: None
Investor Services: Withdraw
Telephone Exchange: Yes
  With MMF: Yes
Registered In: All states

TWENTIETH CENTURY TAX-EXEMPT LONG TERM

Tax-Exempt

Investors Research Corp.
P.O. Box 200
Kansas City, MO 64141
(816) 531-5575

Investment Objectives/Policy: Seeks current income that is exempt from federal income tax. Invests in municipal securities with an average maturity between 15 and 25 years.
Year First Offered: 1987
Distr: Income: Monthly
    Capital Gains: Annually

12b-1: No
Minimum, Initial: None
    Subsequent: None
Investor Services: Withdraw
Telephone Exchange: Yes
    With MMF: Yes
Registered In: All states

USAA INCOME STOCK

Growth & Income

USAA Investment Mgmt. Co.
9800 Fredericksburg Rd.
San Antonio, TX 78288
(800) 531-8000/(512) 498-8000

Investment Objectives/Policy: Seeks current income with the prospect of increasing dividend income and the potential for capital appreciation. Invests in the common stocks of well-established, large companies that pay higher-than-average dividends. May also invest in convertibles.
Year First Offered: 1987
Distr: Income: Quarterly
    Capital Gains: Annually

12b-1: No
Minimum, Initial: $1,000
    Subsequent: $25
Min IRA, Initial: $1,000
    Subsequent: $25
Investor Services: IRA, Keogh, 403(b), SEP, Withdraw
Telephone Exchange: Yes
    With MMF: Yes
Registered In: All states

US REAL ESTATE FUND

Growth

United Services Advisors
P.O. Box 29467
San Antonio, TX 78229
(800) 873-8637/(512) 696-1234

Investment Objectives/Policy: Seeks long-term capital appreciation. Invests at least 65% of its assets in companies that have 50% of their assets or derive 50% of their revenues from the ownership, construction, management or sale of residential, commercial or industrial real estate. May write covered call options.
Year First Offered: 1987
Distr: Income: Semiannually
    Capital Gains: Annually

12b-1: No
Minimum, Initial: $100
    Subsequent: $50
Min IRA, Initial: None
    Subsequent: None
Investor Services: IRA
Telephone Exchange: Yes
    With MMF: No
Registered In: All states

VANGUARD LIMITED-TERM MUNICIPAL BOND

Tax-Exempt

Vanguard Group
Vanguard Financial Center
Valley Forge, PA 19482
(800) 662-7447/(215) 648-6000

Investment Objectives/Policy: Seeks to provide investors with the highest available level of interest income that is exempt from federal income tax and that is consistent with both preservation of capital and the maturity and quality standards prescribed. Invests in investment-grade municipal bonds and expects to maintain an average maturity of two to five years.
Year First Offered: 1987
Distr: Income: Monthly
    Capital Gains: Annually

12b-1: No
Minimum, Initial: $3,000
    Subsequent: $100
Investor Services: Deduct, Withdraw
Telephone Exchange: Yes
    With MMF: Yes
Registered In: All states

Funds Not Listed In Data Pages

We base our mutual fund guide on the listings that appear in the newspaper; we select only no-load funds. Some of the funds listed in the newspaper are not true no-loads despite their designation as "N.L.," while others are inappropriate for individuals or are not available to individuals for other reasons. In this section, we list the funds designated as no-loads in the financial press but not in the main part of this book, and we state the reasons why those funds are not included.

Key to Reasons for Exclusion:

- **BB:** Can be bought only from a bank or broker.
- **C:** Closed to new investors.
- **DE:** For corporations taking advantage of dividend exclusion tax rules.
- **I:** For institutional or corporate investors only.
- **L:** Limited to employees or members of a particular organization.
- **M:** Minimum investment is greater than $25,000.
- **NS:** Information not supplied in time for publication.
- **R:** Redemption fee does not disappear after 6 months.
- **SC:** Front-end sales charge.
- **T:** Tax-free exchange—not available for purchase by individuals.

R	Advest Advantage Government	R	Clipper Fund
R	Advest Advantage Growth	R	Columbia Municipal
R	Advest Advantage Income	R	Cowen Income & Growth
R	Advest Advantage Special	R	Criterion Special Convertible
R	Alger Growth Portfolio	R	Criterion Special Global Growth
L	American Capital Exchange	R	Dean Witter American Valued
L	American Capital Growth	R	Dean Witter Calif. Tax-Free
NS	American Heritage	R	Dean Witter Convertible
R	American Pension Investors	R	Dean Witter Develop. Growth
L	AMEV Special	R	Dean Witter Dividend Growth
L	Bankers System Granit Growth	C	Dean Witter Government Plus
M	Bartlett Corporate Cash	R	Dean Witter Natural Resources
SC	Blanchard Strategic Growth	R	Dean Witter N.Y. Tax-Free
R	Boston Growth and Income	R	Dean Witter Option Income
R	Calvert Washington Growth	R	Dean Witter Sears Tax-Exempt
L	Cheapside Dollar	R	Dean Witter Tax Advantaged
T	Chestnut Street Exchange	R	Dean Witter U.S. Government
L	Citibank IRA CIT: Balanced	R	Dean Witter Value Added Eq.
L	Citibank IRA CIT: Equity	R	Dean Witter World Wide Inv.
L	Citibank IRA CIT: Income	C	Destiny I
L	Citibank IRA CIT: Short-Term	BB	Destiny II

I	DFA Fixed Income Portfolio	I	Fidelity Tax-Exempt Ltd. Term
I	DFA Small Stock	R	First Eagle of America
L	DIT Capital Growth	M	Flag Investors: Corporate Cash
L	DIT Current Income	M	Flagship Corporate Cash
L	DIT OTC Growth	DE	Franklin Corporate Cash
L	DIT U.S. Gov't. Securities	R	Freedom Equity Value
R	Drexel Fenimore Int'l.	R	Freedom Global
R	Drexel Series Trust Bond	R	Freedom Global Income Plus
R	Drexel Series Trust Convertible	R	Freedom Gold and Gov't.
R	Drexel Series Trust Emerg. Gr.	R	Freedom Government Plus
R	Drexel Series Trust Gov't. Sec.	R	Freedom Regional Bank Fund
R	Drexel Series Trust Growth	R,M	Gabelli Asset Fund
R	Drexel Series Trust Option Inc.	DE	Geico Adj. Rate Preferred
R	Drexel S.T. Priority Selection	BB	General Aggressive Growth
R	E.F. Hutton Basic Value	L	General Electric Elfun Income
R	E.F. Hutton Bond	L	G.E. Elfun Tax-Exempt
R	E.F. Hutton Gov't. Securities	L	G.E. Elfun Trust
R	E.F. Hutton Growth	L	G.E. S&S Long-Term
R	E.F. Hutton Option Income	L	General Electric S&S Program
R	E.F. Hutton Precious Metals	BB	General Tax Exempt Bond
R	E.F. Hutton Special Equity	M	Gintel Fund
R	Eaton Vance Calif. Muni.	M	Govaars Investment Trust
R	Eaton Vance High Income	L	Guardian Bond
R	Eaton Vance High Yield Muni.	L	Guardian Stock
R	Enterprise Growth Portfolio	SC	Hartwell Growth
R	Equitec Siebel Agg. Growth	SC	Hartwell Leverage
R	Equitec Siebel High Yield Bond	R	Horace Mann Growth Fund
R	Equitec Siebel Total Return	R	IDS Aggressive
R	Equitec Siebel U.S. Gov't.	R	IDS Income
C	Equity Strategies	R	IDS Strategy: Aggressive Equity
R	Farm Bureau Growth	R	IDS Strategy: Pan Pacific
C	Federated Bond Fund	I	IFG Diversified
I	Federated Cash Mgmt. Trust	I	IFG Intermediate
I	Federated Exchange	I	IFG International
I	Federated Floating Rate	NS	Industry Fund of America
I	Federated F.T. International	R	Integrated Resources Cap. App.
I	Federated GNMA Trust	R	Integrated Res. Home Investors
I	Federated Government Trust	R	Integrated Resources Inc. Plus
I	Federated Growth Trust	R	Investment Portfolios Equity
I	Federated High Yield	R	Investment Port. Gov't. Plus
I	Federated Income	R	Investment Port. High Yield
I	Federated Intermediate Gov't.	R	Investment Port. Option Inc.
I	Federated Intermediate Muni.	R	Investment Port. Total Return
I	Federated Short Inter. Gov't.	I	Ivy Institutional
I	Federated Short Inter. Muni	R	Kaufman
I	Federated Stock & Bond	R	Keystone Amer.: Equity Income
I	Federated Stock Trust	R	Keystone Amer.: High Yld. Bd.
T	Fidelity Congress St.	R	Keystone Amer.: Tax-Free Inc.
I	Fidelity CT ARP	R	Keystone Custodian B1, B2, B4
I	Fidelity Equity Portfolio Gr.	R	Keystone Custodian K1, K2
I	Fidelity Equity Portfolio Inc.	R	Keystone Custodian S1, S3, S4
C	Fidelity Exchange	R	Keystone International
I	Fidelity Fixed Inc. Ltd. Term	R	Keystone Precious Metals
I	Fidelity Fixed Inc. Short Gov't.	R	Keystone Tax-Exempt
I	Fidelity Qualified Dividend	R	Keystone Tax-Free

R	Kidder Peabody Equity Income	M	Pilgrim Group: Corporate Cash
R	Kidder Peabody Gov't. Income	R	Prudential-Bache Adj. Rate
R	Kidder Peabody Special Gr.	R	Prudential-Bache Calif. Muni
L	Landmark Capital Growth	R	Prudential-Bache Equity
L	Landmark Growth and Income	R	Prudential-Bache Flexi Agg.
L	Landmark N.Y. Tax Free Inc.	R	Prudential-Bache Flexi Cons.
L	Landmark U.S. Gov't. Income	R	Prudential-Bache Global
C	Lindner†	R	Pru-Bache Global Nat. Res.
M	Ltd. Mat. Bd.: Neuberger Ber.	R	Prudential-Bache GNMA
C	Loomis-Sayles Cap. Dev.†	R	Prudential-Bache Gov't. Plus
R	MacKay Shields Capital App.	R	Prudential-Bache Gov't. Sec.
R	MacKay Shields Convertible	R	Prudential-Bache Growth Opp.
R	MacKay Shields Corporate Bd.	R	Prudential-Bache High Yield
R	MacKay Shields Global	R	Pru-Bache Inc. Vertible Plus
R	MacKay Shields Gov't. Plus	R	Prudential-Bache Muni Arizona
R	MacKay Shields Tax Free Bd.	R	Prudential-Bache Muni Ga.
R	MacKay Shields Value Fund	R	Prudential-Bache Muni Md.
R	Meeschaert Cap. Accum.	R	Prudential-Bache Muni Mass.
R	Merrill Lynch Calif. Tax-Ex.	R	Prudential-Bache Muni Mich.
R	Merrill Lynch Euro Fund	R	Prudential-Bache Muni Minn.
R	Merrill Fd. for Tomorrow	R	Prudential-Bache Muni N.Y.
I	Merrill Lynch Inst. Inter.	R	Prudential-Bache Muni N.C.
R	Merrill Lynch Muni. Inc.	R	Prudential-Bache Muni Ohio
R	Merrill Lynch Natural Res.	R	Pru-Bache Muni Oregon
R	Merrill Lynch New York Muni	R	Prudential-Bache Nat. Muni.
R	Merrill Lynch Retire. Ben.	R	Pru-Bache Option Growth
R	Merrill Lynch Retire. Eq.	R	Prudential-Bache Penn.
R	Merrill Retire. Global Bd.	R	Prudential-Bache Research
R	Merrill Lynch Retire. Income	R	Prudential-Bache Utility Shares
R	Merrill Lynch Strategic Div.	R	Putnam Capital
BB	Metlife State Street Gov't. Inc.	R	Putnam Mass. Tax-Exempt Inc.
R	MFS Lifetime Cap. Growth	R	Putnam Mich. Tax-Exempt Inc.
R	MFS Lifetime Div. Plus	R	Putnam Minn. Tax-Ex. Inc.
R	MFS Lifetime Emerging Gr.	R	Putnam Ohio Tax-Exempt Inc.
R	MFS Lifetime Global Equity	R	Putnam Tax-Free High Yield
R	MFS Lifetime Gov't. Inc.	R	Putnam Tax-Free Insured
R	MFS Lifetime High Inc.	R	Royce Equity Income Series
R	MFS Lifetime Manag. Muni.	R	Royce High Yield Series
R	MFS Lifetime Manag. Sectors	C	Royce Value
L	MSB	C	Sequoia†
M	Mutual Beacon	SC	Shearson ATT Growth Fund
R	Nationwide Funds: Tax-Free	SC	Shearson ATT Income Fund
M	Pacific Inv.-Low Duration	M	Shearson Multiple Opp.
M	Pacific Investment-Total Return	R	Shearson Special Portfolio
R	Paine Webber Asset Allocation	R	Southeast Growth
R	Paine Webber Master Ener.	M	Southeastern Asset Man. Value
R	Paine Webber Master Growth	L	State Farm Balanced
R	Paine Webber Gr. & Inc.	L	State Farm Growth
R	Paine Webber Master Income	L	State Farm Municipal Bond
R	Pasadena Growth	T	State Street Exchange
R	Pennsylvania Mutual	T	State Street Growth

†*Fund performance included in table for closed funds in performance ranking section—see Chapt. 6.*

R	Thomson McKinnon Global	C	V.E.–Fiduciary Exchange
R	Thomson McKinnon Growth	C	Vance Exchange–Fund
R	Thomson McKinnon Income	C	V.E.–Second Fiduciary Exch.
R	Thomson McKinnon Opp.	DE	Vanguard Adj. Rate Pref.
R	Thomson McKinnon Tax-Ex.	C	Vanguard Explorer†
R	Thomson McK. U.S. Gov't.	C	Vanguard High Yd. Stock†
I	Trust Funds Bond	DE	Vanguard Pref. Stock
I	Trust Funds Equity Index	R	Vanguard Specialized Portfolios
I	Trust Fds. Inst. Man. Trust Val.	C	Vanguard Windsor†
I	Trust Funds Inter. Gov't.	R	Venture Advisers Retire.–Bond
R	United Services Prospector	R	Venture Retire.–Equity
C	Vance Exchange–Capital Exch.	R	Venture Municipal Plus Fund
C	V.E.–Depositors of Boston	R	Winthrop Growth
C	V.E.–Diversification	I	WPG Growth
C	V.E.–Exchange of Boston		

†*Fund performance included in table for closed funds in performance ranking section—see Chapt. 6.*

Mutual Fund Families

Below we present a list of mutual fund families that are primarily no-load. We have listed all funds within a family, including those with loads and redemption fees.

AMA
5 Sentry Pkwy. W., Suite 120
P.O. Box 1111
Blue Bell, PA 19422
(800) 262-3863/(215) 825-0400

AMA Classic Growth
AMA Classic Income
AMA Emerging Medical Technology
AMA Global Growth
Medical Technology
Money-Prime
Pro Money—Treasury

American Investors
D.H. Blair Advisors
777 W. Putnam Ave.
Greenwich, CT 06836
(800) 243-5353/(203) 531-5000

American Investors Growth
American Investors Income
American Investors Money
American Investors Option

Axe-Houghton Management, Inc.
400 Benedict Avenue
Tarrytown, NY 10591
(800) 431-1030/(914) 631-8131

Fund B
Income
Money Market
Stock

D.L. Babson
3 Crown Center
2440 Pershing Rd.
Kansas City, MO 64108
(800) 821-5591/(816) 471-5200

Bond Trust
Enterprise
Growth
Money Market—Federal
Money Market—Prime
Shadow Stock
Tax-Free Income Funds:
  Shorter-Term Portfolio
  Longer-Term Portfolio
  Money Market Portfolio
UMB Bond

UMB Money Market
UMB Qualified Dividend
UMB Stock
UMB Tax-Free
Value

James Baker & Company
1601 Northwest Expressway
20th Floor
Oklahoma City, OK 73118
(405) 842-1400

Baker Equity Series
Baker U.S. Government Series

Bartlett & Company
36 E. Fourth St.
Cincinnati, OH 45202
(800) 543-0863/(513) 621-0066

Basic Value
Corporate Cash
Fixed Income

Benham
755 Page Mill Rd.
Palo Alto, CA 94304
(800) 227-8380/(415) 858-3600

California Tax-Free—High Yield
California Tax-Free—Insured
California Tax-Free—Intermediate
California Tax-Free—Long Term
California Tax-Free—Money Market
Capital Preservation
Capital Preservation II
Capital Preservation Treasury Note
GNMA Income
National Tax-Free—Intermediate
National Tax-Free—Long Term
National Tax-Free—Money Market
Target Maturities Trust

Boston Co.
One Boston Place
Boston, MA 02108
(800) 343-6324/(800) 225-5267

Capital Appreciation
Cash Management
GNMA
Government Money

Managed Income
Massachusetts Tax-Free Bond
Massachusetts Tax-Free Money
Special Growth
Tax-Free—Bond
Tax-Free—Money

Bull & Bear Funds
11 Hanover Square
New York, NY 10005
(800) 847-4200/(212) 363-1100

Bull & Bear Capital Growth
Bull & Bear Dollar Reserves
Bull & Bear Equity-Income
Bull & Bear Gold Investors Ltd.
Bull & Bear High Yield
Bull & Bear Special Equities
Bull & Bear Tax-Free Income
Bull & Bear U.S. Gov't. Sec.

Calvert
1700 Pennsylvania Ave., N.W.
Washington, DC 20006
(800) 368-2748/(301) 951-4820

Cash Reserves
Equity
First Variable Rate
Income
Social Investment Managed Growth
Social Investment Money Market
Tax-Free Reserves:
    Limited-Term
    Long-Term
    Money Market
U.S. Government
Washington Area Growth

CCM Partners
44 Montgomery Street
San Francisco, CA 94104
(800) 225-8778/(415) 398-2727

Calif. Ginnie Mae
Calif. Tax-Free Income
Calif. Tax-Free Money Market
Calif. U.S. Government Securities

Columbia
1301 S.W. Fifth Ave.
P.O. Box 1350
Portland, OR 97207-1350
(800) 547-1037/(503) 222-3600

Daily Income
Fixed Income Securities
Growth
Municipal Bond

Special
U.S. Guaranteed Gov't. Sec.

Counsellors
Warburg, Pincus Counsellors, Inc.
466 Lexington Avenue
New York, NY 10017-3147
(800) 888-6878/(212) 878-0600

Capital Appreciation
Cash Reserve
Fixed Income
New York Municipal Bond
New York Tax-Exempt

Delaware Management Company
Ten Penn Center Plaza
Philadelphia, PA 19103
(800) 523-4640/(215) 988-1333

Cash Reserve
Decatur Fund—I Series
Decatur Fund—II Series
Delaware Fund
Delcap Concept I
Delchester Bond Fund
Delta Trend Fund
Gov't. Fund—GMNA Series
Gov't. Fund—U.S. Gov't. Series
Tax-Free Insured Series
Tax-Free Money Fund
Tax-Free New York
Tax-Free Pennsylvania
Tax-Free USA
Treasury Reserves Cashier Series
Treasury Reserves Investor Series

Dividend/Growth
107 N. Adams St.
Rockville, MD 20850
(800) 638-2042/(301) 251-1002

Dividend Series
Government Obligations
Laser & Advanced Technology

Dodge & Cox
One Post St., 35th Fl.
San Francisco, CA 94104
(415) 434-0311

Balanced
Stock

Dreyfus
600 Madison Avenue
New York, NY 10022
(800) 645-6561/(718) 895-1206

A Bonds Plus

Calif. Tax Exempt Bond
Calif. Tax Exempt Money Market
Capital Value
Convertible Securities
Dreyfus Fund
GNMA
Growth Opportunity
Insured Tax Exempt Bond
Intermediate Tax Exempt Bond
Leverage
Liquid Assets
Mass. Tax Exempt Bond
Money Market Instr.:
　　Government
　　Money Market
New Jersey Tax Exempt Bond
New Leader
N.Y. Insured Tax Exempt Bond
N.Y. Tax Exempt Bond
Short Intermediate Tax Exempt Bond
Strategic Income Fund
Strategic Investment Fund
Tax Exempt Bond
Tax Exempt Money Market
Third Century
U.S. Gov't. Intermediate Securities

Evergreen
Saxon Woods Asset Mgmt. Corp.
550 Mamaroneck Ave.
Harrison, NY 10528
(800) 235-0064/(914) 698-5711

Evergreen
Evergreen Total Return
Evergreen Value Timing

Fidelity
82 Devonshire St.
Boston, MA 02109
(800) 544-6666/(617) 523-1919

Aggressive Tax-Free
Balanced
CalFree—High Yield Port.
CalFree—Insured Port.
CalFree—Money Market
CalFree—Muni Bond
CalFree—Short-Term
Capital Appreciation
Cash Reserves
Congress Street
Contrafund
Convertible Securities
Daily Income Trust
Daily Money
Daily Tax-Exempt Money

Destiny
Equity-Income
Europe
Exchange
Fidelity Fund
Flexible Bond
Freedom
Ginnie Mae
Global Bond
Government Securities
Growth Company
Growth & Income Port.
High Income
High Yield Municipals
Insured Tax-Free Portfolio
Intermediate Bond
International Growth & Income
Limited Term Municipals
Magellan
MassFree:
　　High Yield
　　Money Market
Mercury
Michigan Tax-Free
Minnesota Tax-Free
Money Market Trust:
　　Domestic
　　U.S. Government
　　U.S. Treasury
Mortgage Securities
Municipal Bond
N.Y. Tax-Free—High Yield
N.Y. Tax-Free—Insured
N.Y. Tax-Free—Muni Bond
N.Y. Tax-Free—Money Market
Ohio Tax-Free
OTC Portfolio
Overseas
Pacific Basin
Penn. T-F—High Yield Port.
Penn. T-F—Money Market
Puritan
Real Estate Investment
Select Portfolios:
　　Air Transportation
　　American Gold
　　Automation & Machinery
　　Automotive
　　Biotechnology
　　Broadcast and Media
　　Brokerage & Investment Cos.
　　Capital Goods
　　Chemicals
　　Computers
　　Defense & Aerospace

Electric Utilities
Electronics
Energy
Energy Services
Financial Services
Food & Agriculture
Health Care
Health Care Delivery
Housing
Industrial Materials
Leisure & Entertainment
Life Insurance
Money Markets
Paper & Forest Products
Precious Metals & Minerals
Property & Casualty Insurance
Regional Banks
Restaurant Industry
Retailing
Savings & Loan
Software & Computer Services
Technology
Telecommunications
Transportation
Utilities
Short-Term Bond Portfolio
Short-Term Tax-Free Portfolio
Special Situations
Tax-Exempt Money Market Trust
Texas Tax-Free
Trend
U.S. Government Reserves
Value

Fiduciary
222 E. Mason St.
Milwaukee, WI 53202
(414) 271-6666

Capital Growth
ValQuest

Financial Programs
P.O. Box 2040
Denver, CO 80201
(800) 525-8085/(303) 779-1233

Bond Shares:
  High Yield
  Select Income
  U.S. Government
Daily Income Shares
Dynamics
Industrial
Industrial Income
Strategic Portfolios:
  Energy

European
Financial
Gold
Health Sciences
Leisure
Pacific Basin
Technology
Utilities
Tax-Free Income Shares
Tax-Free Money
World of Technology

Flex-Fund
R. Meeder & Associates
6000 Memorial Dr.
P.O. Box 7177
Dublin, OH 43017
(800) 325-3539/(614) 766-7000

Bond
Capital Gains
Corporate Income
Growth
Income and Growth
Money Market
Retirement Growth

44 Wall Street
One State St. Plaza
New York, NY 10004
(800) 221-7836/(212) 808-5220

44 Wall Street
44 Wall Street Equity

Founders
3033 E. First Ave., #810
Denver, CO 80206
(800) 525-2440/(303) 394-4404

Blue Chip
Equity Income
Frontier
Growth
Money Market
Special

Fund Trust
Furman Selz
230 Park Ave.
New York, NY 10169
(800) 845-8406/(212) 309-8400

Aggressive Growth
Equity Trust
Growth
Growth & Income
High Yield Investment Trust
Income

International Equity Trust
Money Trust
Tax-Free Trust

Gateway Investment Advisors
P.O. Box 458167
Cincinnati, OH 45245
(800) 354-6339/(513) 248-2700

Growth Plus
Option Index

Gintel
Greenwich Office Park OP-6
Greenwich, CT 06830
(800) 243-5808/(203) 622-6400

Gintel
Gintel Capital Appreciation
Gintel Erisa
Parkway

GIT
Bankers Finance Investment Mgmt.
1655 N. Fort Myer Dr.
Arlington, VA 22209
(800) 336-3063/(703) 528-6500

Cash:
  Government
  Regular
Equity Income
Government Investors
Income:
  A-Rated
  Insured Money Market
  Maximum
Select Growth
Special Growth
Tax-Free High Yield
Tax-Free Money Market

Gradison
The 580 Bldg.
6th & Walnut St.
Cincinnati, OH 45202-3198
(800) 543-1818/(513) 579-5700

Cash
Established Growth
Opportunity Growth
U.S. Government

IAI
1100 Dain Tower
P.O. Box 357
Minneapolis, MN 55440
(612) 371-2884

Apollo

Bond
International
Regional
Reserve
Stock

Ivy Funds
Hingham Management Inc.
40 Industrial Park Rd.
Hingham, MA 02043
(800) 235-3322/(617) 749-1416

Ivy General Money Mkt.
Ivy Growth
Ivy International
Ivy Tax-Exempt Money Mkt.

Janus
100 Filmore St. #300
Denver, CO 80206-4923
(800) 525-3713/(303) 333-3863

Janus Fund
Janus Value
Janus Venture

Kleinwort Benson International
200 Park Ave. Suite 5610
New York, NY 10166
(800) 237-4218/(212) 687-2515

Transatlantic Growth
Transatlantic Income

Legg Mason Wood Walker
7 E. Redwood St.
Baltimore, MD 21202
(800) 822-5544/(301) 539-3400

Cash Reserve
Special Investment
Tax Exempt
Total Return
Value Trust

Lehman
55 Water Street
New York, NY 10041
(800) 221-5350/(212) 668-8578

Capital
Corporation
Investors
Management Cash Reserves
Management Gov't. Reserves
Management Tax-Free Reserves
Opportunity

Lexington
P.O. Box 1515
Park 80 W. Plaza 2

Saddle Brook, NJ 07662
(800) 526-0056

GNMA Income
Goldfund
Government Securities Money Mkt.
Growth
Money Market Trust
Research
Tax Exempt Bond
Tax Free Money

Lindner Management Corporation
200 South Bemiston
P.O. Box 11208
St. Louis, MO 63105
(314) 727-5305

Lindner
Lindner Dividend

Loomis-Sayles
P.O. Box 449
Back Bay Annex
Boston, MA 02117
(800) 345-4048/(617) 578-4200

Capital Development
Mutual

Merit Investment Center
121 South Broad Street
Philadelphia, PA 19107
(800) 992-2206

Merit Growth Opportunities
Merit Money Market
Merit Pennsylvania Tax-Free Trust
Merit Tax-Free:
    Tax-Free Income Portfolio
    Tax-Free Money Market Portfolio
Merit U.S. Government

Mutual Shares Corporation
26 Broadway
New York, NY 10004
(800) 553-3014/(212) 908-4047

Mutual Beacon
Mutual Qualified Income
Mutual Shares

Neuberger & Berman Management
342 Madison Ave.
New York, NY 10173
(800) 367-0770/(212) 850-8300

Energy
Guardian Mutual
Liberty
Limited Maturity Bond

Manhattan
Money Market Plus
Neuberger Gov't. Money Fund
Neuberger Tax-Free
Partners

New Beginning
Sit Investment Associates, Inc.
1714 First Bank Place West
Minneapolis, MN 55402
(612) 332-3223

New Beginning Growth
New Beginning Income & Growth
New Beginning Investment Reserve
New Beginning Yield

Newton
330 E. Kilbourn Ave.
Two Plaza East, #1150
Milwaukee, WI 53202
(800) 247-7039/(414) 347-1141

Growth
Income
Money

Nicholas
700 N. Water St., #1010
Milwaukee, WI 53202
(800) 227-5987/(414) 272-6133

Nicholas
Nicholas II
Nicholas Income
Nicholas Limited Edition

Northeast Mgmt. & Research Co.
50 Congress Street
Boston, MA 02109
(617) 523-3588/(800) 225-6704

Northeast Investors Growth
Northeast Investors Trust

100 Fund
Berger Associates
899 Logan St., Suite 211
Denver, CO 80203
(800) 333-1001/(303) 837-1020

100 Fund
101 Fund

Park Avenue Inc.
600 Madison Ave.
New York, NY 10022
(800) 848-4350/(718) 895-1219

N.Y. Tax Exempt Intermediate
N.Y. Tax Exempt Money Market

T. Rowe Price
100 E. Pratt St.
Baltimore, MD 21202
(800) 638-5660/(301) 547-2308

CalFree Bond
CalFree Money
Capital Appreciation
Equity Income
GNMA
Growth & Income
Growth Stock
High Yield
International Bond
International Stock
Maryland Tax-Free
New America Growth
New Era
New Horizons
New Income
New York Tax-Free Bond
New York Tax-Free Money
Prime Reserves
Reality Income I
Reality Income II
Reality Income III
Science and Technology
Short-Term Bond
Tax-Exempt Money
Tax-Free High Yield
Tax-Free Income
Tax-Free Short-Intermediate
U.S. Treasury Money

Reserve Equity Trust
810 Seventh Avenue
New York, NY 10019
(800) 421-0261/(212)977-9675

Dreman Contrarian Portfolio
Growth Portfolio

Rightime Econometrics
The Benson East Office Plaza
Jenkintown, PA 19046
(800) 242-1421/(215)927-7880

Rightime
Rightime Government Securities

Rushmore
Money Management Associates
4922 Fairmont Avenue
Bethesda, MD 20814
(800) 343-3355/(301) 657-1500

Over-the-Counter Index Plus
Stock Market Index Plus

Safeco Securities
Safeco Plaza
Seattle, WA 98185
(800) 426-6730/(206) 545-5530

Calif. Tax-Free Income
Equity
Growth
Income
Money Market Mutual
Municipal
Tax-Free Money Market
U.S. Government Securities

Scudder Fund Distributors
175 Federal St.
Boston, MA 02110
(800) 453-3305/(617) 439-4640

AARP Capital Growth
AARP General Bond
AARP GNMA & U.S. Treasury
AARP Growth & Income
AARP Insured Tax Free Bond
AARP Insured Tax Free Short-Term
AARP Money Fund
Calif. Tax Free
Capital Growth
Cash Investment
Development
Equity Income
Global
GNMA
Government Money
Growth & Income
High Yield Tax Free
Income
International
Japan Fund
Managed Municipal
N.Y. Tax Free
Rodney Square Benchmark
Rodney Square Growth
Target
Tax Free Money
Tax Free Target
Zero Coupon Target

Selected Funds
Vincent, Chesley Advisors
230 W. Monroe St., 28th Fl.
Chicago, IL 60606
(800) 621-7321/(312) 641-7862

American Shares
Money Market:
   General

Government
Special Shares

Steadman
1730 K. St., N.W.
Washington, DC 20006
(800) 424-8570/(202) 223-1000

American Industry
Associated
EhrenKrentz—Growth
EhrenKrentz—Undiscovered Equity
Financial
Investment
Oceanographic, Technology & Gr.

Stein Roe & Farnham
150 S. Wacker Dr.
Chicago, IL 60606
(800) 621-0320/(312) 368-7826

Capital Opportunities
Cash Reserves
Discovery
Government Plus
Government Reserves
High-Yield Bonds
High-Yield Municipals
Intermediate Municipals
Managed Bonds
Managed Municipals
Prime Equities
Special
Stock
Tax-Exempt Money Mkt.
Total Return
Universe

Stratton
Plymouth Meeting Exec. Campus
610 W. Germantown Pike
Suite 361
Plymouth Meeting, PA 19462
(800) 634-5726/(215) 941-0255

Growth
Monthly Dividend Shares

Strong/Corneliuson Capital Mgmt.
815 E. Mason St.
Milwaukee, WI 53202
(800) 368-3863/(414) 765-0934

Government Securities
Income
Investment
Money Market
Opportunity
Short-Term Bond

Tax-Free Income
Tax-Free Money Market
Total Return

20th Century
Investors Research Corp.
P.O. Box 200
Kansas City, MO 64141
(800) 345-2021/(816) 531-5575

Cash Reserve
Giftrust
Growth
Long-Term Bond
Select
Tax-Exempt Intermediate
Tax-Exempt Long Term
Ultra
U.S. Governments
Vista

Unified Management Corporation
429 N. Pennsylvania St.
Indianapolis, IN 46204-1897
(800) 862-7283/(317) 634-3300

Amana Income
Growth
Income
Liquid Green Trust
Liquid Green Tax-Free Trust
Municipal:
    General
    Indiana
Mutual Shares

United Services
P.O. Box 29467
San Antonio, TX 78229-0467
(800) 873-8637/(512) 696-1234

US GNMA
US Gold Shares
US Good & Bad Times
US Growth
US Income
US LoCap
US New Prospector
US Prospector
US Real Estate
US Tax Free
US U.S. Treasury Securities

USAA Funds
9800 Fredericksburg Rd.
USAA Building
San Antonio, TX 78288
(800) 531-8000/(512) 498-8000

Cornerstone
Gold
Growth
Income
Income Stock
Money Market
Sunbelt Era
Tax Exempt Funds:
    High Yield
    Intermediate-Term
    Money Market
    Short-Term

U.S.T. Master
One Boston Place
Boston, MA 02108
(800) 233-1136

Equity
Government Money
Income and Growth
Intermediate Tax-Exempt Bond
International
Long Term Tax Exempt
Managed Income
Money
Short Term Tax-Exempt

Value Line
711 Third Ave.
New York, NY 10017
(800) 223-0818/(212) 687-3965

Aggressive Income
Cash
Centurion (Limited)
Convertible
Income
Leveraged Growth
Special Situations
Tax Exempt Funds:
    High Yield
    Money Market
U.S. Government Securities
Value Line Fund

Vanguard Group
Vanguard Financial Center
Valley Forge, PA 19482
(800) 662-7447
(215) 648-6000

Adjustable Rate Preferred Stock
Bond Market
California Tax-Free Insured

Convertible Securities
Explorer
Explorer II
Fixed Income Securities:
    GNMA
    High Yield Bond
    Investment Grade Bond
    Short-Term Bond
Gemini
Gemini II
High Yield Stock
Index 500
Money Market Trusts:
    Federal
    Insured
    Prime
Municipal Bond Funds:
    High Yield
    Insured Long-Term
    Intermediate-Term
    Limited-Term
    Long-Term
    N.Y. Insured Tax-Free
    Penn. Insured Tax-Free
    Short-Term
Money Market
Naess & Thomas Special
Preferred Stock
PrimeCap
Quantitative Portfolios
Specialized Portfolios:
    Energy
    Gold & Precious Metals
    Health Care
    Service Economy
    Technology
Star
Trustees' Commingled Equity Int'l.
Trustees' Commingled Equity U.S.
U.S. Treasury Bond
W.L. Morgan
Wellesley
Wellington
Windsor
Windsor II
World Portfolio—International
World Portfolio—U.S.

Viking Equity Index Fund, Inc.
232 Lakeside Drive
Horsham, PA 19044
(800) 441-3885
(800) 222-3429

Equity Index
Money Market

Weiss, Peck & Greer
One New York Plaza, 30th Fl.
New York, NY 10004
(800) 223-3332/(212) 908-9582

Tudor
WPG
WPG Government
WPG Growth

**Wood Struthers & Winthrop
  Management Corp.**
140 Broadway
New York, NY 10005
(800) 225-8011/(816) 283-1700

Neuwirth
Pine Street
Winthrop Growth

INDEX

EDUCATIONAL PROGRAMS
FROM THE
AMERICAN ASSOCIATION OF INDIVIDUAL INVESTORS

The American Association of Individual Investors, a non-profit educational association, offers a variety of products and programs to assist serious investors to better manage their assets.

Ongoing investment education is provided through the *AAII Journal*, home study materials, special publications, traveling seminars, national meetings, and local chapters in major metropolitan areas. Many of these benefits are provided free with membership or at reduced prices.

Following are brief descriptions of some of the educational materials. For further information on AAII's membership and other educational programs and services, write to:

American Association of Individual Investors
625 North Michigan Avenue, Suite 1900
Chicago, Illinois 60611
(312) 280-0170

Continued on next page

The Individual Investor's Microcomputer Resource Guide,
Sixth Edition

A complete, updated reference source describing the latest software, hardware, and financial information services available for the individual investor. Two easy-reference grids are included. One covers all available software for each of the major computer systems; the other covers on-line databases and services. This latest edition of the **Guide** also includes a new chapter which presents a detailed spreadsheet template for fundamental stock analysis.

Investing Home Study

This **new** and **updated** 10-lesson home study course for the serious investor explains investment theory and provides practical applications for constructing and managing an investment portfolio. Completely updated for the tax law changes, this comprehensive course covers:

Concepts of investment, risk, and return
Investment alternatives
Stocks -- common and preferred
Stock options and hedging
Debt instruments and time deposits
Mutual Funds
Currencies, metals, and gems
Commodities and futures
Real Estate
And, other investments

Available in loose-leaf, binder format.

Continued on next page

Investing Fundamentals: A 6-hour Video Course

A six-hour, three-tape videocourse on the fundamentals of investing. The tapes cover the basic financial concepts and theories needed to make informed, independent investment decisions.

While this is a comprehensive investing fundamentals course, concepts and mathematical formulas are clearly explained with examples. The video is further supported with a workbook containing additional examples and problems.

The **Investing Fundamentals** videocourse presents:

Reading financial statements
Using financial statements to determine stock value
Evaluating investment vehicles
How unit trusts and other packaged investment products work
Developing a financial plan
And much more

For further information on these and other programs for the serious investor, contact:

American Association of Individual Investors
625 North Michigan Avenue, Suite 1900
Chicago, Illinois 60611
(312) 280-0170